*Macropolitics of
Nineteenth-Century
Literature*

NEW AMERICANISTS
A Series Edited by Donald E. Pease

Macropolitics of Nineteenth-Century Literature: Nationalism, Exoticism, Imperialism

Edited by Jonathan Arac
and Harriet Ritvo

Duke University Press
Durham and London 1995

Susan Meyer's "Colonialism and the
Figurative Strategy of *Jane Eyre*"
first appeared in *Victorian Studies*
33:2 (Winter 1990), pp. 247–268.

Contents

*Macropolitics of
Nineteenth-Century
Literature*

Jonathan Arac and Harriet Ritvo

Introduction

THE TWELVE CHAPTERS of this volume work together to define a rapidly emerging but still relatively unrecognized field of contemporary scholarly inquiry in literary studies—what we are calling "macropolitics." The term itself is coined in polemical contrast to Michel Foucault's "micropolitics." The value of Foucault's work for American literary studies has been diminished because many who invoke it become entangled in the meshes of his key term, "power." Much "new historicist" work, however fine its local analysis, comes to little conclusion except that any significant cultural practice is complicit in the power it might think to be opposing, for resistance is itself built into the power relation. In contrast, macropolitics finds more useful the perspective afforded by Antonio Gramsci's notion of hegemony, developed for Anglo-American use by Raymond Williams in "Base and Superstructure in Marxist Cultural Theory" (*New Left Review*, 1973) and Eugene Genovese in *Roll, Jordan, Roll* (1974). This perspective allows a level of detail, specificity, and attention to process compatible with Foucault's practice, while also emphasizing that the resistances within a system of power may change that system. In particular, by acknowledging the partial independence that exists among the nonetheless related systems of culture, economics, and politics, this way of understanding grants significance to certain threshold transformations that have not typically engaged the attention of American Foucaldians, especially changes in sovereignty.

The contributors to this volume share an understanding that politics at the level of the state has great importance for many of the major developments in nineteenth-century writing, including the definition of what shall be valued as "literature." Literature, and any other writing in a culture, cannot be assured the innocence and purity of radical autonomy, yet it is not on that account simply to be condemned. The relation of writing to power makes it possible for the activity of writing and the products of writing to help bring about change. Language is socially formed, and thus to some degree limited, and even predetermined, in its possibilities; yet language is also socially formative. To bring into existence some of the possibilities for change within a language and its conventions of use carries unpredictable effects. Those effects may be very different from what was intended by their producers, yet this unpredictable structure of history does not demand a tragic understanding. The riskiness of human action need not be understood as our doom; instead it may provide us room.

By "macropolitics" we also allude to the global transformations of the last five decades, which have powerfully challenged the sovereignty of white, Western males. In considering these changes, we cannot ignore the economic expansion of multinational capital and the culturally pervasive growth of media, but we also cannot ignore the successful political decolonization of Africa and Asia—and, since this volume was substantially completed, the renewal of national political aspirations around the periphery of the Soviet Union. The growth in twentieth-century studies of the field of postcolonial literature (marked in recent special issues of *Cultural Critique* and *South Atlantic Quarterly,* among others) requires explorations of the cultural-political nexus that defined the previous historical phase of colonization itself. By the same token, the global struggles of the last decades for the rights of women and of people of color have led to much scholarly attention to current writings, and have made clear the need for studies that allow for a deeper-rooted historical understanding of the issues. The wide concern with the macropolitics of twentieth-century culture helps motivate the study of nineteenth-century cultural macropolitics.

Certain major publications of the last decade display the iceberg-tips of the much larger macropolitical mass that we are trying to bring into visibility. *Orientalism* by Edward W. Said (1979) formulated the crucial link between representation and domination—the active role of culture in politics—in studying the relations of France and Britain to the lands and peoples of the southern and eastern Mediterranean. In discussing Joseph Conrad in *The Political Unconscious* (1981), Fredric Jameson proposed important reasons for associating imperialism and modernism and thus opened paths of inquiry into earlier correlations between politics and culture. Benedict Anderson argued in *Imagined Communities* (1983) for the fundamental significance of eighteenth-century colonial elites in forming the model for what became the nationalism of nineteenth-century European states, thus placing nationalism within imperial perspective. The "macro" level of the state is itself only part of a larger, macropolitical world-system. Essays by Mary Louise Pratt and Gayatri C. Spivak, such as those collected by Henry Louis Gates in *"Race," Writing and Difference* (1986), signal important work in progress that will join the conversation proposed by our volume.

The topics that we have chosen for our particular focus—nationalism, exoticism, imperialism—are closely interrelated. In the nineteenth century, imperialism (the "macropolitical" term par excellence) names a historically crucial process by which an "other" conceived as exotic is represented and subordinated for the purpose of strengthening the worldly place of a metropolitan nation-state. Adding the term of imperialism greatly enhances the significance of nationalism and exoticism, two topics that have a long-established tradition within comparative literary studies but that have generally been separated from each other, because thematic studies have been more taxonomical than argumentatively conceptual, with the result that these topics have not been made to count in a way that corresponds to the importance we find in them. In "Jane Austen and Empire," part of his forthcoming *Culture and Imperialism,* Edward Said recalls a pregnant formula from J. A. Hobson's seminal study *Imperialism* (1902): Imperialism is the expansion of nationality. Exoticism, in turn, is the aestheticizing means by which the pain of that expansion is converted to spectacle, to culture in the service of empire, even as it may also act to change the originating national culture.

The dozen chapters assembled here range over the whole nineteenth century. Adopting the titles of E. J. Hobsbawm's great synoptic trilogy on Europe in the world, chapters one through four fall within the "Age of Revolution," chapters five through nine in the "Age of Capital," and the last three chapters in the "Age of Empire." They begin in the shadow of Napoleon, move through the emergence of Great Britain as the world-dominant power of the nineteenth century, and end in the age of generalized Western imperialism. Yet crucial concerns recur across these divisions, including the political functions of aesthetic containment; the redefinitions of nationality under pressure of imperial ambitions; and the coexistence of imperial with revolutionary tendencies. These chapters cover a wide variety of types of writing, including poetry, drama, fiction, nonfiction, and translation. For sound historical reasons almost half of them focus on England, but the overall coverage includes Spain, France, and the United States, along with Scotland, Ireland, Mexico, the Caribbean, India, and parts of both northern and southern Africa. These macropolitical inquiries investigate such highly canonical works and writers as *Dombey and Son, Jane Eyre, Moby-Dick, Heart of Darkness,* Shelley, Wordsworth, and Flaubert, but they also include explorers' reports, Bible translations, popular theater, and folklore.

The contributors bring to bear new historical data and new interpretive perspectives to change our understanding of established masterpieces and to provoke fresh thought about works that have been neglected, or relegated to purely historical rather than literary and cultural study.

This volume takes its beginnings from the Modern Language Association meetings of 1985 and 1986, at which the division for Comparative Studies in Romanticism and the Nineteenth Century devoted sessions to "Macropolitics of Nineteenth-Century Literature: Nationalism, Exoticism, Imperialism." Four of the chapters included here grew from papers presented then; the rest have been developed from the dozens of valuable proposals submitted in response to the announced topic. What this collection records and amplifies, then, is the growing importance of macropolitical concerns to professional students of nineteenth-century literature. Proposals came from critics of many colonial and colonizing literatures (a wider range than the final selection could accommodate) and from exponents of differing theoretical positions (as is still visible in this volume); from interpreters of canonical texts and from expanders of the canon; from readers primarily interested in class, in race, and in gender. Yet perhaps as significant as this intellectual range is the demographic profile of both the proposers and the smaller group of actual contributors to this volume. Like the themes that unite their work, most of them entered the professional academy only in the last dozen years.

This rough and ready prosopography suggests why compiling this volume seemed not only an attractive project, but a very useful one. The diverse backgrounds of people writing criticism that is in some sense macropolitical clearly indicates the broad appeal—even the urgency—of the issues it raises. At the same time, however, given the fragmentation that literary study shares with all contemporary humanistic disciplines, this same diversity makes it likely that writers who have much in common will remain unaware of each other's work. Examining the footnotes, which function as skeleton intellectual histories or autobiographies, provides suggestive evidence that the communality of interests demonstrated by the essays collected here is largely the result of convergence—an example of evolutionary analogy rather than homology. No work or author is cited by more than four of the twelve contributors, and only Edward Said's seminal *Orientalism* is cited that often. Three contributors cite the theoretical work of Michel Foucault, and three cite the exemplary work of Patrick Brantlinger (*Rule of Darkness: British Literature and Imperialism, 1830–1914*).

This very lack of consensus may be another indication of the appropriateness of collecting these essays at this time. If their thematic interrelation-ships and resonances cannot be explained by common ancestry, they may reflect similar responsiveness to a shared cultural and political environment in which the idea of nationhood has become increasingly problematic and troublesome. This volume thus correlates an emergent focus of academic criticism with developments compellingly presented by contemporary global politics.

The essays have been arranged in roughly chronological order. This is not the only way they could have been arranged. Geography and language would have been possibilities, as would a bipartite division based on the kind of texts (canonical or otherwise) that the authors choose to interpret. But the overlap and interpenetration of themes among the essays is so complex that a minimalist principle of organization seemed best—anything else might obscure some potential resonances in emphasizing others.

The essay that begins the collection demonstrates the material collabora-tion of rhetoric in the American project of nationalist expansion. In "The Problem of the Discoverer's Authority in Lewis and Clark's *History*," Bruce Greenfield argues that this founding document of American expansionism also reveals that the explorers' actual experience of the North American continent undermined their initial understanding of their mission. The empty land, ripe for colonization, of official mythology turned out to be populated by a mosaic of indigenous peoples, many of whom Lewis and Clark found to be courteous, helpful, and in many ways admirable. This recognition did not prompt the explorers to repudiate their purpose, but it did, in Greenfield's view, strongly condition their language. In the account of their expedition (compiled by Nicholas Biddle and published in 1814), their authority—and, synecdochically, that of their country—seems con-stantly at issue. Because of the ambivalent import of the evidence, the explorers were reluctant to ground their right to appropriate solely on their observation of the land and its people; instead they routinely invoke the rhetoric of aesthetic response to validate their claim (and that of their race and nation) to the land.

At about the same time, rhetoric played a similarly important role in expressing and constituting the emergent national identity of Mexico, although, as Nancy Vogeley's "The Discourse of Colonial Loyalty: Mexico, 1808" shows, analogous ends do not require analogous means. The texts she interprets—a range of occasional pieces in prose and verse—are paradoxi-cal. Produced in response to the Napoleonic conquest of Spain, they seem to celebrate the colonial relationship in the stereotyped terms of subordination and loyalty, and yet they also, she argues, embody the feelings that were soon to lead to Mexican independence. Indeed, the very genre of colonial declarations of loyalty to the threatened mother country may be intrinsically subversive. No matter how repressive the linguistic and political tradition to which such declarations belong, the mere presentation of Mexico as a separate political entity amounted to a declaration of literary independence; a population whose decision to express loyalty is presumed to inspire confidence and gratitude may inspire other feelings when it makes different decisions. And the effusive reminders of the cultural patrimony that Mexicans shared with Spaniards pointed to the unstated maternal heritage that they shared only with each other.

The new nations of the western hemisphere were not the only ones to experience literary reformulation in the early nineteenth century. The established European powers found their traditional self-definitions challenged by the imperatives of capitalism and empire. That is, expansion—incorporation of the alien, either territorially or economically—was necessary to maintain preeminence, but that same expansion could diffuse or undermine the common culture on which the sense of shared nationality ultimately depended. The resulting strain may have been particularly acute in Great Britain, threatened externally by Napoleon as well as by its own internal dynamics. In "Romancing the Nation-State: The Poetics of Romantic Nationalism," Marlon B. Ross interprets Sir Walter Scott's *Rokeby* and William Wordsworth's *The White Doe of Rylstone* as unacknowledged attempts to resolve this contradiction by regrounding nationhood in a kind of tribalism. In a move that is both sentimental and conservative, both authors use plotting characteristic of romances to emphasize the enduring connection of a people to its land; further, the form itself—poetic romance has strong affinities to the traditional ballad—connects their nineteenth-century readers to the national past that implicitly defines them.

Less conservative contemporaries of Scott and Wordsworth also used the past to buttress their alternative macropolitical notions, but they were drawn to different times and places. Thus Percy Bysshe Shelley wrote *Hellas,* as Mark Kipperman points out in "Macropolitics of Utopia: Shelley's *Hellas* in Context," not only in explicit support of the Greek struggle against the Ottoman Empire, a cause that engaged the sympathies of many European and American liberals, but also as an implicit endorsement of a kind of popular national self-definition that could challenge either the legitimacy of the ways that traditional powers like Great Britain defined nationhood, or the specific imperial interests of those powers. Kipperman also argues that the kind of utopian idealism that dominates *Hellas* need not compromise its claim to political engagement, as some recent radical critics have maintained, perhaps projecting backward the ideological standards of the late twentieth century.

A rather different text, British only by adoption, that figured prominently in the macropolitical constructions of the nineteenth century was the Bible. Although the Bible was not explicitly valued for its political relevance, as Sue Zemka suggests in "The Holy Books of Empire: Translations of the British and Foreign Bible Society," that apparent absence cloaked a pervasive, if deeper presence. Indeed, the crucial role of religion in defining both the nation and the empire made the efforts of the Bible Society somewhat paradoxical from the beginning. Especially in its efforts to disseminate Bibles around the globe, it mediated imperial culture and authority to peoples who were actual or potential imperial subjects. Yet the human agents of this mediation, the organizers and proselytizers, were often themselves outside the mainstream of political power; they were predominantly dissenters, and frequently women. This paradox is a recurrent presence in the official histories of the Bible Society that are Zemka's primary texts. Another issue is yet more problematical: the ambiguity of the *word*, whether capitalized or not. The role of Bible reading and interpretation was contested within English society—it was a major point of difference between the kinds of people who belonged to the Bible Society and the Anglican establishment that often disparaged them—and questions that were vexed in Britain became still more complex and difficult when transposed into exotic languages and alien societies. So this kind of imperial proselytizing turned out to be a double-edged sword: to spread the message of empire abroad was to destabilize the social order at home.

Jeff Nunokawa's essay further explores the way that imperialist cultures were shaped by their contact with the exotic, and like Zemka, he draws directly upon the work of Edward Said. In "For Your Eyes Only: Private Property and the Oriental Body in *Dombey and Son*," he argues that a series of orientalist images and allusions allows Dickens to conflate the threatening forces of capitalism and sexuality, and to figure their defeat, at least for the purposes of the plot, in the destruction of an exotic incarnation. This defeat prepares the way for the domestic idyll with which the novel closes. But the defeat is not total. As the rhetoric celebrating the family ownership of the firm of Dombey eclipses, but cannot deny, the fact that its wealth is drawn from alien sources, so the enclosed domesticity of the insular romance implies and requires the dangerous forces that it ostensibly shuts out.

If the exotic is a latent, if ominous, presence in *Dombey and Son,* it is strongly manifest in *Jane Eyre*. According to Susan Meyer's "Colonialism and the Figurative Strategy of *Jane Eyre,*" Brontë makes colonialism the basis for an extended metaphoric and literal critique—not primarily of colonialism itself, although such a critique is not difficult to extrapolate from the novel's many references to Britain's exotic possessions, but of the oppression of women and of members of the lower middle class at home. The dark "other" therefore most frequently figures (in the haunting shape of Bertha Mason) the analogy between women's oppression by men and the enslavement of blacks. But Meyer argues that since certain imperious members of the British upper classes are also represented as disturbingly dark, although certainly not as racially other, that darkness represents the taint of colonialism or even of the colonized on the colonizers. Thus Brontë's reservations about colonialism in *Jane Eyre* are ultimately conservative (and thus related to the reactions described by Ross), based not on the sufferings of the exotic oppressed, but on the distortion of social relations at home. Meyer closes by suggesting that the act of writing about such subjects is itself a kind of colonialism.

This suggestion resonates strongly with the argument of Wai-chee Dimock's "Ahab's Manifest Destiny," which conflates text, self, and nation as loci of empire, freedom, and doom. In particular she draws a parallel between Captain Ahab's fate in *Moby-Dick* and that of the Native Americans dispossessed as the growing United States appropriated and settled Indian territories. The language in which both are described—Ahab by Melville, and the Indians by politicians and others concerned both to justify this expansionism and to distinguish it from the apparently similar behavior of more culpable empires—stresses the inevitability of the final result. This inevitability results from the nature of the subject, and so, ultimately, by the logic of what Dimock terms "negative individualism," the victims must bear the responsibility for their own demise.

Although macropolitical discourse in nineteenth-century literature (as in later literature) frequently reinforced the self-aggrandizing impulses of the cultures that produced it, it was not exclusively hegemonic, celebratory, or apologetic. Often, especially in the latter part of the nineteenth century, it also incorporated self-conscious reflections, reservations, and doubts. In "Nationalism and Exoticism: Nineteenth-Century Others in Flaubert's *Salammbô* and *L'Education sentimentale*" Lisa Lowe examines Flaubert's repeated and varied use of orientalist images in order to challenge the dominant late twentieth-century critique of orientalism. She argues that by presenting orientalism as a monolithic discourse, completely successful in its manipulation of the other (however embodied), this critique enhances the power of the discourse it intends to expose or subvert. Flaubert's work, on the contrary, demonstrates the multivalence of orientalism, sometimes figuring others defined (conventionally) by race and gender, sometimes according to class or national or international politics. Not only is orientalist discourse more heterogeneous than is generally acknowledged—and this heterogeneity may include the voices of ostensibly suppressed others; it may also be self-undermining. Thus Lowe urges that the rigid binary opposition implied by the widely used notion of oriental as other be replaced by a mode of analysis more open to the variety of actual discourse.

Like most of the contributors to this volume, Lowe has chosen to explore the rhetorical means by which a dominant culture or class differentiated itself from a perceived other. In "Attending (to) the National Spectacle: Instituting National (Popular) Theater in England and France," however, Loren Kruger illustrates the reciprocal concern among imperialists to construct a unified national image that would submerge troublesome divisions at home, especially those based on class. National theater was perceived as a way of representing (in several senses) the nation itself, although this rather slippery generalization barely concealed the difficulty of defining what was being represented. At issue was exactly the excluded category. Middle class advocates of national theater were apt to define it in classical terms that precluded any proletarian contribution (although not necessarily proletarian audiences); advocates identified with the working class were more likely to propose public spectacles or stage productions that drew on vernacular genres like the music hall. That the latter were taken more seriously in France than in England reflects the popular definition of the French nation established during the Revolution, but Kruger argues that, despite this tradition, by the end of the nineteenth century the participation of the people in the theatrical representation of their nation was no greater in France than in England.

Like Dimock, Chris Bongie maps the discourse of imperialism onto the discourse of individualism in "Exotic Nostalgia: Conrad and the New Imperialism," but in his reading the ultimate triumph of the imperial enterprise had impoverished the world of the colonizers as well as of the colonized. He argues that Conrad perceived his time as one of undifferentiated modernity, in which the rapacious European appropriation of formerly unknown territories had expunged otherness and replaced it with dreary sameness. The savages with whom the old heroic imperializers had to contend have ceased to exist; in the bureaucratic new empires where everything is known and organized they have been transformed into subjects of paternalistic benevolence or exploited laborers. As parts of this reconstituted discourse they may be no less troublesome, but in Conrad's view they have become less mysterious and meaningful. Thus Kurtz's sensibility in *Heart of Darkness* is an anachronism (in comparison, for example, with that of the efficient modern Marlow), because he can sense the fascination of a primitive world, the passing of which Conrad ambiguously regretted.

The final chapter in this collection, James Knapp's "Irish Primitivism and Imperial Discourse: Lady Gregory's Peasantry," explores the appropriation of imperialist discourse by the imperial subject. But the subject in question is an unusual and complicated one: as a member of the Anglo-Irish Ascendancy, Lady Gregory occupied a position of social and ethnic privilege in relation to the "people" whose cause she championed, as well as a position of political and economic disadvantage in relation to the metropolitan center of empire. These highly mediated positions helped determine her representation of the Irish peasantry in such works as *Poets and Dreamers*. On the one hand, she presents her folkloric sources as both inspired and humble, worthy of admiration but no challenge to the existing Irish social structure. On the other hand, by comparing the agricultural peasantry to the roving tinkers, who are both culturally and ethnically different from them, she places the peasants in an intermediate and compromised position like her own—both colonizer and colonized. Similarly indeterminate are the political implications of the celebration and reconstruction of peasant culture in which she participated along with other members of the Irish Literary Revival; it could lead to either rebellion or quiescence. Knapp argues that the multiple possibilities latent in this single imperial relation— this intersection of what seem to be human universals (as embodied in the discourse of primitivism) and historical specifics—show the difficulty of generalizing from one macropolitical situation to another. The role of context is as large as that of structure; the identification of otherness is the beginning of analysis, not the end. In this, perhaps, his reading of the Irish struggle against English imperialism can serve as preparation for understanding the various rewritings and resistances of the twentieth century.

In concluding this introduction, it seems important to note a major division that cuts across the volume and demonstrates again that "macropolitics" is no new orthodoxy but rather a perspective shared by scholars with quite different procedural techniques, which in turn are often strongly at odds within the profession as a whole. One group of chapters might be especially linked with "cultural studies" in its concern for precise institutional specifications of the means by which various kinds of writing and related practices are produced and used in a given historical situation. This group would include the contributions by Greenfield, Vogeley, Zemka, Kruger, and Knapp. In contrast, another group of chapters begins from canonically established literary masterpieces and is most concerned to excavate the meaning of what might be called after Jameson their political unconscious. Here the relation between text and history is mediated more through a theoretical model than through institutional analysis. This group would include the contributions by Ross, Nunokawa, Meyer, Dimock, and Bongie. The distinction is emphatically not between "historicist" and "textualist" commitments but rather between different emphases in historical study. The emphasis of the first group falls on interpreting historical actions, that of the second group on interpreting historical structures (in this case textual structures). On this understanding, then, the chapters by Kipperman and Lowe would fall with the first group, even though they share with the second group attention to canonical masterpieces, because they emphasize the critical actions Shelley and Flaubert perform in their writing. These two chapters further demonstrate that macropolitical analysis of canonical works does not require a predictable stance. Here, as in the profession at large, debates over fundamental issues are still going on, and we hope that this volume will further provoke them.

Bruce Greenfield

The Problem of the Discoverer's Authority in Lewis and Clark's *History*

THE *HISTORY OF THE LEWIS AND CLARK EXPEDITION* (1814) was assembled by Nicholas Biddle mainly from the journals and records of the two commanders. It is a complex document, in terms both of how it was derived from its journal sources and of how it undertook to mediate the westering ideology of its American audience and the western conditions encountered by Lewis and Clark. The second kind of complexity is the subject of this essay, but the first kind, the complexity of the text's creation, needs a brief explanation initially in order that my approach to it as a document may be understood.

The Biddle *History* was the only published account based on the two commanders' journals available during most of the nineteenth century.[1] What all but the few who had seen the holograph journals knew of the explorers' experiences and achievements stemmed from Biddle's collation and abridgement of the expedition records, and, as Gary E. Moulton, editor of the new *Journals of the Lewis and Clark Expedition,* points out, "many readers believed that in it they were reading the actual journals of the captains" (37). Biddle omitted much of the scientific information included in the journals, even though it was conventional in narrative accounts to include such material, but he retained the journal format in which the narrative proceeds day by day, in sections headed by a date. Biddle is credited with scrupulous accuracy when he summarized and rewrote (Moulton, 37), and in many sections, especially when he is following Lewis's entries, his account is almost verbatim that of his source. As was common in accounts of explorations written by a third party, Biddle retained the journalist's use of the first person, and since both Lewis and Clark habitually used the plural "we," referring variably to the two commanders and to the whole group, Biddle, in retaining the first person plural, could mask his switching back and forth between the journals of the original writers. (In fact, Moulton's account of Lewis and Clark's journal-keeping methods reveals such extensive collaborating and copying between the two that it seems clear they had a collective sense of their reportorial function [8–34].) The result is an oddly impersonal but nonetheless fairly unified narrative voice, one which keeps the experience of traveling in the foreground and which has invited many readers' imaginative participation in the progress of the expedition. The continuity of this voice and its attendant point of view is largely Biddle's creation, but its character clearly derives from the events, factual details, and occasional personal reactions recorded in the journals themselves. Despite the complexity of the *History*'s creation, I think it is fair to say that, for its original audience especially, it was presented and perceived as the coherent story of the two leaders' journey, their representation of themselves in relation to the lands and peoples they encountered.[2]

The *History*'s mediation of westering ideology and western experience is guided and propelled by the military, diplomatic, scientific, economic, and symbolic errands with which the authors were charged. Moreover, underlying such specific categories of responsibility was the pervasive sense that these men were approaching the republic's future as they departed into western space. Jefferson's projected information-gathering expedition, although planned before the Louisiana Purchase, took on even greater political importance after that clear signal of the nation's western designs. But pre-dating this legal claim to lands west of the Mississippi, there are many indications that the Pacific Ocean was seen as the natural boundary of the Republic and that Euro-Americans imagined themselves in the West more as the result of an unfolding of, than an addition to, the nation, that they anticipated not a transformation but an expansion of their polity (Jehlen, 9). In a 1786 letter, for example, Jefferson asserts that "our confederacy must be viewed as the nest from which all America, North and South, is to be peopled" (218); and in his "Memoir of Meriwether Lewis" that prefaced the original edition of the *History,* Jefferson claims that the expedition's return in 1806 excited more joy than any similar event in the history of the United States, and that "the humblest of its citizens had taken a lively interest in the issue of this journey" (xxxvi). Presumably these citizens anticipated something like what Timothy Dwight prophesies in *Greenfield Hill* (1794): that there will be "white spires" "imaged on the wave" after America's "sons across the mainland roam;/ And claim on far Pacific shores their home" (52–53).[3] "Roam" is rather a casual verb to denote the taking possession of an entire continent—Dwight apparently envisioned few obstacles—and "claim," as opposed to "make" or "build," suggests that the "home" already in some sense existed and only awaited taking up.

To say that the Lewis and Clark expedition both grew out of and served the view that the ultimate boundaries of nation and continent were congruent is not to make any new claim for Lewis and Clark. If anything, subsequent commentary on their journey has magnified its historical significance by routinely locating it within a national teleology in which their "first sight" of the western lands began the process which culminated in statehood within the federation.[4] Lewis and Clark have become icons of an America at last ready to discover itself; they are seen both as acting for the nation and as individuals identified with the nation, which through them in turn is identified with the land it was undertaking to subsume. Yet the habit of identifying continental America and discovering America tends to conceal the tenuousness and difficulty of Lewis and Clark's relationship with western lands and peoples and the conflicts and contradictions which permeate their report. Myra Jehlen reminds us how the American individual left behind older European societal definitions of the self, becoming instead "incarnate" in the American continent (Jehlen, 4), but she and we all know that it was not a virgin birth. Reading the *History* with the ensuing decades of conflict among the United States, British, Spanish, and Indian competitors in mind, one is able to recover how difficult it was then to write a narrative which would fulfil these kinds of national expectations. The Lewis and Clark expedition was more or less successful, depending on how one defines its goals, but despite its achievements, the *History* did not manage univocally to prophesy the realization of the United States' continental errand, even though it is full of evidence that such a story is what its authors would have liked to have told, and even though subsequent generations have tended to view their report in these terms. The author/heroes of the *History*, in trying to be the American people's factotum in the West, ended up displaying in a particularly vivid way the contradictions inherent in Euro-Americans' developing imperialist relationship with the continent, and in this sense their narrative is a valuable resource for the understanding of an ideology that later would assume a much more coherent literary expression. The Lewis and Clark legend, as opposed to the *History*, is a particularly clear example of what Wayne Franklin calls "those bland fictions which later generations . . . have projected onto earlier times." "Too often," he argues, the "plotting of the American past . . . stresses the abiding realization of original design," eliding "the plain discontinuities, the terminations of American experience" (155). The *History* itself, by contrast, retains clear evidence of the discontinuities and terminations which were part of Euro-American expansion into the West, terminations not only of indigenous ways of life but of modes of Euro-American experience, which gave way as a dominant Western rhetoric emerged.

It is important to distinguish between contradictions in the way Euro-Americans understood the West, and the actual conflicts that arose in the course of establishing their presence. Their conflicts were very like those of other Europeans expanding into inhabited lands, but their contradictions were particular to their own sense of destiny. The conflicts stemmed from the United States' competition with Britain, Spain, the descendants of the French, and, most importantly, the Indian peoples present in the West for control of their lands. The *History* itself, as an official publication, was an assertion of the presence and power of the United States; it was also an account of many instances in which that presence and power were wielded against groups with conflicting claims. In this sense it typified accounts of numerous contemporary American and British expeditions which understandably met with resistance. The overt or implied story of most such accounts of early expeditions to the West is the overcoming of obstacles, both natural and human, to the imperial ambitions of the sponsoring society. Conflict is a normal part of these accounts, and thus when we read of Lewis and Clark's putting the Sioux momentarily in their place (133), or of Alexander Mackenzie's evading the violent designs of villagers on his route through the Bella Coola valley (381), our responses are guided by our knowledge of both imperialist politics and literary conventions. Our view of the history of the continent and our sense of literary convention lead us to expect the resolution of these conflicts through the use of the European's superior power.

The contradiction in the way Euro-Americans imagined the West, however, could not be resolved through action. As both Jefferson's and Dwight's comments suggest, many thought it natural that Euro-Americans would inhabit the West. For many the West was already in some sense American, and for these, increasing contact with the land would make manifest a condition that was as yet but immanent. Actual conflict over possession, however, raised doubts about this continental identity, doubts that did not necessarily disappear once physical possession had been secured. The very existence of conflict contradicted the underlying assumption of American identification with the West, that the land was a vacant entity waiting to be discovered. History could not proceed as a development of this identity of people and place if the process itself turned up evidence that conflicted with its assumptions. Because the Lewis and Clark *History* presents a remarkably copious and conscientious inventory of the

West, more evidence than any other American exploration narrative that the western continent was a mosaic of peoples and not an empty landscape, it embodies this contradiction which is at the heart of American continentalist ideology.

In the present discussion of how the Lewis and Clark *History* functions as a text, this contradiction can be construed as a problem of authority, as, in fact, one voice competing with another for influence. Cultural contradictions are internal to the individual as well as to his society, so that the resolution of competing authorities is a matter of choosing the voice that is somehow more fundamental and reliable as a basis for one's sense of integrity and direction. American explorers needed to be able to establish how, as Americans, they were entitled to assert their claims on western lands. As writers, perhaps more than as men of action, they confronted directly the complexities of the relationship between their subject (the lands they explored) and their audience (the society that sponsored their travels). They needed to find the way of speaking that would allow them to proclaim most effectively the link between "unknown territory" and themselves, their sponsors and their readers.

The conflict inherent in any imperial initiative required that the recounting of officially sanctioned exploration have a clear sense of the writer's authority. Without such authority, the writer's ability to portray his assertion of power in what were by definition unknown territories was compromised, and heroic action in the face of resistance appeared as simply foolhardy or selfish individualism.[5] In part to establish their own authority, many exploration narratives of the period were dedicated to a respected public figure, prefaced by copies of the traveler's instructions, and clearly identified with an official sponsoring government or legally constituted body such as the Hudson's Bay Company.[6] It was as an agent of such public figures and institutions that the explorer was able to act aggressively in what were—and until the mid-nineteenth century were portrayed as—inhabited lands. The exploration narrative's conventional "I" speaks from faraway lands as the sanctioned representative of its audience, and expects to be judged according to public criteria. The rhetoric of the exploration narrative asserts a relationship between the sponsoring group or society and what is being explored in which the former's power is seen to be both effective and legitimate.

Logistically and politically the Lewis and Clark expedition was very ambitious, and for that reason alone its authority was very unstable. Only

Alexander Mackenzie's party was known previously to have crossed the continent north of Spanish territory, but as a fur trader acting more or less as a private citizen Mackenzie could not really be said to have had a nation behind him as Lewis and Clark had. Though their survival and material success were often in doubt, Lewis and Clark's assertion of the United States' relation to the far West strained even the traditionally hyperbolic rhetoric of European exploration writing. As self-conscious representatives of a self-conscious new society their presence in the West bristled with possibilities, and they invoked every means to buttress their authority. Because the United States' claims on these western lands were so large, yet Euro-Americans' presence in them so recent, the explorers' presentation of the sponsoring society's relation to the western lands and peoples is remarkably variable, even contradictory. The first-person "we," retained by the editor from various journals and records, asserts the coherence of the explorers' point of view, but the text in fact shows us different and unreconcilable modes of linking Euro-American society and the western territories.

I have identified four modes of rhetoric in terms of the authority each invokes, for in spite of the first-person voice and chronological plotting typical of the travel adventure narrative there is nothing of the picaresque in Lewis and Clark. Their *History* is a solid thatch of purposes and responsibilities, even, as we shall see, when the two leaders respond aesthetically to qualities of the landscape. The first mode invokes the official authority stemming from their sponsorship by a nation. In this mode, Lewis and Clark undertake to show themselves advancing their country's legitimate interests in the West. In a second mode, they present themselves as servants of scientific knowledge, disinterested data-gatherers relying on the authority of European categories of learning to impose order on western lands and peoples. A third mode of authority develops from Lewis and Clark's reporting of their exchanges with western peoples, what I have called their "local" authority. Last, Lewis and Clark also speak from their feelings about the landscape, invoking their own aesthetic responses as an authority for their presence in what they know are inhabited lands. These rhetorics in part reflect what was conventional in contemporary exploration writing, the asserting of legal rights over land and peoples and the collection of scientific data, for example. But the particular circumstances of Lewis and Clark's journey resulted in their relying, less conventionally, on personal responses to natural beauty and grandeur as an authorization of their presence (and their society's future) in the western countries. I shall argue that this rhetoric of personal, primarily aesthetic, discovery becomes priv-

ileged because it offers a way of obviating the conflict between imperial
authority over the land and the cooperative relationship Lewis and Clark
developed with local peoples during their twenty-nine months in the West.

The earliest and clearest basis upon which to approach western lands and
peoples was the official. Captains Lewis and Clark led a military expedition
and were authorized to treat with the Indian peoples they encountered, and
in their writing they go to some trouble to show themselves behaving as
empowered envoys. They record, for example, that on July 22, 1804, "we
camped [on the Missouri, ten miles from the mouth of the Platte] intend-
ing to make the requisite observations, and to send for the neighboring
tribes, for the purpose of making known the recent change in the government [from French to American], and the wish of the United States to
cultivate their friendship" (52). At the subsequent meeting with six chiefs of
the Ottoes and the Missouris, all the Lewis and Clark party "paraded for the
occasion." "A speech was then made announcing to them the change of
government, our promise of protection, and advice as to their future
conduct" (65). Lewis and Clark never show themselves slighting the for-
malities on such occasions, or understating their authority. From such a
basis they feel secure in characterizing western peoples in terms of their
friendliness or hostility, their potential usefulness in trade, their amenability
to settled patterns of land tenure, their attachment to competing European
powers. The explorers had clear instructions to assert United States legal
authority in Louisiana, and their narrative makes such assertions unequivocally.

An equally clear basis of authority lay in their roles as natural scientists
and ethnographers. The collection of scientific data had long been understood as part of the explorer's role, and formalized categories of knowledge
had been established to organize the traveler's reporting.[7] Whatever the
immediate economic or political motives of the venture, scientific description was an accepted mode of reporting and an implicit assertion of the
traveler's power over lands and peoples. Jefferson carefully defined Lewis's
responsibilities to science in his written instructions to him, insisting that
his observations were "to be taken with great pains and accuracy; to be
entered distinctly and intelligibly for others as well as yourself" (xxvii).
Lewis was to observe and record the longitude and latitude of the places
visited; the possessions, relations, languages, traditions, monuments, oc-
cupations, food, clothing, shelter, diseases, moral and physical circumstances, laws, customs, dispositions, commerce, morality, and religion of

the peoples who inhabited the western countries; the soil and face of the country; the growth and vegetation; animal life; remains of extinct animals; mineral productions; volcanic appearances; and climate (xxvii–xxviii; Jackson, *Letters,* 62–63). These instructions were referred to by later American explorers as a model of how to conceive of their role.

It is in the *History*'s ethnographic observations that the linking of knowledge and power is especially apparent. The writers of the Lewis and Clark *History,* like those of contemporary and earlier travel reports, did not really try to disguise this linkage. Whereas later anthropological writing would shift toward a stance of disinterested objectivity, the political context of Lewis and Clark's ethnography is explicit.[8] Thus Jefferson ends his list of ethnological categories by asserting "the interest which every nation has in extending and strengthening the authority of reason and justice among the people around them," concluding that knowledge of these people "may better enable those who may endeavor to civilize and instruct them, to adapt their measures to the [people's] existing notions and practices" (xxvii–xxviii). Lewis and Clark categorized the peoples of the Missouri, for example, according to the extent to which they were agricultural, that is, prepared for a future in which they would be confined to small pieces of land. The narrative up to their winter with the Mandans on the upper Missouri contains frequent mentions of land "susceptible of cultivation" or "better calculated for farms," as well as of sites for trading forts, towns, and mills, and the explorers used the extent to which Indian groups relied on agriculture as a rough index of the difficulty they would present to United States citizens moving west (5, 28, 30, 35, 117). Indian peoples who stayed in one place could be isolated and avoided. The Mandans, who lived in semi-permanent villages and who relied to some extent on corn and vegetables, presented few problems. Similarly, the Osages, "residing . . . in villages, and having made considerable advance in agriculture," are "less addicted to war"; but the "Kaninaviesch," an offshoot of the Pawnee nation, "have degenerated from the improvements of the parent tribe, and no longer live in villages" (12, 57). While considering an agricultural life as a possible future for the Missouri peoples, Lewis and Clark also, less optimistically, adverted to the widely held view that Indian societies in general faced inevitable decline. The Missouri section of the journey seemed to provide abundant support for this notion. "The history of the Mandans," they say, ". . . illustrates more than that of any other nation the unsteady movements and tottering fortunes of the American Indians" (196–97). Similarly, the story of the "Chayennes [sic] . . . is the short and melancholy relation of the calamities of almost all the Indians" (147). The reasons for the "tottering fortunes" and the "calamities" are left unspecified, although Lewis and Clark certainly knew that they and their countrymen were deeply implicated. Here and elsewhere their descriptions of Indian cultures show a strong tendency to coalesce around theories in which their decline was inevitable, and the whole process appeared as a natural rather than a political phenomenon.

The United States' legal claims and the conventions of ethnology and the natural sciences are Lewis and Clark's securest sources of authority. The legal rhetoric stemmed from the highest levels of public policy making, while the scientific was a well established tradition in exploration writing, in which the gathering of information not immediately related to an expedition's economic and political motives was given a privileged status. The rhetorics of legal and of scientific authority were both powerful tools for objectifying inhabitants of the West and controlling, indeed minimizing, their status in the land. Writing in these rhetorics alone, the traveler could present the peoples as well as the places and resources of the West as the subject matter of a report, rather than as participants in a dialogue (or even a dispute).

Lewis and Clark's portrait of their interaction with western peoples is, however, much more complex than these two rhetorics alone would allow. They recorded much more about their relations with western inhabitants than they were able to categorize legally or scientifically, for a great deal of their time was spent on the day-to-day business of feeding, moving, and directing their party, in all of which they relied heavily on local peoples for advice and material assistance. Their expedition's success owed much to their ability to drop their diplomatic and ethnological tools and communicate in local terms about matters which were, first of all, local, such questions as how far it was between the eastern and western watersheds. We can isolate a third rhetoric for the recording of this kind of practical interaction with local peoples. It is characterized by a sense of time and a set of goals which are comprehensible to native inhabitants. It does not subordinate the Mandans within the terms of the binational agreement negotiated between Washington and Madrid, nor does it group them ethnologically with other peoples, perhaps unknown to them, who shared similar ideas about "the deity." Rather, it engages them in the next step of the expedition and thereby shows the expedition reconciling its goals to local logic and experience. It is in this local mode that we see Lewis and Clark getting where they want to go, especially after they leave behind the navigable waters of the

Missouri, where they were able to carry provisions and equipment in boats, and begin the journey on foot and horseback during which they were almost entirely dependent on local supplies.[9]

Once Lewis and Clark reach the village of the Shoshonees, cross the divide, and enter the Columbia River valley, the terrain becomes difficult and unfamiliar, and food scarce, so that the travelers enter into close relations with many groups. They become accomplished traders and adapt to such local customs as the eating of dog flesh. They frequently express their appreciation of the hospitality, kindness, and intelligence of their hosts and guides, recording their progress down the Columbia more in terms of movement from village to village than in terms of natural landmarks. Their gratitude for such welcome as they receive is directed more toward the people than toward an abstract sense of nature's bounty, as it had been in the lush foothills east of the mountains where the party had seen great herds of grazing elk, deer, and buffalo, the last "so gentle that the [men] were obliged to drive them out of the way with sticks and stones" (303).

Whereas Lewis and Clark's relation to the tribes of the Missouri suggested a kind of vassalage, a stable hierarchy, their interactions with the peoples of the Columbia are much more volatile, and at times, dangerous. As a small isolated party, Lewis and Clark were dependent on the Columbians as trading partners. The easterners had to adapt themselves to the local economy, making the most of whatever advantage their weapons and trade goods offered in order to gain a passage through the western countries. They describe the lives and culture of the Columbia Indians largely in terms of their commerce. Game from the mountains, fish from the rivers, roots and vegetables from the meadows, European manufactures from the ships at the river-mouth, all circulated in a system of exchange which both linked and distinguished the dozens of villages along the river valley. The explorers express surprise at the ubiquity and complexity of Indian commerce, and they complain several times that they "are never freed from the visits of the natives" (935). Nonetheless, they render a very thorough account of the workings of that commerce, and they habitually include trading patterns in their accounts of particular groups of residents.[10]

In numerous instances Lewis and Clark express gratitude and affection toward their Indian hosts. They say that the Wallawallas, for example, "of all the Indians whom we have met since leaving the United States, . . . are the most hospitable, honest, and sincere" (980). They are an "honest, worthy people" (978), who graciously render the travelers many services. In addition, it seems that Lewis and Clark appreciate these kindnesses the more because they are aware of the fragility of these peoples' limited prosperity. Their relationships develop local contexts and histories. They observe, for example, upon returning through their lands, that the Walla-wallas "seem to have been successful in their hunting during the past winter," for they "are much better clad" than when they saw them previously (977). The Multnomah women of the Willamette Valley also elicit their sympathy for having, in winter, to stand chest deep in water in order to gather with their feet the wappatoo root, a valuable staple and the basis of their commerce (929). The leaders of the expedition take pride in always paying in some way for what they receive from local peoples. This insistence, together with their recognition of gifts freely given, are consistent with the spirit of their careful and detailed observations of the way the western peoples lived.

Lewis and Clark's account of the differences among Columbian peoples displays a remarkably sympathetic understanding of their day-to-day life. They never doubt the superiority of their own civilization, but they are long enough in the Indians' worlds, and dependent enough on their knowledge and good will, to extend credit for many virtues which transcend cultural peculiarities. It is also clear that they appreciated that the arrival of Americans in the West would be a distinct event in the history of each of the region's societies. Few observers since Lewis and Clark have realized to a comparable degree the complexity of human life in this theoretically empty land, and yet these sophisticated interpreters of its native peoples were simultaneously committed prophets of the American destiny in the West. We see both aspects of Lewis and Clark's achievement in the following passage, in which they describe a complex meeting during their return journey:

> We . . . collected the chiefs and warriors and having drawn a map of the relative situation of our country on a mat with a piece of coal, detailed the nature and power of the American nation, its desire to preserve harmony between all its red brethren, and its intention of establishing trading houses for their relief and support. It was not without difficulty, and not till nearly half the day was spent, that we were able to convey all this information to the Chopunnish, much of which might have been lost or distorted in its circuitous route through a variety of languages; for in the first place, we spoke in English to one of our men, who translated it into French to Chaboneau; he interpreted it to his wife in the Minnetaree language; she then put it into Shoshonee, and the young Shoshonee prisoner explained it to the Chopunnish in their own dialect. At last we succeeded in communicating the impression we wished, and then adjourned the council. (1004–5)

As the committed envoys of their own society, they deliver the "message," the imperial motive of their journey. In order to carry out their errand, however, they have had to become initiates of the complex world of the western Indians, arranging simultaneous translation through three intermediate languages; and as initiates, they perhaps understand more of the eventual impact of their message than is comfortable for them.

This third rhetoric implicitly acknowledges what the legal and scientific deny, that the western continent is a mosaic of inhabited lands whose peoples have their own senses of history and destiny independent of that of the United States. Whereas the legal and scientific modes are intended to subordinate western lands and peoples with respect to the United States' vision of itself as a continental nation, the mode of practical exchange portrays a quotidian reality of shared space in which the explorers' action stems not exclusively from imperial intentions predating their arrival in the west, but in part from their exchanges with local peoples. There is no authority for this mode beyond the travelers' presence in the West. The problem is that this mode has the potential to contradict the subordination that is asserted or implied by the other rhetorics. If the legal and scientific modes are intended to extend themselves over that land by means of their authorized spokesmen, the practical mode shows these agents developing themselves as alternative authorities and their errand as a thing in itself, taking its definition from its enactment rather than from its design.

The challenge that this local mode offers the official and the scientific is not simply that of new data requiring the alteration of the categories in which they were collected; it implies another basis altogether for imagining the Euro-American relationship with the western continent. The fundamental assumption of the official and scientific modes is that the inherent superiority of Euro-American institutions is to be made manifest through their imposition on the lands and peoples of the western continent. The local mode, however, recognizes the otherness of the western peoples and portrays, if only as a transient thing, Americans in a relationship of near equality with them. This contradiction is not resolved in the narrative. Lewis and Clark do not end by reflecting on how their initial sense of their authority to discover and announce an immanent America to both East and West has been undermined by their two-year relationship with western countries. They do not retreat from the teleology of their original errand. The official, scientific, and local modes of relating to the western continent assert their respective authorities simultaneously, and no synthesis is really possible. The incompatibility of these modes of authority reflects the contradition inherent in early nineteenth-century Euro-American culture as it continued its westward expansion: its sense of national identity depended more and more on the image of the continent, but "discovering" the continent unavoidably turned up evidence of its serving as home to hundreds of unassimilable peoples.

This contradiction, and the political choices it demanded, are to a large extent evaded by another authority for the Euro-American's presence in the West. This fourth mode was independent of both the imperial and the local contexts, and it offered to transcend the knowledge that two societies could not occupy the same space simultaneously and that the displacement of the one by the other involved a denial of one aspect of the Euro-American's experience of his world. This fourth mode of authority places the explorer in direct contact with the land itself. There are no local peoples to direct him through it, and there are no eastern sponsors to tell him what to see in it.

The rhetoric of this mode of authority makes personal testimony as to the beauty and grandeur of the land itself into a transcendent authority for the viewer's presence. It has much in common with what Wayne Franklin calls the "discovery account" of the early voyagers, and perhaps, as he suggests, this rhetoric and its attendant pose survive in later narratives as one of the basic tropes of New World writing. Franklin's discoverer stands "before a purely present landscape," that is, one whose history is unknown or suppressed and whose future is therefore available. His discoverer "achieves through perception alone a communion" with an America seen as "a vast emblem of rejuvenation" (23). Such discoveries acquire new political implications as Europeans begin to settle the land: In the writings of American-born Europeans this communion comes to serve as a kind of entitlement, a transcendent authority for claims to the land. Emerson, for example, expresses such a claim in a very pure form in his notion of "Commodity" as developed in the essay "Nature." Here the "green ball" of the earth is made not only for our "delight" but for our "support," and the natural world is a "divine charity" to "nourish man" (Franklin, 83). "Man" here, of course, means Emerson's new man, capable of experiencing the kind of fundamental delight in himself and in nature which makes him truly at home in America, for it is upon "delight" in the land that Emerson's claim to "nourishment" is founded.

This rhetoric develops most clearly in the *History* after Lewis and Clark recommence their journey in the spring of 1805, after the winter spent with Mandans on the upper Missouri. Whereas the Mandans inhabited a country with a visible history, where there were remains of previous villages, and where the current inhabitants were able to recount their past to the visitors who passed the long winter with them, the foothills to the west were only seasonal hunting grounds through which the expedition happened to pass without meeting any hunting parties. "Beyond this," they say shortly after leaving the Mandans, "no white man had ever been except two Frenchmen," setting up their own fitness to see and discover definitively.

Part of this vision of the high prairies of the upper Missouri is in the pastoral mode: "The country," they say, "is beautiful in the extreme" (296). It "presented the usual variety of highlands interspersed with rich plains," which were "level and fertile" (276). Suggestions of an easy grazing life abound. The travelers are surrounded by placid, grazing buffalo, elk, and deer, which provide them plenty of food. They believe that the wool of the buffalo "resembled that of the sheep, except that it was much finer and more soft and silky," and they have no doubt that an "excellent cloth may be made" from it (276). They say that usually "the game . . . is so abundant that we can get without difficulty all that is necessary" (300, 303, 308). Overall it is a country which yields its abundance to the travelers without much struggle, and they seem to relax and expand with the plentiful food, the relatively easy traveling on the river, and the absence of serious resistance to their presence. This is also country which yields itself easily to the travelers' imaginations. The river, in a typical calm stretch above the great falls, seems to offer the abundance of nature to those who follow it:

> The Missouri itself stretches to the south in one unruffled stream of water, . . . and bearing on its bosom vast flocks of geese; while numerous herds of buffalo are feeding on the plains which surround it. (370)[11]

There are no competing siblings at this bountiful "bosom." What they see is all for them.

As they proceed, however, and the river becomes more broken by rapids and the banks steeper and more treacherous, their response to the landscape changes. Pastoral images give way to visions of the sublime; gentle plenty yields to awesome, frightening beauty, and the travelers catch their first view of the "Rock mountains—the object of all [their] hopes, and the reward of all [their] ambition" (328). Lewis's response to the grandeur of the Missouri Breaks, a portion of the river which frequently required the men to tow the canoes while wading up to their armpits in the cold water, is conspicuously aesthetic, in spite of the hardships they suffered there:

> These hills and river-cliffs exhibit a most extraordinary and romantic ap-
> pearance. They rise in most places nearly perpendicular from the water, to the
> height of between 200 and 300 feet. . . . In trickling down the cliffs, . . . water
> has worn the soft sandstone into a thousand grotesque figures, among which,
> with a little fancy, may be discerned elegant ranges of freestone buildings,
> with columns variously sculptured, and supporting long and elegant galler-
> ies, while the parapets are adorned with statuary. On a nearer approach they
> represent every form of elegant ruins—columns, some with pedestals and
> capitals entire, others mutilated and prostrate, and some rising pyramidally
> over each other till they terminate in a sharp point. These are varied by niches,
> alcoves, and the customary appearances of desolated magnificence. (338–39)

The self-conscious resort to the vocabulary of art—a terminology rarely
used in the narrative—suggests Lewis's powerful personal response and his
desire to convey the scene's effects on a civilized observer. This aesthetic
response to a natural scene is even more strictly a response of the non-
Indian than the pastoral imagery invoked in the foothills. One presumes
that Indians, too, could appreciate the fertility and abundance of the land
and make use of it in their way. Here, however, the language of artifice, the
references to "elegant galleries," "parapets adorned with statuary," to "col-
umns," "pedestals," and "capitals," denote a kind of perception which only
the heirs to Mediterranean civilization could bring to bear on rocks.

In another passage describing the Great Falls of the Missouri, Lewis
makes clear the ideological context of his aesthetic:

> [S]eating himself on some rocks under the center of the falls, Lewis enjoyed
> the sublime spectacle of this stupendous object, which since the creation had
> been lavishing its magnificence on the desert, unknown to civilization. (365)

The word "desert" is a value term, not to be taken literally, for Lewis knows
that other people have often seen this same sight. Lewis highlights the
particular significance of his viewing through reference to positioning
himself for the sole purpose of taking in the sight; he has detached himself
from the party and is exploring the falls alone. Such a moment had not
occurred since "the creation," and he seems to feel that his presence begins a
new era. That "Indians" and a few "Frenchmen" have seen these falls before
only serves to highlight the significance of Lewis's arrival. This passage,
dealing with perhaps the most intense and personal of his encounters with
the land, continues as he proceeds upstream past the several cataracts which
make up the series known as the Great Falls. Conventional references to the

beautiful and the sublime continue to mark each encounter with a new sight as a special act of appreciation. The upper cataract, he says, "was indeed beautiful, since, without any of the wild, irregular sublimity of the lower falls, it combined all the regular elegances which the fancy of a painter would select to form a beautiful waterfall" (368–69). Finally, at the head of the falls, Lewis notes what can hardly be an accidental detail:

> Here on a cottonwood tree an eagle had fixed her nest, and seemed undisputed mistress of a spot, to contest whose dominion neither man nor beast would venture across the gulfs that surround it, and which is further secured by the mist rising from the falls. (369)

The eagle—adopted in 1786 as the central motif of the United States seal—here calls attention to the national meaning of Lewis's personal encounter with the land. It is not just a civilized person who has come to fulfill the destiny of the place, but a civilized American, whose totem, the eagle, is also the presiding spirit of the place. The eagle, here a maternal one, presides like a nurturing goddess over the American explorer's appropriation of the western landscape as an aspect of American national identity.

Lewis later describes the sources of the Missouri as "chaste" and "hidden" because they had "never yet been seen by civilized man." When the travelers drank from it "they felt themselves rewarded for all their labors and all their difficulties" (484). Here the river is a synecdoche for a land innocent of human associations, even though Lewis knows that it is known to the local inhabitants. The narrative itself offers copious evidence of native peoples' incorporating the land as a part of their culture; Lewis and Clark relied on these peoples for food, information, and transportation, and in other modes of discourse they did not overlook them. Dealing with dozens of Indian groups along their way, it required a special rhetoric to respond to the land as essentially empty and waiting to be discovered, while daily documenting their exchanges with its inhabitants.

General and scholarly treatments of the Lewis and Clark narrative have sometimes effaced this conflict over the land when they assess Lewis and Clark's achievement. They see the subsequent course of the western empire in this mode of merely visual contact with the land. Elliott Coues, one of the most important of the narrative's editors and commentators, says in his "Preface to the New Edition" (1893) that when Lewis and Clark made their journey, "none but Indians had navigated the Missouri river to the Yellowstone, and none had navigated the Columbia to the head of the tidewater." That Coues does not equate Indians' knowledge of these lands with his explorers' vision is made clear when he dedicates his edition to "the people of the Great West," and exhorts them: "Honor the statesmen who foresaw your West. Honor the brave men who first saw your West." For Coues, this first sight is not only a step toward actual possession but a figuration of the whole history of European expansion. "Seeing" the land in his sense obviates the conflict in the historical process through which it came to be part of the United States, even though the conflicting claims of Euro-Americans and Amerindians are clearly represented in the contradictory modes of the Lewis and Clark *History*. In Coues's preface we see an excellent example of what Sacvan Bercovitch describes as a trope using an historian to enforce a certain view of the past (637). What one might call the "first white man to see" trope encapsulates the key ideological features of the teleology. The figure insists on sight as the signifier for imperial possession, in a metaphor that masks the fact that one people's possession is another's dispossession. Yet the color white signals that this sight is laden with significance for subsequent generations.[12] Those who identify themselves as white are meant to see their present dominance of the continent in the succession of white sightings that until fairly recently have constituted our histories of the earlier stages of European expansion into the Americas, even though the whiteness of these sightings can also, of course, be a reminder of the visions that are no longer represented. Coues's sense of what Lewis and Clark saw is not unusual in western historiography, but it is a simplification of the view offered in his original source. Lewis and Clark see "America," and thus themselves, in the western lands, but in their writing this vision is side by side with the other modes of discourse we have discussed above, in which something of the actual processes and costs of taking over is recorded.

Coues is really the heir of generations of writers about the West who isolated the aesthetic and personal mode of authority we have seen in Lewis and Clark as the best way to tell the story of Euro-Americans taking possession of their present territory. Even in the works of Lewis and Clark's immediate successors the legal, scientific, and local modes recede into the background as the authority of stories of western travel comes more and more from the individual American's recognizing himself in a landscape he has already identified as American, and from which local inhabitants have been abstracted. The most powerful assertion of authority in these later writers is the trope of aesthetic appreciation that we have already seen as transcendent in the Lewis and Clark *History*. These later explorers often placed themselves on the tops of hills or mountains in order to obtain a sweeping view of the surrounding country.[13] Zebulon Pike, for example, surveys the Mississippi valley from a hill near present-day Winona, Minnesota:

> When we arrived at the Hills we ascended them, from which we had one of the most beautiful and sublime prospects. On the right we saw the mountains which we passed in the morning, and the Prairie in their rear. . . . On our left and under our feet, the Valley between the two barren hills, through which the Mississippi wound itself, as far as the eye could embrace the scene, by numerous channels forming many beautiful islands. Our four boats under full Sail, with their flags displayed before the Wind, was altogether a prospect so variegated and romantic, that a man may scarcely expect to enjoy such a one more than once or twice in his life. (31)

As in Lewis's reactions to the landscape, references to the sublime and the beautiful signal the "civilized" personal response to the land, but it is a moment when personal experience takes on historic significance, for the individual traveler's response brings his society's values to bear on the new country, and the land itself seems to acquiesce. Pike's eye "embrace[s] the scene," which in turn seems to open itself to the "four boats under full Sail, with their flags displayed before the Wind."

In a similar situation, Pike renders the view from the top of a hill in Colorado, which is again "one of the most sublime and beautiful inland prospects ever presented to the eyes of man":

> The main river bursting out of the western mountain, and meeting from the north-east, a large branch, which divides the chain of mountains, proceeds down the prairie, making many large and beautiful islands, one of which I judge contains 100,000 acres of land, all meadow ground, covered with innumerable herds of deer; . . . this view combined the sublime and the beautiful; the great and lofty mountains covered with eternal snows, seemed to surround the luxuriant vale, crowned with perennial flowers, like a terrestrial paradise, shut out from the view of man. (375–76)

The sweeping vision suggests control of what is seen, and as is often the case, the passage includes a temporal dimension in which the explorer provides for the future implications of the present scene. The "terrestrial paradise, shut out from the view of man" has, of course, been unseen only by Europeans, as Pike himself, on some level, knows. Pike's first "white sight" is that Adamic moment when the creation is turned over to its intended master, the moment of recognition when "the 100,000 acres of land, all meadow ground," the "innumerable herds of deer," the "luxuriant" state of the valley, all point to the fruitful agricultural society that is Pike's ideal union of people and place.

Like Lewis and Pike, John Charles Fremont also isolated the unique moment when the land, through its beauty, seemed to make a special revelation to him. Fremont's *Report* is rhetorically more unified than most earlier such accounts. His tone is simultaneously the most confident, personal, and self-consciously representative of the American exploration writers up to his time. He writes as an American speaking to other Americans about something that concerns them all. He renders his landscape with an enthusiastic, painterly eye, describing not only the elements of the scene but his own avid involvement with them:

> Viewed in the sunshine of a pleasant morning, the scenery was of a most striking and romantic beauty, which arose from the picturesque disposition of the objects, and the vivid contrast of colors. I thought with much pleasure of our approaching descent in the canoe through such interesting places. (143)

The political implications of these aesthetic perceptions are often evident in the text. Leading up to his climactic description of the view from the top of a peak near the summit of the South Pass, Fremont describes the approach as more a beckoning gateway than the "winding" and "gorgelike" ascents that Americans had encountered in crossing the Alleghenies. It is like the "ascent of the Capitol Hill from the Avenue, at Washington" (161–62). Fremont makes his achieving the top of the peak, the westernmost and highest point on his journey, as well as the rhetorical climax of his narrative, the moment of his clearest assertion of the connection between his personal experiences and his nation's future in the West:

> I sprang upon the summit, and another step would have precipitated me into an immense snow field five hundred feet below. To the edge of this field was sheer icy precipice; and then with a gradual fall, the field sloped off for about a mile, until it struck the foot of another lower ridge. . . . We mounted the barometer in the snow of the summit, and, fixing a ramrod in a crevice, unfurled the national flag to wave in the breeze where never flag waved before. . . . A stillness the most profound and a terrible solitude forced themselves constantly on the mind as the great features of the place. Here, on

the summit, where the stillness was absolute, unbroken by any sound, and the solitude complete, we thought ourselves beyond the region of animated life; but while we were sitting on the rock, a solitary bee (Bombus, the humblebee [sic]) came winging his flight from the eastern valley, and lit on the knee of one of my men.

It was a strange place, the icy rock and the highest peak of the Rocky Mountains, for a lover of warm sunshine and flowers; and we pleased ourselves with the idea that he was the first of his species to cross the mountain barrier—a solitary pioneer to foretell the advance of civilization. (175–76)

Initially alone on the summit, Fremont experiences a moment of communion with the "profound and terrible solitude," which "forced itself constantly on the mind." Loneliness, here, is not threatening, however; it is the state which prepares him for a transforming experience. Soon his solitude, and vertigo, are given national historic significance as he plants the flag "where never flag waved before," and sees that the bee, also solitary, is like himself a "pioneer to foretell the advance of civilization." Fremont understands his experience as both unique and typical. He is "the first white man" to set foot on this peak and to envision this landscape, but he understands the significance of this moment as his being the first of many. His solitary identification with the land is a model for each westering American who can discover himself as he discovers the "solitude" of the West.

Writing almost forty years after Lewis and Clark, Fremont relies much more than they on the authority of his personal response to natural beauty. Although Stephen Fender argues that ultimately Fremont felt more secure in the scientific descriptive mode, turning to it much more in his second *Report* (48–49), I think that in the first *Report* at least, his most overt and vigorous assertions of an American's right to these western lands rely on the authority of what I have called the aesthetic mode. In conjunction with this mode of authority, Fremont demonizes and trivializes the Indian inhabitants, and his narrative offers nothing like Lewis and Clark's mode of intimate contact and shared experience. Reading Fremont after Lewis and Clark we sense an American who is much more confident about his and his country's western presence, and the popularity of Fremont's narrative among overland travelers, despite its relative lack of new or practical information, suggests that his pose of confident personal possession of the landscape, was by this time familiar, reassuring, and easy to imitate.

Some of the implications of treating the West as pure landscape emerge in Stephen Fender's interesting discussion of forty-niners' journey accounts. Fender argues that for forty-niners trying to recount their overland journeys to California the problem lay in writing about a place that had no particular reality in existing writing, and which for that very reason was liable quickly to become what anyone said about it (12–13). If the West of these narratives oscillates between enigma and cliche, it is, perhaps, because its history has been almost completely obscured by the rhetoric, by then dominant, of personal response to landscape. The forty-niner with pen in hand was painfully aware that the spectacular, "wild" country he saw had been described as such by hundreds who had preceded him along the trail. For many travelers in the early 1850s, the West was a landscape with little history apart from its role as a setting for repetitions of the primal encounters of "the first white man." Fender suggests that these writers experienced a similar uneasiness confronting the emptiness of both place and page (3–4). If this was so, then we perhaps see the ultimate achievement of the "first white man" rhetoric in this generation for whom the West was primordially empty, so much so that they had trouble even experiencing it. Their encounters appeared to threaten a blankness which perhaps reminds us of the white fog engulfing the narrator at the end of Poe's *Pym,* after the protagonist has blown much of Tsalal's native population to atoms and resumed his obsessive southward journey. Having been taught to conceive of the West as an empty land into which they could project their own futures, Americans of the 1850s, like Poe's explorer, were confronting an ambivalent blankness that resulted from ignorance of their own history in this region.

In Lewis and Clark, however, we find writers whose breadth and scope are such that they cannot manage to attain a unified tone regarding the lands they are seeking to encompass. They teach us immeasurably more about the West than Fremont because they were not as confident about how to write about themselves there. Their uncertainty is a virtue in that it is an accurate reflection of the relationship of the eastern imperialist ideology to the western territories at the time of their writing. The complexities and the contradictions of their report are those of the historical situation of which they were a part. On the one hand they were committed to the assertion of United States legal authority over these territories and their inhabitants, and they describe their performance of these duties confidently and clearly. They were also well prepared to invoke the authority of the categories of contemporary science as another, if less direct, assertion of their control. The circumstances of their survival and movement in the West, however, demanded close cooperation with local peoples, and as a result of their reporting of these exchanges Lewis and Clark opened up a mode of relationship with the West which contradicted the authority of the legal and scientific. This local mode created for the traveling Euro-American a west-ern discourse of shared experience with local peoples, and such a discourse threatened, or at least complicated, the basis on which the United States' expansion into the West could be imagined. Finally, what distinguishes the fourth, aesthetic mode from the others, and what is responsible for its success in later western writings, is that it obviates the contradictions among the other history-based claims. In this mode the American observer in the West is given a clear title to the land, irrespective of legal claims, through the ritual identification of American self and the land. That the land has been waiting for the first white man to recognize it is confirmed by the emotion of the viewer himself upon seeing it.

Notes

1. The *Journal* (1807) of expedition member Patrick Gass preceded the authorized history into print by seven years, but it was not an adequate substitute for the records of the two commanders. There were also numerous "apocryphal" accounts of the expedition based in part on Jefferson's 1806 *Message* to Congress and on material lifted from older western accounts such as those of Jonathan Carver. (See Coues, "Bibliographical Introduction," cvii–cxxxii.) Elliot Coues's edition of the *History* was published in 1893, and Reuben Gold Thwaites's edition of the *Original Journals* in 1904–05.

2. In discussing particular passages from the *History*, I refer where possible to the author of the journal record upon which the passage is based.

3. In discussing the 1790 debate over the location of the American capital, Meinig comments on the new nation's imperial outlook: "If there was reason to doubt whether an Atlantic America could extend and sustain itself as a viable geopolitical system across half a continent, there was no doubt at all about Americans themselves spreading across such an expanse, for they were busily doing so. The only uncer-tainty about that advance was how far they might go, for there was little reason to think that they might halt at the Mississippi or be deterred by the bounds of any other political claims. Fervent spokesmen were already declaring a transcontinental destiny for the American people and asserting that 'westward course of empire' must indeed soon take its way" (367–69).

4. See, for example, Elliott Coues's dedication, "To the People of the Great West," at the beginning of his edition (1893) of the *History:* "Jefferson gave you the country. Lewis and Clark showed you the way. The rest is your own course of empire. Honor the statesmen who foresaw your West. Honor the brave men who first saw your West. May the memory of their glorious achievement be your precious heritage!"

5. Zebulon Pike, for example, upon hearing that certain "savages" had threat-ened him, asks whether "the laws of self-preservation, would not have justified" his

"cutting those scoundrels to pieces"; but he admits that he dreaded meeting the individuals "for fear the impetuosity of my conduct might not be approved of by my government, who did not so intimately know the nature of those savages" (117).

6. Samuel Hearne dedicated his *Journey from Prince of Wales's Fort in Hudson's Bay to the Northern Ocean* (1795) to the "Governor and Committee of the Hudson's Bay Company"; John Long his *Voyages and Travels of an Indian Interpreter and Trader* (1791) to Sir Joseph Banks, President of the Royal Society. Lewis and Clark's *History* is prefaced by a letter from former President Jefferson explaining the origins and purposes of the expedition and memorializing the by then dead Lewis.

7. See Frantz (15–19) for an account of the effect of the Royal Society and the new science of the seventeenth century on the conventions of travel reporting. In the eighteenth century Cook's voyages set the pace in scientific exploration. Cook's entourages included several highly trained men who issued their own reports, supplementary to the master narratives of the expeditions. His voyages were joint ventures of the British Admiralty and the Royal Society. See MacLulich (10–11, 54–55) for discussions of Cook's impact on travel reporting.

8. Whereas modern anthropology has been much criticized on the grounds that it is complicit with western colonialism, Lewis and Clark were unselfconscious about using ethnographic categories to extend their society's control of others. Nevertheless, as I shall argue, in undertaking to write their reports they confronted a conflict between the relationships they developed "in the field" and those that were prescribed by the conventions of exploration reporting. Johannes Fabian argues that there is a split between modern ethnographic research and anthropological theorizing in this respect. Anthropological writing "creates its object" in part through the distancing effects of temporal categories, especially the "denial of coevalness" or "shared time." Ethnography is often forced to operate in "shared time" through the "cognitive necessity" inherent in research exchanges with the group under study, and this sharing is reflected in the style, especially the verb tenses, of field notes. (Fabian, 21–35.)

9. Although my term for this rhetoric is "local," suggesting a definition in terms of space, time is also a factor. The captains were forced to relate to Indians of the West in terms of their present power and knowledge rather than their belonging to an earlier "age" of prosperity or development. Again, I am indebted to Johannes Fabian's theory that much anthropological writing distances, and thereby disempowers, non-Europeans through the use of temporal categories ("the denial of coevalness"). See note 8 above.

10. See 915–17 for a description of the traffic on the river, and 935 for a typical description of the trading habits of a people.

11. It seems appropriate, too, that throughout this section of the narrative the possible presence of Indians known to frequent these parts is seen as threatening, and even sinister. The Assiniboines, for example, though known to claim this territory, are spoken of as "troublesome" and "vicious" intruders (302, 305).

12. Historian John Bakeless, for example, describes his *The Eyes of Discovery* (1950) as "an effort to describe North America as the first white men in each area saw it." This trope is so crucial that Bakeless explains how even though "the first explorer in

each part of the United States often took but a brief glimpse and then departed before putting on record any detailed account of what he saw," one can "fill in a description of what the first arrival must have seen from accounts given by much later and more leisurely travelers" (Preface). Not knowing what "the first white man" saw, we are required to construct it.

13. Mary Louise Pratt has called this trope the "monarch-of-all-I-survey scene" (146).

Works Cited

Bakeless, John. *The Eyes of Discovery: The Pageant of North America as Seen by the First Explorers*. Philadelphia: J. B. Lippincott Co., 1950.

Bercovitch, Sacvan. "The Problem of Ideology in American Literary History." *Critical Inquiry* 12.4 (1986): 631–53.

Dwight, Timothy. *Greenfield Hill: A Poem*. New York, 1794. Rpt. in *The Connecticut Wits*. Ed. Vernon L. Parrington. New York: Harcourt, Brace, 1926.

Fabian, Johannes. *Time and the Other: How Anthropology Makes Its Object*. New York: Columbia University Press, 1983.

Fender, Stephen. *Plotting the Golden West: American Literature and the Rhetoric of the California Trail*. Cambridge: Cambridge University Press, 1981.

Franklin, Wayne. *Discoverers, Explorers, Settlers: The Diligent Writers of Early America*. Chicago: University of Chicago Press, 1979.

Frantz, R. W. "The English Traveller and the Movement of Ideas, 1660–1732." In *The University Studies of the University of Nebraska*. Vol. 34. Lincoln: University of Nebraska Press, 1934.

Fremont, John Charles. *Narrative of the Exploring Expedition to the Rocky Mountains in the Year 1842. . . .* Washington, 1845. In *The Expeditions of John Charles Fremont*. Ed. Donald Jackson and Mary Lee Spence. Urbana: University of Illinois Press, 1970.

Gass, Patrick. *A Journal of the Voyage and Travels of a Corps of Discovery. . . .* Pittsburgh: Zodak Cramer, 1807.

Hearne, Samuel. *Journey from Prince of Wales's Fort in Hudson's Bay to the Northern Ocean*. Ed. Richard Glover. Toronto: Macmillan, 1958. (1st ed. London, 1795.)

Jackson, Donald. *The Letters of the Lewis and Clark Expedition*. Urbana: University of Illinois Press, 1962.

Jefferson, Thomas. *The Papers of Thomas Jefferson*. Ed. Julian P. Boyd. Princeton, N.J.: Princeton University Press, 1954.

Jehlen, Myra. *American Incarnation: The Individual, the Nation, and the Continent*. Cambridge, Mass.: Harvard University Press, 1986.

Lewis, Meriwether, and William Clark. *History of the Expedition under the Command of Captains Lewis and Clark*. Ed. Elliott Coues. New York: Harper, 1893. (1st ed. Philadelphia, 1814.)

Long, John. *Voyages and Travels of an Indian Interpreter and Trader*. London, 1791.

Mackenzie, Alexander. *The Journals and Letters of Alexander Mackenzie*. Ed. W. Kaye Lamb. Cambridge: Cambridge University Press, 1970. (1st ed. London, 1801.)

MacLulich, Thomas Donald. "The Emergence of the Exploration Narrative in Canada." Ph.D. dissertation, York University, Toronto, 1976.

Meinig, D. W. *The Shaping of America: A Geographical Perspective on 500 Years of History*. Vol. 1, *Atlantic America, 1492–1800*. New Haven, Conn.: Yale University Press, 1986.

Miller, Perry. *Errand into the Wilderness*. Cambridge, Mass.: Harvard University Press, 1956.

Moulton, Gary E., ed. *The Journals of the Lewis and Clark Expedition*. Vol. 2. Lincoln: University of Nebraska Press, 1986.

Pike, Zebulon. *The Journals of Zebulon Pike*. Ed. Donald Jackson. Norman: University of Oklahoma Press, 1966. (1st ed. Philadelphia, 1810.)

Pratt, Mary Louise. "Conventions of Representation: Where Discourse and Ideology Meet." In *Contemporary Perceptions of Language: Interdisciplinary Dimensions*. Ed. Heidi Byrnes. *Georgetown University Round Table on Language and Linguistics 1982*. Washington, D.C.: Georgetown University Press, 1982, 139–55.

Thwaites, Reuben Gold, ed. *The Original Journals of the Lewis and Clark Expedition*. New York: Dodd, Mead, 1904–05.

Nancy Vogeley

The Discourse of Colonial Loyalty: Mexico, 1808

IN MANY CASES the colonial literature to survive in greatest quantity is the laudatory, celebratory material produced in response to some distant occasion at the imperial court. Whether the king's birthday, a royal marriage, some military success, or a Church-related development, such an event usually inspired an outpouring of loyalty in colonial areas. It is easy to dismiss the poetry or theatrical compositions, which is the form these expressions normally took, as pseudo-art, insincere rhetoric, useless exercises by a viceregal elite which soon lost control as a result of later historical changes. However, such discourse is instructively studied to explain why colonial people are often an old regime's staunchest supporters, apologists for its essential structure in the face of doubt and dissent. It may also shed light on how, in spite of its declaredly conservative nature, this linguistic activity helped prepare the way for change to occur. Equally as important as the subversive documents which in retrospect forecast changing attitudes, these loyalist statements define an aspect of colonial thinking which has retarded cultural emancipation even though political ties have been cut.

This discussion will focus on several collections of anti-Napoleon, pro-Fernando VII materials which were published in Nueva España in the last days of July and throughout August 1808.[1] As soon as a ship docked in Veracruz with the news that on May 1–2 the Spanish citizenry had revolted against Napoleon's occupying armies, Mexican poets and playwrights poured forth their support of the monarchy and traditional values. Mexicans still pinned all their hopes for reform on the young king, Fernando VII, who as recently as March had forced his father, the inept Carlos IV, to abdicate. However, on the advice of his prime minister, Manuel Godoy, Fernando VII had permitted French troops to enter Spain, ostensibly to cross over into Portugal so as to end that country's threatening alliance with England.[2]

The official gazette in the Mexican colony printed the news of the Spanish revolt on July 29, and immediately the capital was strewn with poetry. A contemporary account of the scene follows:

> Por todas las esquinas se ponian papelones, carteles, proclamas, versos y bien temprano ya corrian de mano en mano los impresos de las noticias de Veracruz, cuyas primeras palabras son VIVA FERNANDO. Yo vi fixar un soneto, tan bien hecho, que parecia increible se hubiese formado en minutos. En la esquina del portal leí una proclama de tres parrafos, tan bien cortada, y de tan buen pensamiento, que merece muchos elogios [el autor]. . . . Pero ¿quien sería capaz de leer todos los papeles que cubrian las esquinas de Provincia, de Palacio, del Portal, del Empedradillo, del Parian, de la calle de Plateros, S. Francisco, &?

> On every corner one found fastened large sheets of paper, placards, proclamations, verses; and the printed version of the news from Veracruz—whose first words were VIVA FERNANDO—traveled quickly from hand to hand. I saw affixed a sonnet, so well crafted, that it seemed incredible that it had been formed in minutes. At the corner of the Portal I read a proclamation of three paragraphs, so clearly set out and of such thoughtfulness, that [its author] deserves great praise. . . . But, who would be able to read all the papers that covered the corners of Provincia, the Palace, the Portal, the Empedradillo, the Parian, the street of the Plateros, S. Francisco, etc.?[3]

The colonial professions of loyalty seem unusual at this key moment in Mexico's history; two years later Father Miguel Hidalgo's famous "Grito de Dolores" would unleash the hatred and resentment felt by many members of Mexico's diverse population and start a civil war that ended Spanish control in 1821. However, in 1808 most in the upper and middle classes separated the king from his advisers and representatives, blaming the widespread corruption on the latter. These members of the colonial elite, if they wanted change at all, wished for reform and autonomy in the imperial system; the desire for independence only grew with the insurrection fighting in Mexico and Fernando's return to the Spanish throne in 1814.

Neverthelesss, Mexico was shattered by the news in the summer of 1808 that Napoleon was holding Fernando VII prisoner in Bayonne. The faith in a patriarchally ordered universe that most had learned was shaken when this symbol of God's authority was so removed from power and humiliated. Colonial leaders were further confused by conflicting claims from *juntas* or provisional governments in Valencia, Sevilla, then later in Cádiz, Murcia, and Oviedo, that they represented the Spanish crown. The question of a legitimate government was further complicated by Napoleon's appointment of his brother José as administrator in Madrid.

It is understandable that, in their bewilderment, the first reaction of American Spaniards to news of their Peninsular brothers' revolt was expressed in the colonial terms of filial outrage and family protestations of support. Napoleon, who had previously been described admiringly in Mexican newspapers for his military deeds and his war on Protestant England, immediately became a villain; France, with great influence in the Spanish Bourbon court whose culture had been widely held up as enlightened and progressive, at once became an enemy. Overnight England became an ally and a culture based on belief in man's reason was suspect.

*   *   *

The frenzied use of art by many colonials to insist on their loyalty at this moment is itself significant. While to some extent Mexicans were imitating and attempting to outdo their fellow Spanish subjects in their demonstrations, they also felt that the use of words was their designated response. Far away from the fighting, they could contribute only their linguistic artifacts to the struggle. Governing rhetoric during the colonial period had taught them an identity based on the Catholic faith, allegiance to a father/king, and acquisition of the Spanish language; therefore, it was consistent with this identity that they called upon this gift in helping to defend what they perceived as a threat to this unity.

The first decade of the nineteenth century had witnessed an increased use of newspapers and printed materials such as pamphlets and broadsides (Vogeley 1982), thus opening up opportunities for colonial verse-makers. Indeed, in 1806 a writer in the unofficial *Diario de México,* which began publishing several months earlier, complained of "la peste de poetas que se va soltando" "the plague of poets that is being unleashed."[4] Many of these poets were seeing their words in print for the first time, and their authorized topics were religious, moralistic, or politically reflective of events at the distant court. However, a domestic event had also occasioned a flood of poetry when more than two hundred poets responded to a literary competition held when an equestrian statue of Carlos IV was erected in Mexico City on December 9, 1803. Yet the Mexican response to news of Napoleon's treachery and of the Spanish revolt of May 1–2, 1808, was more than a ritual colonial performance. In one collection of poems written between July 29 and 31 and compiled by Josef Agustín de Castro, "escojiendo las que han parecido mas dignas de darse a la prensa" "choosing those that have seemed most worthy of being given to the press," 89 poems by some 34 identifiable writers overwhelmingly repeat the message of loyalty. The format of this 152-page collection—consecutively numbered segments of four pages each—implies that the collection was sold as journalistic literature in installments; an appeal at the end of Segment 1 to those who might have poetry and who wished to have it published suggests that the collection was formed amidst the enthusiasm of the moment. Many other loose poems, variously professing love for and loyalty to Fernando and hatred of Napoleon, appear in the collections of Mexican Independence materials; the terms of their discourse are relatively uniform, although the tone may range from the exalted to the obscene and the form from the ode to the march. An eight-page report detailing an allegorical masque put on by the town of Valladolid (Morelia) on August 6 also survives.[5] In it colonials seem concerned with establishing the loyalty of all sectors of the population; for example, among the symbolic characters an Indian represents American allegiance to Spanish reign. The precise dating here and in other works where even the time of the composition is recorded suggests that these artistic compositions were not only addressed to a home audience but also written to reassure a distant officialdom.

The artistic power of the May 2 uprising was manifest both in the colonies and on Spanish soil; two of Goya's most famous canvases depict fighting in Madrid's Puerta del Sol on that day and a scene early the next morning when patriots stood before a French firing squad. Later, an elegy by the Spanish poet Juan Nicasio Gallego, "El dos de mayo," was widely reprinted and became known in Mexico in January, 1809. However, innocent of these other artistic expressions, the first Mexican response to the news seems to have been a combination of dictated fealty and genuine sympathy. Apart from the fact that the expression of loyalist feeling guaranteed approval by the censors and ready publication of one's work, this exaggerated use of art in the colonial world at such an historic moment invites explanation.

That such art was meant to function as part of public spectacle is clear. That such art seems to spring from a need to proclaim Mexico's loyalty when disloyalty was rampant is also clear. A report of Mexico City's reaction to the news, entitled "Lealtad Mexicana" "Mexican Loyalty" and published in the July 30 edition of the *Diario,* registers the surprising mood of jubilation. The article also records how the painted image of Fernando, colorful banners on public buildings, and the music of the Te Deum inspired the people to rally.

Ayer à las cinco de la mañana se anunciò solemnemente en ésta capital la plausibilísima noticia . . . Los nobles sentimientos de los mexicanos, merecen el universal aprecio de las naciones, y ésto vamos à describir, para satisfaccion de nuestros espìritus inflamados.

Con el grandioso anuncio de la artilleria y repique general, se extendió el regocijo en todo el pueblo de ésta capital, y concurrio en tropas à la frente del real Palacio, repitiendo sus vivas y aclamaciones al deseado FERNANDO VII, Rey de España y de las Indias. El Exmô. Senor Virrey saliò al balcon, acompañado de varios Señores ministros, militares y personas distinguidas, para recibir los vivas del noble y leal pueblo de Mexico. Una union notable-mente desordenada de Españoles, europeos y americanos, pedian à voces, que se repitiese la salva de la artillería. . . . La naturaleza y la humanidad se veía en los semblantes de un pueblo inmenso, que no respira mas que patriotismo, fidelidad y acendrado amor a su Soberano. El mismo pueblo sacò la artillerìa para hacer la salva, y los vivas subian hasta el trono de la Providencia, unidos con los mas afectuosos votos por la prosperidad y felicidad de las armas Españolas.

Cuando estaban en la fogosidad y entusiasmo de la salva, traxo una porcion de pueblo el retrato del amable FERNANDO, y lo conduxeron al real Palacio, sin que la tropa pudiese poner en òrden á la multitud. El Señor Oydor Don Josef Arias Villafañe, y el Alcalde . . . baxaron hasta el primer descanso de la escalera principal, para recibir el retrato, y lo conduxeron en medio de la multitud al Exmô. Señor Virrey, quien lo recibió lleno de regocijo mas fiel. Inmediatamente se adornò el balcon principal del real Palacio, y se colocó el retrato: à consecuencia, dicho Señor Exmô. y demàs ministros, unidos con los votos de èste noble pueblo, manifestàron su júbilo tirando una porcion considerable de pesos, que parece fueron dos mil, y lo mismo se repitió en la Diputacion, y por muchos particulares.

Así que estuvo un gran rato en el balcon el real retrato, lo pidiò el pueblo, para pasearlo en triunfo por las calles de la ciudad. En efecto lo baxò el Sòr. Villafañe, y otros Señores de la corte, y lo entregaron al pueblo, y éste lo arrebatò lleno de ternura, y baxo de palio lo llevò por todas las calles de ésta capital; . . . en medio de los vivas mas patéticos y hasta las mugeres, echaban al ayre los pañuelos y basquiñas en señal de su regocijo. VIVA FERNANDO VII, muera el Emperador de los franceses: esta es la expresion del patri-otismo, éste el desahogo de la lealtad mexicana. . . . En todos los templos se cantó el Te Deum, habiendo comenzado en la Metropoli con tanta concu-rrencia del pueblo y de la nobleza, que no habia un lugar vacio en todo el templo. . . . La ciudad se adornò con tapiceria, y se ha puesto en las mas partes el retrato del Soberano aclamado. Las estatuas y retratos de Napoleon han sido abrasadas por el pueblo. . . .

Yesterday at five in the morning the most commendable news was announced in this capital. . . . The noble sentiments of the Mexicans deserve the universal appreciation of the nations, and this we are going to describe for the satisfac-tion of our inflamed spirits.

With the splendid announcement of artillery and widespread ringing of bells, the jubilation was spread to all the people of this capital. [The crowd] gathered in front of the royal palace, repeating its *vivas* and acclamations to the beloved FERNANDO VII, king of Spain and the Indies. His Excellency the Viceroy came out onto the balcony, accompanied by various ministers, military men and distinguished persons, in order to receive the *vivas* of the noble and loyal people of Mexico. A notably disorderly collection of Spaniards, Europeans and Americans yelled for the artillery salvos to be repeated. . . . Character and humaneness were visible in the faces of this immense horde that only breathed patriotism, loyalty and pure love for its Sovereign. The very same people pulled out the artillery in order to fire the salvo, and their *vivas* ascended to the throne of Providence, united with the most affectionate pleas for the success and happiness of the Spanish forces.

While they were in the vehemence and enthusiasm of their salvo, a portion of the people brought out a portrait of the beloved FERNANDO, and took it to the Royal Palace without the soldiers being able to control the multitude. His Excellency the Judge Don Josef Arias Villafañe and the Mayor . . . came down to the first landing of the main staircase in order to receive the portrait, and they took it from amidst the horde to his Excellency the Viceroy, who received it with the greatest delight. Immediately the main balcony of the Royal Palace was adorned and the portrait was positioned: then, His Excellency and the remaining ministers, joined by the wishes of this noble people, showed their jubilation by throwing a considerable amount of *pesos*, which it seemed was almost 2,000; and the same thing was repeated in the Congress and by many private citizens.

After the royal portrait had been on the balcony for a long while, the people requested it so as to carry it in triumph throughout the streets of the city. In fact Señor Villafañe and the other gentlemen of the court took it down, and they gave it over to the people who, full of tenderness, seized it and, placing it under a canopy, took it throughout the streets of the capital; . . . in the midst of the most heart-rending *vivas,* and even the women threw their kerchiefs and petticoats into the air in a sign of rejoicing. LONG LIVE FERNANDO VII, death to the Emperor of the French: this is the expression of patriotism, this is the venting of feelings of Mexican loyalty. . . . In all of the churches the Te Deum was sung, having begun in the city with such an attendance of people and nobility that there was no empty place in any church. The city was decorated with tapestries, and the image of the acclaimed Sovereign has been placed everywhere. The statues and portraits of Napoleon have been burned by the people. . . .

The great bulk of these pro-Fernando, anti-Napoleon poetic compositions seems to have served the purpose of tangible, material artifacts in celebratory rites, described by social anthropologists such as Victor Turner. Caught up in the spirit of "communitas" (Turner 1969 Ch. 4) palpably put forth in the streets, domestic poets produced "key symbolic objects" (Dorson) which could be felt to have some magical-sacred value in mediating between potentially disruptive forces and thereby in protecting the structure. Examples of this sense of drawing-together are abundant in the poetry; the following composition shows how elements within Mexico were wishfully reconciled to one another in the act of being bound to a foreign king:

El nombre *Gachupin,* queda extinguido,
   El de *Criollo,* tambien es sepultado,
   El de *Indio* y demás ya no es mentado
   Quando en FERNANDO todos se han unido:
Unanimes por él hemos gemido,
   Por su causa inocente hemos rogado,
   Formando un cuerpo en todo tan amado
   Que maridage tal ha confundido;
Admirandonos mas que en lo alocado
   Del gozo en que han estado aquestos dias,
   El Lepero mas ruin no se ha embriagado,
   Desgracia no se há visto, ni porfias;
Casa de pobre ó rico no han robado,
   Esto sí no es violar las alegrias.
   En lo que advertirás Joven FERNANDO
   Quanto todos te estamos venerando.

The name of *hated Spaniard* is extinguished,
   That of *Creole* also is buried,
   That of *Indian* and the rest is no longer mentioned
   When all have been united in FERNANDO:
Unanimous for him we have wailed,
   For his innocent cause we have pled,
   Forming a body in all so loving
   That it can be confused with a marital bond;
Admiring ourselves more than in the crazy
   Pleasure of what have been those days,
   The lowest rabble-rouser hasn't gotten drunk,
   Or fallen into disgrace or obstinacy;
No house of a wealthy man or a poor man has been robbed,
   That indeed means not violating everyone's happiness.
   In all of this the young FERNANDO
   Will know how much we are venerating him.[6]

The words on the pieces of paper tacked up in public places may have been legible to only the literate few, yet it is probable that semi-literates at least recognized in the print of this and other poems the capitalized name of FERNANDO and recalled the chant "VIVA FERNANDO, muera Napoleon" set up in the streets of the capital the day the news broke. The capitalized name, as in the *Diario* article, suggests its articulation in many throats. In addition, the larger letters of the king's name reinforced the message of the king's stature and conveyed a sense of his physical presence, which the use of direct address in this and many other poems rushed out in these days enhanced. Illiterates attributed their own meaning to the paper displayed prominently; such usage was always reserved for the educated elite and would have been associated with recent events.

Most significant, however, is the way in which the colonial world converted a tragedy into a joyous celebration. An event which Spanish artists and writers understandably saw darkly was transformed by Mexico's patriotism into an opportunity for demonstrating self-pride; the writer in the *Diario,* for example, gives eloquent testimony of how a rowdy populace, under the spell of Fernando's portrait and shouts of his name, adhered to the values of God and king. Mexico thought itself a shining example of loyalty in the eyes of civilized people throughout the world, and its poets immediately sought to publicize its worth. They used flattering epithets like "Mexicanos ilustres" and "nobles Mexicanos"[7] to suggest Mexico's moral superiority. They characterized the colony as a fortunate and wealthy land whose mines must contribute to the struggle in Europe.[8] In rallying Mexicans behind national symbols, they sang of "la patrona Guadalupana" (Mexico's patron saint, the Virgin of Guadalupe).[9]

One can read this discourse of colonial loyalty, of course, in several different ways. The rhetoric of praise to Fernando may be seen as a veneer concealing a basically subversive expression of Mexican nationalism. Seizing the extraordinary moment, writers who were at heart insurgents gave voice to suppressed desires. In anticipation of indigenous events such as the overthrow of the Viceroy Iturrigaray on September 15–16, 1808 (albeit at the hands of ultra-conservatives), and Hidalgo's Independence movement begun on September 15–16, 1810, their nationalist language may be considered revolutionary.

However, the statement of colonial loyalty in this body of poetry must also be taken at face value, as a true expression of royalist support. Yet who could be considered a royalist at this time was a troublesome question since, only a month and a half later, loyalists who professed respect for the divine right of kings and the traditional juridical system would depose by illegal or extra-legal means the duly appointed viceroy in Mexico City (Villoro 57, Anna 58). The answer must partially lie in the individual's public use of language.

If one thinks of the activity of writing political poetry at this time—and of having it published—as still tied closely to colonial artistic rituals, then the discourse of colonial loyalty must be understood unequivocally—as an example of how powerful interests may so preempt language that thinking of one's identity in any other terms is impossible. It is true that the many poets responsible for the poems came from the Mexican-born population as well as the Spanish, were lay and clergy and represented differing economic interests; thus their motives for expressing themselves, and in this one way, must have varied. Yet all were literate in Spanish, educated sufficiently to use Spanish metric patterns and politicized to the extent that distant political developments moved them to this investment in time and energy. Poetry or literature, which is very often thought of as privately produced and privately consumed, in this case seems to have been the result of a social experience, destined to play a part in the public display.

*   *   *

Loyalty, then, emerges as a secondary feature of this communal voicing. The psychoanalyst's explanation of such activity arising out of the fear and displaced aggression of a dependent people may indeed be valid; similarly, an historical analysis based on material concerns, which finds loyalist poetry and prayers to be a response equivalent to volunteering the colony's mineral wealth, is also correct. An especially interesting example of a poet's experiment with using words to respond to a distant crisis is the first poem supposedly published in Mexico City on July 29, 1808; its author, a Peninsular-born Spaniard, apparently prided himself on his fast action. Yet, as the choking close of the following selection makes clear, this verbally active colonial was not satisfied by this opportunity to release his emotions:

Gota á gota mi sangre
Derramarla quisiera
Por mi amado FERNANDO;
Mas dista mucho el teatro de la guerra
No tengo mas desahogo
Que el de esa Arma ratera;
Mas palabra a palabra

Exhausto he de quedar en la contienda.
Mi natural idioma
Pobre se me presenta:
¡Oh si de todos ellos
Las voces mas valientes consiguiera!
Aunque mudo quedára,
Diera esa fina muestra,
De mis anhelos nobles,
Ya que al Ibero acompañar no pueda.
Como volar quisiera
Al suelo de mi origen,
Fuente de mi lealtad y mi Nobleza! . . .
Mas ¡ay! hablar no puedo . . .
Aunque esa es una Guerra
Para mi imaginária,
En el efecto es real y verdadera.
Muero, mas no á los tiros
De la gente francesa,
Sino de pura rabia
Contra el cruel Napoleon y su caterva,
Solo ese impedimento
Suspenderá mi lengua:
Bien se ha visto que hasta ohora
No ha habido dia sin versos de mi vena.
Yo soy el B.J.V. [B. Josef Valdés]
Que he puesto varias piezas
En públicos parages
Que al Galo Omnipotente incienso prestan.
Ni entonces ni ahora el *Dixi*
He usado en todas ellas.
Pues corto, mas no acabo,
Y por ahora esperad me restablezca.

Drop by drop
I should like to spill my blood
For my beloved FERNANDO;
But the theater of war is far away.
I have no other means of expression
Than this dishonest weapon [of my poetry];

But word by word
I am to remain exhausted in the fray.
My natural language
Reveals itself impoverished;
Oh, if from among all of them [other languages]
I could claim the bravest words!
Although I remained mute,
I would give a fine showing
Of my noble desires,
Since I cannot accompany the Iberian.
How I should like to fly
To the soil of my birthplace,
Source of my loyalty and my Nobility! . . .
But ay! I cannot speak . . .
Although this is a War
Which is imaginary for me,
In fact it is real.
I die, not because of the shots
Of the French soldiers
But out of pure rage
At cruel Napoleon and his mob.
Only that impediment
Will suspend my speech;
It has already been proven that until now
There has been no day without verses from my mood.
I am B.J.V.
Who has placed various artistic compositions
In public places
So as to lend incense to the Gaul's omnipotence.
Neither then nor now
Have I written *Dixi* to them.
However, here I stop but I do not finish,
And for now wait until I recover myself.

The metropolitan-centered identity of B.J.V. is deeply felt; his moral
fiber and his sense of his own worth ("mi lealtad y mi Nobleza" "my loyalty
and my Nobility") are rooted in his homeland. His "natural idioma" is the
only thing he has to defend himself with in distant lands. Yet it is probable
that a *criollo* (Creole, an American-born person of European blood) or

anyone indoctrinated by state, Church, or controlling economic interests to participation in the colonial structure, would have expressed a similar, and even deeper, sense of a derived identity. For such linguistically enslaved colonials words must have assumed powerful proportions. For B.J.V. the words of public poetry were the only weapon at hand to use against the enemy in an imagined war; yet words publicly uttered had also betrayed him as a result of his previous pro-Napoleonic statements. Thus, using the language he was taught led him, for the moment, to silence. One assumes that B.J.V. and others like him soon underwent a rite of passage as a result of questioning and independent thought.

As Edward Said has written, it is wrong to generalize about the colonial and the post-colonial experience (45); rather, each oppressed individual or group, according to his/her/its own development, records its peculiar history. Yet some aspects of colonial loyalist discourse may at this point begin to emerge as common denominators. As in the Mexican experience, the discourse often originates in crisis. It frequently patterns itself ritualistically after older responses. Whether "Viva Fernando, muera Napoleon"—or even "John loves Mary"—it is inscribed publicly to reassure the union. It is acutely self-conscious, perhaps because of an awareness of inferiority and dependency; the colonial feels the eyes of the world on him. Because the yardstick the Enlightenment offered the Mexican, based on the polarities of civilization and barbarism, was no longer an applicable measurement of status among the world's nations because Napoleon had made the French ideal untenable, the colonial had to fall back on the only other model for behavior the outside world had taught him, that is, loyalty to traditional political and religious values.

Art at this key moment in Mexico's history was very much the prerogative of the ruling classes. A small number of Spanish-speaking, European-blooded individuals in the capital and outlying provincial cities mainly consumed what passed for art. Their education was often poor, consisting merely of learning to parrot impressive-sounding words. Their culture was based almost totally on imported books and ideas (Vogeley 1987). Yet there is evidence that many of these colonials saw the need for translating foreign concepts into their own terms and for then extending a new national culture by means of art forms to the larger population of Indians, blacks, and persons of mixed caste, who were usually illiterate and who spoke Spanish either badly or not at all. The colonials' awareness of the importance of sermons and the visual arts, such as theater and architecture, reveals not just an understanding of art's utilitarian value, which a Neo-classic aesthetic had taught, but also their own understanding of art's capacity to mediate between cultures and classes.

Somehow the quickening of Mexico's loyalty caused an examination of the linguistic means by which loyalty is expressed. While in the past loyalty had seemed to be acquiescence in exploitation, acceptance of the religious and political discourse of submission, now loyalty to Fernando demanded that Mexicans learn a new, active language of loyalty to fellow Mexicans. If they hoped to aid the Spanish empire in a moment of crisis, they needed to assume strength by quelling any dissent at home and coming together as a nation. Such a colonial leader as Francisco Manuel Sánchez de Tagle, who wrote Arcadian poetry for an intimate circle of devotees, realized the need for political poetry which would communicate to Mexico's linguistically diverse population. In one of his pro-Fernando, anti-Napoleon pieces he sought to help his less-skilled readers to understand the allusive intricacies of his poetry by providing a list of explanatory footnotes.[10] Another manifestation of upper-class interest in giving the masses lessons in loyalty is the staged allegorical pageants[11] and the poems obviously written for oral performance, for example, the marches—one to be sung to a well-known drinking song.[12]

It is difficult to know how and to what extent these printed poems entered the oral culture of the literate and illiterate classes, yet it is clear that their writers intended them to be simple in their meaning and to give auditory pleasure. Many of the poems may have been designed primarily for the *criollos* whose schooling was not up to European standards and whose inferior economic condition and American birth caused them to be more critical of Spanish domination. An interesting example of a poem written with sound effects suggestive of its recitation appeal follows:

¿Pensarás, majadero Napoleon,
  Que es España lo mismo que *Austerlitz?*
  ¿Pensarás, patarato, que es *Dantzik*
  Que es *Gena,* ó qualquiera ruin Nacion?
Te engañas, presumido fanfarron,
  Hipocrita, el mas vil, mas infelíz,
  Que en el valor de España hay un *mís mís*
  Que quando dice *sás,* dá el bofeton:
Muy bien lo tiene ya experimentado
  El cobarde Berg, pues èste ha huido
  Al verse por España derrotados:

Bien que parece, nada le ha valido,
   Pues si la ira española le ha alcanzado
   Sin duda en los infiernos lo ha metido.

Do you think, pesty Napoleon,
   That Spain is the same as *Austerlitz?*
   Do you think, Mr. Politeness, that it is *Danzig*
Or *Jena,* or any little old Nation?
You deceive yourself, conceited blusterer,
   Hypocrite, scum, unfortunate,
   [In thinking] that in the valour of Spain there is a kitty kat
That when it says POW, delivers the blow:
The coward Berg had experienced it very well,
   For he has fled
   When he found himself defeated by Spain;
It seems that nothing has rescued him
   For if Spanish rage has found him
   Doubtless it has put him in hell.[13]

The poem's careful use of foreign place names and political actors indicates that the poet may be teaching Mexicans of various classes the current European litany of hatred for Napoleon.

However, this consciousness of class levels of language, of differences between European and American terms of loyalty, produced similar but different results a few months later. Whereas the tone of the poetry written immediately after word arrived of the May 2 uprising is relatively high and exalted, later in August and then through September and October, when news came that Napoleon had named his brother José as governor in Spain and Spanish possessions overseas, the loyalist poetry included some significant examples of satire and low usage. In one poem the anonymous poet provided a list of footnotes explaining his use of *mexicanismos* and colloquial expressions to Pepe Botellas, the derogatory name given José Bonaparte; here, in a reversal of the Sánchez de Tagle poem, the Mexican poet defiantly upholds the value of the Mexican language to readers outside the Mexican speech community.[14] In another poem the anonymous poet playfully glosses a verse in which a toilet is named a "Napoleon."[15]

The metaphors of the French Revolution of 1789 have been instructively studied by Jean Starobinski; Ronald Paulson has also examined one of Goya's paintings on the May 2 theme as a representation of revolution. Yet what is startling to learn is that colonials themselves may have been aware of the very processes shaping their thinking. Telling evidence of this is the attention paid in this pro-Fernando, anti-Napoleon loyalist poetry to communication and to language. That such consciousness and demystification was in the air is borne out by the appearance of an article, "Discurso sobre el uso de la mitologia en las composiciones poeticas" "Discourse on the Use of Mythology in Poetic Compositions," in the September 20 and October 6–7, 9, 1808, issues of the *Diario*. Its relevance for contemporary political events is spelled out in a footnote: "Aunque éste discurso está un poco dilatado lo insertamos por las diversas instrucciones que encierra, para formar la crítica de los varios ingenios que se han dedicado à la poesia en ésta América" "Although this discourse is a little delayed we insert it because of the diverse instructions it contains, so as to form a critique of the various minds that have dedicated themselves to poetry in this America." In this unsigned essay the writer rejects the use of mythological language in poetry as unnatural, improper, and a hindrance to the expression of the truth. These ideas were pursued even further in various articles published in the *Diario* in May 1809, where the mythical language commonly used to treat the king and royal topics is traced to forms of expression used to refer to the gods. This writer says that when Greeks and Romans adopted the symbols of rule of eastern religions, they failed to understand the allegory these linguistically impoverished peoples had created and thus took literally their "ficciones poéticas" "poetic fictions." Since then a marvelous tradition was passed on uncritically. Although ostensibly a study of ancient history, this discussion in the *Diario* reveals that colonials were beginning to be aware that inherited language could disguise errors in thought and that a taste for mythological references in poetry—or obfuscating usage—could serve the interests of the powerful classes.

Loyalty at this moment in Mexico's history meant not only affirming the legal right of the king to govern but also agreeing to extend his legal authority to larger areas of the society through the use of an increasingly outmoded set of reverential metaphors. Secular and national adherence was only beginning to win respectability in the colony when Napoleon's actions discredited this modernizing thought and awakened a fear of chaos among the colony's leaders. Therefore, their response repeated earlier paternalistic doctrine and was blindly reactionary in insisting on obedience. It is a linguistic fact that those areas first colonized by an empire, remote from changes in the capital, often preserve usages which are regarded as archaisms in the light of later developments; Spain itself, for example, an outpost in the Roman empire, retained many older word forms which the emerging Italian language cast aside. A people stripped of its language and given a foreign discourse can only with difficulty begin to formulate an independent system of thought.[16] Albert Memmi has shown how a portrait of the colonizer must always include those members of the domestic elite most in thrall to foreign customs who totally reject the ways of their compatriots (65) and therefore cooperate in their country's exploitation. They are often fascists, he says, because they are incapable of thinking anything else but that everything good is associated with the motherland and everything bad with the homeland.

Memmi especially remarks on the power of the metaphor of the family to impose harmony and enforce bondage. Loyalty is part of the vocabulary which kinship relationships often require for personal bonding. What is a functional, if not intrinsically positive, quality to be encouraged in a small-scale society, where other values contribute to a sense of mutual obligation among equals, may be inappropriate and even dangerous in a larger, impersonal structure such as an empire or nation-state. As Bertolt Brecht wrote in *Mother Courage,* "Whenever there are great virtues [such as loyalty, bravery and courage] it's a sure sign something is wrong . . . In a good country virtues wouldn't be necessary." (39) That the language of virtue is still being used to justify colonial exploitation is apparent in the recent statement by a Francophile writer that France did not colonize; instead it civilized, it humanized (Rosenblum).

Clearly the pro-Fernando, anti-Napoleon loyalist rhetoric of the poetry produced in Mexico in 1808 paved the way for political events in 1810 which led to the colony's independence from Spain. In the discussion of Spain's freedom from the French, Mexico learned the terms necessary for thinking about its own freedom. In being taught to hate Napoleon, the colony acquired the experience of turning angrily on a previously respected figure. As a result of describing itself and its population with pride, Mexico appropriated from the center the vocabulary of decency and nobility that it needed to create a local ethos. Poetic language which sought to win loyalty to the Spanish cause by addressing Mexicans as "hijos del bravo Cortés" "sons of the fierce Cortez"[17] instead awakened many to the question of legitimate rule and the reality of their equal identity as children of Indian mothers (Alamán 190).

Mexico's discourse of loyalty in the last years of colonial rule reveals how a seemingly repressive and paralyzing language has the potential to stimulate a critical reexamination of the bond being ratified. If some Mexicans' awareness of the metaphors sanctifying political structures at that time was later lost in history, it may be that the ensuing powerful nationalism was only what Michel Pêcheux describes in his discourse analysis[18] as "counter-identification"—a mode negating the earlier form of subjection but still operating according to the same terms. Proof of this is the Mexican experience; when the colony declared independence in 1821, prominent elements in the country established a Mexican empire and brought a general, Agustín de Iturbide, to head the government as Emperor Agustín I.

Notes

1. I am drawing on 25 such poems and a theatrical allegory, explicitly published in Mexico and dated during this month (or, by internal evidence, showing they belong to this time period), which are to be found in the British Library under Shelf No. 11451. bbb.6. Thirteen of these are also to be found in scattered volumes in the Sutro collection of the California State Library System. The sizable collection formed by Josef Agustín de Castro, which I discuss later, is also to be found in the Sutro collection.

2. For a full account of Napoleonic activity in Spain see Lovett.

3. "J.S.E.," *Diario de México* August 5–9, 1808. Here and elsewhere I reproduce the spelling and accent patterns of the original language.

4. "El Antipoeta," "Poesia," *Diario* January 18, 1806. This reformed poet writes: "sané de la manía de hacer versos" "I was cured of the mania of writing verse."

5. "Mascara alegorica que la noble Juventud de Valladolid representó en las calles de esta Ciudad, en celebridad y regocijo de haber sacudido la Peninsula del yugo frances."

6. This "irregular sonnet" appears unsigned in the Josef Agustín de Castro collection and in the *Diario* on August 5, 1808.

7. See the "Romance endecasílabo que en motivo de las circunstancias del dia, tiene el honor de dedicar a los nobles y fidelisimos mexicanos, el Capitan Conde de Colombini, Ayudante mayor de la Plaza de esta Capital, y Academico de honor de la Real Academia de las tres nobles Artes de San Carlos de esta Nueva España," [n.d., n.p.] 9 pp.

8. See "Marcha de los voluntarios," [n.d., n.p.] 4 pp.; see also Agustín Pomposo Fernandez de S. Salvador, "Silva libre," July 30, 1808, 32 pp.

9. See "Romance endecasilabo. En elogio del que acaba de publicar el Sr. Capitan y Conde de Colombini, por el Br. D. Josef Valdés," [n.d., n.p.] 4 pp.

10. "Oda" (undated). However, the reference Sánchez de Tagle makes in a note to the haste with which he wrote the poem and the urgency demanding its publication suggests the poem dates from late July or early August, 1808.

11. In late July and early August the official *Gaceta de México* records *representaciones* or public demonstrations of loyalty in Puebla, Veracruz, and Zacatecas. It also reports programs staged in the theaters in Mexico City.

54 Nancy Vogeley

12. "Himno de la victoria, para puesto en musica, y cantado a la entrada de los victoriosos exercitos de la provincia por Don Juan Arriaza" "Dado a luz por el editor de la Gazeta D. Juan Lopez Cancelada" (undated). This poem, seemingly coming from Spain, was nevertheless reprinted in Mexico for it was obtainable at the printing house of Doña María Fernández de Jáuregui.

13. This is the last of four sonnets by an anonymous poet appearing in a collection by Josef Agustín de Castro. An introduction states that they were composed at 10:00 A.M., July 29, 1808. [n.p.]

14. "Llanto de la America por el decreto imperial y real que le quita a PEPE BOTELLAS," [n.d., n.p.] 7 pp.

15. "Justa ridiculizacion imperial y real del grande Trapoleon, en una decima, escrita por un amigo y glosada por otro: con aplicacion a toda la Napoleonera; especialmente al Rey de las once noches, por quien lloraron de gozo los Napolitanos quando tuvieron el imponderable de verse libres de S.M. Chispona," [n.d., n.p.] 4 pp.

16. For a discussion of the American as Caliban, see Fernández Retamar.

17. See "Marcha de los voluntarios."

18. For a discussion of Pêcheux's work I have relied extensively on Macdonell (39–40).

Works Cited

Alamán, Lucas. *Historia de Méjico desde los primeros movimientos que prepararon su independencia en el año de 1808 hasta la época presente.* 5 vols. 1849–52. Méjico: Imprenta de J. M. Lara. Vol. I, 1849.

Anna, Timothy. *The Fall of the Royal Government in Mexico City.* Lincoln: University of Nebraska Press, 1978.

Brecht, Bertolt. *Mother Courage.* Trans. Eric Bentley. New York: Grove, 1966.

Diario de México October 1, 1805–12.

Dorson, Richard M. "Material Components in Celebration." In *Celebration: Studies in Festivity and Ritual.* Ed. Victor Turner. Washington, D.C.: Smithsonian Institution Press, 1982, 33–57.

Fernández Retamar, Roberto. "Caliban: Notes towards a Discussion of Culture in Our Americas." Trans. Lynn Garafola, David Arthur McMurray, and Robert Márquez. *Massachusetts Review* 15 (1974): 7–72.

Lovett, Gabriel H. *Napoleon and the Birth of Modern Spain.* 2 vols. New York: New York University Press, 1965.

Macdonell, Diane. *Theories of Discourse: An Introduction.* New York and Oxford: Basil Blackwell, 1986.

Memmi, Albert. *The Colonizer and the Colonized.* Boston: Beacon Press, 1967.

Paulson, Ronald. *Representations of Revolution (1789–1820).* New Haven and London: Yale University Press, 1983.

Rosenblum, Mort. *Mission to Civilize: The French Way.* New York: Harcourt, Brace, Jovanovich, 1986.

Said, Edward. "Intellectuals in the Post-Colonial World." *Salmagundi* 70–71 (1986): 44–64.

Starobinski, Jean. *1789: The Emblems of Reason*. Trans. Barbara Bray. Charlottesville: University Press of Virginia, 1982.

Turner, Victor W. *Dramas, Fields, and Metaphors: Symbolic Action in Human Society*. Ithaca and London: Cornell University Press, 1974.

―――. *The Ritual Process: Structure and Anti-Structure*. Chicago: Aldine Publishing Co., 1969.

Villoro, Luis. *El proceso ideológico de la revolución de independencia*. 2d ed. México: Universidad Nacional Autónoma Metropolitana, 1977.

Vogeley, Nancy. "Defining the 'Colonial Reader': *El Periquillo Sarniento*." *PMLA* 102 (1987): 784–800.

―――. "Mexican Newspaper Culture on the Eve of Mexican Independence." *Ideologies and Literature* 4 Second Cycle (1982): 358–77.

Marlon B. Ross

Romancing the Nation-State: The Poetics of Romantic Nationalism

HOW DOES A NATION GROW to become itself? Must it seek its limits by expanding to the point of its own potential dissolution, losing its sense of oneness demarcated originally by the closeness of its geographical borders and loosening its bonds to that indigenous tradition that initially marked its sense of self-identity? This question, a specter haunting Britain at the verge of the nineteenth century, appears on the threshold of Britain's modernization of itself as a nation-state. The concept of national development cross-breeds the notion of territorial acquisition, born during the Renaissance, with the notion of historical progress, born during the Enlightenment, and grafts both onto the notion of the folk as an organic entity with a natural relation to the nurturing place, the motherland, or the place of dissemination, the fatherland, a notion born during the Romantic period. Given the spatial and the temporal aspects alone, nationalism as we know it could not have materialized from its "germinal" state at the end of the eighteenth century. Given life and form by a "mere" metaphor, that of organic growth, the nation-state could blossom, could grow into itself. Looking out on a moment of revolutionary crisis and a horizon of territorial expansion, the British needed somehow to organize this experience of rapid change and rapid expansion, to justify their development into a modern nation-state while retaining the sense of inherently ordained order that characterized the then eroding socio-economic structure.

Whereas growth, both temporal and spatial, implies natural continuity and preformation, like the predestined movement from birth to maturity or the form of the body predetermined by the enlargement of the cell, change and expansion are inherently discontinuous and disruptive. Whereas growth stresses how the child is father to the man, change and expansion are distressing phenomena, disrupting the relation between past and present, between internal and external, between native and exotic. Keeping a steady eye on France, the British were confronted with the question of their country's relation to itself: its relation to its past menaced by the French Revolutionary zeal to begin anew, to abolish tradition; its relation to its borders menaced by Napoleon's empire-building, by its own conflictual desire to mimic Napoleon and to silence him, to enlarge its own borders but without losing its identity in relation to the exotic-external that defines its nationality. What is the difference between civil revolution, which threatens to tear the state from its past and thus from its proper path, and mere civil dissension, which can be seen as a tradition native to the English state and thus viewed as necessary growth pains? What is the difference between Napoleonic aggression, which disrupts the geographical integrity of the state's body, crushing independence abroad and liberty at home, and British expansion, which can be seen as integral growth, preordained by England's glorious past? Is the nation that grows into itself necessarily an empire? If the change is as efficient as industrialization or the expansion as bloodless as capitalizing on world trade, then national growth should be, like Adam Smith's magical hand, invisible, invincible, and inviting.

*　　*　　*

When Edmund Burke sounds the alarm that a revolution in France must be seen as aggression against Britain, he sets the tone that reverberates throughout future discourse on Britain's fate as a nation. For a modern nation to progress, he claims, it must never lose touch with its past; for it to expand, it must never lose sight of its center. Burke indulges in romance: he constructs a pleasing fiction in which conflict naturally gives way to rightful resolution and in which higher love (patriotism of the citizen for his motherland) can only be achieved through honorable warfare against the evil that threatens the kingdom from without (Britain going to war against France). *Reflections on the Revolution in France*, like romance, bases its appeal on values that are simultaneously lost and always about-to-be-lost, but must be recovered and retained. The age of chivalry may be gone, but the principles that made chivalry possible are the ones on which the modern nation-state must ground itself. Burke's romance foregrounds loyalty to the past, for in the ideal state, as in the fantastic world of romance, it is possible to have progression without change. The present, for Burke, is a recurrent version of the past refined. Likewise like romance, the state is an internally harmonious whole, despite its apparent variety. The threat of disruption is always external, an evil that can be seen, though it may at times beguile the innocent and virtuous, just as the British are initially beguiled by France. Finally, the state functions, like knights of romance, through a hierarchized network of static relations, binding each to the other, vassal to lord, lord to lord, lord to king, in a concentrically ordered web of kinship, based on the prototype of the patriarchal clan. This network of kin relations reaches out, like concentric circles, to bring the whole together and to determine its growth as a natural process of accretion, the way a tree grows upward and outward by adding layers of bark and by extending branches from the central trunk. Like Wordsworth's spot of time, or the generic romantic poem itself, Burke's state becomes a living body, an organic form that grows into itself by feeding on its origin. It is a metaphor that seems more appropriate for the rise of the monarchic state toward the end of the middle ages, as can be seen in Burke's antecedent, Thomas Hobbes's *Leviathan,* for what Burke and the romantics tend to suppress is the *machinery* of modern nationalism, the fact that it functions like a series of interlocking cogs, fueled by coal and capital, rather than like a patriarchal tribe, motivated by the instinctual love of kin that spreads out into loyalty for the national kind.

As the appeal to origins usually does, Burke's argument naturalizes and mystifies the development of the nation-state. Its power becomes its own internal harmony, its own past strength. A self-correcting system in which error is not possible, unless it comes in the guise of an intrusion from the external-foreign, Burke's tribal body tends to heal miraculously all the wounds that afflict Britain as it moves into modern statehood and empire. Not only are present fractures—Tory vs. Whig, aristocracy vs. bourgeoisie, manufacturers vs. laboring class, women vs. men, conservative agrarians vs. utilitarian industrialists, and so on—magically mended, but also past conflicts, like England's civil war, become performative signs of natural growth. It is only one conflict, jacobin vs. anti-jacobin, that threatens the security of the body, like a virus that must find a point of entry. Ironically, because Burke's conception is so inwardly focused on the origin-center, the problematic relation of internal to external, which is being called into question by capitalist trade and colonization, becomes the primary concern: how to shore up the borders at the very point when the borders need weakening in order to expand.

Attending to Burke's alarm, Wordsworth echoes Burke's analysis of the nation-state. Even in his earliest works, such as "A Letter to the Bishop of Llandaff" and the Salisbury Plain poem, where he is attempting to argue against Burke and for the jacobin cause, Wordsworth views the modern nation-state as an organic body, motivated by instinctual, tribal affection. Wordsworth's focus, however, is the supposedly *original* and *natural* attachment of the folk to the land that they inhabit. Aware that the function of land is rapidly changing, Wordsworth is concerned about the effect of this change on the harmony and morality of "the people." Just as the natural landscape is the source that nurtures his ordination as a poet, guiding him toward human love and productive social intercourse, so the land is the source of national harmony, liberty, and virtue. Thus, even as he takes on the disinterested language and reasoning from abstract principles characteristic of the philosophes and their jacobin descendants, pointedly opposing these to Burke's inflammatory prose, Wordsworth grounds his argument in a kind of Burkean romance:

> [A]s governments formed on such a plan [universal representation] proceed in a plain and open manner, their administration would require much less of what is usually called talents and experience, that is of disciplined treachery and hoary machiavelism; and, at the same time, as it would no longer be their interest to keep the mass of the nation in ignorance, a moderate portion of useful knowledge would be universally disseminated. If your lordship has travelled in the democratic cantons of Switzerland you must have seen the herdsman with the staff in one hand and the book in the other. In the constituent assembly of France was found a peasant whose sagacity was as distinguished as his integrity, whose blunt honesty overawed and baffled the refinements of hypocritical patriots. (*Selected Prose* 148)

Wordsworth's portrait suppresses the question of how literacy, once it is accomplished, feeds itself, because he needs his herdsman to be naturally bonded with the land, not corrupted by the "talents and experience" that accompany the highly literate. "A moderate portion of useful knowledge" is difficult to gauge, and it assumes a stable relation between the benefactors who disseminate and those who benefit from such dissemination. The dynamic of this relation—between lord and peasant, between more and less literate, between peasant and land—becomes more clearly defined, of course, in the preface and poems of *Lyrical Ballads*. What remains constant from beginning to end for Wordsworth is the folk's mediating function, enabling an organic-pastoral vision of nationality in which the natural attachment to land stabilizes a nation in the midst of rapid change and expansion.

Ironically, the growth of Britain into a modern nation-state is based on the radical change in the function of land that Wordsworth resists. Industrialists, utilitarians, scientists, economists, state functionaries, capitalists, the bourgeoisie all view land, not as a constant that is to be held onto, passed on through primogeniture, stabilizing the relations among the classes, seasonally producing the fertility of the whole, and determining the values of the whole in consonance with that stability, but rather as property to be exchanged, expanded, and improved for the sake of profit and national growth. Wordsworth, intensely aware of this changing function of land, senses the conflict between his romance of natural attachment to the land and his jacobin principle of equality:

> It cannot be denied that the security of individual property is one of the strongest and most natural motives to induce men to bow their necks to the yoke of civil government. . . . The history of all ages has demonstrated that wealth not only can secure itself but includes even an oppressive principle. Aware of this, and that extremes of poverty and riches have a necessary tendency to corrupt the human heart, he [a legislator] will banish from his code all laws such as the unnatural monster of primogeniture, such as encourage associations against labour in the form of corporate bodies, and indeed all that monopolising system of legislation whose baleful influence is shewn in the depopulation of the country and in the necessity which reduces the sad relicks to owe their very existence to the ostentatious bounty of their oppressors. . . . [Our legislators] have unjustly left unprotected that most important part of property, not less real because it has no material existence, that which ought to enable the labourer to provide food for himself and his family. (*Selected Prose* 152–53)

Partly on target in seeing "arbitrary wages" as a source of the problem, Wordsworth nonetheless, in his fervor for the revolutionary cause, attacks one of the primary principles that later serves to help him reclaim the constancy of land as an intrinsic value to the people: primogeniture. It is not primogeniture (an ancient system that helped to keep landlords, freeholders, and agrarian laborers rather harmoniously dispersed across the English countryside) that depopulates the land, but the new bourgeois enterprises (those "corporate bodies" that "encourage associations against labour"). As Wordsworth sheds the clothing of jacobin reasoning, which was rather thinly worn in the first place, he also sheds the confusion displayed in this passage. In the poems of *Lyrical Ballads* and later, he not only celebrates what he considers the naked truth of natural ownership; he also reclaims the naturalness of primogeniture, as the new system of land use becomes the "unnatural monster" that scares "the people" away from their roots in nature.

Always at stake for Wordsworth is the difference between the "material existence" and the "immaterial." Land is valuable in his view, not because of its materiality, as the solid basis for all economic exchange, according to the economists, but rather because of its immaterial origin and effect. It is the attachment to the land that sustains a tribal and thus a national organic whole, not the profitability of the land itself. This paradox accords with his view of poetic productivity: it is not the natural landscape that makes him a poet, but his attachment to the landscape, his imaginative perception of it. Coming to his Burkean senses, after the superficial delirium of jacobinism, Wordsworth realizes the significance of his relation to the "native soil." Appropriately, this realization is most ardently expressed in the sonnet "Composed in the Valley near Dover, on the Day of Landing." During the short peace of Amiens, Wordsworth makes a four-week trip to Calais to settle accounts with Annette, his French lover, and Caroline, their "natural" daughter, before his marriage to Mary Hutchinson, a woman raised on his "native soil" and whom he knew from childhood. As is usual for Words-worth, the sonnet, then, correlates the personal with the political, the native son with the national cause. The first quatrain sets up the return home as pastoral harmony, closing itself with the source of such perfect union between the people and their land, the Englishness of it all:

Here, on our native soil, we breathe once more.
The cock that crows, the smoke that curls, that sound
Of bells;—those boys who in yon meadow-ground
In white-sleeved shirts are playing; and the roar
Of the waves breaking on the chalky shore;—
All, all are English.   (*Poetical Works* 243)

The all-inclusiveness of Englishness—nothing in England can be alien to him or to England itself—not only serves as totalizing harmony for the pastoral union of people and land; it also serves as the turning point of retrospection with the beginning of the next quatrain: "All, all are English. Oft have I looked round / With joy in Kent's green vales; but never found / Myself so satisfied in heart before." By lengthening the first quatrain so that it lingers into 5.5 lines and dissolves itself into the next quatrain, Words-worth demonstrates the interdependence between present and past, be-tween his original perception and his intensified fulfillment, between origi-nal attachment to the local habitat and ongoing national pride. Of course, the source of this intensified satisfaction (one is even tempted to say complacency) is the foreign, specifically France, Annette, Caroline, all embodiments of past affection, intimately tied to him, but having threat-ened, by their foreignness, his attachment to the native soil:

Europe is yet in bonds; but let that pass,
Thought for another moment. Thou art free,
My Country! and 'tis joy enough and pride
For one hour's perfect bliss, to tread the grass
Of England once again, and hear and see,
With such a dear Companion at my side.

The only note of dissatisfaction comes appropriately at the conventional turning point of the sonnet, but instead of formal resolution, we get dismissal of the conflict itself. The formal harmony of the sonnet is jarred by that flippant dismissal: "but let that pass, / Thought for another moment." A sonnet so engaged in its own pastoral unity can manage that unity only by dismissing unconventionally the very conflict that should serve as the sestet's harmonizing movement toward closure. Another moment? Another sonnet? Another country. Clearly not "My Country!" Distinguishing England from Europe, Wordsworth also separates England from France's "bonds," so different from his bond to his own native soil. To be away from England is to be blind and deaf; to return is to "hear and see." The "perfect bliss" that he once erroneously felt in his first trip to France, his fervor for the French cause, was misplaced bliss, now redirected toward its proper English end. Even the peace of Amiens cannot trick him into reconciliation with France, though it allows him to resolve (or dismiss) his personal ties to France by monetarily discharging his duty to his French-born child. Just as his personal life will be consummated in perfect union with "a dear Companion" (Dorothy standing in for Mary) of English kin, so his national pride achieves its too perfect (since the conflict is dismissed rather than engaged) resolution (as closure and as determination) in the form of the sonnet. The threat, purely Burkean in nature, is external-exotic, and by reclosing the borders and transforming all within those borders into totally harmonious Englishness, Wordsworth manages to dispel all those real threats—potential love for his "*illegitimate*," unnatural French child, potential revolution within Britain—that lie within, within him and within Britain. Only by denying the problematic relation of past to present—his past relation with Annette conflicting with his present engagement to Mary, England's agrarian past conflicting with the rapid change toward profitable, industrialized land-use—can Wordsworth constitute his intensified national pride. But as he elides the relation between past and present, he necessarily simplifies the relation between internal and external, making that boundary between England and all else, especially France, clearcut exactly at the time when France and England can be identified as twin countries battling for possession of the world.

The immaterial bond tying Wordsworth to England is stronger than the material bonds that chain Europe to France because it is original and organic, growing out of tradition and attaching the people to the land that they inhabit. Like Burke, he looks backward/inward toward the origin/ center in order to justify the organic growth of the state. In another sonnet (#29 under "Poems Dedicated to National Independence and Liberty") Wordsworth again stresses the immateriality of national strength, even to the point of absurdity: "O'erweening Statesmen have full long relied / On fleets and armies, and external wealth: / But from *within* proceeds a Nation's health" (*Poetical Works* 254, Wordsworth's emphasis). In addition to the dichotomy of external (foreignness) and internal (nativity), Wordsworth posits a dichotomy of material (external wealth) and immaterial (inner strength). Not only should a country's wealth come from within its own borders (from the fertility of the land), its wealth should rely on the immaterial richness of the spirit, the fertile attachment to place. In an apparent reversal from his opinion in the "Letter to the Bishop of Llandaff," it no longer matters whether there is a great disparity between rich and poor, as long as this attachment is maintained, as long as "poor men cleave *with pride* to the *paternal* floor" (my emphases). "The walks of gain," commercial and industrial profit, do not guarantee national strength, but a "Soul by contemplation sanctified" does. Although these sentiments are addressed specifically to the Catholics in Spain whose nation is at "strife" with France's domination, it obviously equally applies to the British, who are "free," but expanding their borders to bind the "external wealth" of their ever-growing colonies.

In another sonnet (#32 under "Poems Dedicated to National Independence and Liberty") the full logic of Wordsworth's nationalism is evident. The sonnet brings together all his Burkean notions: progress without change, the internal harmony of the state, the natural organicity of the state's body, the elision of past and present, the externality of all danger to the state's well-being, the self-correcting capability of native tradition. With these Burkean notions are synthesized his own Wordsworthian ideas: the immateriality of national power, the attachment to land as the source of harmony, and the natural organicity of "the People."

The power of Armies is a visible thing,
Formal, and circumscribed in time and space;

But who the limits of that power shall trace
Which a brave People into light can bring
Or hide, at will,—for freedom combatting
By just revenge inflamed? No foot may chase,
No eye can follow, to a fatal place
That power, that spirit, whether on the wing
Like the strong wind, or sleeping like the wind
Within its awful caves.—From year to year
Springs this indigenous produce far and near;
No craft this subtle element can bind,
Rising like water from the soil, to find
In every nook a lip that it may cheer.   (*Poetical Works* 255)

It is no coincidence that Wordsworth resorts to the same imagery that he uses at the beginning of *The Prelude* to ordain his natural vocation as a poet. This power, this spirit, can be correlated to imagination itself. Just as the poet's power surpasses that of scientists, the inner spirit of the "People" surpasses all "external" signs of power. This power grows by a natural process of accretion, and, whether on the wing or sleeping, it cannot blow in the wrong direction, any more than the wind can, any more than the natural poet can lose his way. The People's "indigenous produce" springs "far and near." While the external threat is diminished by shoring up the borders and totalizing the internal harmony of the "People," the national spirit itself knows no such bounds; it flows naturally, "[r]ising like water from the soil." Wordsworth's apologetics for nationalism may start at the origin-center, the attachment to the local native soil; it, however, "spreads itself wide," as Wordsworth says of the spirit of poetry, finding "[i]n every nook" its destined fulfillment.

*   *   *

Hazlitt, who also hears Burke's alarm, but with more skeptical ears, attempts to unravel the contradictions that reside at the heart of modern nationalism. In his fragment "On Patriotism" he explains in his usual bluntly lucid terms the impossibility of Burke's and Wordsworth's romance of the pastoral nation-state. "Patriotism, in modern times, and in great states, is and must be the creature of reason and reflection, rather than the offspring of physical or local attachment" (*The Round Table* 67). Focusing on the present and on those states claiming world power, Hazlitt recognizes the problem of maintaining "physical or local attachment" as the source of nationalism. Patriotism is artificially constructed—a "creature"—rather than naturally inseminated—an "offspring." Hazlitt further writes:

> Our country is a complex, abstract existence, recognised only by the understanding. It is an immense riddle, containing numberless modifications of reason and prejudice, of thought and passion. Patriotism is not, in a strict or exclusive sense, a natural or personal affection, but a law of our rational and moral nature, strengthened and determined by particular circumstances and associations, but not born of them, nor wholly nourished by them. (67)

Clearly countering Burke's argument, Hazlitt bases the drive toward nationalism on that foundation of enlightenment-jacobin discourse: reason. As a "law of our rational and moral nature," nationalism must be taught; it does not grow into itself, although it is "strengthened and determined by particular circumstances."

> The common notions of patriotism are transmitted down to us from the savage tribes, where the fate and condition of all was the same, or from the states of Greece and Rome, where the country of the citizen was the town in which he was born. Where this is no longer the case,—where our country is no longer contained within the narrow circle of the same walls,—where we can no longer behold its glimmering horizon from the top of our native mountains—beyond these limits, it is not a natural but an artificial idea, and our love of it either a deliberate dictate of reason, or a cant term. (67)

Bringing the question of national development back into historical perspective, rather than relying on the romance of Wordsworthian retrospection, and bringing it back into its social context, rather than relying on the romance of Wordsworthian organicism, Hazlitt points to the limits of the old forms of nationalism. "[T]he fate and condition of all" is no longer the same in Britain, for factions of every kind, geographical, political, class, gender, economic, actually constitute the "numberless" conflicting interests of the modern nation-state, which is defined not by its organic wholeness, but rather by "a deliberate dictate of reason."

But this does not mean that Hazlitt is able to smooth out the contradictions inherent in modern nationalism. The contradictions return with the power of the repressed as soon as Hazlitt brings into his purview those far-flung colonies that his "deliberate dictate of reason" serves to justify:

> It is not possible that we should have an individual attachment to sixteen millions of men, any more than to sixty millions. We cannot be *habitually*

attached to places we never saw, and people we never heard of. Is not the name of Englishman a general term, as well as that of man? How many varieties does it not combine within it? Are the opposite extremities of the globe our native place, because they are a part of that geographical and political denomination, our country? Does natural affection expand in circles of latitude and longitude? What personal or instinctive sympathy has the English peasant with the African slave-driver, or East Indian Nabob? Some of our wretched bunglers in metaphysics would fain persuade us to discard all general humanity, and all sense of abstract justice, as a violation of natural affection, and yet do not see that the love of our country itself is in the list of our general affections. (67, Hazlitt's emphasis)

Reducing to absurdity the Burkean concentric circle of affection and the internal harmony of his traditionary state, Hazlitt replaces these with "varieties" and "opposite extremities" attached by the abstract value of "reason" itself. Hazlitt's state is the cause and effect of *naming;* we are what we denominate ourselves. The "English peasant" has no reason to have "instinctive sympathy" for the "African slave-driver, or East Indian Nabob." Surely, Hazlitt, an ardent opponent of the slave trade and a libertarian in principle, is here objecting to both the slaver and the nabob, both functionaries of the state, whether indirectly or directly. And yet in taking away that "instinctive sympathy" that would force the "English peasant," who profits little from the efforts of the slaver and nabob, to embrace the oppressors, rather than the slaves and East Indians, just because the oppressors are English and the "others" are not, Hazlitt ironically gives *reason,* instead of Burkean prejudice, as a justification for identifying with the Englishness of the slaver and nabob. The peasant may not have reasons for his patriotic identification, but he does have reason, which enables him to understand the abstract relation between himself and his patriots toiling for England in a foreign land. The English peasant is thus able to name himself, while the slave and the East Indian remain unknowns at the outer edge of rational Englishness.

When "justice" becomes this "abstract," then nationalist imperialism itself can wear a benign face. Hazlitt ends the fragment with this observation:

It was said by an acute observer, and eloquent writer (Rousseau) that the love of mankind was nothing but the love of justice: the same might be said, with considerable truth, of the love of our country. It is little more than another name for the love of liberty, of independence, of peace, and social happiness. We do not say that other indirect and collateral circumstances do not go to the superstructure of this sentiment (as language, literature, manners, national customs), but this is the broad and firm basis. (67–68)

Slipping so easily from the love of mankind to the love of England is perhaps one of those "indirect and collateral circumstances" that disables Hazlitt from seeing the logical flaw in his "reason." To love mankind out of an abstract sense of justice requires the refusal to make distinctions of kind, including national distinctions. Loving one's country is exactly the opposite: it requires a distinction of kind that potentially excludes all others from the justice so freely given to one's fellow citizens. Indeed, if the country "is little more than a name for the love of liberty, of independence, of peace, and social happiness," then who names this love for the slave and the East Indian? Hazlitt's liberal reasoning, in the long run, becomes more dangerous to those others who are not British, for it eventually becomes a more powerful way of naming the expanding limits of the nation-state than Wordsworth's and Burke's straightforwardly nostalgic and reactionary appeals, and in fact such logic becomes the rationale for Britain's empire-building.

*   *   *

What Hazlitt does is to dissolve the problematic relation between external and internal, focusing instead on the radical difference between the past notion of nationalism and the modern notion. Operating within history, conversely to Wordsworth and Burke, he nonetheless ignores the resistance of the external-exotic in the present, an alienating resistance that can function within the borders of the country through the "English peasant" as much as at the borders through the slave and East Indian. In his verse romances, Walter Scott grapples with these same relations, attempting to negotiate the junctures of external-internal, past-present, native-exotic, personal-national, examining the social circumstances of growth as change, expansion, crisis, and disruption. Being trained in the Scottish Enlightenment tradition, he brings the same enlightenment mentality that Hazlitt employs, foregrounding the sway of history and circumstance. But he, an admirer and disciple of Burke, also brings a desire for romance, for the formal resolution of social disruptions and historical change into the harmonies of organic growth based on traditional values. By focusing on *Rokeby*, his fourth verse romance, published in 1813, we can see how the romance form helps him to negotiate these contradictions through a process of *transference* in which past civil discord is rewritten from the unavoidable context of Scott's own present ambivalence toward his personal circumstances and the disruptions occurring in Napoleonic Europe. "'Transference' is bound up with a notion of time not as simple continuity or discontinuity," according to Dominick LaCapra, from whom I am borrowing the term as a historical-critical concept, "but as repetition with variation or change—at times traumatically disruptive change." LaCapra continues:

> Transference causes fear of possession by the past and loss of control over both it and oneself. It simultaneously brings the temptation to assert full control over the "object" of study through ideologically suspect procedures that may be related to the phenomenon Freud discussed as "narcissism."
>
> Narcissism is a one-sided but alluring response to the anxiety of transference. It involves the impossible, imaginary attempt totally to integrate the self; it is active in the speculative effort to elaborate a fully unified perspective, and its self-regarding "purity" entails the exorcistic scapegoating of the "other" that is always to some extent within. (*History and Criticism* 72)

LaCapra's description of the historian's project accords well with Scott's own romance project in *Rokeby*. Scott's vehicle of narcissism, however, is romance form itself, whereas the object of Scott's study is the English Civil War, which itself is a projection of the Scottish-English conflict before the union, which Scott writes about directly in most of his other romances, and which itself is a projection of Britain's internal struggle to achieve modernized nationalism. Not only is Scott's resorting to romance an "alluring response to the anxiety" of socio-historical disruption, activating "the speculative effort to elaborate a fully unified perspective" from which the nation can view itself, but also it represents an "impossible, imaginary attempt totally to integrate the self," which microcosmically participates in the social, political, economic, and literary crises in which the national interest is engaged macrocosmically.

As Horace E. Scudder points out, "Scott palpably connected the writing of the poem *Rokeby* with the enlargement of his domain" (*Scott's Complete Poetical Works,* ed. Scudder 226). In a letter of 1812, addressed to Morritt, the lord of the estate that gives the poem its name, Scott says, "My work *Rokeby* does and must go forward, or my trees and enclosures might, perchance, stand still" (*Letters,* ed. H. J. C. Grierson 3: 88). In the same letter, Scott writes, "I shall keep off people's kibes if I can, for my plan, though laid during the civil wars, has little to do with the politics of either party, being very much confined to the adventures and distresses of a particular family"

(88). Writing about the composition of *Rokeby* twenty years later, Scott dismisses the distressful realm of national politics, and focuses his readers' attention instead on his own personal distresses in attempting to write the romance, not only the distresses of attempting to build his domestic empire, Abbotsford, but also the distresses of his literary empire. Byron, he reminds his faithful readers, had taken the wind out of his sails, and a plethora of Scott imitators had threatened the distinctiveness of Scott's own voice, not to mention the fact that they also had threatened his capacity to make money on his romances, money needed to finance the expansion of his dream estate.

According to Scott's own logic, his attempt to finance a great estate causes him to write yet another metrical romance, to choose a familiar English subject for the sake of novelty, and to suppress politics from the poem. His desire for Abbotsford also causes him to compete with Byron when it may have been wiser for him to exit the stage. "I was as likely to tire of playing the second fiddle in the concert, as my audience of hearing me," he says (*Complete Poetical Works* 230). And so we come full circle in his logic: The very thing which causes him to write yet another romance is the thing which disables him from competing with the "formidable" Byron. Scott writes, "I had around me the most pleasant but least exciting of all society, that of kind friends and an affectionate family. My circle of employments was a narrow one; it occupied me constantly, and it became daily more difficult for me to interest myself in poetical composition" (230). The estate he desires to finance through writing romance is the domain that causes him to lose interest in writing romance.

In other words, cultivating a great estate is, like the cultivation of a great national culture itself, a duplicitous activity. Even as it enables the individual to be ensconced in the securely narrow comforts of domestic harmony at home, it requires him to venture out toward the dangerous territory beyond his castle's moat. Perhaps more disturbingly, it requires him to expand his domain—whether it be a *bourgeois* estate or a capitalist nation-state—in order to assure the continued health of that domain. This fact would perhaps be more palpable in Britain than in a nation like France, for Britain's island-determined borders accentuate the limits of its national resources. Britain's growth, especially toward the end of the eighteenth century, must be reconceptualized, displacing the idea of actual territorial acquisition with a more complex kind of imperial desire, the desire to monopolize the *sources* of acquisition—to control the waterways, to control international trade, including slavery, and to control the import of raw materials needed to fuel industrial expansion. By Scott's time, it has become glaringly clear, despite Wordsworth's contrary pastoral vision, that prosperity at home is not simply a matter of internal resources—rich land and a steadily-increasing, productive population—which until the latter part of the eighteenth century were considered the sole sources of national wealth. Since it has become increasingly clear that national growth relies instead on the incorporation of external resources into the nation through trade or preferably through expropriation, the nation must be willing to send out its best as envoys to compete for those resources. Those alien resources beckoning outside the nation's borders constitute both an opportunity for economic expansion and necessarily a threat to the homogeneity of national culture itself. Therefore, just at the point that the external-exotic must be absorbed in order for industry and trade to proceed apace, the nation is being defined as a harmonious, homogeneous living whole; this paradox enables and justifies the *innate* difference between the patriot nabob and the foreign Indian he rules, between the patriot slaver and the foreign slave he objectifies.

Although Napoleon is a military threat to Britain's national sovereignty, an ideological threat to Britain's sense of its own sacred national tradition, and an economic threat to Britain's capitalist expansion, his subversiveness goes further. On the one hand, Napoleon tries to build an empire in the old-fashioned Roman way, through tyranny and territorial acquisition, without attention to the distinctions of national borders. Napoleon liberates people from the constrictions of their own nation-states in order to bind them either to himself or rhetorically to abstract principles of pan-nationalism, using the same kind of liberalizing logic we saw at work in Hazlitt. On the other hand, he builds his empire on principles of nationalism, claiming to return autonomy and authority to the folk by deposing monarchs who rule without popular consent. Thus, in the first case he can be seen as a threat to the validity and vitality of nationalism itself. In the other case, he raises the question of the actual rights of those others whom Britain is seeking to dominate. If nationalism is a sound principle, should not the indigenous traditions of Africans and Indians be left intact; should not those others be allowed to name themselves? No wonder his cause promotes so much internal dissension within Britain as a result of those who sympathize with that cause, if not with his method, threatening the nation from within and from without.

It goes without saying that both Scott and Wordsworth are alarmed by Napoleon's imperialism (as opposed to Hazlitt, whose glorification of

Napoleon remained constant). Their complicated feelings about Napoleon, however, indicate that it is not so much imperial power itself that unnerves them as the anti-nationalist implications of Napoleonic imperialism. More subtly, however, Napoleon embodies the very conflict at the heart of this new nationalism. Scott projects onto Napoleon the dissonance felt within his own nationalist ideology. As his romances look back nostalgically at the harmony and loyalty of feudal relations, they look out ambivalently at Napoleon, whose ambition in actuality accords quite well with the unchecked conquests of knights before the emergence of the modern nation-state. At the same time that prenationalist conquest counters Scott's modern conception of liberty, it also counters his modern conception of nationalism. And at the same time that Scott's conception of nationalism counters prenationalist conquest, it ambivalently condones industrial-capitalist conquest, potentially thwarted by Napoleon's anachronistic *and* prescient intervention. Since imperial conquest cannot be justified in Napoleonic terms, in terms that question the priority of the nation-state and raise the issue of the rightful autonomy of the colonized, then it must be justified in other terms, in terms that circumvent—or at least sublimate—the conflict between national sovereignty and capitalist expansion, between national liberty and capitalist conquest.

This socio-historical context suggests how Scott's desire for Abbotsford, his need to depoliticize the romance, and his fear of competing with Byron and losing his position as supreme romancer are all charged and mangled wires in a dense network of transferential signification. The basic pattern of that network is determined, like Britain's course itself in this period, by the ideology of monopoly capitalism. He is compelled to enlarge his estate so as to prevent stagnation. Either his romance readership must grow in relation to Byron's, or it will not be worth keeping. When confronted with Byron's threat, Scott both self-consciously and unconsciously begins to incorporate Byronic elements into his own romances. He unwittingly writes a romance called *Harold the Dauntless,* a mistake he later admits since it leads his readers erroneously to expect another Childe Harold (*Complete Poetical Works* 369). In *Rokeby* he more subtly invades Byron's territory, placing his tale in England and coloring it with Byronic tints of frustrated young love, aborted ambition, and light-hearted adventure in the midst of despair. Mortham, one of several heroes in *Rokeby,* could easily be called a Byronic figure.

Scott wants to prevent us, however, from viewing his romance impulses in a context more significant than the ephemera of purely *personal* needs. He presents his motives to himself and to others as simply and even crudely personal: to get some land to do with what he will. His choice of locale is similarly motivated by simple affection and aesthetics: "the grounds belonged to a dear friend" and "the place itself united the romantic beauties of the wilds of Scotland with the rich and smiling aspect of the southern portion of the island" (*Complete Poetical Works* 229). He claims that an English subject will ironically be more novel than his original exotic choice of a Scottish subject, and so it will sell better. Scott's logic here is blatant, if flawed. Because the poem is supposedly derived from crudely personal motives, the poem must not be seen to have any ulterior or higher aims. Therefore, it is not about parties—not about fiercely opposed Cavaliers and Roundheads or about Tories and Whigs of Scott's own time. Instead, *Rokeby* is simply a pleasant tale about a particular family, written to make his own life more pleasant. Anyone who attempts to inject the monumental and momentous world of politics into the romance misreads both the poem itself and the innocence of Scott's romance motives. The charm of romance, for Scott and for his readers, as I have argued elsewhere, is exactly this innocence of purpose, this sheer pleasure of nostalgia ("Scott's Chivalric Pose"). Conventional romance operates by shutting out the mundane problems that press in on the poem, externalizing mundane reality in order to construct an internally harmonized, though varied, whole within the poem itself. Therefore, when concerns from the external present cross over into the poem, they must do so clandestinely, so to speak, as transformed phenomena serving the fantasy of formal harmony and thematic pastness through the internalizing past of the poem.

*   *   *

A few years before Scott starts writing *Rokeby,* Wordsworth is at work on a poem about another English civil conflict. And, like Scott, Wordsworth wants to claim that his romance is not really about civil war, about the politics of the nation-state, but rather about a particular family. A brief look at Wordsworth's claims about his project can help elucidate Scott's tangled web of motives, *concordia discors*-like, since Wordsworth's claims contradict Scott's only to prove similar. Wordsworth describes his romance *The White Doe of Rylstone* in this way:

> It suffices that everything tends to account for the weekly pilgrimage of the Doe, which is made interesting by its connection with a human being, a Woman, who is intended to be honoured and loved for what she *endures,* and

the manner in which she endures it; accomplishing a conquest over her own sorrows (which is the true subject of the Poem) by means, partly, of the native strength of her character, and partly by the persons and things with whom and which she is connected; and finally, after having exhibited the "fortitude of patience and heroic martyrdom," ascending to pure etherial spirituality, and forwarded in that ascent of love by communion with a creature not of her own species, but spotless, beautiful, innocent and loving. (*Letters of William and Dorothy Wordsworth*, 2:222)

Just as Scott is interested only in the historical reconstruction of a specific family's trials, Wordsworth is interested only in the value of suffering as evidenced by a particular family, especially by one woman. Whereas Scott claims to be interested merely in outward beauty, in locale, Wordsworth is interested only in inner value, in the spirit of place. Scott claims that he writes the poem solely in order to describe a specific place that he happens to love; Wordsworth writes his romance to evoke a transcendent love for a representative place. Wordsworth goes so far as to discount the importance of objects in the romance; in effect, he claims that objects do not exist as objects: "objects . . . derive their influence not from properties inherent in them, not from what they are actually in themselves, but from such as are bestowed upon them by the minds of those who are conversant with or affected by those objects" (*Letters* 3:276). As opposed to Scott's crude interest in enlarging his property by romanticizing the external properties of objects, Wordsworth suggests that he is interested in superseding property (in the sense of owned space and of physical substratum) in order to elucidate the life of the unencumbered soul.

Scott and Wordsworth, then, seem to be at opposite ends of the spectrum, one honoring the temporal, the ephemeral, the specific, the arbitrary, the other "apotheosizing" (to use Wordsworth's own word for it [*Letters* 3:276]) a place in order to embody the transcendent, the permanent, the universal, the ordained. Despite the apparently divergent motives and aims claimed by these two romancers, their discourse, as well as the rules that govern that discourse, moves according to the same implicit design. Both romances, and the authorial commentary surrounding them, are dictated by patterns of enlargement and enclosure, aggression and domination. Behind Wordsworth's anti-materialist metaphor is a grounding metaphor, which derives from the very valuation of property that the metaphor supposedly supersedes. The *White Doe* records a woman's "conquest over her own sorrows." Spiritual endurance is expressed as aggression and domination, as overcoming and ruling. What the woman learns to rule is what at first appears alien to her own being, the emotional anxiety that threatens to weaken her own control over herself. However, Wordsworth's romance attempts to teach us how to rule more than ourselves; it teaches us to view our own special experience as universal, to conquer all spiritually so that nothing remains alien to us. According to Wordsworth, we lay waste our powers when we concern ourselves with materiality, and conversely we empower ourselves when we move beyond mere territorial acquisition to a sublimer form of conquest. Wordsworth, like Scott, is replacing one form of control, the kind that stresses actual physical domination, with what he considers a higher form, spiritual domination.

Whereas Scott's monopolizing drive ambivalently takes number or size as the source of greater and more creative control, Wordsworth's is grounded in control through qualitative superiority. This difference can be seen concretely in each writer's relation to his readership. Scott always makes a point of applauding the accessibility of his romances, and usually by stating exactly how many copies have been sold. Also, he attempts to maximize his profit by controlling the market process itself, from composition to publication (unfortunately for him an enterprise that results in his own bankruptcy, not an unusual outcome for capitalist risk). Wordsworth, on the other hand, says that he hopes his romance "will be acceptable to the intelligent, for whom alone it is written" (*Letters* 3:276). By educating the few who are capable of visionary conquest, Wordsworth hopes to sustain the "native strength" of his people, encouraging the capable—fit, though few—to take on a responsibility that the common folk derive more naturally from their more direct relation to the land itself. Wordsworth's romance dynamic also, however, accords with his contradicting concept of how the more literate must disseminate what he calls "a moderate portion of useful knowledge" to the folk, who must remain innocently less literate in order to mediate between the civilizing expansiveness of the literate and the stabilizing origin-center, the native land.

The conflict between nostalgia for feudal forms of control and the need for capitalist modes of monopoly expansion expresses itself in diverse ways. Scott repeatedly applauds his own dominance over the publishing market and even goes so far as to suggest that Southey and Wordsworth fail to sell their poems because they do not know the "bookselling animal well enough" (*Letters* 1: 385–88). Yet he also repeatedly apologizes for his own popularity, suggesting that his superior understanding of "the great mass of mankind" will give him only a "temporary superiority over men . . . I scarcely thought myself worthy to loose the shoe-latch" (*Complete Poetical*

Works 228). Even in Scott's attitude toward his new estate, we see this conflict. He prides himself on how he manages his enclosures through the most advanced technological means, and yet he stresses that his relation to his dependents is characterized by ancient feelings of feudal loyalty. The romances themselves, though obsessed with feudal, prenationalist conquest and clan warfare, repeatedly celebrate the emergence of nationalism from competing tribes.

Each poet would have us believe that his respective romance rejects the politics of nationalism, Scott by refusing to move beyond the merely local, Wordsworth by forcing us above the local to a transcendent domain. But if we turn to the romances themselves, and to the specific socio-historical conditions under which the poets labor, we find a different, more complex story. Both poems are about the potential contraction of domain, about the potential loss of property. Indeed, we can be more precise. Both poems relate how, in the midst of a factious, violent war that tears the nation—which is represented in both poems by an ancient landed family—apart, "property" is reclaimed and expanded, instead of lost. Both poems record, in disparate ways, how the nation, in a crisis of potential breakdown, actually expands its sense of place, actually intensifies its sense of identity in order to prevent fragmentation and disruption from within and thus the inevitable conquest that would follow from without. Both poets seem at first to trivialize the function of property—Scott by making it merely a personal comfort, Wordsworth by making it insubstantial in relation to cognitive victory over the external world—but in doing so each actually reincorporates the function of property in a more crucial sense.

*   *   *

Scott's obsession with containment of family, enclosure of property, and enlargement of domain is transferred to the structure of *Rokeby* as the ideology of nationalist evolutionary growth. The conflict at the heart of the romance revolves around these questions: will the Rokebys and Morthams be able to sustain control over their own tribal identity: will they, despite fierce ideological tensions and military bombardments, be able to retain their ancient property: and perhaps most important, will they be able to maintain the health of their place (their property and their position) by expanding to incorporate the external forces that seem to threaten them? The frenzied plot, with all its complex goings-on and entanglements, while explicitly celebrating the victory of organic harmony and completion, also expresses fear of the tensions bred by a changing sense of national autonomy and growth. The socio-historical contradictions of Napoleonic Europe that are apparently suppressed from the objective (the object-content) of the poem resurface in the frantic activity of the plot and in the ideological maneuvers that structure the romance.

Rokeby begins in a condition of divisiveness. We are introduced first to the man who embodies the ultimate threat to Rokeby, Oswald. Oswald fulfills not only the structural role of a romance villain, the major obstacle that must be overcome in order for the romance to complete itself; he also plays a complex ideological role. The first images we encounter in the poem are ancient tower and rolling river (the same images that initiate the *White Doe*). The tower represents stability, the river, change, but they are combined into a single image to represent the interconnection of tradition with change and civil with natural orders. The tower lends meaning to the river by giving it a history; the river lends credence and viability to the tower, for as the tower survives the changes of nature, it takes on nature's natural vitality and partakes of nature's natural authority. Instead of change remaining a threat, it becomes an active part of tradition itself. Oswald's place in the tower, in the civil sphere, mirrors his place in the natural sphere. In both spheres, there is turmoil, a distress that invades Oswald's sleep and that forces him, by the end of the poem, out of the ancient tower that he so unnaturally aspires to rule. So Oswald's distress at the beginning of the poem signals that he is the source of the poem's distress, and once he is ousted, the poem can achieve its final harmony.

Those towers, which in the changeful gleam
Throw murky shadows on the stream,
Those towers of Barnard hold a guest,
The emotions of whose troubled breast,
In wild and strange confusion driven,
Rival the flitting rack of heaven.
Ere sleep stern Oswald's senses tied,
Oft had he changed his weary side,
Composed his limbs, and vainly sought
By effort strong to banish thought.   (I.23–32)

The shadows that tower over the river project Oswald's "wild and strange confusion." Oswald is attempting to usurp the power of the tower, and as a result, his sleep becomes confused, changeful, disruptive, unnatural. The ancient towers are haunted by confusion and they haunt Oswald because he is a villain plotting to kill the lord who has entrusted him with the estate. More crucially, however, his sleep is unnatural because he is attempting to enjoy the comforts of his lord's estate while Mortham, the fit master of the tower, is away fighting to maintain that estate. Scott does not want us to miss this irony, for he has Bertram, the man Oswald has commissioned to kill Philip of Mortham, say to Oswald:

"Here, in your towers by circling Tees,
You, Oswald Wycliffe, rest at ease;
Why deem it strange that others come
To share such safe and easy home,
From fields where danger, death, and toil
Are the reward of civil broil?"   (I.211–16)

Like Scott, who must leave the narrow comforts of his domain to compete in the larger world in order to maintain and expand his domain, so Philip of Mortham is compelled to leave his domain behind and do battle in the world. Oswald represents the potential subversion of this law of tribal or national growth. Oswald wants to expand his empire, but to do so, like Napoleon, by expropriating alien property without going through the evolutionary process whereby property is expanded through the gradual harmonization of differences. Oswald also ignores the loyalty to tribe which must ground ownership and must precede expansion of property. In other words, Oswald is, once again like Napoleon, an anti-nationalist. He uses the very moment of the nation's self-crisis as a moment of personal advancement. Opportunistically, he accentuates the unnatural factions within the nation in order to gain property from each faction, in order to satiate his own ambition, rather than to fulfill natural dictates of national growth.

The ultimate impotence of Oswald's ideological position is exemplified in the romance plot. The Morthams and the Rokebys are two ancient neighboring families pitted against each other in the civil war. It appears as though these two families are fated to remain separate clans both because of the circumstances of civil disturbance and for a natural cause: Mortham has no heir. (The cultural and the natural always conveniently correspond in this way in the poem.) These two families, however, as we sense from the very beginning of the poem, should be conjoined. They are neighboring families with an incestuously intertwined, though factious, history. Rokeby has married Mortham's sister; Rokeby's daughter, Matilda, is Mortham's niece. But by the end of the romance, we realize that the two families' interconnection is more complicated than this. Mortham does indeed have a son, but because of past sins, his heir has been lost to him. Mortham had eloped with the daughter of an Irish chief O'Neale against the Irishman's wishes. O'Neale, seeking reconciliation with his daughter and her new husband, sends his son secretly to Mortham's estate. In a fit of jealousy Mortham, given misinformation by none other than Oswald, mistakes his wife's brother for a treacherous suitor, and, finding the siblings in an embrace, shoots the brother, mistakingly also killing his own wife. The Bryonic Mortham grows even more melancholy and desolate when his only son is kidnapped, not realizing that O'Neale has stolen the boy and has had him sent to Rokeby. And so Rokeby unknowingly raises Redmond, Mortham's son, as his own. What the romance dictates is that the two heirs, Matilda and Redmond, raised as sister and brother, be united, representing the natural growth of two neighboring tribes—England and Ireland or England and Scotland—into a single national entity.

At every juncture of the plot Oswald threatens to subvert this process of natural growth by displacing it with unnatural expansion motivated by personal greed and ambition. He manages to persuade Rokeby, who does not realize that his adopted son is the true heir of Mortham's tower, to accept Wilfrid, Oswald's son, as Matilda's suitor and as eventual heir to Rokeby-Hall. After Oswald has learned the true identity of Redmond, the civil war provides him the perfect context for having his supposed ally Mortham secretly killed in combat and for having Rokeby and Redmond, captured Cavaliers under his charge, executed—thus garnering for himself both Mortham Tower and Rokeby-Hall. That his machinations are futile goes without saying. Not even through the factiousness of civil war can Oswald disrupt the natural course of tribal growth. Mortham, having secretly escaped Oswald's murder attempt, returns to save the day. True identities are revealed, and the two estates become one through the marriage of Mortham's and Rokeby's heirs. Past redeems present; internal dissension is transformed into natural (familial) harmony and organic (human reproduction) growth.

But the fate of the Mortham-Rokeby domain, symbolizing the destiny of Britain itself, is not all that is at stake in the romance. Also at stake is the fate of imperial spoils, the internal-external, native-exotic problem. Having killed his wife and lost his son, Mortham becomes estranged from his own tribe. Emotionally abandoning his family and friends, he also abandons his estate and his nation-state. In effect, he becomes a potential Oswald, an anti-nationalist, motivated by melancholy and the desire for revenge that unhinge him from home and homeland. Mortham also becomes, in his melancholic state, an opportunist like Napoleonic Oswald. He finds himself in Spanish America, fighting in the wars there, and winning a great treasure chest of wealth. As Oswald has attempted to exploit civil discord to satisfy his own greed, Mortham successfully exploits international rivalry for dominion in the New World, but his imperial wealth brings no satisfaction. Because he has lost his tribal identity, he has no true loyalty to the country for which he supposedly conquers. As Scott had learned from Burke, the prosperity of the nation-state begins at home with the instinctive loyalty dictated by prejudice for one's own blood kin, and as he may have learned from Wordsworth's political sonnets, not from "external wealth: / But from *within* proceeds a Nation's health." Accordingly, Mortham's imperial wealth becomes, not a means of prosperity for him, but a reminder of his estrangement, of his emotional poverty, and so he hides it away until he can be restored to his natural self, to his estate, to his heir, to his nation. It is difficult not to suggest, in this parable, a transferential relation to Scott's own financial predicament. If it is true that external wealth cannot heal the divisions within the self or within the nation because it tends to disrupt the tradition on which health and unity are based, it may be natural that Scott's attempt to commemorate his national aristocratic tradition through the building of Abbotsford should cause so much tension within the self exactly because he must rely ironically on "external wealth," the *bourgeois* commerce of the "bookselling animal," rather than on the entailed, inherited income that would serve to complete the fantasy of an ancient, aristocratic British line.

The treasure chest spurs factiousness within the nation, spurs anti-nationalism, as it becomes the object of greed for various villains in the poem, including most crucially Oswald himself. For instance, a group of deserters from the war, both Cavaliers and Roundheads, band together to raid Rokeby-Hall, where they think the chest is hidden; because Rokeby's lord has been captured and the hall lies virtually unprotected, the bandits reckon that they can easily take the imperial wealth before Oswald has time to complete his own evil scheme. These men commit double-treachery, at first joining in the factions of civil war, and then betraying their factions in order to grasp what appears to be wealth made vulnerable because of that civil war. The imperial treasure chest, then, represents a potential threat to national harmony, rather than an enrichment of it. It represents Napoleonic imperialism, a drive for conquest that is motivated by greed and desire for power and that tramples on and subordinates alien countries in order to fulfill that greed and desire for power. It is conquest by tyrannical domination rather than by the natural evolutionary growth of native wealth.

Scott highlights the difference between these two imperialist impulses by displaying for us the conversion of Mortham from Napoleonic imperialism to organic national growth. Mortham "spoke of wealth as of a load / By fortune on a wretch bestowed, / In bitter mockery of hate, / His cureless woes to aggravate" (V.668–71). The treasure is a mockery of the happiness that the security of wealth should bestow. This is because he is driven to those foreign lands, not from loyalty to his kin and country, not from a desire to extend to other lands the values of liberty and abundance at the heart of his own culture, but instead from the derangement of his own egomania. The civil war proves an opportunity to Mortham as much as it does for Oswald, but for Mortham, it is a chance to reverse his destiny and to return to tribe and nation. After repenting and confessing his sins to Matilda, Mortham commits himself to the Puritan cause, announcing that he is "Moved by no cause but England's right. / My country's groans have bid me draw / My sword for gospel and for law" (V.692–93). To confirm this conversion, he entrusts his imperial wealth to Matilda and tells her that if he is killed in combat and his heir does not return in three years, she should use the wealth to heal the wounds of the nation: "So spoils, acquired by fight afar, / Shall mitigate domestic war" (V.707–08). Mortham's conversion is necessarily accompanied by a new commitment to finding his lost heir. If he does survive the war, he says, he shall seek his son through "Europe wide."

In entrusting the imperial wealth to Matilda, in regaining loyalty to his tribe and nation, Mortham purifies that wealth. It gains the power to heal a nation, temporarily wounded by the incisions of civil discord. Matilda represents the untouched purity of the nation, its impregnable and unfragmentable soul. As the object of desire for both Redmond and Wilfrid, she purifies and completes them, just as she purges the sin of Napoleonic imperialism. Wilfrid, the unwilling progeny of Oswald, must die as surely as Oswald, yet because of his love for Matilda, his death helps to re-unite the nation. Broken by his father's evil and his unrequitable love for Matilda, he dies so that Matilda's true love, Redmond, may live. Only Matilda can effect this national union, only she is worthy of hearing Mortham's confession, only she is worthy to purge imperial error, only she can purify and complete the tribal ambition.

*   *   *

Similarly, Wordsworth uses his heroine Emily in the *White Doe* as an emblem of purification. Along with the doe, who represents both the naturalness of Emily's conquest and the exotic other with whom "communion" must be sought, Emily is the only pure presence in the poem. When her brother Francis, refusing to choose sides, feels obligated by conscience to follow, unarmed, his kindred rebels, he entrusts the tribal identity to his sister: "For thee, for thee, is left the sense / Of trial past without offence," (II.521–22) he says. Even though Rylstone-Hall itself, once the men have deserted it in their zealous cause, "must fall," Emily can, Francis suggests, through her feminine endurance, possess for them a greater domain. She can become "A Soul, by force of sorrows high, / Uplifted to the purest sky / Of undisturbed humanity!" (II.585–87). Like Scott, Wordsworth brings a higher harmony from the disturbances of national conflict through his heroine, who represents the ideal of English culture, the soul of England, the motherland. Even as the tribe seems to defeat itself through "ill-advised" and "unfortunate" factiousness, the soul of the nation endures unharmed, for the nation itself is greater than the sum of its parts. When Wordsworth says that Emily endures partly by "native strength," then, he means both by natural strength (as represented through her relation to the doe) and by the strength granted her by birth, by having been born into a uniquely strong place, into a culture that provides her the sustenance for spiritual conquest even in the midst of apparent dissolution of property. What makes such spiritual endurance and conquest possible, even ordained, is this special relation to the unique origin-center, what Wordsworth calls in "The Convention of Cintra" "the green fields of Liberty in this blessed and highly-favoured Island which we inhabit" (*Selected Prose* 171). The romance pretends to move beyond the arbitrariness of the specific, beyond the arbitrariness of English culture, but actually it universalizes and apotheosizes the values of that specific place. The folk who come to fill the chapel in response to Bolton tower's summons draw strength from Emily's example and experience their own "native strength" through her visionary conquest, even though they are *not* aware of Emily's story and how it relates to their own.

While composing the *White Doe* (1807–1808), Wordsworth is also deeply interested in the problem of nationalism, as is evident in his tract, "The Convention of Cintra," composed during the same period (1808–1809). Wordsworth is trying to understand how a nation can survive both internal conflict (which seems to contradict his organic, spiritual conception of nationalism) and external assault, and, more subtly, he wants to understand how a nation can change and expand while remaining stable and unified. His attention is brought to this problem both by Catholic Spain's predicament during the Peninsular War and by Britain's potential division as a result of French cunning. This concern is transferred to his "object of study" in the poem, an attempt at civil war waged by disgruntled Catholics during the reign of Elizabeth: "It was the time when England's Queen / Twelve years had reigned, a Sovereign dread; / Nor yet the restless crown had been / Disturbed upon her virgin head" (II.360–63). Wordsworth chooses the Elizabethan era because it was a time of great national growth and prosperity when England's triumph over France, Spain, and the Pope was assured, and the internecine disruptions of religious and political factions experienced under Henry VIII and Bloody Mary had abated into relative calm. In the *White Doe* Francis Norton, torn between loyalty to his rebel father and brothers and loyalty to his country, urges his father not to join Neville and Percy, "Two Earls fast leagued in discontent" (II.368). Francis pleads: "A just and gracious Queen have we, / A pure religion, and the claim / Of peace on our humanity" (II.386–88); his plea, however, is futile, and, as he prophesies to Emily, the family is "doomed to perish utterly" (II.521–87) for their "misled" rebellion against the state. Thus, through the voice of Francis, Wordsworth issues a warning to jacobin sympathizers or other disgruntled factions threatening civil discord, as he transfers the anxieties of a prosperously expanding nineteenth-century Britain back to the ideal past of an Elizabethan England, expanding and yet stable.

The advice that Wordsworth gives the Spaniards (and the British) in "The Convention of Cintra" correlates exactly with the exemplary behavior of Emily and Francis in the romance:

[T]he *professional* excellencies of the soldier must be contemplated according to their due place and relation. Nothing is done, or worse than nothing, unless something higher be taught, *as* higher, something more fundamental, *as* more fundamental. In the moral virtues and qualities of passion which belong to a people, must the ultimate salvation of a people be sought for. . . . They must now be taught, that their strength *chiefly* lies in moral qualities, more silent in their operation, more permanent in their nature; in the virtues of perseverance, constancy, fortitude, and watchfulness, in a long memory and a quick feeling, to rise upon a favourable summons, a texture of life which, though cut through (as hath been feigned of the bodies of the Angels) unites again. (*Selected Prose* 182, Wordsworth's emphases)

This is exactly what Francis and ultimately Emily represent, the higher power of the immaterial unity of a nation's soul that cannot be cut through, even by Napoleon's own sword. Wordsworth asserts that there are only two instances when "a People may be benefited by resignation or forfeiture of their rights as a separate independent State": when it is conquered by a superior country and when "two contiguous or neighbouring countries, both included by nature under one conspicuously defined limit—the weaker is united with, or absorbed into, the more powerful" (226). This is because "the People," like the poet, is not only a natural, organic entity, but a divinely ordained one. "This was the feeling of the people; an awful feeling: and it is from these oracles that rulers are to learn wisdom" (217).

These higher and fundamental spiritual qualities that make the people into a single, harmonious, inviolable, oracular entity also make it unlikely for them to go astray. Canto First of the *White Doe* is devoted to the multitude who have come to worship in a chapel near the mound that shelters Emily's grave fifty years after the fateful battle that wiped out the Norton family. Seeing the white doe, which comes to the mound each Sabbath, each of the worshippers, of different ages, ranks, and conditions, has a legend, a superstition, or a recollection that explains the white doe's Sabbath journey to the mound. A "slender Youth, a scholar pale, / From Oxford," for instance, "has come to his native vale," and devises an elaborate pastoral "conceit" to make sense of the white doe's habit. Because the people are tied naturally to their habitat, their explanations, all of them *factually inaccurate*, are nonetheless *spiritually accurate*. The worshippers transfer to the doe and the mound their own particular histories, so that even in their diversity and factual error, they reconfirm the native tradition that binds them to the land and to one another as a living whole, a people. In other words, they practice *within* the romance what the narrator practices *as* romance: they transform potentially conflicting histories into a single collective story/history, just as Wordsworth transforms the potential disruption of the Nortons into a story/history of internally harmonized endurance.

While stand the people in a ring,
Gazing, doubting, questioning;
Yea, many overcome in spite
Of recollections clear and bright;
Which yet do unto some impart
An undisturbed repose of heart.
And all the assembly own a law
Of orderly respect and awe.   (I.314–21)

As the worshippers form a circle around the doe, they, in their differences, form a natural assembly that is a law unto itself, that orders itself, through awe and respect of its own natural bonds, represented by the doe, which binds itself to Emily's mound, at the heart of the circle. This valuation of the folk in relation to the land explains why both Wordsworth's and Scott's romances tend always toward ballad, the form that both poets turned to originally. The balladic internalized by romance not only represents the binding of high to low, of artifice to nature, of literate to oral culture, of master to peasant, but also seeks literally to embody the origin-center of the nation itself. Ballad returns them to the origin of popular tradition from which the nation grows, while romance brings into harmony even that silenced other—the illiterate peasant—whose relation to the land inspires patriotism at its best. "The poorest Peasant, in an unsubdued land, feels this pride," Wordsworth says in the "Convention of Cintra":

> In fact: the Peasant, and he who lives by the fair reward of his manual labour, has ordinarily a larger proportion of his gratifications dependent upon these thoughts—than, for the most part, men in other classes have. For he is in his person attached, by stronger roots, to the soil of which he is the growth: his intellectual notices are generally confined within narrower bounds: in him no partial or antipatriotic interests counteract the force of those nobler sympathies and antipathies which he has in right of his Country. (*Selected Prose* 230–31)

That this sort of pastoral nationalism is itself factually inaccurate, a romance of the nation-state, as Hazlitt points out, makes it no less powerful a call to British imperialism. In fact, as romance it may exert its greatest power.

Works Cited

Burke, Edmund. *Reflections on the Revolution in France*. Ed. Conor Cruise O'Brien. 1790; New York: Penguin Books, 1968.

Hazlitt, William. *The Round Table and Characters of Shakespear's Plays*. Introduction by Catherine M. Maclean. Rpt. London: J. M. Dent and Sons, 1964.

Hobbes, Thomas. *Leviathan*. Ed. C. B. MacPherson. 1651; New York: Penguin Books, 1968.

LaCapra, Dominick. *History and Criticism*. Ithaca, N.Y.: Cornell University Press, 1985.

Ross, Marlon. "Scott's Chivalric Pose: The Function of Metrical Romance in the Romantic Period." *Genre* 19 (1986): 267–97.

Scott, Walter. *Complete Poetical Works*. Ed. Horace E. Scudder. Boston: Houghton Mifflin, 1900.

———. *The Letters of Sir Walter Scott*. Ed. Herbert J. C. Grierson et al. 12 vols. London: Constable & Co., 1932–37. Rpt. New York: AMS, 1971.

Wordsworth, William. *The Letters of William and Dorothy Wordsworth*. 7 vols. Ed. Ernest de Sélincourt. 2d ed. Oxford: Clarendon Press, 1967–1988.

———. *Poetical Works*. Ed. Thomas Hutchinson, rev. by Ernest de Sélincourt. New York: Oxford University Press, 1904.

———. *Selected Prose*. Ed. John O. Hayden. New York: Penguin Books, 1988.

Mark Kipperman

Macropolitics of Utopia: Shelley's *Hellas* in Context

"WE ARE ALL GREEKS," said Shelley in his Preface to *Hellas,* "Our laws, our literature, our religion, our arts have their root in Greece. . . . The modern Greek is the descendant of those glorious beings whom the imagination almost refuses to figure to itself as belonging to our Kind, and he inherits much of their sensibility, their rapidity of conception, their enthusiasm, and their courage." Shelley's idealism here echoes the excited report of the Greek revolution by Leigh Hunt in the *Examiner.* But, as historian William St. Clair records in his withering and often sad critique of philhellenism, *That Greece Might Still Be Free,* nearly identical sentiments were voiced in pamphlets and lectures all over Europe by suddenly politicized classics professors at the outbreak of the 1821 revolt.[1] What is remarkable to St. Clair is how utterly wrong, even preposterous, such statements were; how little knowledge they reflected of the loosely knit bands of marauding tribes, unconcerned with the modern nation-state and as savage in their warfare as the Turks themselves, who then inhabited the ancient territories of the city-states and their heroes.[2] From slender knowledge, though, came the great utopian propaganda of Shelley's *Hellas,* a work that in one sense is historically myopic, even deluded by its liberal philhellenism; and yet in another sense it is precise, even radically visionary in its opposition to Ottoman imperialism and its support for a people struggling toward identity in a modern constitutional state—in 1821 a progressive idea. How would we today evaluate the political alignment of this romantic utopia?

At stake are our theoretical assumptions as well as our practical judgments in reading a text across its own historical moment, and, too, our ways of aligning that moment itself within our own historiography. From one perspective, Shelley's conception of Greek "nationhood" is anti-historical rather than progressive—will seem even imperializing to some—since it assumes a "Greek" continuity in a realm of classical ideas rather than in the realities of ethnohistory. Yet from another perspective, despite the philhellenic ideology, Shelley's *Hellas* aligns itself with the historical moment of insurgency in 1821, in Spain, in Naples, and among the westernized Greeks, against the Holy Alliance and for constitutional nationhood. (It is easy to forget that despite internal contradictions the bourgeoisie in the decade after the Congress of Vienna could still be called a revolutionary class.) And, as with all good revolutionary propaganda, *Hellas* associates this progressive movement with the utopian evolution of mankind in general.[3]

These tensions and contradictions make *Hellas* particularly challenging to situate politically, and although this may seem to be an extra-literary matter, in fact the success of the work's intended or non-intended political ideology has inspired interesting theoretical debate among Marxist and historicist critics. I will suggest, however, that the precise relation of a single text (especially, as in this case, a propagandistic one) to the macropolitics of its age is a practical judgment of the degree to which ideological elements disguise or distort its overt historical commitment. Often, the question turns on whether utopian language is judged as futurist flight from history or as exhortation to mobilize in a period of transformation. Either way, however, it must be acknowledged that utopian language, in its explicit ahistoricality, risks an unselfconscious escapism, denying its grounding in the history it demands to transform.

I would like to begin with Jerome McGann's mordant response to a long line of liberal critics on the politics of *Hellas*:

> Although [Kenneth Neill] Cameron represents the Greek Revolution as a significant crack in the Holy Alliance, it was far from being that. Rather, it represented the beginning of the end of the Turkish Empire and the definitive emergence of European imperialism—at the head of which was England—into world history.[4]

I do not see how such an outcome could have been clear (or historically inevitable) *from the perspective of 1821*, but McGann's real point is that Shelley's idealist philhellenism is "open to a political exploitation by Europe's imperialist powers" out of blindness to the objective forces of politics and history. McGann is at the same time attacking idealist *critics* for assenting unreflectively to this escapism. And no doubt there is something vulnerable in the near contempt for "mere" history shown by a purely idealist reader of Shelley such as Earl Wasserman: "Only in a nearly trivial way is *Hellas* a propagandistic call to rally to the Greek cause; in its true scope, it centers upon the Greek revolution to validate Shelley's confidence in an imminent and ineluctable universal transformation." He concludes that Shelley's (Hegelian) aim is to locate the drama in "recurrent historical cycles and therefore to transform merely temporal events into an eternal truth."[5]

I would like at once to distinguish between critics' idealism and Shelley's. I do not believe Shelley would completely recognize his political aims in Wasserman's breathless transcendentalism. But McGann's historicist attack accepts critics' exaggeration of this strain in the poem as representing Shelley's own sense of politics. For McGann, idealist escapism does indeed reveal Shelley's commitment to politics, but only negatively as a "reflex" against the despair of facing up to history: a notion that denies to Shelley any meaningful radicalism in his own local circumstances. I do agree with the aim of embedding the idealism within its historical horizons, but I am less anxious to condemn Shelley's utopian language as escapist or even "open to exploitation by Europe's imperialist powers." I doubt such ideological appropriation would have occurred to conservative readers—much less to the nervous publisher who in 1820 deleted the radical attack on the Holy Alliance from the Preface.[6] And, of course, the play is dedicated to Prince Mavrocordato, whom Shelley had known well in Pisa and who left to join the uprising initiated by his cousin Ypsilanti in March. Shelley and many of his readers believed a massive rebellion was beginning on Europe's southern flank, and Shelley urged Ollier to publish *Hellas* immediately: "What little interest this poem may ever excite, depends upon its *immediate* publication."[7] If *Hellas* is filled with atemporal ideals, they had timely urgency for Shelley.

That urgency can be appreciated only by a keener sense of the history of the revolt than McGann's, who seems to believe that Hellenism was clearly the ideology of choice for British imperial aims. In fact, the relationship between ideology and historical fact was, from the perspective of 1821, interdetermining, causal relationships confused and not open to clear scientific specification. Philhellenism was an idealism rooted in nationalism, and the applicability of nationalism to a "Greek" people emerging from Ottoman domination was radical, even shocking. For Turkey was still a great power in 1821 and Greece only an ideal, her people (beyond the Peloponnese) little more than disorganized tribes, her leaders living abroad out of touch with local chieftains. And yet the ideal of a nation was crucial to the success of the guerilla struggle. Was nationalism, then, a romantic mystification manipulated by the elites of the great powers for macropolitical ends? Or was it the rallying cry for a new historical order that threatened the Holy

Alliance? The question cannot be posed outside an historical perspective: however "romantic" or conservative nationalism may seem to appear over its nineteenth-century development, and no matter how much classicist nostalgia was invoked by British elites, *in 1821* the cause of the Greeks did also emblematize a broader, radical call for a new world order. The significance of philhellenism, according to historian C. W. Crawley,

> was quite independent of the character of the Greeks and the real conditions of Levantine politics; it lay in the European appeal of classical tradition and of Christendom oppressed, and above all in the discovery of an outlet for energies compressed by the Conservative Alliance—an outlet the more welcome because relatively unconnected with the dangers of revolutionary movements at home. Every statesman in England, and many abroad, had been brought up in Classical studies, and some of them felt a warm personal concern in the fate of Greece, whatever their view of public duty. . . . In the age of Sir Walter Scott, with the passing of the eighteenth century and the end of the stern struggle against Napoleon, there was renewed among Englishmen, official and unofficial, of every political creed, a strain of fine Quixotism, a temper ready to admire adventure. . . . It manifested itself in different forms; not merely in the avowed romantics and philhellenes—men like Lord Guilford and Sir Richard Church—but in the zeal of the anti-slavery group, in the warm-hearted impulsiveness of Stratford Canning, in the fervor of Urquhart, a convert to the "Spirit of the East," in Palmerston himself, the apostle of "British common sense," and strangest of all, in those who professed themselves least moved by sentiment, such missionary disciples of Bentham as Sir John Bowring and the "typographical" Colonel Stanhope.[8]

The British elites found themselves divided. Shelley's poem appeared at a crucial historical moment, when the classicist sympathies of statesmen like Canning were in conflict with British imperial interests. Not that those interests were exactly clear at the time: both Castlereagh and Canning played a delicate diplomatic game, attempting to preserve neutrality, the navigability of Ionian waters, and the trust of both Russia and the Turks. Castlereagh refused to intervene, in order to avoid being sucked into a military alliance with Russia to guarantee Greek independence, and indeed there was some sense among the ministers—probably well founded—that if the Greeks could make some advances themselves they were better served than if England and Russia had negotiated a settlement for them at the Congress of Verona in 1822.[9]

Diplomatically, the British did not want to be forced into military action to guarantee a settlement. Politically, Castlereagh as much as his liberal opponents tended to see the Greek revolt as part of a general rebellion against the Holy Alliance. At the same time, he feared that an alliance with Russia against the Turks would in the long run be a danger to British interests in Southwest Asia. For one thing, there was not just important trade with Smyrna in Asia Minor but trade also with Ottoman lands throughout the Levant. The Ionian islands (controlled by Britain) were trade centers, and the British were sensitive to the fact that they were used as refuges by Greek rebels, the waters endangered by warfare and piracy. But most important to British fears of antagonizing the Turks was the common tendency in the period both to overestimate Russian power and to predict the eventual demise of the moribund Ottoman Empire. Turkey was Britain's only defense against Russian advances to the Mediterranean; the collapse of Turkish armed power might mean conflict with Russia. Only when the Russo-Turkish war broke out in 1829 did it become evident that Russia had only limited power to seize and hold territory south of the Danube. It is not surprising, then, that the British ambassador to Constantinople, Lord Strangford, urged Castlereagh to call for immediate Greek surrender and even ordered the local British admiral to assist the Turkish fleet! Even as late as 1827, the British crown apologized for the destruction of the Turkish and Egyptian fleets at Navarino by Admiral Codington, acting independently and impulsively to preserve a declared armistice. Liberals like Lord Holland proclaimed Navarino a "glorious victory"; George IV "lamented" the "untoward event."[10]

In this context, philhellenism could have been seen as nothing less than a challenge to the global order of empires negotiated in 1815. Moreover, as Marilyn Butler has pointed out, Shelley's particular brand of hellenism would have been immediately obvious to his contemporaries as an alignment with republican radicalism. Butler sees Shelley's circle, particularly Peacock, Keats, and Hunt, forming a "left-wing cult of the classical" in conscious response to the conservative "Romanticism" of Coleridge and Wordsworth. And that classicism expressed itself in a fascination with naturalism, paganism, and myth: "In the tradition of learned polemic absorbed by Shelley and Peacock, the classic tale was not poetic fancy but religious myth, a means of conveying a universal truth through allegory."[11] No doubt the urbane classicism of a Peacock or a Shelley carries with it an air of aristocratic idealization. But such class analysis here would be too blunt an instrument; the myth-making here is no mere flight from historicity but a more complex engagement with an Enlightenment and Radical-Dissenter tradition of liberalism, naturalism, and anti-authoritarianism.

Ancient Greece is indeed an enduring, atemporal ideal for Shelley and his circle, but one that can speak to the present era which, as we shall see, Shelley portrays as emerging from authoritarian Christianity to a new pagan-inspired liberality, egalitarianism, and harmony. It is not true that Shelley's romantic utopianism is somehow politically disengaged or confused. In 1821 Shelley's idealism was *both* atemporal *and* rooted in historical progressivism in a way that only art and not politics can be.

McGann's attack on the utopian strains in romanticism resembles Lukács's on literary expressionism in the 1930s, generally that expressions of idealism *in art* are ideological in the same sense as they would be in critical or philosophical propositions about the world. But art is not itself history or politics, retaining enough autonomy to imagine (ideal) potentialities within these that science might not. It is not surprising that critics can situate a work within some historical or political context not consciously (or possibly) perceived by the artist; but this does not imply that any particular poetic treatment of history or myth, idealist or not, has necessarily predictable political implications. Historicists must avoid such claims. This point was made in a famous attack on Lukács by Adorno:

> Lukács would doubtless deprecate as idealistic the use of terms like "image" and "essence" in aesthetics. But their application in the realm of art is fundamentally different from what it is in philosophies of essence or of primitive images, especially refurbished versions of the Platonic Ideas. The most fundamental weakness of Lukács's position is probably his inability to maintain this distinction, a failure which leads him to transfer to the realm of art categories which refer to the relationship of consciousness to the actual, as if there were no difference between them. . . . It is no idealistic crime for art to provide essences, "images"; the fact that many artists have inclined toward an idealist philosophy says nothing about the content of their works. The truth of the matter is that except where art goes against its own nature and simply duplicates existence, its task vis-à-vis that which merely exists, is to be its essence and image.[12]

In Shelley's *Hellas* there is indeed a good deal of Wasserman's kind of transcendent idealism, in the *imagery* of an enduring principle of liberation existing potentially within each moment ("Greece and her foundations are / Built below the tide of war, / Based on the chrystalline sea / Of thought and its eternity" [696–99]). But the *political function* of the imagery is not to deny the meaningfulness of human history but rather to revise both Mahmud's and the reader's conception of history and of the power of empire to control those conceptions. Shelley's idealism here is neither platonic nor escapist but argues that the very shape and realization of human ideals like peace and equality depend on the progress of history; that struggles for liberation are founded in permanent ideals but expressed and defined only within historical contingency; and that these ideals exist as permanent possibilities of social and spiritual progress, so that even as negatives (utopia is not yet) they persist to negate the negations of imperialism with its delusions of permanent power.

Within its own form and the real historical context it evokes, Shelley's idealism in *Hellas* does reflect the constitutionalist, nationalist, and essentially anti-imperialist progressivism of his time. Eurocentric and classicist, yes—and bourgeois nationalism itself would not seem so progressive, perhaps, by the 1840s—but it is worth noting that for all his classicism Shelley was progressive enough to fault the historical Athens for its treatment of slaves and women.[13] The "brighter Hellas" that shall arise in the far future might seem to imply a flight from contemporary history; yet this utopia remains poised upon and defined by historical contingencies rendered urgent for the play's contemporary readers. The Shelley-Peacock circle needed to idealize Hellas in the post-Napoleonic era precisely because they sensed the crisis of culture—for them either a medium of social vision or a means of social control—in a secular age of failed revolutions and imperial reaction. Again, bourgeois nationalism at this time must have seemed the most radical position capable, at a revolutionary moment, of articulating social ideals based on the most enduring yet progressive principles of European civilization.[14] Indeed, our ability to idealize within any historical situation is itself probed in *Hellas* and is essential to the often ironic structure of the drama.

Contributing to that irony, of course, is the sense of potential historical and spiritual progress that contrasts with Mahmud's growing ability to perceive his own necessary defeat; the counterpoint to this parabolic tale is Mahmud's actual victory, now emptied of meaning. The most remarkable dramatic recognition in the play, of course, is Mahmud's dream-vision, induced by the seer, Ahasuerus. His evocation of "the One" that transcends the fleeting moments of life seems to support the view of idealist critics that Shelley's metaphysics etherealizes the historical present:

—this Whole
Of suns, and worlds, and men, and beasts, and flowers
With all the silent or tempestuous workings
By which they have been, are, or cease to be,

Is but a vision—all that it inherits
Are motes of a sick eye, bubbles and dreams;
Thought is its cradle and its grave, nor less
The future and the past are idle shadows
Of thought's eternal flight—they have no being.
Nought is but that which feels itself to be.   (776–85)

But despite Shelley's sympathy with such metaphysical idealism, it should not be seen in isolation from its dramatic context. I would agree with Cameron that the speech is directed at Mahmud's imperial arrogance, producing "visions that will undermine Mahmud's morale by convincing him of the inevitable end of his empire."[15] In this, he functions like Demogorgon in *Prometheus Unbound,* announcing the ineluctable progress of history (conceived of as the progress of human ideals into the real). He is a type of the romantic border-figure, signaling a transition from one stage of consciousness to another. But in the dramatic context, that transition is from one understanding of *history* to another:

Mistake me not! All is contained in each.
Dodona's forest to an acorn's cup
Is that which has been, or will be, to that
Which is—the absent to the present . . .
Knock and it shall be opened—look and lo!
The coming age is shadowed on the past
As on a glass.   (792–95; 804–06)

Such a view of historical necessity should bring to mind an earlier dream-vision, where Ahasuerus makes his first appearance in Shelley, *Queen Mab.* Here the use of dream-vision as aesthetic *form* does not imply any implicit commitment to idealist metaphysics. Quite the contrary: in *Queen Mab* the metaphysics is explicit and materialist. In *Hellas* the relation of ideals to history is more dialectical. But in either case the use of dream-vision is consistent and incidental to idealism or materialism; it serves rather as a utopian form aimed at revising—or "awakening"—the dreamer's sense of history. This rhetorical mode should not be thought of (or abused as) a peculiarly "romantic" ideology: in fact, it is as deeply rooted in D'Holbach, Volney, and the *philosophes* as it is a precursor of later nineteenth-century scientific utopianism. In *Hellas,* the new vision itself concerns the relation of history to civilization's ideals.

Against a backdrop of timeless ideals struggling into history and modified by their incarnation unfolds this drama of new conceptions demanding new historical choices. Historicity and ideality are not so much opposed as interwoven, but not in a way open to theoretical knowledge or a "science" of politics. Their relation is revealed, rather, through the antagonisms of dramatic action; as one critic observes, "lyric drama is used to accentuate the dynamics of antithesis in the context of an unfinished struggle."[16] Thus the complex, tempered, often obscure idealism of the chorus:

Worlds on worlds are rolling ever
   From creation to decay,
Like the bubbles on a river
   Sparkling, bursting, borne away.
   But *they* are still immortal
   Who through Birth's orient portal
And Death's dark charm hurrying to and fro,
   Clothe their unceasing flight
   In the brief dust and light . . .
   New shapes they still may weave,
   New Gods, new Laws receive.   (196–205, 207–08)

Despite their eternal presence, these immortals both affect and are subject to history. Historical evolution in *Hellas* appears as a progression of awakenings into temporality.

Swift as the radiant shapes of sleep
   From one whose dreams are Paradise
Fly, when the fond wretch wakes to weep . . .
   The Powers of earth and air
Fled from the folding star of Bethlehem.   (225–31)

At this historical advent, the Greek gods "Apollo, Pan, and Love"—who designate a benign humanized nature—desert a world awakening to the new "Truth" of Christianity.

Our hills and seas and streams,
   Dispeopled of their dreams,
Their waters turned to blood, their dew to tears,
   Wailed for the golden years.   (235–38)

The imagery is a complex inversion of Milton's "On the morning of Christ's Nativity," and reflects Shelley's ambivalence toward a Christianity whose victory implied centuries of sectarian strife. In Milton, the mountains hear weeping from departing gods (xx), but nature herself rather rejoices in the new spiritual music and is "almost won" now that "her reign had here its last fulfilling" (x). In Shelley's chorus Christian truths waken us "to weep," and although they are "true in their relation to the worship they superseded" do not usher in utopia.[17] In contrast to this cold awakening to "blood" and "tears," *Hellas* hopes for an awakening into history not sorrowful but joyous and humane.

The play itself recalls this wakening "to weep" as Mahmud progressively comprehends his own historical irrelevance; it further encourages *its audience* to a countermovement, a vision of victory even in the face of a temporary setback to the cause of liberation, a Greek failure. The utopian ideal, of course, would be the unification of the realm of Love with real historical advance. In the final chorus the "tears" become votive offerings, and the blood is rejected as Saturn and Love return to fulfill the hope of the first chorus for a history without triumphs, empire, or the blood sacrifice of war demanded by the "thorns of life." And these thorns are not the vague stings of any earthly embodiment to the too-sensitive soul so often associated with Shelley; the rejected "Prologue to *Hellas*" identifies them specifically as "scepters and crowns, mitres and swords and snares" (*Julian* 3:15, lines 153–54).

Saturn and Love their long repose
  Shall burst, more bright and good
Than all who fell, than One who rose [Jesus]
   Than many unsubdued;
Not gold, not blood their altar dowers
  But votive tears and symbol flowers.   (1040–95)

History and ideality converge for Shelley in a moment of political choice, and it is too often forgotten that *Hellas*'s macropolitical vision dawns not only on the immobilized and obsolescent Mahmud but also on the play's audience. *Hellas,* like *The Persians* upon which it is modeled, is a drama of *reports*. As in Aeschylus's play, or as in Shakespeare's *Antony and Cleopatra,* the sense of the reporting is the impinging of historical moment upon idyll, dream, or, in Mahmud's case, the mystification of power and imperial permanence. For Shelley's audience in 1821, the idealization of hellenism would not have been escapist; rather it intensified the sense of the present, where British action could uphold the ideological fantasies of Holy Alliance or intervene on behalf of emergent nationalism. It is precisely at this moment that the drama reaches its ironic climax, as the report reaches Mahmud of his victory over the Greeks, with British aid:

Victory! Victory! The bought Briton sends
The keys of Ocean to the Islamite— . . .
                    O keep holy
This jubilee of unrevenged blood—
Kill, crush, despoil! Let not a Greek escape!   (1016–17, 1020–22)

But Mahmud has already accepted the irrelevance of this victory ("Come what may, / The Future must become the Past" [923–24]), his final words adding an undermining question-mark to his echo of the shouts: "Victory? Poor slaves!"[18]

The victory will belong to the progressive emergence of enlarged human potential, symbolized by ancient Greece but not limited even to that historical example. This larger cause may lose as little by this defeat as the Turks gain:

    If Greece must be
A wreck, yet shall its fragments reassemble
And build themselves again impregnably
    In a diviner clime . . .   (1002–05)

This may seem to be a retreat to otherworldliness—in which case no historical outcome would matter much—but again Shelley here is only invoking the permanence of human ideals as guiding principles of further political struggle:

Let the tyrants rule the desert they have made
    Let the free possess the paradise they claim
Be the fortune of our fierce oppressors weighed
    With our ruin, our resistance and our name!   (1008–11)

That struggle, he does suggest, may take place in other lands than contemporary Greece: "Let Freedom and Peace flee far / To a sunnier strand / And follow Love's folding star / To the Evening-land" (1027–30). But despite the obvious nervousness here at the drama's end, the shifting away from the contemporary political exigency, the suggestion of a new utopian advent ("the folding star") in America does connect Shelley to recent revolutionary history and also, perhaps, to American Philhellenes, whose vigorous fundraising Shelley would have heard of from Byron.[19] Thus, even if Shelley in typical romantic fashion sees ideals as transcending history in their unity and permanence, their function remains radical, demanding political commitments and presenting historical possibilities here and now.

For Shelley, idealization is not ideological mystification if it presents a clarified political choice, an intensification of the present seen against a progressive future. In Ernst Bloch's terms, the future leaves a "trace" on the present, which is interlaced with political possibilities. Shelley's utopianism cannot in these terms be seen only as escapist illusion. But *Hellas,* particularly in its famous final chorus, does pose utopianism's most archly impossible question, Can any event within history conclusively revise our ways both of writing and of making it?

If Shelley demands that utopia emerge within historical struggles, he also insists on annihilating that history whose implicit goal, especially in the West's chiliastic theology, is the triumph and revenge of the good. This demand to remythologize history implies an idealization of the secular both classical in its humanism and Christian in its vision of an end to the past through an advent in the present. But it is more than these in aiming at a human appropriation of the forces of history in an actual moment of radical reconceptualization. Such appropriation interfuses history with mental drama, and it would clarify matters to admit that Marxist critics are correct to say that Shelley's radicalism on this point is unlike Marx's. But radicalism it is—Marx himself, incidentally, found Shelley so—and not a pure escape from politics into ideality.[20]

Here we have identified the romantic paradox of *Hellas*'s politics: that the poem commits itself to a specific progressive political struggle to be resolved by a mental revision, and yet is aware that historical progress has been written in a vocabulary of opposition, of victory, retribution, power divorced from love. How, indeed, given the "degradation" of most contemporary Greeks that even Shelley acknowledges in his Preface, how could even a Greek victory in 1821 avoid the turn to blood revenge and ensuing reactionary oppression? This question, I would argue, would have been obvious, even urgent, for a generation that had venerated and then despised a French revolution turned to empire, and had looked on in greater horror at the brutal irony of the Emperor's defeat by the reactionary Alliance. It would be natural to appeal to enduring ideals of liberation while supporting revolutionary violence. It is, perhaps, a permanent paradox of revolutionary utopianism to demand in advance of attaining political victory a reinvention of history (and culture) in the midst of crisis.

Reenvisioning dominant mythologies, we have come to believe, requires a power more political than cultural, rarely given to poets, rarely taken bloodlessly, rarely held without compromise. We feel this way—if we are to be truly historicist, and fair, in judging Shelley's radical legislator-poet—because we live in an era of state power that has made obsolete Shelley's tyrant kings, whose divinity and power so easily vanish when exposed to romantic mental theater. The bourgeois revolution that dethroned kings replaced them with less demonized powers, the Captains of Industry. The growth of the liberal industrial state in the nineteenth century has permanently changed what we count as radicalism and support for the oppressed: these new victims, as Engels was the first to note, become invisible even to themselves as such, their struggles not obviously dramatic but ideologically effaced in the name of political consensus. Romantic rebellion soon seemed less threatening for most people than just irrelevant. It is a measure of Shelley's real historicity, then, this rather sad tone of irrelevance and apology we hear in Mary Shelley's own note on *Hellas,* written for her 1839 edition: "We have seen the rise and progress of reform. But the Holy Alliance was alive and active in those days, and few could dream of the peaceful triumph of liberty. . . . Freedom and knowledge have now a chance of proceeding hand in hand" (*Julian* 3:63).

But Shelley has left us with an enduring problem, even if we are less sanguine about the political power of literary culture. This is the question of the political power of utopian idealization and radical, humane vision. I have argued that the precise relation of the idealizations of art to politics will depend not on any intrinsic ideological formula but rather on the clarity with which ideals and political "realism" are interwoven to display in art the dialectical relation between utopia and history.

I do not mean this as historical relativism or determinism, however. If there is no escaping history, there is also no escaping Shelley's utopian insistence that our political struggles emerge from reconstructions of history. Such reconstruction is the difficult work of culture itself, a truly discontented struggle between ideologies of power and the hope for a progressive future. Both are culture's dream-work, but Shelley's utopianism strives to awaken us into a world transformed by a dream of love, not a fantasy of power. He thought poets best able to do this—through the mental theater that both awakens us to the limiting paradoxes of our received beliefs and reforms them through new visions, visions of how our present moment might recreate history as the secular unfolding of love.

Notes

1. *That Greece Might Still Be Free* (London: Oxford University Press, 1972), 51–65. Hunt remarks that "We are Greek when we speak of nautical matters with the sailor, of arithmetic with the merchant, of strategems with the soldier, of theatres and dramas with the play-goer, of poetry and philosophy with the man of letters, of theology with the churchman, of cosmetics with the fine lady [Hunt continues in this fashion]. . . . How can any of us pretend to admire the Greek love of liberty, if we will do nothing for it when it revives?" *The Examiner,* no. 718 (October 7, 1821): 626. This was published as Shelley was composing *Hellas.* For the circumstances of its composition, and Shelley's access to contemporary events in Greece through Byron, Hunt, and Mavrocordato (the Greek prince who tutored Mary Shelley in Greek), see Kenneth Neill Cameron, *Shelley: The Golden Years* (Cambridge, Mass.: Harvard University Press, 1974), 375–80, 634 nn.

The text of *Hellas* I have used, unless otherwise noted, is in *Shelley's Poetry and Prose,* ed. Donald Reiman and Sharon Powers (New York: Norton, 1977), 407–40. I have also consulted the Williams transcript, with Shelley's corrections, and the first edition (1822), both in the Huntington Library, HM 329 and 22407.

2. It is true, as Carl Woodring says, that "naturally *Hellas* does not describe the barbaric slaughter then practiced at every opportunity by the Greeks. In this work Shelley tries to persuade" (*Politics in English Romantic Poetry* [Cambridge, Mass.: Harvard University Press, 1970], 315). But it is doubtful that, even through Hunt or Mavrocordato, Shelley would have known of these massacres. Few Europeans did (St. Clair 23–27), and the Westernized educated class of Greeks were interested, of course, in raising money for a glorious cause. Shelley himself apologizes for having to rely on "newspaper erudition" (Preface). Hunt's information does not seem to have been much better: a year after *Hellas* was written he could write to his brother Henry, "I have already inquired about the *Greeks,* and have little doubt that I shall get information for the paper. I have written to Mr. Brown at Pisa, where there are numbers staying, and am going to apply to a merchant at Leghorn who has a Greek connexion." Even by the standards of the day these were poor sources, and he wrote little more about Greece: Letter to Henry Hunt, November 1822, MS in the Huntington Library, HM6601.

3. For Marx it is inevitable that a rising class will represent its interests as a universal advance for "mankind." Hence utopias are always fantasies of a particular class disguised in idealism. This does not, however, make them the less radical. "For each new class which puts itself in the place of one ruling before it, is compelled, merely in order to carry through its aim, to represent its interest as the common interest of all the members of society, that is, expressed in ideal form." But Marx goes on to say that at *the moment of revolution,* "its interest really is more connected

with the common interest of all other non-ruling classes"; that is, is from its own historical vantage universally liberating. See Marx, *The German Ideology*, ed. C. J. Arthur (New York: International Publishers, 1970), 65–66. I am arguing that this was the case, in fact, with the spectrum of liberal and radical opposition to Holy Alliance; it was not until ten or fifteen years later that liberalism might be seen as out for its own nationalist-industrialist interests. (Marx's point, of course, is that it was those class interests and not the ideals, that moved history along. "'Liberation' is an historical and not a mental act" [61]. Shelley, though wanting to move history in much the same direction, would not agree.)

4. *The Romantic Ideology* (Chicago: University of Chicago Press, 1983), 125. Historians might question this history: *in 1821* the "end" of the Ottoman Empire would be generations in the future; and the "definitive emergence of European imperialism" would be difficult to specify, particularly given the scrapping among Holy Allies over this issue in the 1820s. Indeed, in 1821 the Greek revolt was seen by Metternich and the British ministers as potentially revealing "significant cracks" in the alliance—as it did, to some degree. See C. W. Crawley, *The Question of Greek Independence* (Cambridge: Cambridge University Press, 1930), 17–29.

5. *Shelley: A Critical Reading* (Baltimore: Johns Hopkins University Press, 1971), 376. See also the parallels Wasserman finds with Hegel, 402, 411.

6. We should not discount censorship as an index of what was truly threatening or as a force that in itself delimited what could be written, debated, and thought, in the first third of the century. Cameron is correct to remark that Shelley's Preface "contains what is perhaps the most concentrated revolutionary statement of the age" (379). The paragraph, "Should the English people ever become free . . ." threatens to bring the war home to the oppressors; it was deleted by Charles Ollier in the 1822 edition, but proofs containing it were available to Buxton Forman in 1892 (*Poetical Works* 4:40–41), and at least one early printed copy contained this paragraph and the deleted ll. 1091–93 (Huntington 54530).

7. *The Letters of Percy Bysshe Shelley*, ed. Frederick L. Jones (Oxford: Oxford University Press), 2:365.

8. *The Question of Greek Independence: A Study of British Policy in the Near East, 1821–1833* (Cambridge: Cambridge University Press, 1930), 14–15. See also C. M. Woodhouse, *The Greek War of Independence* (London: Hutchinson's, 1952), 57: "few indeed in this country were prepared at the time to see the magnificence of the Greeks' challenge. . . . The preface to *Hellas*, written in the early months of the struggle, is a notable vindication of poetic vision in the practical affairs of the world."

9. Crawley 25–29.

10. Crawley 20; 100–12.

11. *Romantics, Rebels and Reactionaries* (New York and Oxford: Oxford University Press, 1981), 121.

12. "Reconciliation under Duress" (1960), in *Aesthetics and Politics* (London: Verso, 1980), 159. McGann has more recently taken the position that sociohistorical criticism "argues that 'what may be and should be' is always a direct function of 'what is, hath been, or shall be,' and its theory of representation holds that art imitates not merely the 'fact' and the 'ideal' but also the dynamic relation which

operates between the two." He goes on to insist on the "determinate" character of the relation to the "what is," such that there is a "natural or scientific relation" available to critical knowledge: McGann, ed., *Historical Studies and Literary Criticism* (Madison: University of Wisconsin Press, 1985), 14. My own position is more pragmatic and closer to Marilyn Butler's in her essay in the above volume, "Against Tradition: The Case for a Particularized Historical Method," 25–47.

13. A lucid summary of Shelley's attitudes toward ancient Greece and the relation of these to *Hellas* is Timothy Webb's chapter "The Greek Example," in his *Shelley: A Voice Not Understood* (Atlantic Highlands, N.J.: Humanities Press, 1977), esp. 194–203.

14. To clarify: for Shelley these principles would include urbanity, skeptical scientific inquiry, contractual and republican government, liberality and progressivism in the arts and sciences. It would be instructive to compare *this* kind of "political middle ground" in the Regency with the considerably more conservative Hellenism (a static ideal of "perfection," "sweetness and light" *guiding* liberal inquiry) to which Arnold retreats, during the tumultuous days of the reformist parliament of 1869, in *Culture and Anarchy*. For Shelley, culture could still lead a revolution; for Arnold it could only temper one.

15. Cameron 390.

16. Constance Walker, "The Urn of Bitter Prophecy: Antithetical Patterns in *Hellas*," *Keats-Shelley Memorial Bulletin* 33 (1982): 36.

17. Shelley, note to lines 197–238, in *Complete Works of Percy Bysshe Shelley,* ed. Roger Ingpen and Walter Peck, Julian Edition (London: Ernst Benn, 1930), 3:56. Hereafter cited as *Julian* in the text. On the imagery of blood, gold, and awakening, see the valuable article by Walker, 40–44.

18. This line, 930, was later added to the Williams Transcript (HM 329) by Shelley.

19. Or even from Prince Mavrocordato himself. Byron would have known of Philhellenic committees from his friends Sir John Bowring and J. C. Hobhouse, but the London Greek Committee itself was not founded until 1823, eight months after Shelley's death. For a useful history, see Douglas Dakin, *British and American Philhellenes* (Thessaloniki: Institute for Balkan Studies, 1955), esp. 42–62.

20. McGann's is only the most recent of Marxist criticisms of Shelley. See, for instance, the attack on the "bourgeois illusion" in Shelley by Christopher Caudwell, who nonetheless sees Shelley as "the most revolutionary of the bourgeois poets of this era," in "The Bourgeois Illusion and English Romantic Poetry," in his *Illusion and Reality* (1936); rpt. *Romanticism: Points of View,* ed. Robert Gleckner and Gerald Enscoe, 2d ed. (Detroit: Wayne State University Press, 1975), 117. (Caudwell's analysis is often crude, accusing Shelley of "indistinct emotions" and ethereal idealism; but also identifying Prometheus with the "machine-wielding capitalist," an unlikely hero for such a poet.) That Marx and Engels admired Shelley is reported (perhaps unreliably) by Eleanor Marx and E. Aveling, *Shelley's Socialism* (London, 1888).

Sue Zemka

The Holy Books of Empire: Translations of the British and Foreign Bible Society

> My word shall not return to me void, but shall accomplish that
> which I please, and it shall prosper in the thing whereunto I send it
>
> (Isaiah 55:11, quoted by the Madras Auxiliary Bible Society, in
> defense of the Mahratta Bible)

The Bible Famine, the Bible Society, and the Histories of the Bible Society

EARLY IN 1802, the Rev. Thomas Charles, a Methodist minister, approached a group of London dissenters and evangelicals with the problem of a "Bible famine" in his native Wales. Charles had spent over a year trying to get the Society for Promoting Christian Knowledge to begin a program for supplying the poor people of Wales with Bibles. He found the Society, which was the official Anglican organ for the distribution of religious literature, difficult to move and finally unsatisfactory in its response. In contrast, the London evangelicals and dissenters that Charles approached were immediately incited into action by his pleas. After making further inquiries and circulating a questionnaire in evangelical magazines, they decided that Wales was only symptomatic of an alarming shortage of Bibles among the poor, both in Britain and abroad. Encouraged by promises of foreign cooperation and confident that theirs was a divinely inspired task, they decided to organize a Bible Society that would address both national and international needs. Thus the British and Foreign Bible Society was founded in March of 1804 for the purpose of sponsoring translations and cheap editions of Bibles, Testaments, and Psalters in "all the languages spoken by man." As one charter member reportedly said, in a spirit of naive enthusiasm that would largely account for the Society's success, "If for Wales, why not for the world?"[1]

The British and Foreign Bible Society was the third great society for conversions inspired by the Methodist and evangelical revivals and the millennial excitement of the previous decade. (The other two societies were the London Missionary Society, which was mainly a dissenting enterprise, and the Church Missionary Society, which had an evangelical and patriotic character.) Over the next fifty years, the B.F.B.S. would claim full or partial responsibility for the distribution of more than 250,000,000 Bibles, in whole or in part, around the world. These included 125 new translations into languages or dialects in which the Bible had never before been printed. Several factors assisted the Society in this remarkable achievement. First, innovations in the print industry made it possible to mass produce inexpensive editions with standardized texts. Secondly, the Society's aggressive methods of proselytizing, in spite of early opposition from the East India Company, proved to be increasingly suited to England's changing Indian colonial policies.[2] Thirdly, the Bible Society developed an elaborate hierarchical national structure that allowed its middle- and lower-middle-class members, many of whom were women, to exercise control at the regional level.[3] And finally, the Bible Society owed its success to missionaries in India, Africa, and Asia—men like William Carey, Robert Moffat, and Robert Morrison, who assiduously applied themselves to the work of translating the Bible into languages they barely knew, and for people whom they were simultaneously teaching how to read. Aided by the Society's donations of paper, print fonts, and money, these missionaries, most of them dissenters with little formal education, devised orthographies for oral languages, compiled dictionaries and grammars for literate languages, and, assisted by native speakers of the language whom they employed for a minimal sum, composed and often printed and distributed their own Bible translations.

In the Rev. George Browne's two-volume *History of the British and Foreign Bible Society* (1859), letters from missionaries provide the chief source for sensational depictions of the Bible's purportedly unequivocal effect on people of diverse cultural and environmental circumstances.[4] The inhabitants of India, Africa, and Asia become, in Browne's histories, products for an English home audience, images of benighted heathens who acquire, via the agency of the Bible, the familiar attributes of Protestant belief, Victorian domesticity, and biblical literacy: "Friends of the Bible will rejoice to hear that the poor Namacquas, whose days were formerly spent in roaming over mountains and deserts, have learnt from the Sacred Scripture to assemble together to hear the Word of God" (Browne 2:243). The purpose of Browne's history was to update an earlier work, *The Origins and First Ten Years of the British and Foreign Bible Society,* which had been written in 1816 by John Owen, a prominent Evangelical minister and the Society's first secretary. Whereas the bulk of Browne's work focuses on the operations the Society carried out in Europe, Africa, India, and Asia between 1815 and 1850, most of Owen's focuses on the accusations and controversies that troubled the Society in the first decade of its existence.

In this essay, I will develop three arguments about the construction and ideological functions of the histories produced by the British and Foreign Bible Society. The first argument mainly concerns Browne's *History,* which interpolates letters from missionaries and Bible Society workers in such a way as to make cultural difference an opportunity for large-scale cultural displacement. The Bible Society based and justified its existence on the belief that the exposure to Holy Scriptures created an abstract Christian subject with similar attributes of behavior and belief regardless of cultural conditions, material environment, or preexisting religious beliefs.[5] Consequently, although Browne's depictions of Africans, Indians, and Catholic Europeans reading the Bible for the first time provide very little in the way of ethnographic observation, they do provide narrative vehicles through which problems central to English Protestant culture are acted out and resolved. These problems include religious sectarianism, the competing integrity of public (oral) and private (silent) reading, and the threat that differences of language and culture posed to Protestant faith in the Bible's univocal and universally translatable meaning.

Secondly, I will argue that the driving force in the Bible Society's narratives was an anxious desire to believe that English evangelism did not insert itself as an interpretive authority between the Bible and its newly extended world readership. This desire was evidenced in three ways: by both historians' relative inattention to the details of translating and preaching the gospel; by their appropriation of economic metaphors; and by Browne's use and alteration of the traditional evangelical motif of child characters. Both Owen and Browne use economic metaphors to depict England as the invisible "agent" of a divinely monitored "circulation" of the text of Christian revelation. Their reiteration of the terms "agency" and "circulation" works to obscure the several ways in which English missionaries authored that revelation—by authoring alphabets and orthographies for oral languages, by authoring Bibles in such a way as to make them consistent with a particular brand of English faith, and finally by authoring a vision of early Victorian British expansionism as a post-millennial fulfillment of Christian teleology.[6] Browne's history more completely erases the missionaries' intermedial presence by transferring their proselytizing functions to foreign children, whom he portrays as the innocent, honest, and spontaneous agents of a Book whose authority comes from God, not England. Moreover, when these children are girls, as they often are, they become symbols of the conflicted conscience of evangelical imperialism: while their status as powerless and innocent proselytizers hides the problematic power of the missionary endeavor, their gender hides the patriarchal structure of the Bible Society's relationship to its foreign beneficiaries. In this way, Browne's narrative reflects the conventional centrality accorded to children in evangelical narratives and theology, but only to rewrite the motives of that centrality within a new imperialistic context. The religious education that English evangelicals had always been concerned to impart to their children becomes less important than the innocence and divine infallibility that children symbolically bestow upon the labors of their English Protestant elders.

My third argument concerns Owen's and Browne's histories of the Bible Society in their capacity as fund-raising exercises. The method of composition that Owen and Browne executed in their texts created a direct and persuasive correspondence between English contributions to the Bible Society and foreign conversions to biblical literacy. By interweaving the missionaries' accounts of conversions with statistics, lists of new auxiliary societies, new translations, and records of donations or "subscriptions," Owen and Browne inserted their targeted readers (the largely middle- and lower-middle-class members of the Society) as characters in their texts. Consequently, their histories both enact and epitomize the Bible Society's most important function, which was to create a hegemonic cultural practice that afforded middle-class evangelical men and other, more marginalized citizens (women, dissenters, some members of the lower classes) a means of identifying with the English state as beneficent agent of God's will. Apart from the question of how the Society's translations were actually received and interpreted in non-Christian societies, and in spite of the animosities that frequently arose between colonial agents and religious missionaries, the Bible Society abetted and reflected Victorian nationalism and imperialism by offering English men and women a means through which they could think of themselves as active participants in the establishment of a religious empire.

These arguments reflect the degree to which the English evangelicals and dissenters who created the Bible Society invested an entire and complex ideology into a single commodity. The translated Bibles that Owen and Browne tracked around the world returned to their English sponsors reassuring reflections of converted and grateful communities, proofs that the coalition of English religion, culture, and technology could indeed divide the world into the providential symmetry of a "British" and "Foreign" society. When members of foreign communities are depicted displaying an anxious desire for Bibles, they seem to confirm the innocence and integrity of English evangelicalism's own anxious desire for the millennarian expansion of its Christian society. They seem to confirm the reciprocity of that desire, but not without occasional recognitions of unfamiliarity. A Muslim sends his servant thirty miles to buy a Bible, and the Society's colporteur momentarily wonders if their mutual fetishization of this book truly betokens similar motives—"What makes the Mahomedans so desirous to possess the Bible, is not clearly apparent." (Browne 2:161). But as long as foreigners wanted the Society's books and were willing to pay a nominal fee for them (the Society insistently never gave Bibles away), their actions were consistent with the Society's mystical valuation of this good. Alongside the Society's members, foreign purchasers of the Society's Bibles were assigned a fixed role in the new continuations of the Bible, the Bible Society history. These books depict a world being transformed by books, and they cite as their authority for this transformation scriptural passages like the one from Isaiah quoted at the opening of this essay. For the readers of the Society's histories, Isaiah's rhetorical alliance of prosperity and divine intentions had found a new manifestation in the anticipated alliance between capitalist expansion and Protestant evangelism. This new alliance was more than rhetorical—like the translated Bibles themselves, it represented the literalizing word-play of God's ongoing authorship of history.

From Babel to the Mouths of Babes: Problems in Translation and Their Fictional Resolutions

In 1844, the Rev. Barnabas Shaw, a Wesleyan missionary in South Africa, wrote a letter to the British and Foreign Bible Society containing this description of how the Word of God was carried to a tribe of Botswana Bushmen:

two little girls went from my station in Namacqualand to visit a tribe on the borders of the Bushmenland. They carried their Testaments with them, and read among the people. The natives were so interested in what they heard, that they allowed the two children but little time for rest. Day and night they were under the necessity of reading out of the 'Great Word', by which several persons of that tribe were brought under the sound of the Gospel. Thus, 'out of the mouths of babes and sucklings, he has perfected praise.' (Browne 2:255)

Without trying to gauge how much of Shaw's account is fact and how much is fiction, we can still marvel at the simple, anecdotal, and reassuring manner in which it casts a literate culture's mediation of the Bible onto an oral one. There are, in fact, more mediators lurking in this passage than there are messages communicated. The Bible is the primary symbol of communication since it bestows with magical irresistibility the message of Christian revelation. But the young girls are responsible for this communication as well, since they are the ones who, armed with a missionary school education, purportedly go out and read the Bible to the Bushmen for several days in a row. And since this is a translated Bible, there is also the past intermediary of the translator, who in this case must also have devised a system of orthography for the Bushmen's oral language. And finally, there is the concluding quotation of the Bible, with which an innocence as great as that of the babes and sucklings to which it refers, filters out the immense labor and cultural gaps suggested by these other agents and mediates to an English readership the image of more heathen souls brought into the Christian fold.

The presence of the young girls is crucial here for several reasons. First, the fact that they become the teachers of their elders "infantilizes" the Bushmen—the only adult in the story is an absent narrator, the Rev. Mr. Shaw. Consequently, the young girls provide a vicarious innocence for the English missionary, who imaginatively participates in their role as child-preachers, and thus is separated from the aspects of his vocation that, from an English point of view, were controversial and disturbing. (What exactly is Shaw teaching—Anglican or Non-conformist doctrines? How do the Africans interpret what he says? How can they be apathetic to their own need for salvation and western enlightenment?) Childhood becomes the pristine space wherein Christianity and the Bushmen meet, a space distanced from the "adult" world of the mission, where the missionary's presence is more problematic (for himself as for the native population), and less clearly illustrative of divine guidance. In a gesture that became a commonplace in the Bible Society histories, the story displaces the agency of conversion from an English missionary (the single most important mediator in the evangelical encounter) to native children, and the question of interpretive interference in the communication of the Bible is dissolved with a biblical symbol of inviolable immediacy to God's inspiration—the mouths of babes.

Like most stories contained in George Browne's *History of the British and Foreign Bible Society*, Shaw's account does not dwell on insurmountable obstacles posed by the prospect of converting oral cultures to biblical literacy. In part, this is because Browne has reduced the missionaries' experience to propaganda, deflecting attention away from the long years missionaries often had to spend in Africa before they could claim any converts, and from the immense frustration they sometimes expressed in their correspondence and memoirs. Robert Moffat, for instance, spent five years in Namacqualand before he could report a single baptism, and Anne Hodgson, the wife of a Methodist missionary, wrote home of the disillusionment of finding herself "among a people who have never heard the Gospel, and 'are dead in trespasses and sins'; and whose principal requests are 'give me meat—give me tobacco'" (171).[7] And yet in the Society's published accounts, the missionaries present an optimistic picture of recent or imminent progress, and never attribute setbacks to the inaccessibility of their own, highly literate religious culture to oral, non-western cultures. Their writings predate, of course, anthropological debates about the underlying differences or similarities between oral and literal cultures, and the missionaries' attention to the "orality" of African cultures never extends beyond the vague assumption that it is an emptiness waiting to be filled in with the Gospels.[8] What is clear from their writings is the degree to which the missionaries' perceptions were shadowed by their own ambivalence towards the relative benefits of bringing oral cultures within "the sound" of the Gospel and bringing them to read it. For the missionaries, the problematic division was not between orality and literacy—their mission centered, after all, on a Book—but rather between the competing integrity of oral recitation and silent reading in the transmission of the text they regarded as divine revelation.

Their anxiety over the various rhetorical ways that the use of language could distort its message was indigenous to a post-Enlightenment, empirical, and literate conception of language, and, in this case, specifically to the impact of that conception on Protestant attitudes towards the Bible. Like their supporters in England, the missionaries who preached and translated the Bible believed that revelation was singular in its original and ultimate meaning, and that oral and private reading were as necessary to communicating the Bible's divine intentions as they were capable of distorting it.[9] But both oral and private reading allowed for an unfortunate liberty of interpretation, of either inflectional or typographic interference with the meaning of Scriptures.

Within England, the evangelical community increasingly valued private reading of the Bible as the supremely accurate and unmediated form of communication between God and man, although paradoxically, the high value that early nineteenth-century evangelicals and Wesleyans placed on private Bible-reading originated in a tradition of great sermonizers, men like John Wesley and Jabez Bunting, who articulated a religious culture that revolved around the introspective, affective experience of reading the Bible. Private Bible-reading preempted the importance of sermons and corrected their errors: Charles Simeon commented that he never felt closer to God than when he read the Bible (Chadwick 1:442), and an anonymous frame-smith addressing the Bible Society in 1813 said "the pure word of God, I read in my Testament, edifies me more than the vain words I hear from the pulpit" ("Ninth Annual Report" 138). Indeed, the "Bible famine" that the Society discovered in Britain at the turn of the century was in part one of its own making, since the evangelical movement was largely responsible for England's recognition that illiteracy among the poor was an unfortunate condition requiring improvement. (Teaching working-class English children to read had been an evangelical undertaking since the formation of Sunday schools in the mid-1780s.) Globally, however, faith in the transparency of the printed word only made sense by (concealing) the missionary translator, whose presence intruded at every level—as a sermonizer, an oral reader, and an author of the text that literate readers read alone.

The fact that converting the world to the Bible meant first converting much of it to literacy was apparent to Browne and his English readers even if he were inclined to gloss over the time and effort implied by such a massive conversion. The Bible Society's histories depict African and poor Indian adults pursuing literacy with a singlemindedness of purpose that befits an English Sunday school education, because "all have a desire to read the word of God" (Browne 2:278). Children on the Gold Coast, the Society's German affiliates relate, teach their parents to read by coming home from the missionary school and writing the alphabet in the sand. The Rev. Henry Venn composed an alphabet for the Ga language that was used to produce Bibles for several oral languages of West Africa, thereby establishing, in Browne's words, "a system of aggressive evangelization, assuredly destined to gain ultimate possession of all the territories of the sons of Ham" (2:283–84). Venn translates the Bible into Ga and Browne translates Africa into the Bible, justifying "aggressive evangelization" as the fulfillment of a biblical empire where the descendants of Ham are willingly and joyfully converted in the days before the Second Coming.

Similarly, Robert Moffat, a Wesleyan Methodist whose formal education ended at the age of eleven, singlehandedly devised a chirographic system for the oral Tswana language, and used it to make a translation of the Bible from the Hebrew and Greek texts—a project that he worked on from 1829 to 1857. In the 1830s he continued to preach sermons in Tswana explicating the Gospels and Old Testament, and printed copies of his own spelling books to teach the people of Botswana to read along with him (Sandilands 1). Describing the conversions that ensued, Moffat proclaimed "the single reading and study of the Bible alone will convert the world" (Browne 2:248), thus overlooking his own laborious guidance of the Botswana converts' educations. Elsewhere, however, Moffat lamented the physical and mental anguish of his work, commenting that he had often "felt it to be an awful work to translate the Book of God, and perhaps, this has given to my heart the habit of sometimes beating like the strokes of a hammer" (*Life's Labours* 91). But these personal reflections were reserved for Moffat's final memoirs, published much later in the century. In the Bible Society's histories, his labor and disappointments, like those of other missionaries, are eclipsed by claims of rapid progress and providential success. Such claims had a definite appeal for Protestant readers, who donated to the Bible Society because they believed that the unaccompanied Bible had a wondrous ability to inspire universal consent, and gratitude for the Englishmen who brought it.

Despite the outward optimism of the missionaries quoted in Browne's history, it was clear that the Protestant belief in the self-sufficiency of Scriptures for Christian interpretation, a belief fought for and jealously guarded by Dissenters, had met a new challenge in the missionary experience of Asia, Africa, and India. Here the enemy was not the High Church's insistence on the necessity of the Prayer Book and Articles of Faith to a proper understanding of the Bible, but rather the linguistic, cultural, and educational differences that threatened to expose the Protestant Bible as a culturally relative text. The missionaries met this challenge both with direct arguments and (as in Shaw's correspondence) with spectacular anecdotes. Answering the objection that for a "pagan, unacquainted with Jewish antiquities, European history, and Christian doctrine . . . there is much in the Bible that he cannot understand," Dr. Morrison, a distinguished Hindu scholar and a translator for the Bible Society, responded with the Pietistic argument that understanding really depends on the heart of the reader. "The careless, profligate, and proud, in every land, will despise the Bible," Morrison wrote, "but the inquiring mind and the anxious spirit . . . will esteem it a 'pearl of great price'" (Browne 2:205). More sensationally, the Baptist translators at Serampore reported that several Brahmins and members of high caste began to "observe Christian worship on the Lord's day, before they had any intercourse with the Missionaries, *simply by reading the Scriptures*" (Browne 2:116). And a German missionary related the story of a young Hindu who requested to be baptized after purchasing a Persian Testament at a fair: "He has had no teacher, the *reading* of the word alone has converted him" (Browne 2:157).

Without broaching the question of what these Hindus converted to or why, the missionaries' accounts of their conversions verified for English Protestants the clarity, persuasiveness, and self-sufficiency they ascribed to Scriptures. On at least one occasion, a missionary pushed the suspension of disbelief past even the Bible Society's credulity: Robert Yuille, a missionary and translator in Mongolia, was dismissed from service in part because he lied when he wrote to the Directors that the Chief Lama of Khaglan had been reading his translated Scriptures "every morning on his Knees, and with all of the Lamas of the Household with him." Yuille's dismissal was insisted upon by his fellow translators, William Swan and Edward Stallybrass, men of high standards, who surreptitiously informed the London Directors of their colleague's dubious abilities: "test his skills in *any* language he professes to know—*English*—Latin—Greek—Hebrew—Russ—and the result of such examination may lead to something near the truth of his Mongolian scholarship" (Bawden 294–96). But within Browne's history, neither the credibility of the missionaries nor the relative facility of their work is brought into question. Time and time again, the fantasy of the Bible's reception abroad is the same: missionaries find non-Christians in a state of apprehensive desire for religious enlightenment (Morrison's "anxious spirit"), and once they read or hear the New Testament, they spontaneously endorse an understanding of it sympathetic to Protestant faith.

In contrast to the stories of African and Indian conversions, the stories of evangelization in nations that are already Christian involve a greater dramatic tension, because here the millennarian plot is complete with an anti-Christ, the Pope. While the African stories offer an idyllic inversion of Protestant England's own internal religious and social sectarianism, the

European stories offer another kind of symbolic religious unity for their English readers, one that is predicated on the need to unite Protestant forces against a common external enemy. Again, children are crucial to these stories, and their commonality with the native children in the African stories (both are cast as mediators, guardians, and infallible interpreters of the Bible) works, first of all, to minimize the differences between African and European beneficiaries of the Bible Society, and, secondly, to erase the English empowerment and superiority that is implied by the Bible Society's philanthropic relationships with both its beneficiaries and its European auxiliaries.

Browne's chronicle of the Society's activities in the 1830s contains an account of the fate of a certain Belgian Bible, the cherished but outlawed possession of a small group of Protestant villagers. The villagers had managed for some time to outwit the local priests, who knew of the Bible's existence and were on the lookout to confiscate it. One scheme they devised was to leave the Bible buried beneath blankets in a cradle, watched over and rocked by a young girl. Her vigilance eventually became their downfall, however, since a spy for the priests, having noticed her long hours of rocking and watching, guessed that something other than an infant was in the cradle. He gave her away to the priests, who entered the house while the men were out working in the fields and took the Bible, against the girl's protestations (1:454).

The story is a pastiche of competing iconographies. The substitution of a Bible for an infant is inspired by the dual association of the Bible and the Christ child with the revealed Word of God. And, since the confiscated Bible is presumably a translation into vernacular Flemish or French, it shares with the infant the quality of being an incarnation of the Word into a common human form that only those with corrupt or imperfect faith (i.e., Roman Catholics) consider too "vulgar" a vessel for divine habitation. The Madonna figure that guards the cradle is both a child-mother and a mother-child, since she is wrongfully replaced by the Catholic Church's claim to be the only true mother and guardian of the faith. The violence of that replacement, its similarity to a scene of rape, or, in biblical terms, to the slaughtering of the innocents by Herod, signals the selling into slavery of the true Christian faith to the papal imposter, who is of course not only a false mother but a whore. Interestingly, this competition between two symbolic mothers can occur only in the absence of all real mothers, who have been inexplicably vacated from the scene. The most "real" characters in the narrative ("real" in the sense that their ontological status is least complicated by symbolic overtones) are the men, who have had to leave home in order to go to work. This necessity does not bind the priests, whose lives are supported by the workingmen's tithes (an unmentioned detail that would not be lost on contemporary readers), and who ironically are thus free to further prey on Protestant families and possessions. This story is typical of the European stories in Browne's and Owen's histories in that it organizes politically and socially complex material into a confrontation where the operative term is religion—the Bible Society and the Catholic Church fight it out for the power to determine whether or not the Belgians will have the right to read and interpret the Bible.

Like the story of the Belgian Bible, the following story from a missionary in Greece organizes a variety of the Society's conventions (the innate wisdom of children, the impossibility of true converts misinterpreting the Bible, the replacement of backward cultural practices with education and progress, foreign need and gratitude for the Society's work) around an old representative of Catholicism and a young representative of the Bible Society's influence, this time with the victory going to the Bible Society:

> In one of the villages, about four or five hours' distant from Canea, a monk (whose name I do not now recollect) was making his visit for the purpose of collecting oil, money, &c.; and for the better furtherance of his designs, he carried with him the relics of some saint, famous for his godliness and piety; these relics he presented to the people to kiss, and make the sign of the cross over them and afterwards to give him whatever they chose. But wherever he went, he was told . . . that they had learned better than to worship saints and their relics, since they had the Bible introduced among them, and a school established. . . . In revenge for his disappointment, he began to cry out against the school, and the distribution of the Bible. And, as if chance had favored his design, he found a copy of the book of Job in the house of the villager where he was, and, opening it, he read the 17th verse of the 4th chapter; but he read it affirmatively, and not interrogatively, as it is. After he had read it, he turned to those present, and began to speak against the Bible printed and distributed by the Bible Society, saying that it contained many blasphemies and sinful things, and frequently referred to this passage. One of the children, who had learned to read in the school, and had listened to him with considerable attention, when he had finished his discourse, said, he did not know that the Scripture anywhere said that man 'can be purer than his Maker' . . . the boy, taking the book, read the passage interrogatively . . . and observed that it only asked the question, if a man shall be 'juster than God and purer than his Maker, while he sees faults even in his angels?' The monk remained silent, and the people drove him out of their village (Browne 2:58–59).

What were for English Protestants the controversial relations among oral reading, private reading, and the act of interpreting the Bible find in the story of the Greek monk a polarized and morally differentiated formula: proper reading and interpretation is Protestant in origin, while perversion in reading and interpretation comes from the fountainhead of religious corruption, the Catholic church. This differentiation represses, however, a similarity that is implied everywhere else in Browne's text: the Bible operates for the Society as the relics do for the monk, as fetishized commodities that are sold for a price incommensurate with its spiritual dividend.

There is a subtext to this dramatic confrontation between the interpretive powers of an old Catholic monk and a young Protestant convert that goes beyond the religious aspects of the Bible Society's "debate" with Catholicism. The Bible Society and what its stands for (the tacit metonymy that links England's promotion of the Bible as a progressive and liberating ideological commodity with the global expansion of its manufacturing and trade economy) is at war with Catholicism and what its stands for (the more explicit metonymy between the monk and Catholicism's dependence upon ignorance and popular superstition for the maintenance of its ancient clerical and aristocratic privileges). These metonymic associations are elsewhere made more salient by Browne's frequent reiteration of the call for "a free circulation of Scripture"—a slogan that invokes the arguments that English manufacturers and free-trade economists used against trade regulations such as the Corn Laws, which were similarly associated with outmoded aristocratic privileges and were similarly held accountable for hurting the poor by causing disastrous fluctuations in the availability of "vital" commodities. Hence for Browne the Bible Society signals the beginning of a "true Catholic society" where the "free circulation of Scriptures," a circulation that has been checked "by the Ancient court of Rome," will save "unimagined numbers of families" from "the famine of the Word of God." Phrases such as these engraft traditional English hostility towards the Catholic suppression of the Bible upon the hostility that Britain's manufacturers and merchants felt towards the remnants of dynastic feudalism.

In discourse as well as in practice, the Bible Society merged Protestant ideology with the economic rubric and the developing market mechanisms of capitalism. This was true even though in the first three decades of the nineteenth century the East India Company was hostile to missionary intervention in their territories. The Bible Society emulated the structures, policies, and rhetoric of colonial trade even as it was rejected, or at best tolerated by those agents of colonial trade who continued to abide by the religious non-intervention and mercenary attitudes that characterized War-ren Hastings's career.[10] In its conviction that cultural intervention in India was absolutely necessary, the Bible Society (like other evangelical societies for conversion) complemented the direction that the utilitarian influence over colonial policies would take. It was, in a sense, the quintessential Victorian colonial business, combining commercial organization with moral conviction. By identifying itself as a non-intrusive administrative protectorate, and by building its system of distribution on commercial models, the Bible Society simulated in its organization the advantages that England claimed over other European powers in the battle for a superior trading position overseas. This supremacy was based on commercial and maritime control—on exchange and mobility—and consequently it fos-tered a rhetoric of maximum liberality and equality between states even as it disguised the fact of English ascendancy. Hence another common feature of Owen's and Browne's rhetoric is their emphasis on "agency" and "instru-mentality"—terms that tacitly assert the British Bible Society's ascendancy over its foreign auxiliaries as the preferred mediator between God and the nations, races, and languages of the earth. Owen calls England the "chosen agent" through which God will globally reveal his truth, and affirms that the Bible Society cannot "desist from its labour" until "through its instru-mentality . . . the Bible shall accomplish its office" (1:286). British agency is the link between the Bible as a national trust and as a global resource, as in the comment the "Holy Scriptures are not a personal benefit, but a trust to be used . . . for the benefit of others" (Browne 1:3). Elsewhere the idea of instrumentality is communicated with greater patriotic zeal: "let us there-fore rejoice, that, under Providence, England has become the honoured instrument of [Christianity's] dispensations" (Owen 1:419). With these formations the Bible Society conceives both itself and its "parent" nation as agents of a providential source of power: England's claim to global preemi-nence in the work of Bible distribution is based not on executive authority over its foreign auxiliaries, but on its administrative guardianship over the channels of "free circulation."

The B.F.B.S. was always fundamentally a British institution, even though by 1854 there were sixty-four foreign Bible Societies that contrib-uted a large amount of effort and independent initiative. Toward these "native operations" the B.F.B.S. maintained an attitude that was partially fraternal but mainly condescending: in its annual reports, the Bible So-ciety's secretaries diligently chronicle the operations of foreign Societies, but also relegate those operations to the role of channels of circulation that flow outward from the Society's center in London. The rhetorical conventions that typify these reports reflect the patriarchal character of the Bible Society's structure. Most commonly, the Society is described as a fountain with tributaries or a sun dispersing darkness. Such metaphors could be used to the Society's disadvantage by members of foreign auxiliaries who felt that the British brethren exaggerated their importance. In 1813 a "Soldier of the American Revolution" published a letter accusing the Society of falsely projecting itself as "the sole proprietor of God's light to the world" (6). There were other "British lights," he remembers, of which Christians should be less proud—the lights of American churches burnt by British soldiers during the recent war (18). Although the soldier's letter begins on a conciliatory note, by the end of it he seems to want the American Bible Society to wage another war of independence against the patronage of its British parent, arguing (with a phrase that perverts the British secretaries' other favorite metaphor) that "the vile mother and monster Britain has been the source and fountain of all the wars in Europe" (22). Not surprisingly, such inflammatory accusations from within the ranks of affiliated Bible Societies did not find their way into the Bible Society's histories.

Even within the ranks of English Protestantism, not everyone concerned with the Society's objectives accepted its merger of religious, capitalist, and nationalist righteousness without reservation: the writer Henry Drummond accused evangelical missionary movements of an overweening pride that blinded them to the apostasies they engaged in. "The Evangelicals of Britain," he wrote, "assuming that their Bible Societies are going to convert the world . . . will be the first to feel the weighty hand of the Lord's vengeance" (Oliver 108). From Drummond's point of view, the Society was not properly concerned with the theological exigencies of the day—the needs to overcome the papal anti-Christ and acknowledge the sinfulness of the English nation. Judging from their tendency to cast innocent children as missionary proselytizers, Drummond's accusation that evangelicals were oblivious to the potential culpability of their ambitions was overstated. But he was right to sense a different rationale at work in the Society's brand of anti-Catholicism, a secularizing rationale that presented itself as religious but unwittingly helped transform Protestantism from a supernatural theology into a code of behavior and cultural values that would inform England's evolving imperial identity. Even in their most apocalyptic moments, the Bible Society's historians tended to interpret the papal anti-Christ as a metaphor for the repression of language as a tool of civilization's progress. In the story of the Greek monk selling alms, for example, Bible-reading is an occasion for both registering and refuting the old Catholic argument against translations of the Bible into "vulgar tongues."[11] While the Church traditionally argued that the best guard against heresy was to maintain Latin as the privileged language of theological knowledge, the Bible Society believed that translations of the Bible into spoken idioms were the cornerstones of enlightened societies of self-respecting Christian individuals.[12] Drummond would have agreed that every man and woman should be able to read the Bible in his or her first language, but he disagreed with the logic that treated religion as the tool of a cultural progress orchestrated by a fallible mankind.

By adopting empirical and rationalist philosophies of language, the Society symbolically conflated the Bible with another English text of mythical proportions, the Social Contract. When it targeted for Bible translations the languages of Mohawks, Hottentots, and other "neglected little tribes," the Bible Society created an opportunity to relive not only the Christian myth of apostolic origins but also the Enlightenment myth of a consensual passage from natural to rational society. In a speech to the London Missionary Society, a Christian Hottentot reportedly called the Bible "a charter of human liberties" that had taught his tribe to "live like civilized men," and thus saved them "from the self-destruction of the state of nature" (Browne 2:246). His language suggests he had been reading at least as much Rousseau as Christian Scriptures. At the Great Exhibition of 1851 the Hottentot's words were reiterated by the banner proposed for the Society's booth: "The Charter of human liberty—the Book by which England has become great."[13] Here the Lockean source of consent—the protection of life and property—is replaced with a consensual text, one that merges a religious with a secular tradition and assimilates images that carry both democratic and imperialistic significances. The multiplicity of languages, like the multiplicity of Bibles, is merely a nominal plurality—every language has its idiom of unadorned, plain style prose, free from rhetorical embellishment (the universal idiom of rational, empirical communication). And every Bible translated into these idioms will have the uniform effect of leading its readers to the recognition that God's textual intentions are identical with the intentions of English Protestant culture.

The Society's growing concern that its translators aim for an "easy and simple" diction reflects what I described earlier as the decline of oratory and rhetoric as valid forms of communicating knowledge. This decline is further exemplified by the Bible Society's attitudes toward its own historical textualization. When George Browne updated John Owen's history, he took considerable pains to clarify where he was indebted to Owen and where he departed from Owen's example. The difference between them, as Browne sees it, is the difference between an orator and an historian: Owen has "composed in an ardent strain" and with "eloquent statements" that display "the copiousness of the orator," rather than "the calm recital of the historian." To make his text more credible, Browne has tried to avoid "the warm and glowing character of [Owen's] narrative" and "has purposefully guarded against amplification" (1:vii). These passages suggest that for Browne and his readers the form of prose writing which was most believable, which was least capable of distortion or falsification, was the form of writing associated with the emerging mode of mass communication: the silent reading of print, a silence in which both the reader and the writer participated. Browne's cautious introduction registers the way in which reading itself was changing, becoming more purely a cognitive activity severed from its oral and aural affinities. And, in turn, it registers the tension he and his readers felt between the impassioned rhetorical embellishments that characterized traditional evangelical discourse and the empirical diction and objective tone that distinguished the type of discourse toward which some of them, Browne included, aspired—plain-style nonfiction prose.[14]

Although Browne goes to some pains in the introduction to distinguish his "historical" text from Owen's "rhetorical" one, his inability to make a similar distinction in regard to the Bible implicitly points to important questions ignored by the remainder of his text. Have the various translators whom the Society has sponsored been careful to guard against amplification in their translations? And if they have, doesn't this imply some alteration of the Scriptures, which already contain rhetorically "ardent strains" within them? Most importantly, how can amplification be guarded against, since the main way in which these translations have become known around the world is through oral reading?

As these questions suggest, if some of the difficulties of converting the world to print could go unmentioned, there were other and related questions that continued to be raised by the ongoing task of converting the Bible to print. The Bible was an eminently unstable text: the multiplicity, ambiguity, and complex history of the Bible's manuscripts, combined with the problematic relationship between the Old and the New Testament, and with Protestantism's valorization of a single, divine text, made for ongoing debates about the Authorized Version, debates that were aggravated in the early nineteenth century by the philological study of biblical manuscripts.

The Bible Society initiated its work believing that innovations in print technology would help resolve some of these debates by making it possible to mass produce exact reproductions of the A.V. In its first year of operations, the Society sponsored the first edition of the King James Bible using stereotype print, a system that they celebrated as the source of a "correct and standard text" and "a regular and permanent supply" of Bibles (Browne 1:21). At the same time, the Society began to collect approved editions of the A.V. for comparison so as to continue modifying the stereotyped version and thus proceed towards a "perfect" text (Browne 1:31). The Bibles they printed were always, as members were proud of pointing out, "without note or comment," thereby emphasizing that this was a non-partisan venture, one that every Protestant to the left of the High Church could respect: an attempt to establish an original, uninterpreted text—an unmediated line to God's word.

However, as the Society ventured into other languages and other Bibles, the unity of its Protestant coalition was undermined by the inability to separate a fundamental biblical text from the task of translation. Compiling editions of the A.V. that would please all the sects cooperating in the Society was difficult enough, but once they ventured into other languages and other Bibles, agreement began to seem impossible. The conclusion which the Society worked desperately to avoid was that there was no pure, "uninterpreted" Bible, that in fact every translation was already an interpretation. In 1839, a splinter organization, the Trinitarian Bible Society, was formed of ex-Bible Society members who objected to the use of the Latin Vulgate to translate a Bible for European Roman Catholics. In another incident, a group of London patrons insisted on cutting off funds to the Baptist translators at Serampore, whom, they discovered, had translated "baptize" into a Hindustani word for immersion. In the 1820s, the two British missionaries in Siberia, Edward Stallybrass and William Swan, began to complete a Mongolian translation of the New Testament that had been begun in 1807 by Moravian missionaries (one of whom was a celebrated Dutch Orientalist, I. J. Schmidt). Stallybrass and Swan found that the Moravians' translation often "did not give the *whole sense* to any particular passage"; for example, their rendering of the creation story in Genesis failed to give sufficient emphasis to the sacred nature of the Sabbath (Bawden 284). In still other instances, the problem was not with translators who manipulated a foreign language to convey a specific doctrinal charge, but rather with the refusal of some non-European languages to conform to a primary tenet of Christian teaching. Work on a Chinese Bible was plagued for years by a debate on the best way to render the various biblical names for God in Chinese. The missionaries wanted a generic term for God that, like the English word, could be used in the plural as well as the singular, thus including false Gods as well as the one Christian God. They limited their choices to "Shin" and "Shangti," but found both inadequate: "Shin" conveyed a rather abstract idea of the nature of the Divine Being, whereas "Shangti," the proper Chinese word for God, was never used to refer to false or evil Gods. After several years of deliberation, the Society sponsored two different versions, one using "Shin" and the other "Shangti." The holy Book of empire was beginning to fracture into a number of texts.

The Society's remarkable successes (109 new translations by 1809) and its ostentatious appeals for support were sometimes greeted by English scholars and High Churchmen with suspicion, and sometimes with outright disdain. Neither Owen nor Browne omits these charges from his history of the Society, but, rather, each uses them to the rhetorical end of portraying attacks on the Society as negligible setbacks in an overall picture of dramatic progress. Hence criticisms from High Churchmen (more frequent in the first twenty years of the Society's histories) are interpolated with answers from tracts written by the Society's supporters. As Owen relates, a conservative spokesman for the Society for the Promotion of Christian Knowledge suggested that in giving the A.V. to the poor, the B.F.B.S. gave too little, since for doctrinal purposes the Bible was complete only when it was circulated with the Prayer Book (1:164–65). Meanwhile, another Anglican theologian charged that the Bible Society gave too much, because only seven books of the Old Testament and six of the New were "suitable for the study of the unlearned" (Owen 2:205). Thus the Society's diplomatic policy of printing "only" the Bible was undermined by the question of which Bible to print, and High Churchmen refused to suffer in silence the dismay they felt for the Society's ideas of what constituted the Bible of Protestant faith. The Society's strongly evangelical bias was further demonstrated by their policy of always privileging the New Testament, which for the purposes of conversion, they considered sufficiently comprehensible even without the Old Testament. Perhaps the most energetic of the Society's critics was the High Churchman Rev. Herbert Marsh, the Lady Margaret Professor of Divinity at Cambridge, who between 1811 and 1812 produced one speech and three pamphlets condemning its existence. In his third and most extensive pamphlet, Marsh leveled the scathing charges that the Bible Society sponsored unqualified translators, produced translations that were detrimental to faith, and moreover made spurious claims to translations for which it was not responsible.[15]

One attack on the Society that George Browne neglected to mention in his history was an 1828 review of Owen's book written by a frequent contributor to the *Quarterly Review,* the Rev. Edward Edwards. Taking up a charge that had been raised in 1812 by Dr. Marsh, Edwards accuses the Society of rapidly producing poor translations and of claiming responsibility for new translations that, in fact, were merely publications of preexisting and sometimes questionable manuscripts. Edwards cites the example of the Society's Mohawk translator, a convert named Teyoninhokarawen (aka "John Norton"), whose New Testament was suspect not only because it was executed from the English A.V. instead of the original Greek, but also because no one except Teyoninhokarawen was capable of judging the fidelity of the translation (9). Edwards incorporates this example into a picture of the Society as a corrupt, lower-middle-class scam for power and money—a kind of early Victorian precursor to television evangelism. According to Edwards, every new translation is an advertisement for donations that "increase the coffers of the Society's funds" (6). In 1819, he relates, the Society went so far as to print a Turkish New Testament that was taken from the eighteenth-century manuscript of a "Polish renegado." When the translation was criticized for its "florid style and affectation," the Society responded by printing up new leaves for the most offensive pages and then "having them distributed to those who had bought them in Turkey" (19). No explanation is given, Edwards complains, of how these customers were found, or how they were persuaded to unbind their books and insert the improved pages.

Although, like Dr. Marsh, Edwards accused the Society of occasionally allowing old translations to masquerade as new ones, what is at stake in his argument has as much to do with dead foreign translators as with living English ones, and with the doctrinal, interpretive, or simply sloppy alterations of Scriptures which the latter could perform. But it is not clear whether Edwards is more afraid of the threat posed to Scriptures by these translators or of the fact that they signaled a threat to the cultural and political hegemony that traditionally controlled such scholarly labor. The contempt for the Society's translators expressed in his essay seems at once scholarly and social, fueled by the recognition that through the Bible Society a class of "self-educated missionaries" were garnering some degree of worldly influence. None of these men, Edwards complains, has had "the benefit of a regular or learned university education" (23). And, of course, many of them did not have the benefit of an Oxford or Cambridge education (presumably the only ones that would qualify them in this Anglican minister's eyes) because even if they had the necessary financial resources, as dissenters they were not allowed to matriculate.

Marsh's and Edwards's criticisms suggest that the dismay which England's cultural elite felt when regarding the Bible Society was at once religious (pertinent to the Anglican Church's doctrinal control of the religious literature circulated by English institutions) and political (pertinent to the social and cultural establishment that determined who received a classical education, and who was qualified to represent English interests in the public capacities of a clergyman, a university scholar, or a government official). Although both Owen and Browne omit this information, much of the momentum for the Bible Society's marathon translations came from devoted dissenters, most of them working-class, and only a few of them with extensive university educations. They included the Baptist translators at Serampore, William Carey, who had been apprenticed as a shoemaker, and Joshua Marshman, a weaver; Henry Martyn, the son of a miner who obtained a scholarship to Cambridge, where he was inspired by Simeon to become a missionary, and who afterwards translated the New Testament and Psalms into both Hindu and Persian; Robert Morrison, the Presbyterian son of a boot-tree maker who authored a Chinese translation of the Bible in twenty-one volumes; the Methodist Robert Moffat, who had been apprenticed to a gardener before he went to Africa as a missionary and translated the entire Bible into the Tswana language; and the two translators of the Mongolian Bible, the Congregationalist Edward Stallybrass and the Scottish "free-thinking" William Swan, both of whom had studied classics and theology for two years at Homerton College. All of these men, to varying degrees, were politically and socially disadvantaged at home— and all of them went to their foreign missions with the belief that their right to influence the course of empire came from God. Undeterred by continual difficulties (lack of supplies, censorship, interference from the English colonial governments, their own limited abilities in the languages they were translating), these men spent years writing the Books that they believed with all sincerity, and with more philanthropic idealism than most of their secular counterparts in colonial trade, would contribute to England's millennarian enlightenment of "poor," "barbaric," and "heathen".nations.

This motive might account not only for the missionary translators but also for the middle-class men (dissenters or evangelicals) who contributed

to the Society at home and to the women who worked in or ran the
Associations. Edwards thought he could persuade people to stop subscrib-
ing to the B.F.B.S. by demonstrating that its historian, John Owen, did not
describe how the translations were executed but rather reduced them to
sensational statistics. He was mistaken, however, because for many of the
subscribers these numbers were symbolic registers of their role in the
progress towards a Christian fulfillment of history. Each Bible, Testament,
and Psalter that Owen records equals one more soul won for God, one
more soul bought with subscriber's donations: 4,210 Bibles and Testaments
are distributed in and round Bristol in 1810; 500 Bibles are distributed in
Mauritius in 1812; 73,000 rupees are raised in British India in 1811; 3,000
Testaments are sold in Germany in the same year; 2,000 copies of the
Chinese Gospel of Luke are printed in January 1814. In this ideological
economy, numbers are abstract signifiers that erase the distinction between
poor Englishmen, rich Englishmen, Europeans, non-Europeans, donations, and Bibles—all are quantitatively assessed as incremental contributions to a Protestant British and Foreign totality. Far from arousing universal suspicion, Owen's (and later Browne's) numerical pyrotechnics worked
to attract contributions from some English men and women by implicitly
expressing Protestant imperial power as a formulaic equivalency between
English donors, translated Bibles, and converted citizens of the world.

What made this equation persuasive was the Bible Society's ability to
extrapolate from evangelical faith affective associations with the Bible that
were independent of its nature as a text. Consequently, far from reflecting a
textual orientation toward Scripture, Owen's and Browne's histories reflect
a belief that the interpretation of the Bible has already been absorbed into
its psychological and social itinerary, and that the Bible universally affects
its readers in a predictable and univocal way. In this way, the cornerstone of
English faith—you are what you read—became the fallacy of evangelical
philanthropy's presumption that it knew what its subjects around the world
read. And although in England, subversive and radical interpretations of
the Bible were inescapably apparent (one need only think of Blake, Joanna
Southcott, Edward Irving, or the anti-Christian pamphleteer Richard Car-
lile), upon the unseen narrative stage of the colonies and Catholic Europe
the Bible Society could project its utopian dream of societies transformed
by Bible-reading into paragons of Protestant middle-class culture without
too much cognitive dissonance, and what dissonance there was could
barely be distinguished beneath the fictional vignettes that are continually
replayed in Browne's histories. Put a translated New Testament into the

hands of a non-Christian who knows nothing about the Old Testament or European history, or of a Catholic who has never read the Bible in his or her native dialect, and the result will be a grateful Protestant.

Despite the repetitive simplicity of these plots, many of them work, as we have seen, to condense various anxieties (linguistic, doctrinal, political, and economic) into symbolic forms. The main argument that I want to make about these stories, based on the suggestion with which this section began, is that the child is the crucial figural motif in this condensation, not only because the child is a conventional vehicle for evoking religious sentimentality in Victorian and evangelical literature, but also because the child eclipses the exchanges of power that are implicit on several levels in the missionary encounters contained in Browne's history. The fictional substitution of a child for the missionary, for the Bible Society, or, in the largest sense, for Christian imperial England, acquits all of these purported agents of divine will of the charges of self-interest, of undue cultural interference, of exploitation, and of perversion of the meaning of the Book whose evangelical interpretation bestowed divine agency on these entities in the first place. Children always speak the truth, they never distort, even when, as in the case of the Bushmen, their elders make them stay up all night to read to them. Children have a special insight into the spirit of Protestant Scripture, as in the case of the Greek boy who corrected the monk on the proper reading of Job 4:17. And children are the trusted guardians of the Bible, even when they are robbed of their holy commission like the Belgian girl, whose vigilance makes her the symbol of embattled Protestantism under siege by the Antichrist. In all of these instances, children vicariously validate the divine agency of the Bible Society because their incorruptible literacy and good intentions prove that the missionary impulse comes from God.

But most importantly, the displacement of the English missionaries' mediative function onto children does not negate the fact that these children are all foreigners. Thus the child symbolically blurs the boundaries between the identity of the English missionary and that of the foreign beneficiary. And, since the majority of the proselytizing children in Browne's text are girls, the identities of missionaries and foreigners are blurred along the lines of gender. The female child hides the fact that the relationship between England and its colonies is a patriarchal one, while her proselytizing actions (she is never represented talking to missionaries, but only to other or potential converts) confirm the belief that English authority does not assert itself through a master-slave dialogue, but rather through a linear, steadily expanding transmission of Protestant enlightenment. The female children of the missionaries' stories, all of them sympathizers with the missionary cause, allow the English readers of the histories to identify simultaneously with the providential privilege of their country and with the special power of "powerlessness" that symbolically belongs to women and children—those who come first in Christian ethics precisely because they come last in patriarchal society. In this way, the missionaries' stories represent a religious discursive formation that is analogous to the economic discursive formation of "free circulation." Both participate in imperial ideology as overt assertions of a self-effacing, disinterested ethical position that is also a covert assertion of English cultural supremacy.

There is one last child, again a female, that is particularly important to the Bible Society's tradition. This child was purportedly present at the "initial scene" that inspired the Rev. Thomas Charles to suggest a Bible society, although she does not make a textual appearance until 1904, when the third of the Bible Society's histories was published. As the story goes, there was a sixteen-year-old named Mary Jones who lived near Charles's parish in Bala, Wales. Following her conversion, Mary Jones began to "so thirst for the Water of Life" that she walked twenty-eight miles across the Welsh countryside to Mr. Charles's parsonage to see if she could purchase a Bible. When he told her that there were no Bibles to be had, she was reduced to tears, and Charles was so moved by this display of her disappointed hopes that he sold her a Bible from his own bookshelf, vowing never to forget the incident in his quest to relieve the Bible famine of Wales (Canton 1:465).

It is not an exchange of power or knowledge that is at issue in this transaction but rather an exchange of innocent desire. The story confirms the necessary desire, the spiritual hunger, that the Bible Society had, in 1904, been assuming for years in all of the designated recipients of its philanthropy. But at the same time, the true desire that moved the Society and its missionaries—religious zeal, the desire to evangelize—is displaced onto the one child who is only a beneficiary and does not partially "stand in" for a missionary, the one child who does not deliver, read, interpret, or guard a Bible, but rather requests one. And because Mary Jones pays for her Bible, she proves herself in middle-class terms as one of the deserving poor. Her fictional treatment reveals the thoroughness with which commodification and religious sentimentality were integrated in the Bible Society, because the moment of her initiation into evangelical citizenship is marked by both tears and a purchase. From the "beginning," the Bibles that pass hands in the Society's histories do not represent the text of Christian faith (indeed, it seldom matters whether they are opened or closed) so much as they do the ambivalent motives which comprise imperial-evangelical ideology—motives which are symbolically divided into the various parties that handle these books. In this story of origins, for instance, the roles that typify the histories' conversion narratives are at once simplified and reversed, and the child-missionary becomes the child-convert, the female subject whose pure and suppliant desire starts (and ends) this signifying chain, Mary Jones coming to the Rev. Thomas Charles of Bala, Wales, looking for a Bible.

Conclusion: Reading the Bible and Writing the Empire

When Thomas Charles called upon the London Tract Society to help him relieve the "Bible famine" of Wales, he helped initiate a movement that brought together two of the most powerful motivations in early Victorian middle-class culture: Protestant bibliolatry and philanthropic concern for the poor. Slogans such as "the Bible famine," "the destitution of Scriptures," and "starvation for the word of God" affixed a metaphorical hunger to the physical hunger that the poor were suffering, more often than not, in the first four decades of the Society's operations. By a generous interpretation, the energies that Society members expended on ministering to a metaphorical hunger for Bibles reflected their belief that in the face of helpless conditions, spirituality and inspiration are as fundamental to human survival as material goods. In 1831 the Bible Society's Auxiliaries distributed 19,600 Testaments and Psalters to working-class families in anticipation of a cholera epidemic, and in Paisley in 1837, the starving unemployed were assiduously supplied with Bibles. But such efforts often only aggravated the anger of working-class individuals who saw themselves victimized by evangelical hypocrisy. Louis James states that novelists writing for the working-class were quick to point out the vicious folly of giving poor people Bibles and tracts instead of food, clothing, and sanitation. He cites as an example J. M. Rymer, the popular writer of penny-issue novels, who "can think of no better way of illustrating Sweeney Todd's demonic hypocrisy than having him distribute tracts to the orphan of the man he had murdered" (115). That Rymer would attach evangelical hypocrisy to a stock villain suggests the depth of resentment that separated missionary evangelism from many of its hoped-for beneficiaries.

To a large extent, those who participated in the B.F.B.S.—as members, donors, colporteurs, translators, or local organizers—found in their work a sense of importance, of opportunity, and of patriotic participation in the growth of an enlightening empire. Many of these rank and file members were disadvantaged elsewhere in English society, because of their class, their education, or (in the case of the many women who directed the Society's associations) their gender. And yet the fictive conversions that the Society's historians produced reflect not so much a celebration of religious might and influence as an ambivalence towards it, for repeatedly the deliverers of the Word retreat from their own authority. The children who replace them are drawn from a variety of nations and circumstances, but they share with each other a supernatural power—a power that is efficacious, incontestable, and entirely non-threatening. None of these children will grow up to challenge their religious or colonial guardians; none of them will ever regard English missionaries or merchants as adults of equal stature. In this way, the children of Bible Society's narratives perform a miraculous dual function: they affirm that the missionary influence does not claim patriarchal power, and they confirm that England does.

Whereas domestically, the Bible Society's chief nemesis was a growing working-class disinterest in religion, internationally one of its chief opponents was the growing European interest in Eastern cultures and religions. The Society met this challenge by promulgating descriptions of Hinduism as a barbaric religion. Claudius Buchanan, for instance, whose translating projects in Bengal were cut short in 1807 by the East India Company, wrote a book condemning the Company's policy of collecting taxes from pilgrims to maintain the temples of Juggernaut, where the pilgrims engaged in "lascivious" and "obscene" rituals (*Christian Researches* 32–34). Such terms became commonplaces as Society tract writers continued to dwell on images of Hindus "throwing themselves to sharks, hanging children [and] burning widows" (Owen 1:355). It was senseless and unfair, they argued, to regulate the importation of Christianity into India at a time when European Orientalists were exporting Hinduism: "If we acquaint ourselves, through the medium of translation, with their mythical absurdities and amatory trifles," one tract writer claimed, "it is but fair that we should afford them an opportunity of becoming acquainted, through the same medium, with the august mysteries of the Gospel" (Owen 1:344–45). Here the Society emulated its free-market role models in practice as well as philosophy, attempting to engineer the deflation of competing Indian cultural goods.

Its success in that deflation was partial and short-lived. In the 1830s, the Bible Society's interpretation of Hinduism as representing a Christian moral emergency complemented the utilitarian project to bring western culture to India. Consequently, the opposition the Bible Society had previously received from the East India Company was dramatically reduced after the Company lost its remaining commercial functions in 1833 and became a governing body representing the interests of "enlightened" commerce and utilitarian reform.[16] Under the viceroyalty of Lord William Bentinck, the Bible Society and the colonial government emerged as tacit allies, because despite the ideological differences between them, the utilitarian desire to impart English culture to the Indian colonies accorded with the similar desire of missionary evangelism.[17] The colonial government launched campaigns to anglicize Indian custom and law more aggressively: the practice of *sati* was outlawed in 1828; measures were passed protecting the rights of Indian converts to Christianity; English was declared the official language of education; and Thomas Macaulay was assigned the formidable task of reforming the Indian Penal Code.

At a later point in the century, the blatant cultural disdain towards Hinduism expressed in the Bible Society's publications would be eclipsed by the growth and popularity of Orientalist studies, but in the first decades of its existence the Society maintained an aggressive front against western intellectual interest in the East. Edward Said has suggested that academic Orientalism operated for its practitioners in part as a displaced supernaturalism (120–23). Conversely, the Bible Society's apparently religious discourse operated as a displaced secularism. It mediated the East to English Protestants not through a discourse of theological or spiritual attitudes but rather through a discourse that reduced both Christianity and Hinduism to ascertainable and easily judged codes of behavior and political standing.

The Bible Society contributed to nineteenth-century imperial ideology by textualizing the world as a Protestant and British totality. The histories that it produced were books that tried to "write" an empire inspired by, structured by, and comprised of the Bible. Consequently, the problems George Browne met with in structuring his Bible Society history reflect the difficulty of structuring, at mid-century, England's colonization of the world. In his Preface, Browne writes that he will replace John Owen's method of chronicling the annual activities of the Society with a broader perspective, "dividing the history into two principal compartments, the home and the foreign." The efficacy of this division is sabotaged, however, by the intricate architecture and overweening growth of the Society's posts, missions, and foreign Auxiliaries. The refusal of these heterogeneous and overlapping details to organize themselves into an organic totality becomes an inescapable fact as Browne continues to describe his plan, noting that "the divisions and sub-divisions" of the Society's various operations cannot keep pace with "the wide field of operations" and "the voluminous records" that he has tried to organize into "a comprehensive impression" (1:v–vi). God, the unrepresentable, has become commensurate with empire, which similarly eludes apprehension.

In this way, the final nemesis that haunts the Society at every turn—the Malthusian proliferation of races, tribes, and "societies," the escalating mutations of languages and dialects that forever add to the Bible translator's labor—is internalized in the Society in the form of its own textually uncontrollable details, divisions, records, and operations. While supporters of the Bible Society's work in the 1840s had seen its translations as proof of the Bible's "adaptability" and power "to accommodate" itself to foreign cultures, by the early 1850s the beneficent power of adaptation seemed less decisive than the fear of the uncontrollable fecundity of linguistic and cultural differences. Evaluating the Society's progress in its first fifty years of existence, one essayist wrote:

> when we glance at the researches of those ninety-two eminent linguists, geographers, and men of science, who enabled Mr. Balbi to present in so accurate a form his invaluable Atlas of languages, in which it is shown how these languages are constantly breeding new offspring, we fear that if the income of the Bible Society be tenfold, at its second Jubilee, what it is now, there will still be more languages into which it will be the duty of the Christian to translate the Scriptures, and millions of the human race will still be ignorant of the Lord of heaven and earth; unless Providence should, as it has often done before, anticipate human plans, by some overwhelming display of its power to dispense, in whole or in part, with human agency ("The British and Foreign Bible Society," 387).

Against a singular "Atlas," a singular "Christian" translator, a singular "Providence," and a singular "human agency," the "millions of the human race" deploy themselves like a Satanic coalition of differences designed to defer the millennium indefinitely. The "others" of the Bible Society's quest, the colonial and foreign objects of conversion that must be brought into the community, not only escape assimilation but counteract with their own form of power—the diabolical opposite of translation—the power of linguistic multiplication. This power returns to English evangelical culture an inverted image of ameliorative progress, threatening to counteract the spread of biblical-imperial literacy with a chaos of voices that cannot be controlled or understood.

In the 1850s, the British Empire was politically still on the rise; the cultural totalitarianism anticipated by its Bible Society contributors, however, was on the decline. Confronted with the fact that several decades had passed without the wholesale conversions they expected, the surviving supporters of the B.F.B.S. lowered their millennial expectations and regrouped behind a philosophy of incremental progress, of ongoing diligent labor against insurmountable odds. Browne's history of the B.F.B.S. was published two years after David Livingstone's best-selling *Missionary Travels and Researches in South Africa,* and it was the latter text, with its subordination of religious to ethnographic interest, its emphatic faith in the necessity of promoting commerce in Africa, and its presentation of an indefatigable Briton at home among the exotic dangers of a distant land which won the imagination of a broader English audience than the B.F.B.S. had ever commanded. When Livingstone first sailed for the Cape of Good Hope in 1841 he brought with him five hundred copies of Robert Moffat's Tswana New Testament. When he returned to London in 1856, he brought the massive information that he would spend a year compiling into his memoirs. Of this literary challenge Livingstone remarked that he "would rather cross the African continent again than undertake to write another book" (7). Many more books would be written about the British empire, but after the Bible Society's histories, none would be based on the belief that the book of God could contain the world.

Notes

1. The quotation might be apocryphal, but it became part of the Bible Society tradition, as A. P. Smit's 1970 account of the Bible Society's first meeting demonstrates (1–3).

2. In the early 1800s, the Board of Control of the East India Company was divided over the advisability of "evangelicizing the Hindoos," and in effect a war was waged between missionaries who favored aggressive cultural and religious intervention and company agents who preferred either no religious interference or only the reserved demeanor of the Anglican missionary tradition. The first victory went to the conservatives in 1807, when missionary operations at the College of Fort William in Bengal were greatly curtailed, and its department for translating the

Bible was abolished. Dr. Claudius Buchanan, the evangelical vice-provost of the college, was dismissed, and afterwards he launched a polemical campaign against the East India Company. In the same year that Buchanan was dismissed, Thomas Twining, an agent of the Company, lost his bid to prohibit the B.F.B.S. from operating in the Company's territories. Twining's arguments exemplify the combination of religious tolerance and business rationale that informed most of the Company's policies: Twining said he could not be "a mere spectator in the attempt to wound the tenderest feelings of the natives of India," and additionally he feared such a disturbance "would drive us from the portion of the globe with as much ease as the sands of the desert are scattered by the wind" (28–29). The Board of Proprietors decided against Twining's resolution. Missionaries tended to claim that their efforts were seriously impeded by the Company—John Clark Marshman, for example, complained that at no time in his sixty-year experience did the Parliament, the press, or the Board of Control take the side of the missionary cause (2:470–72). But in the early nineteenth century, Parliament and the Board of Control passed several actions protecting and at times supporting the rights of missionaries in India. And in 1813, after the Company was deprived of its commercial monopoly, Dr. Buchanan attained his longstanding desire to see the establishment of an Indian episcopacy.

3. Initially, the B.F.B.S. was patronized almost exclusively by evangelical clergy, dissenting ministers, and upper-middle-class laity. As it developed, however, it became more of a middle- and lower-middle-class organization. Among the Society's first members were the Rev. Charles Simeon, the popular Cambridge theologian, and several members of the wealthy evangelical Clapham sect, including William Wilberforce. After Lord Teignmouth, a former Governor-General of Bengal, accepted the post of President, the Bishops of London, Durham, Exeter, and St. David's sent in their names as subscribers. The original costs of subscription, ranging from one guinea to fifty pounds, were prohibitive for lower middle class incomes, but as early as 1805 an Auxiliary Bible Society was formed in London offering memberships ranging from two to seven shillings. In 1854, the British and Foreign Bible Society reported 3,315 domestic Auxiliaries, Branches, and Associations. The Auxiliaries operated in much the same fashion as the "parent" institution in London, while the Associations, which made only group contributions to the Society's general funds, did not give official memberships and were primarily distribution centers for the Society's Bibles. While the members of the Auxiliaries were most often clergymen and affluent middle class evangelicals and dissenters, the majority of the participants in the Associations came from the lower middle class. Women were most active at the level of the Associations, probably because there they could serve in a higher capacity—of the 2,482 Associations reported in 1854, over half were conducted by women.

4. Missionaries to India and Africa equally emphasized the behavioral and religious aspects of the conversions they sought—indeed, their concern with inculcating European manners often eclipsed the religious side of their work. As one missionary from Tanjore wrote the Society, "the moral conduct, upright dealing, and decent dress, of the native Protestants of Tanjore, demonstrate the powerful influence and peculiar excellence of the Christian religion. It ought, however, to be

observed, that the Bible, when the reading of it becomes general, has nearly the same effect on the poor of every place" (Owen 1:323). From South Africa, Robert Moffat wrote of the civilizing effect that his translation of Luke had on the Botswanas, concluding "thus, by the slow but certain progress of Gospel principles, whole families become clothed and in their right mind" (*Missionary Labours* 505).

5. For this observation I am indebted to Regenia Gagnier's argument that, in the context of Victorian literary autobiography, the tradition of bourgeois subjectivity assumes "an abstract individualism" independent of "material conditions and social environment" (12).

6. Both Owen's and Browne's histories reflect early Victorian preoccupations with prophecy, and specifically with the spirit of "post-millennialist" optimism that fueled the activities of evangelical reform. Unlike some of their evangelical and dissenting brethren who ascribed to a "pre-millennial" interpretation of the Second Coming, post-millennialists stressed that Christians themselves were responsible for achieving the massive global conversions which would precede Christ's return to earth. Pre-millennialists had the truly apocalyptic vision—they expected that Christ's sudden and dramatic return in glory would vindicate their disdain for the self-congratulatory optimism of those who celebrated progress, embraced democracy, and overlooked the sinfulness of the English nation. Post-millennialists, in contrast, were embarrassed by such prophetic excesses, and identified wholeheartedly with England's providential role as a global disseminator of Christian enlightenment. It was this component of "post-millennial" rhetoric—a combination of avowed faith in Christian teleology and certain faith in English cultural superiority—that gave the middle- and lower-middle-class reforming societies their distinctive character, separating them from both the more politically-inclined chiliasm of working-class prophetic thought and from the similarly reform-minded but secular attitudes of the utilitarians (Oliver 20–24).

7. Although in their memoirs the missionaries were fairly candid about their experiences, they often expressed their doubts only retrospectively, after they began to enjoy some success. Robert Moffat, in one of his published memoirs, noted after the end of his first ten years among "indifferent" Botswanas that "the moral wilderness was now about to blossom. . . . The simple Gospel now melted their flinty hearts; and eyes wept, which never before had shed the tear of hallowed sorrow" (*Missionary Labours* 496). In a gesture that typifies missionaries' writings, Moffat reads the otherness of the Africans as evangelical allegory—the cold heart of the inaccessible heathen needs the emotional stimulation of the Gospels to acquire the sentimentality that makes him recognizable in western eyes. Evidence that the Bible was not taking root in an area was often viewed through the screens of nationalism. Claudius Buchanan observed that in India, Christian missions flourished more where there were few French inhabitants, since French Christians set such an unfavorable example (54–55). In fifty years of "sporadic campaigning" in Mongolia, Moravian missionaries attracted only "a few unfortunates" into the Church, but a lot of hostility from the Kalmucks—failures that the Bible Society attributed in part to the laziness of the Moravians (Bawden 45–46). In contrast to Moffat's and Buchanan's nationalistic processing of frustration, Mrs. Anne Hodg-

son, who spent several years in Africa as the wife of a Wesleyan missionary, concluded that there was something insidiously disingenuous about the way the Missionary Societies in England depicted missionary life in Africa: "Our eyes are not
gladdened with seeing multitudes flock to the standard of the cross, nor our ears
with the interrogatory 'What must I do to be saved?' A very difficult language is to
be acquired, with a poor interpreter, who is of a dreadfully bad temper; sometimes
he will answer a question, and sometimes he will not" (Shaw 171). The misguided
domestic belief in progress in the work of foreign conversions was aided by the fact
that missionaries seldom returned to England to speak about their adventures in
person, and, if they had, Elisabeth Jay conjectures that they "would have found
scant welcome from crowds accustomed to hearing of the Society's achievements
from the noble and famous rather than the labourers in the field" (169).

8. James Clifford cites Derrida as the catalyst for a recent debate that has unset-
tled "the sharp distinction of the world's culture into literate and pre-literate; the
notion that ethnographic textualization is a process that enacts a fundamental
transition from oral experience to written representation" (118). Hence, Clifford
argues, there is less of a distinction between literate and non-literate societies than
anthropologists traditionally presume, because "non-literate cultures are already
textualized; there are few, if any, 'virgin' lifeways to be violated and preserved by
writing" (117). The "other side" of this argument is perhaps best represented by
Walter Ong, who emphasizes essential differences between oral and literate cultures
and notes that, among other things, oral cultures rely solely on memory, do not
conceive of language in visual terms, and tend to use concepts in a situational as
opposed to an abstract frame of reference. However, these considerations have led
Ong to a conclusion that Clifford might find sympathetic, insofar as it describes
orality and literacy as interactive rather than polarized conditions: "without textualism, orality cannot even be identified; without orality, textualism is rather opaque
and playing with it can be a form of occultism, elaborate obfuscation—which can be
endlessly titillating, even at those times when it is not especially informative" (169–
70).

9. The Bible Society's attitude toward translation straddles the two poles that
George Steiner identifies in linguistic theory as the "relativist" and "universalist."
On the one hand, insofar as the Society's translators sought analogies between
Scriptures and the target languages, their translations reflect the emphasis placed by
contemporary linguists and cultural historians (Herder, Mme de Stael, Humboldt)
on the reciprocities between language and "national" character and habits of belief
(Steiner 73–85). On the other hand, the unique universality that Society translators
attributed to the Bible overrode these relative conditions of language. In the mid-
century writings of the Society, this mixture of relativist and universalist views was
harmonized through quasi-evolutionary terminology, where the Bible was frequently described as an ideal type that entered into various linguistic species with
more or less representational success. As an essay in the *Edinburgh Review* put it, "it
has not been given to any other *book* of religion, thus to triumph over national
prejudices . . . varying by every conceivable diversity of language. . . . [the Bible]
adapts itself with facility to the revolutions of thought and feeling . . . and flexibly

accommodates itself to the progress of society" ("The Vanity and Glory of Literature" 316–17). Although the Bible Society's concern with the relativity of languages was informed by contemporary trends in linguistic and cultural theory, their belief that the Bible was still absolutely translatable was not unique either to their era or to Christianity in general. Their belief exemplifies what Walter Benjamin says of all translations of "Holy Writ," that "where a text is identical with truth or dogma, where it is supposed to be 'the true language' in all its literalness and without the mediation of meaning, this text is unconditionally translatable." Even though there was no single Bible in early Victorian England—the discovery of new manuscripts and debates over textual variations were constantly challenging the integrity of both the King James version and the Hebrew and Greek texts—Protestants still maintained faith in an ideally authoritative text, wherein, as Benjamin says of all holy writings, "language and revelation are one" (82).

10. Throughout the nineteenth century, Victorians posited a radical shift towards philanthropic improvement in England's rule of India after Hastings's trial revealed the abuses that were performed under the mandate of turning profits. John Seeley, the Cambridge professor of History who was cynical enough to proclaim "we seem . . . to have conquered and peopled half the world in a fit of absence of mind (12)," still held in 1881 by the interpretation that in dissolving the East India Company the English government had effectively subordinated its commercial to its philanthropic interest in India: "[In the eighteenth century] it was no affair of ours whether the Hindus had a bad Government, or had no Government at all and were merely the prey of armed plunderers. . . . Adam Smith, writing in the eighties at the end of the reign of Warren Hastings, says there never was a Government so wholly indifferent to the welfare of its subjects. . . . But since 1851 it has been removed. The very appearance of a selfish object is gone. The Government is now as sincerely paternal as any can be, and, as I explained, it has abandoned the affectation of not imparting the superior enlightenment we know ourselves to possess on the ground that the Hindus do not want it" (205).

11. Other stories illustrate this point more graphically. A few pages earlier, Browne cites the example of an old Greek priest who went to observe a missionary school where young girls were learning to read the Bible. At the end of his visit, the monk is quoted as saying: "I only learned to read a little and became a priest, and although I read at Church prayers and portions of the Bible, they are in Ancient Greek, and I cannot understand them . . . I, who have grey hairs upon my head, have been receiving lessons from children. How I would like to sit down with these children, and learn the Scriptures!" (2:45–46). Still other stories assume a tone more polemical than sentimental: "A zealous Roman Catholic priest, afterwards a no less zealous Protestant, was brought to examine one of our Flemish Testaments, in the following singular manner.—A Colporteur had sold a copy to one of his parishioners. The poor man, frightened by a violent sermon preached by another priest, hastened home, took his Testament, and carried it to his own priest (the one in question) and begged him to burn it. . . . The priest, it appears, was afterwards induced to read the Testament left with him. Afterwards . . . he became a Protestant minister" (Browne 1:456).

12. Owen includes two letters that praise the Society's translations for their unembellished, simple, and easily accessible style. The curious thing about these letters is that both come from authorities whose own cultures still maintained a distinction between the "vulgar" tongue of common intercourse and an erudite written language reserved for the court and religious writings. One letter is from the King of Persia, who praises Henry Martyn's Modern Persian Gospel because it is written in "a style most befitting Sacred Books, that is, in an easy and simple diction." A note from the translator of the letter explains that the King has honored the translation by using the word "tilawat" for "read"—"tilawat" usually being reserved for the act of "reciting or perusing the Koran" (2:265–67). Thus the Society's desire to treat the Bible as information that must be rendered in every pedestrian dialect finds, in the King of Persia's letter, a word of praise ironically rooted in a tradition that treats sacred writings in an opposite vein, as privileged texts which should be protected from common linguistic intercourse.

13. At first the Bible Society's application for a booth at the Great Exhibition was refused by Prince Albert, who objected to the implied association of the Bible with the proclaimed subject of the exhibition, modern industry. A long correspondence ensued, and the booth was approved (Chadwick 2:461–62).

14. A *Blackwood's* essay on the Bible Society in 1825 charged that the style of the evangelical clergy was out of step with modern modes of speech—although, as the quotation makes clear, what distinguishes "modern speech" is its resemblance to the style and diction of print: "The preaching of many of the evangelical clergy . . . uses the quaint, obsolete, luscious, obscure language of the old religious divines, and assigns too many words, such as faith, love, and grace, etc., a meaning very different from that which the dictionary gives them. This we conceive to be a very great fault. Why do not these clergymen use the style of the present day, as it is found to be among our best writers? Were they to do this, it would render their sermons infinitely more useful" ("Bible Societies" 624).

15. In December of 1811 Marsh addressed a public meeting in the Cambridge Town Hall to argue against the establishment of a Cambridge Auxiliary Bible Society. Marsh's "violent language" had the undesired effect of arousing "a strong feeling in favour of the Bible Society, and after an enthusiastic town-hall meeting, the auxiliary was established against his wishes ("Marsh" 36:213). In the following month Marsh continued his campaign against the Society with two pamphlets. Among the respondents to these pamphlets was Charles Simeon, whose considerable influence at Cambridge was responsible for the Auxiliary in the first place. Owen summarizes Marsh's arguments, along with lengthy excerpts from the rebuttals of the Society's spokesmen, in 2:143–211.

16. Seeley argued that English trade in India did not begin to prosper until after the Company was deprived of its monopoly in 1813, and that "great trade" with India only began after 1833. In his lectures at Cambridge, he used this point to demonstrate the superior efficacy of a system that did not engage in "sordid rapacity," but rather maintained separate channels for governmental and commercial activities (209–15).

17. Patrick Brantlinger describes the relationship between missionary Evangeli-

cals and utilitarian colonialism as one with more important similarities than differences: "the Evangelicals and utilitarians insisted that the chief objects of British imperialism were the conversion and civilization of India. The utilitarian project of social reform often conflicted with the Christian conversion advocated by the evangelicals, but both goals involved a belief that ran counter to the most extreme form of racism: no matter how benighted or tyrannized by custom and false religion, Indians were capable of education, improvement, progress" (106). Along similar lines, Eric Stokes has argued that utilitarians assimilated aspects of the evangelical missionary tradition to produce a philosophy of government that coupled an elaborate legislative system with a centralizing commitment to the necessity of supervision.

Works Cited

Bawden, C. R. *Shamans, Lamas and Evangelicals.* London: Routledge and Kegan Paul, 1985.

Benjamin, Walter. "The Task of the Translator." In *Illuminations.* Trans. Harry Zohn. New York: Schoken Books, 1969, 69–82.

"The Bible Societies." *Blackwood's Edinburgh Magazine* 18 (1825): 621–31.

Brantlinger, Patrick. *Rule of Darkness: British Literature and Imperialism, 1830–1914.* Ithaca, N.Y.: Cornell University Press, 1988.

Browne, Rev. George. *The History of the British and Foreign Bible Society, from Its Institution in 1804, to the Close of its Jubilee in 1854.* 2 vols. London: Bagster and Sons, 1859.

Buchanan, Rev. Claudius. *Christian Researches in Asia.* 2d American ed. Boston: Samuel T. Armstrong, 1811.

Canton, William. *A History of the British and Foreign Bible Society.* 2 vols. London: John Murray, 1904.

Chadwick, Owen. *The Victorian Church.* 2d ed. 2 vols. London: Adam and Charles Black, 1970.

Clifford, James. "On Ethnographic Allegory." In *Writing Culture.* Ed. James Clifford and George E. Marcus. Berkeley: University of California Press, 1986, 98–121.

[Edwards, Edward.] "British and Foreign Bible Society." *Quarterly Review* 36 (June 1827): 1–28.

Gagnier, Regenia. "The Literary Standard, Working-Class Lifewriting, and Gender." In *Revealing Lives: Gender in Autobiography and Biography.* Ed. Marilyn Yalom and Susan Groag Bell. Urbana: University of Illinois Press, 1989.

"Herbert Marsh." *Dictionary of National Biography.* Vol 36. London: Smith, Elder, and Co., 1897, 211–15.

James, Louis. *Fiction for the Working Man, 1830–1850.* London: Oxford University Press, 1963.

Jay, Elisabeth. *The Religion of the Heart: Anglican Evangelicalism and the Nineteenth-Century Novel.* Oxford: Clarendon Press, 1979.

Livingstone, David. *Missionary Travels and Researches in South Africa* (1857). New York: New Amsterdam Book Co., n.d.

Marshman, John Clark. *Life and Times of Carey, Marshman, and Ward.* 2 vols. London: Longmans, Green, 1859.

Moffat, Robert. *A Life's Labours in South Africa.* London: John Snow, 1871.

————. *Missionary Labours and Scenes in South Africa.* London: John Snow, 1842.

"Ninth Annual Report of the British and Foreign Bible Society" (1813). Stanford, Calif.: University Microfiche.

Oliver, W. H. *Prophets and Millennialists.* Auckland, New Zealand: Auckland University Press and Oxford: Oxford University Press, 1978.

Ong, Walter J. *Orality and Literacy.* New York: Methuen, 1982.

Owen, Rev. John. *History of the Origin and First Ten Years of the British and Foreign Bible Society.* 2 vols. London: Tilling and Hughes, 1816.

Said, Edward. *Orientalism.* New York: Random House, 1979.

Sandilands, A. "The Historical Background of the Tswana 'Centenary' New Testament." *Botswana Notes and Records* 3 (1971): 1–5.

Seeley, J. R. *The Expansion of England.* Ed. John Gross. Chicago: The University of Chicago Press, 1971.

Shaw, William. *Memoirs of Mrs. Anne Hodgson.* London: J. Mason, 1836.

Smit, A. P. *God Made it Grow: History of the Bible Society Movement in South Africa.* Trans. W. P. DeVos. Cape Town: The Bible Society of South Africa, 1970.

A Soldier of the American Revolution. "Letter in Answer to the Speech of Dr. Mason at the Thirteenth Anniversary Meeting of the British and Foreign Bible Society." Elizabeth Town, N.J. (1818). Stanford, Calif.: University Microfiche.

Steiner, George. *After Babel: Aspects of Language and Translation.* London: Oxford University Press, 1975.

Stokes, Eric. *The English Utilitarians and India.* Oxford: Clarendon Press, 1959.

Twining, Thomas. "A Letter to the Chairman of the East India Company, on the danger of interfering in the Religious Opinions of the Natives of India; and on the Views of the British and Foreign Bible Society, as directed to India." 2d ed. London: Hazard and Carthew, 1807.

"The Vanity and Glory of Literature." *Edinburgh Review* 89 (1849): 309–23.

Jeff Nunokawa

For Your Eyes Only: Private Property and the Oriental Body in *Dombey and Son*

AT THE END OF *The Country and the City,* Raymond Williams describes a remarkable fantasy entertained by officers of the British empire during the nineteenth century, an idealized vision of "rural England . . . its green peace contrasted with the tropical or arid places of actual work."[1] The rustic conception of the homeland harbored by the expatriates who worked in Britain's third world colonies is puzzling, since, as Williams notes, "the society from which these people had come was, after all, the most urban and industrialized in the world, and it was usually in the service of just these elements that they had gone out" (282). Williams suggests that the pastoral pleasures remembered or anticipated by the armies of the British empire described no actual landscape, but rather a dream of carefree homeowning:

> [T]he reward for service . . . anticipated more often than it was gained, was a return to a rural place within this urban and industrial England: the 'residential' rural England, the 'little place in the country'. . . . The country, now, was a place to retire to. (282)

The connection that Williams notices here between working in exotic colonies and acquiring embowered estate is an ideological fantasy which English novels of the mid-nineteenth century both reflect and help to form. In novels like *Vanity Fair* and *Jane Eyre* characters maintain or secure the integrity of domestic property through work, theft, or trade that takes place in the colonies. I am going to plot one mid-century novel's especially complex version of this link between foreign places and safe property, a version of this link which involves intricate intimacies between Victorian constructions of property, capital, sexuality, and race.

Dickens's *Dombey and Son* (1848) creates a form of estate that is sheltered from various forces that threaten private property, and this construction requires a strategy of containment and catharsis which takes the "orient" as its scapegoat. However, before we get global, we first have to survey the condition of the local economy; we need to figure out why property is endangered in the novel.

In *Dombey and Son*, to own is to own alone. "Partner[ship]" in the family Firm is "reserved solely to inheritors of that great name" (722), and this restriction is even narrower than it looks; it diminishes the number of eligible partners to one, since Dombey and Son, in the annals of the Firm, are indifferent instances of a single person, the corporate proprietor who is the lone subject of House correspondence:

> He will be christened Paul . . . of course . . . His father's name . . . and his grandfather's! . . . There is some inconvenience in the necessity of writing Junior . . . but it . . . doesn't enter into the correspondence of the House. *Its* signature remains the same.[2]

The rule of exclusive access applies as well to the "Home Department" of the Firm, where Dombey's "sense of property in his child" (70) receives "a rude shock" (70) when he is compelled to share his son, even with a wet-nurse.

Dombey's "haughty dread of having any rival or partner in the boy's respect and deference" (103) measures more than the eccentricities of pathological jealousy. The definition of ownership as the right of exclusive access is an ideological construct whose force appears in our inability to imagine an alternative description of the term, in our sense that the phrase *private property* is redundant. Ownership, in the words of one character in *Dombey and Son*, appears to be nothing other than "[e]xclusion itself" (159). Theorists of property such as C. B. Macpherson characterize this conception of property as a crucial contraction of its meaning, a narrowing of the category concomitant with the ascendancy of capitalism. The canonization of private property as the sole form of possession is cast by such theorists as a construct that appears and cooperates with capitalism, situated as an integral element of an economy dominated by commodity exchange.[3]

Dickens's chronicle of the fortunes of Dombey and Son describes an antagonism between the concept of ownership as exclusive access, and the workings of commodity exchange. In *Dombey and Son,* such property is the casualty, rather than the condition of capitalism. To get at this, we first need to notice how the novel radicalizes the boundary of proprietarial exclusion.

Dickens's novel escalates the conception of ownership as exclusive access to the uses of property by extending the ensemble of those uses to include even its cognitive apprehension. If, in *Dombey and Son,* to own is to own alone, to own alone is to own in secret.

The bleakness of the House of Dombey reflects the "blankness" that conceals and thus preserves all that belongs to Dombey: "It was as blank a house inside as outside . . . Mr Dombey ordered the furniture to be covered up . . . to preserve it for the son" (75). A common figure of speech encapsulates the philosophy of property in *Dombey and Son:* "[H]e is going to have . . . the books kept closer" (99). Fortune's closeness shades the novel's account of London's financial district in a chapter ironically entitled "More First Appearances." Near the offices of Dombey and Son, "the Royal Exchange was close at hand; the Bank of England, with its vaults of gold and silver 'down among the dead men' underground, was their magnificent neighbour" (87). Both the Royal Exchange, "close at hand," and the crypt that covers and protects the gold and silver of the bank of England instate an affiliation of secrecy and security.

Conversely, if to "preserve" property is to "cover it up," the loss of property occurs when it is made available to the apprehension of others. It is to defend against the alienation of publication that one character declines to mention the name of Dombey's future wife in the presence of others: "he holds that name too sacred to be made the property of these fellows, or of any fellows" (455). The loss of property in the floodlights of publicity appears on the grandest theater when Carker, the capitalist's treacherous assistant, manages Dombey's loss of fortune not by stealing it, but by staging it, "exhibit[ing] it in magnificent contrast to other merchants' Houses" (843).

Edith Dombey's hold on her "accomplishment[s] or grace[s]" is cancelled when they are broadcast on the marketplace:

> I have been offered and rejected, put up and appraised, until my very soul has sickened. I have not had an accomplishment or grace that might have been a resource to me, but it has been paraded and vended to enhance my value, as if the common crier had called it through the streets. (856)

Since they are "paraded and vended," her accomplishments and graces cannot be a resource for her. This alienation of potential property results not from its sale, but merely from its *availability* for sale.[4]

The broadcasting that cancels the privacy of property and thus abrogates ownership clusters around a particular form in the novel, a form that appears when Edith Dombey is exhibited on the auctioneer's block: she is offered—at once "put up and appraised." This phrase implies not only that the capital value of Edith Dombey's resources is exhibited, her "accomplishment[s]" and "grace[s]" "paraded and vended to enhance [her] value," but also that her translation into value that can be bought with money is *itself* a kind of spectacle.

In all of its forms, capital is exhibition. It composes the collective speech that is the noise of the novel; its "voices" (87), the "uproar of [its] streets" (87), are the shouts of perambulating merchants and the "suggestions of precious stuffs" (87). "[S]uggestions" are issued *by* "precious stuffs"; "gold and silver" themselves offer "demonstration[s]" (584); "commodities [are] . . . addressed to the general public" (237). As Dombey's definition of money suggests—" 'a very potent spirit . . . that cause[s] us to be honoured, feared, respected . . . and ma[kes] us powerful and glorious in the eyes of all men' " (152–53)—capital is a means of communication that may best be described as publication.

Capital is a sign, not a substance; the "image" of the "Son of the Firm" is indistinguishable from the "impression" that it communicates: "If there were a warm place in [Dombey's] frosty heart, his son occupied it; if its very hard surface could receive the impression of any image, the image of that son was there . . . as the 'Son' of the Firm" (151). Similarly, the novel defines the "vast resources" of Dombey and Son endangered by Carker's exhibition of them as the "credit" of the House, and thus describes the capital displayed by Carker as an instance, rather than the object of communication. Dombey and Son consists of "bankers' books, or cheque books, or bills, or such tokens of wealth rolling in from day to day" (92).[5]

Thus the ownership of capital is a self-canceling term in *Dombey and Son*, since capital is exhibition, and as such dismantles the boundary of secrecy that defines possession.[6] The "capital" which is the "Firm's name" is "known and honoured in the British possessions abroad" (188); and if, in the words of one sycophant, "[n]o one can be a stranger to Mr. Dombey's influence," the horde that divests Dombey of his private sorrow for the death of his son indicates that no one can be *kept* a stranger to Dombey's estate: "From high to low . . . everyone set up some claim or other to a share in his dead boy" (353). Dombey's loss of "his sense of property in his boy," a loss that results from the flood of publicity, results inevitably from the boy's character as part of the "capital of the House's name," his character as the " 'Son' of the Firm." "Everyone's share" in the dead boy is, more specifically, every *reader's* share. Dickens announces as much in his preface to *Dombey and Son,* when he speaks of the novel's fabulously popular account of Paul Dombey's death: "If . . . my readers . . . have felt a sorrow in one of the principal incidents on which this fiction turns, I hope it may be a sorrow of that sort which endears the sharers in it" (41).

Dombey's interest in the progress of the "Son of the Firm," part of the "capital" of the Firm's name and "title" (937), is the fascination of the novel reader:

> [Dombey] loved his son with all the love he had. If there were a warm place in his frosty heart, his son occupied it; if its very hard surface could receive the impression of any image, the image of that son was there; though not so much as an infant, or as a boy, but as a grown man—the 'Son' of the Firm. Therefore he was impatient to advance into the future, and to hurry over the intervening passages of his history. (151)

The capital which is the name of the House is identified as a novel, a "history," much like *Dombey and Son* itself, whose extreme length (Dickens's longest work) might tempt an "impatient" reader to "hurry over [its] intervening passages." Like the clamor of commodities that inhabits it, the novel itself is a kind of commodified speech addressed to the general public. And if the novel is like capital, capital, in *Dombey and Son,* is like the novel, a form of publicity available to anyone who can read it.

*   *   *

In keeping with the Victorian designation of the domestic sphere as a sanctuary from commerce, *Dombey and Son* establishes, within "the home department," a space for covert possession, sheltered from the alienating floodlights of capital. This domestic estate consists of an idealized woman (Florence Dombey), a fantasy of femininity which consists of a chaste image that the novel's hero (Walter Gay) embraces first in his mind, and finally in marriage: "the woman's heart of Florence, with its undivided treasure, can be yielded only once" (902). Conflating, as it does, exposure to view, and the transfer of property, the term "yield" effectively registers capital's aspect in *Dombey and Son,* an aspect from which the "undivided treasure" of Florence is exempted. She is her lover's secure because covert estate, at once an object for his eyes only and a possession securely fastened to him.

Gay's "undivided treasure" must be cleansed not only of the taint of capital, but also of sexuality. This is so because sexuality, like capital, is defined in Dickens's novel as a form of publicity. *Dombey and Son* thus participates in something Michel Foucault calls "peculiar to modern societies": "What is peculiar to modern societies is not that they consigned sex to a shadow existence, but that they dedicated themselves to speaking of it *ad infinitum,* while exploiting it as *the* secret." Foucault argues that sexuality is constituted as a secret that can't be maintained by being cast as a form of display: "sex had to be put into words." Sexuality in "modern societies" becomes a secret that cannot be kept, because it becomes "something to say. . . . Whether in the form of a subtle confession in confidence or an authoritarian interrogation, sex—be it refined or rustic—had to be put into words."7 As the drift of this remark suggests, sexuality is not simply an object observed, according to Foucault's account, but a subject that displays by its very nature; sexuality is not a substance, but a sign, a means of appearance.

The aspect of sexuality that Foucault describes here appears in *Dombey and Son,* where sexuality, like capital, is inherently indiscreet. Edith Dombey's erotic emanations make this clear to us. The "base and wretched aim of every . . . display" that she "learnt" was the "artful . . . laying [of] snares for men" (472–73). Edith Dombey's "beauty," that which "calls forth admiration" (367) from "all kinds of men" (473), is "a badge or livery she hated" (466).

The shows and signs which work through the figure of the woman are like the landscape that adorns Carker's domicile: "The lawn, the soft, smooth slope, the flower garden, the clumps of trees where graceful forms of ash and willow are not wanting . . . bespeak an amount of elegant comfort within" (553). The rumor of an erotic body lying in the shape of the "soft, smooth slope" and "graceful forms" of this passage again designates sexuality as a kind of display, or a form of address.

Moreover, sexuality, like capital, is nothing in *Dombey and Son* but a form of exhibition. Like the "credit" that constitutes the "resources" of the House, the "elegant comfort" signaled by these sexual shapes, the "[r]ich colours, excellently blended," that "meet the eye at every turn," "the furniture—its proportions admirably devised to suit the shapes and sizes of the small rooms," the "few choice prints and pictures" are themselves "one voluptuous cast—mere shows of form and colour" (554).

Sexuality and capital are not merely analogous in *Dombey and Son:* in various ways, the novel charts the merging of these forms of exhibition. Capital's sexualization and sexuality's capitalization together compose the spectacle of Edith Dombey, "offered" on the "market" at once as a commodity, "appraised, hawked and vended," and as an erotic entity, "the bye-word of all kinds of men" (473). The financial transactions of the Firm appear to an observer in the shape of a body "laid bare before him" (722); and everywhere in the novel, commodities are caught in the act of disrob-ing: "Riches are uncovering in shops" (902). Thus, for property to be secret and therefore secure, it must be cleansed of both capital and sexuality.

And the taint of these things pervades the novel. The chaste entity that eludes the alienating publicity of capital and sexuality, the innocent estate that Gay preserves in his mind and encircles in his arm is made, rather than found. It depends upon the extinction of a sexualized, commodified version of Florence—a story, a widely available "adventure," in which the youth takes a "delightful interest":

> That spice of romance and love of the marvellous, of which there was a pretty strong infusion in the nature of young Walter Gay . . . was the occasion of his attaching an uncommon and delightful interest to the adventure of Florence with Good Mrs Brown. He pampered and cherished it in his memory, especially that part of it with which he had been associated; until it became the spoiled child of his fancy, and took its own way, and did what it liked with it. The recollection of those incidents, and his own share in them, may have been made the more captivating, perhaps, by the weekly dreamings of old Sol and Captain Cuttle . . . the latter gentleman had even gone so far as to purchase a ballad . . . that had long fluttered among many others . . . on a dead wall in the Commercial Road: which poetical performance set forth the courtship and nuptials of a promising young coal-whipper with a certain 'lovely Peg,' the accomplished daughter of the master and part owner of a Newcastle collier. In this stirring legend, Captain Cuttle descried a profound metaphysical bearing on the case of Walter and Florence; and it excited him so much, that on very festive occasions . . . he would roar through the whole song in the little back parlour; making an amazing shake on the word Pe-e-eg, with which every verse concluded, in compliment to the heroine of the piece. (172)

The "captivating" "adventure of Florence with Good Mrs Brown" is the centerpiece of a general atmosphere of sexual excitation that culminates in Captain Cuttle's "amazing shake." Our sense of the sexual character of this adventure is supported by its figuration as the "spoiled child of his fancy," a characterization that *Dombey and Son* reserves for its prostitutes, Alice Marwood and Edith Dombey. The sexuality of this adventure also suggests itself in the source of Gay's interest in them, the "spice of romance and the love of the marvellous" instilled in him by his uncle, a "secret attraction" towards "books" and "stories" that "lure" and "charm" (96).

As the economic language that describes Gay's relation to it suggests, this erotic fantasy merges with the commodity to which it is attached. Their radical identification is registered by the passage when it casts the commodity that Cuttle purchases on Commercial Road as an agent of eroticization; the rehearsal of the ballad of "lovely Peg" makes, or would make, the adventure of Florence and Good Mrs Brown more "captivating."

And, in keeping with the publicizing character of capital and sexuality, this eroticized, commodified "adventure of Florence with Good Mrs Brown" is widely available. The closeness between Walter Gay and the young coal-whipper is the distance between these boys and the girls in whom they take "interest": Gay is a lowly employee of Dombey and Son, as much removed from Florence as the coal-whipper is from lovely Peg. But just as the gap between Peg and her proletarian paramour is closed *within* the ballad, the gap between Walter Gay and the eroticized, capitalized figure of *his* master's daughter is closed *by* the "adventure," a form of publication in which even the otherwise unenfranchised can take "interest."

As the boy grows, these exciting fantasies give way to a chaste conception of Florence that we have seen, or, more precisely, *not* seen, before. The sexualized, capitalized adventure gives way to an "indefinite image" of innocence that Gay keeps to himself:

> He could do no better than preserve her image . . . precious . . . unchangeable, and indefinite in all but its power of giving him pleasure, and restraining him like an angel's hand from anything unworthy. (288)

This "indefinite" image of Florence is radically privatized: We have no access at all to this angelic, "indefinite" sight; like the view offered by the fortress walls of an estate, a view which only serves to confirm the exclusion of those who are confronted by it, our conception of Gay's image is restricted to the recognition that it is harbored by, and directed to Gay. In contrast to the obscurity of this "image," the "exciting" "romantic" fantasies which precede it are described in great detail:

> They set off Florence very much, to his fancy. . . . Sometimes he thought (and then he walked very fast) what a grand thing it would have been for him to have been going to sea on the day after that first meeting, and to have gone, and to have done wonders there, and to have stopped away a long time, and to have come back an Admiral of all the colours of the dolphin, or at least a Post-Captain . . . and have married Florence (then a beautiful young woman) in spite of Mr Dombey's teeth, cravat, and watch chain, and borne her away to the blue shores of somewhere or other, triumphantly. (173–74)

Like the "adventure of Florence with Good Mrs Brown," which first appears as an episode within the narrative of the novel itself (Chapter 6), this fantasy is as available to us as it is to Gay. The chaste figure of Florence Dombey, the chaste figure which replaces Gay's interesting fantasy, is "borne away triumphantly" from the edge of the novel where she is situated when, with lovely Peg, she is cast in the publicizing shape of capital and sexuality.

*   *   *

I want now to situate the novel's establishment of secure, secret property in a wider context. Like the Indian fabrics that adorn the houses of Victorian novels, the day-dream and the white bride that Walter Gay "garners up" first in his mind and then in his arms involve a dark foreign relation. The recession of the capitalized, sexualized "adventure" which precedes Gay's private treasure of chastity, the passing away which enables the covert possession that follows, depends upon the "orientalization" of the boy's early fortunes.

Before I proceed to consider how Gay's erotic adventures are "orientalized," and how this "orientalization" enables their demise, I need first to rapidly define and survey the "oriental" presence in Dickens's writings. By "oriental," I rely on Edward Said's designation of the broadest meaning of the term, "the demarcation between East and West," and refer to a heterogeneous cluster of discursive "sites" associated with regions and cultures that are now sometimes called collectively the "third world."[8] It will be my task throughout this section to justify the use of this comprehensive term by isolating common features that draw together Dickens's various accounts of the non-western, accounts ranging from recognizably fanciful versions of the "orient," to pseudo-ethnographic descriptions of Dark Continents, populated by squalid Savages. Mrs Jellyby's reverse myopia in *Bleak House*—"[her] eyes . . . had a curious habit of seeming to look a long way off . . . [a]s if . . . they could see nothing nearer than Africa!"—may speak poorly for her capacity as domestic monitor, but it speaks well for the drawing power of the African spectacle.[9] The distant object of the philanthropist's fascination describes generally the geography of the "oriental" in Dickens's work, where the east is an exhibition.[10]

Things "oriental" join the gallery of capital and sexuality in *Dombey and Son;* their exotic hues are spectacular:

> the rich East India House, teeming with suggestions of precious stuffs and stones, tigers, elephants, howdahs, hookahs, umbrellas, palm trees, palanquins, and gorgeous princes of a brown complexion sitting on carpets, with their slippers very much turned up at the toes. (87)

The wealth displayed by the East India House is a wealth of display, a wealth composed of curious objects and fabulous colors that invite the gaze.

Like capital and sexuality, the "oriental," for Dickens, displays by its nature. The tigers and elephants that take part in the spectacle of the East India House help us to think of this catalogue of curious sights as a kind of parade, like the one that the opium addict sees at the beginning of *The Mystery of Edwin Drood:*

> The Sultan goes by to his palace in long procession. Ten thousand scimitars flash in the sunlight, and thrice ten thousand dancing girls strew flowers. Then follow white elephants caparisoned in countless gorgeous colours.[11]

And the Indian or Arabian parade is matched by the African theater described by Dickens in an essay entitled "The Noble Savage" (1853). The Savage is always "exhibited" in England, sometimes in "a picturesque and glowing book," sometimes "in an elegant theatre, fitted with appropriate scenery."[12] More strikingly, the Savage is pictured by Dickens as a figure for a landscape, or a player for a stage even in his natural habitat. The African is not only the object of occidental surveillance, according to Dickens's account; like sexuality and capital, the savage is not only an object scrutinized, but also a character whose native aspect is an exhibition:

> The women being at work in the fields, hoeing the Indian corn, and the noble savage being asleep in the shade, the chief has sometimes the condescension to come forth and lighten the labour by looking at it. On these occasions he seats himself in his own savage chair, and is attended by his shield-bearer: who holds over his head a shield of cowhide—in shape like an immense mussel shell—fearfully and wonderfully, after the manner of a theatrical supernumerary.

This passage casts both the fields of labour at which the Noble Savage directs his gaze, and the Savage spectator himself, adorned by stage scenery and "a theatrical supernumerary," as the object of exhibition: the landscape of the "oriental" is comprehended by the frame of the picture, or the space of the stage.

The Noble Savage lightens the site of toil by looking at it, and this suggests what is true about the "oriental" landscape generally: it is a sight that is shaped by its apprehension. Like the other forms of publication that I have examined, the "oriental" cannot be separated from its appearance; its purely spectacular character is suggested by its frequent shape as hallucination—the "arabesques" and "miniature tigers and lions" that only Paul Dombey discerns in the "paperhanging in the house" (234), or the opium vision that John Jaspers entertains in *The Mystery of Edwin Drood*.

There is a difference between the "oriental" exhibition and those of capital and sexuality. *Drood's* "oriental" parade features the Sultan himself at its center; the riches of the East India House culminate with "gorgeous princes of a brown complexion, sitting on carpets, with their slippers very much turned up at the toes"; other "oriental" displays in the novel include a "fierce idol with a mouth from ear to ear, and a murderous visage" (330), "two exhausted negroes holding up two withered branches of candelabra on the sideboard" (509), and a barber's waxen effigy, "bald as a Musselman": unlike the displays of sexuality and capital, "oriental" exhibition is always incarnated.

Before I detail the embodiment of "oriental" display, I need to consider again the exhibitions of capital and sexuality in *Dombey and Son,* exhibitions whose detachability from the body renders them similar to the oracular voice of Bunsby, Captain Cuttle's laconic prophet, "[a] deep, gruff, husky utterance, which seemed to have no connexion with Bunsby, and certainly had not the least effect on his face." Money's status as "spirit" (rather than flesh) manifests the metaphysical nature that characterizes capital, generally, in the novel. Dombey's identification with another sign of capital is affiliated with the apotheosis of Christ:

> A.D. had no concern with anno Domini, but stood for anno Dombei—and Son. He had risen, as his father had before him, in the course of life and death, from Son to Dombey, and for nearly twenty years had been the sole representative of the Firm. (50)

To be the representative of the Firm is to be he who rises after a course of life and death; to be the sole representative of the Firm is to be the Firm's soul representative. The hint offered by this passage, that Dombey leaves the body behind to become the representative of the Firm is repeated by the novel's dark description of the Son's christening, the solemn ceremony in which he assumes the name of the House. Paul Dombey's interpolation as a sign of capital merges with his funeral:

> 'Please to bring the child in quick out of the air there,' whispered the beadle, holding open the inner door of the church. Little Paul might have asked with Hamlet, 'into my grave?' so chill and earthy was the place . . . Then the

clergyman . . . appeared like the principal character in a ghost story, 'a tall figure all in white;' at sight of whom Paul rent the air with his cries, and never left off again till he was taken out black in the face. (114)

The boy's position as "Son of the Firm" is called his "after-life" (103): the capital of the House's name appears after death.

These accounts of the career of Dombey and Son as characters that take place in "after-life," these depictions of capital as ghosts or epitaphs (someone in the novel aptly notices the difficulty in distinguishing the family from tombstones), dramatize the discrepancy between the displays of capital and the fleshly body. This distinction is registered in different terms in the passage we considered earlier, where the "Son of the Firm" is made the subject of a novel:

> [Dombey] loved his son with all the love he had. If there were a warm place in his frosty heart, his son occupied it; if its very hard surface could receive the impression of any image, the image of that son was there; though not so much as an infant, or as a boy, but as a grown man—the 'Son' of the Firm. (151)

As the quotation marks that surround the "Son" of the Firm indicate, the maturation figured here is a kind of textualization which transcends the flesh: the "warm place" that can shelter the body of the son is replaced by a blank slate that can receive the imprint of his image.

The "after-life" of capital shadows, but remains separate from the fleshly body; correlatively, the "badge or livery" of sexuality is adjacent to, but distinct from it. If the erotic verges or impinges on the bodily form in *Dombey and Son,* it nevertheless falls short of incarnation. Edith Dombey's beauty is a costume *attached to* her figure, a "badge or livery she hates." She sees "*upon* [a prostitute's] face some traces which she knew were lingering in her soul, if not yet written *on* that index" (662, my emphasis). But if the body serves as surface or mannikin, the body remains separate from the words or clothes that constitute sexual display.

While the exhibitions of capital and sexuality are different from the flesh that they work through in *Dombey and Son,* the body itself composes the spectacle that inhabits the dark landscape of Africa, according to "The Noble Savage":

> He sticks a fishbone through his visage, or bits of trees through the lobes of his ears, or birds' feathers in his head . . . he flattens his hair between two

boards, or spreads his nose over the breadth of his face, or drags his lower lip down by great weights, or blackens his teeth, or knocks them out, or paints one cheek red and the other blue, or tattoos himself or oils himself, or rubs his body with fat, or crimps it with knives.

Sexuality is a garment or a text that adorns or inscribes the body; the savage exhibition penetrates and merges with the savage physique. Savage display is a body show, and Dickens's antipathy towards the display which is "the noble stranger" is body hatred:

> Think of the Bushmen. Think of the two men and the two women who have been exhibited about England for some years. Are the majority of persons— who remember the horrid little leader of that party in his festering bundle of hides, with his filth and his antipathy to water, and his straddled legs, and his odious eyes shaded by his brutal hand . . . conscious of an affectionate yearn-ing towards that noble savage, or is it idiosyncratic in me to abhor, detest, abominate, and abjure him? I have no reserve on this subject, and will frankly state that, setting aside that stage of the entertainment when he counterfeited the death of some creature he had shot, by laying his head on his hand, and shaking his left leg—at which time I think it would have been justifiable homicide to slay him—I have never seen that group sleeping, smoking, and expectorating round their brazier, but I have sincerely desired that something might happen to the charcoal smouldering therein, which would cause the immediate suffocation of the whole of the noble strangers.

Dickens's Savage is not merely contained in carnality, wrapped in "a fester-ing bundle of hides," but composed of it: "straddled legs," "odious eyes," "brutal hand," "sleeping, expectorating." The Savage embodiment of ex-hibition is most dramatically enacted when he performs a pantomime: "that stage of the entertainment when he counterfeited the death of some crea-ture he had shot, by laying his head on his hand, and shaking his left leg." Even when the exhibited entity is represented *by,* rather than contained *in* the Savage's physical form, Dickens dwells on and emphasizes the body that presents it.

It is this bodily persistence which makes "dramatic expression" impossi-ble for the "Noble Savage":

> There was Mr. Catlin, some few years ago . . . who had lived among more tribes of Indians than I need reckon up here, and who had written a pictur-esque and glowing book about them. With his party of Indians squatting and spitting on the table before him, or dancing their miserable jig . . . he called, in all good faith, upon his civilized audience to take notice of their symmetry

and grace and perfect limbs, and the exquisite expression of their pantomime. . . . Whereas, as mere animals they were wretched creatures very low
in the scale and very poorly formed; and as men and women possessing any
power of true dramatic expression by means of action, they were no better
than the chorus of an Italian Opera in England—and would have been worse
if such a thing were possible.

The attribution of abstract values ("symmetry," "grace") to the physical
shape of the Noble Savage is given the lie by his actual body—"spitting,"
"squatting," "poorly formed"—just as abstract expression produced "*by
means* of dramatic action" is outside his strictly carnal capacity.

Dickens's insistence on the bodily character of "oriental" exhibition is
most noticeable when it is superimposed on versions of "oriental" spectacle
which were previously identified with the transcendence of the body. The
decline of the flesh of a character called Cleopatra in *Dombey and Son* is
underwritten by her decline *into* flesh: This "wrinkled" and "haggard"
impersonation of the queen of the Nile "certainly [does] not resembl[e]
Shakespeare's Cleopatra, whom age could not wither" (367). The painted
face of the savage has its counterpart in Cleopatra's body: "Such is the
figure, painted and patched for the sun to mock, that is drawn slowly
through the crowds from day to day" (673).

Again, paint not only dwells on the surface of the "oriental" body, it also
penetrates it: "She was soon able to sit up . . . to have a little artificial bloom
dropped into the hollow of her cheeks" (614). "Arranged as Cleopatra," the
entire "oriental" body is directed and defined by the work of exhibition:
"slightly settling her false curls and false eyebrows with her fan, and showing her false teeth, set off by her false complexion" (361–62). In order to
make a spectacle, her languishing "figure" is situated on the death bed once
occupied by Paul Dombey: "the figure . . . substituted for the patient boy's
on the same theatre, once more to connect it . . . with decay and death is
stretched there" (671–72). Here the verb that describes Cleopatra's arrangement characterizes this body as a kind of canvas, a "figure painted and
patched for the sun to mock, drawn slowly through the crowds." "Cleopatra" is not only a body painted, but a body consisting of paint, a drawn
figure.[13]

Instances or inhabitants of the soul, the shows of capital and sexuality are
exempted from the accidents of the flesh. In contrast, "oriental" exhibition
is subject to the susceptibilities and boundaries of the body. "[C]ertainly
not resembling Shakespeare's Cleopatra, whom age could not wither"
(367), Dickens's Cleopatra decays and dies. And her demise is everywhere

defined as the collapse and conclusion of the spectacle with which her body is radically identified. In her twilight, "the eastern star" is like the "exhausted negroes" who hold up the withered candelabra in her house, a decaying display, "a patched and peeling" exhibition, "drawn" "for the sun to mock." Cleopatra's collapse into a "cadaver" is everywhere defined as the collapse of "show": "Mrs Skewton . . . smirk[s] at her cadaverous self in the glass" and then "suffers her maid to prepare her for repose, tumbling into ruins like a house of painted cards" (513).

Dombey and Son's account of Cleopatra's nightly demise suggests that the death of this "oriental" exhibition bears with it the death of exhibition *per se:* "the painted object shrivelled; the form collapsed." I mention the synechdochical force that the novel attributes to Cleopatra's collapse, because it points to the eastern route by which the abstract exhibitions of capital and sexuality are terminated: through their "orientalization," these things, elsewhere separate from the body, merge with it, and are thus subject to bodily death.

The "orientalization" of capital arrests the "process of sublimation" by which Dombey and Son become a name, the "course of life and death" which constitutes capital formation in the novel. Consider the exhibition of Dombey's body in "a dark brown room":

> Mr Dombey . . . finding no uncongeniality in . . . the room, in colour a dark brown, with black hatchments of pictures blotching the walls, and twenty-four black chairs, with almost as many nails in them as so many coffins, waiting like mutes on the threshold of the Turkey carpet; and two exhausted negroes holding up two withered branches of candelabra . . . The owner of the house lived much abroad. . . . and the room had gradually put itself into deeper and still deeper mourning for him, until it was become so funereal as to want nothing but a body in it to be quite complete.
> No bad representative of the body, for the nonce, in his unbending form, if not in his attitude, Mr Dombey looked down into the cold depths of the dead sea of mahogany (509–10)

This passage situates the "body" that Dombey represents as the culmination and center of a dark exhibition that begins with the "black hatchments of pictures blotching the walls," and goes on to gain focus as a solemn ceremony. The body, which, as we have seen, is elsewhere in the novel contradistinguished from the garments of spectacle, is here cast as the "complet[ion]" of the costume of mourning that the room "puts itself into." When it dwells in an "oriental" region, the body is itself made the material of display, rather than merely supplying the surface on which display is worn or inscribed.

And the corpse that completes this dark exhibition is the now embodied form of the abstract display which is capital. In an "oriental" theater, the capital of the House's name, the "sole" and, by implication, the soul representative of the Firm is cast as flesh. The ghostly representative is "orientalized" in a "dark brown room," made part of a landscape inhabited and defined by "exhausted negroes" and Turkish carpets, and, in this dusky context, incorporated.

As Cleopatra indicates, sexuality is similarly incarnated in Dickens's novel when it is cast under the sign of the "orient." The "oriental" embodiment of sexuality is dispersed throughout *Dombey and Son,* sometimes in odd peripheral figurations; it is intimated, for example, in the landscape of Paul Dombey's "arabesque fancies": "[Paul] found out miniature tigers and lions running up the bedroom walls, and squinting faces *leering* in the squares and diamonds of the floor-cloth" (234, my emphasis). And, amongst the "prints and pictures of one voluptuous cast" that festoon Carker's domicile "is the figure of a woman, supremely handsome, who, turning away, but with her face addressed to the spectator, flashes her proud glance upon him. . . . Perhaps it is . . . Potiphar's Wife" (554). In the story of this Egyptian temptress, sexuality is decisively located with the body that is covered by clothes, rather than in the clothes themselves: "And it came to pass . . . that his master's wife cast her eyes upon Joseph; and she said, Lie with me . . . And she caught him by his garment, saying, Lie with me: and he left his garment in her hand, and fled . . ." (Genesis 39:7, 12).[14] Edith's body is sexualized only once in the novel, and that is when it is tied to the "slave market": "There is no slave in a market . . . so shown and offered and examined and paraded . . . as I have been," Edith declares, and here, she is "submitted to the *license* of look and touch" (473, my emphasis). In the African or Near Eastern slave market, the body ceases to be the surface of sexuality and becomes its form, the fleshly object of the licentious touch and gaze.

When the representative of the House is cast as a body by the edge of a sea of mahogany, he is cast as a corpse; when sexuality is figured in the frame of an Egyptian temptress, it decays and dies; when the abstract exhibitions of capital and sexuality are "orientalized" and thus embodied, they are subject to the limits of the flesh. With this in mind, it is time now to return to the scene in *Dombey and Son* where Gay's capitalized, sexualized fantasies disappear, in order to discover an "oriental" body left behind on the path that leads to the secret site of secure estate.

The "oriental" character of Gay's "marvellous" "adventures" appears in a faint but crucial figure that underlies these fantasies:

Walter, so far from forgetting or losing sight of his acquaintance with Florence, only remembered it better and better. As to its adventurous beginning, and all those little circumstances which gave it a distinctive character and relish, he took them into account, more as a pleasant story very agreeable to his imagination . . . than as a part of any matter of fact with which he was concerned . . . Sometimes he thought . . . what a grand thing it would have been for him to have been going to sea on the day after that first meeting, and to have done wonders there . . . to have come back an Admiral . . . and have married Florence (then a beautiful young woman) . . . and borne her away triumphantly . . . So it was that he . . . entertained a thousand indistinct and visionary fancies of his own . . . (173–74)

The boy's daydreams are "a thousand indistinct and visionary fancies" that he "entertains." This phrase alludes to the center of Dickens's fabulous "orient," the locus from which most of its pageantry proceeds in his work, the "Entertainment" that he situates as a primal scene of storytelling, "The Arabian Nights": "The Thousand and One Nights," which, as the title page of Edward William Lane's 1838 translation notes, were "Commonly Called, In England, The Arabian Nights' Entertainments."[15] "Everybody is acquainted with that enchanting collection of stories, the Thousand and One Nights, better known in England as the Arabian Nights' Entertainments," Dickens writes in 1855,[16] and nobody was better acquainted with them than Dickens himself, who, throughout his life, made his writing thick with allusions to "this gorgeous storehouse of Eastern riches."[17]

And these Arabian adventures come to a close in the shape of an insensate body:

[F]lorence gave him her little hand so freely and so faithfully that Walter held it for some moments in his own, and could not bear to let it go.

Yet Walter did not hold it as he might have held it once, nor did *its touch* awaken those old day-dreams of his boyhood that had floated past him sometimes even lately, and confused him with their broken and indistinct shapes. The purity and innocence of her endearing manner, and its perfect trustfulness, and the undisguised regard for him that lay so deeply seated in her constant eyes, and glowed upon her fair face through the smile that shaded—for alas! it was a smile too sad to brighten—it, were not of their romantic race. They brought back to his thoughts the early death-bed he had seen her tending, and the love the child had borne her; and on the wing of such remembrances she seemed to rise up, far above his idle fancies, into clearer and serener air. (335, my emphasis)

The elegiac atmosphere of this passage derives most apparently from the death of Paul Dombey. But even before these lines reach Paul's death bed, they offer the rumor of a death in the "old day-dreams" that Florence's touch does not "awake[n]." The connection between the death of the boy and the stillness of the "old day-dreams" suggested here is extensive in this passage. Consider the conflation of the "romantic race" of Gay's fantasies with the emissary of solemnity, that which "brought back to [Gay's] thoughts the early death-bed." While the "they" that "brings back to his thoughts the early death-bed" refers to the sadness of the dead boy's sister, this antecedent is confused with the "romantic race" of Walter's adventures, as if the early death-bed accommodated these puerile fabulations.

The confusion of Gay's "thousand indistinct and visionary fancies" with a corpse signals and intensifies a similarity between these things. Like the dead boy, the Arabian adventures are a body: the touch of the hand that cannot awaken Gay's day-dreams indicates the fleshly character of their "shape," the bodily character that is the signature of "oriental" exhibition in *Dombey and Son*. And the proximity of this body to Paul Dombey's death brings into play a subsidiary meaning of "awake," a meaning which suggests that Florence's touch does not rouse the body, because no touch could. The early death-bed that Florence tends at the end of this paragraph casts its light back on the body that she touches, but does not awaken; an elegy for a boy extends to become as well an elegy for a boy's fantasies.[18]

Thus the extinction of capital and sexuality, the extinction which makes way for private domestic property in *Dombey and Son*, is figured as the death of an "oriental" incarnation. Like the corpse of the House amongst "exhausted negroes," or the body of Cleopatra, "stretched" on a death-bed, Gay's "delightful adventures"—exhibitions of capital and sexuality, exhibitions elsewhere abstract—are here subject to a bodily demise. If the "transactions of the House" of Dombey and Son involve "most parts of the world" (843), the secure estate that replaces it depends no less on distant regions; the "hushed child" who constitutes this estate rests on the stilled body of the "orient."

Notes

1. Raymond Williams, "The New Metropolis," in *The Country and the City* (New York: Oxford University Press, 1973), 281. All subsequent citations of *The Country and the City* refer to this edition.

2. Charles Dickens, *Dombey and Son* (New York: Penguin Books, 1984), 50. All subsequent citations refer to this edition.

3. This position is first elaborated by K. Marx, *Early Manuscripts*, trans. Martin

Milligan (New York: McGraw-Hill, 1964). For a compact and lucid presentation of an argument that affiliates the identification of private property as exclusive access with the rise of capitalism, see C. B. Macpherson, "The Meaning of Property," in *Property, Mainstream and Critical Positions* (Toronto: University of Toronto Press, 1978). According to Macpherson, property was a heterogenous category prior to "the emergence of full market capitalism," which Macpherson, following Marx's historical narrative, designates as the stage when all value has become governed by the marketplace of capital exchange. While the concept of private possession has always been part of the definition of property, prior to the hegemony of capitalism "theorists, and the law, were not unacquainted with the idea of common property." Even if the category of collective ownership was an idealized or marginalized concept, it nevertheless prevented the equation of property with *private* property. The narrowing of the definition of ownership to private ownership, which he defines as "an exclusive individual right, my right to exclude you from some use or benefit of something," a narrowing which abandons "common ownership . . . the guarantee to each individual that he will not be excluded from the use or benefit of something," assists the ascendancy of full market capitalism with which it coincides: "This of course was exactly the kind of property right needed to let the capitalist market operate. If the market was to operate fully and freely, if it was to do the whole job of allocating labour and resources among possible uses, then all labour and resources had to become, or be convertible into, this kind of property."

4. In "Secret Subjects, Open Secrets" (*Dickens Studies Annual: Essays on Victorian Fiction*, vol. 14 [Carbondale: Southern Illinois University Press, 1985] 17–38) D. A. Miller detects a psychology in *David Copperfield* that is affiliated with the economy in *Dombey and Son*:

> It is as if Heep and Ham, Betsey Trotwood and Jane Murdstone, however much the ethical content of their inwardness may differ, agreed on the paranoid perception that the social world is a dangerous place to exhibit it, and on the aggressive precautions that must be taken to protect it from exposure. To be good, to be bad are merely variants on the primordial condition which either presupposes: to be *in camera* (25).

In this way, I am attempting to register the effort to protect the privacy of the subject of the novel in economic terms, to assess the connection between privacy and property, and between surveillance and capital.

5. The novel's conception of capital as a form of communication accords with the postmodern economics charted by Jean Baudrillard, who argues that the various instances of economic value that inhabit capitalism are all contained as elements in the functioning of the sign, contained as means of signifying value. The terms that constitute the dichotomy of economic value—called variously, exchange value versus use value; the commodity versus labor—and the terms that Baudrillard helpfully collates with the terms of the Saussurian sign—signifier versus signified— are mutually constitutive. Thus, for example, if the exchange value of an object serves to signify its use value, conversely, its use value functions as a referential alibi

which acts to enable the practice of signifying. For Baudrillard, the semiotic character of economic value is manifested most fully in "a fetishism of the signifier." The fetish object is not the site of projected and alienated qualities, "not a fetishism of the signified, a fetishism of substances and values . . . which the fetish object would incarnate for the alienated subject. . . . It is not the passion . . . for substances that speaks in fetishism, it is the *passion for the code*" ("Fetishism and Ideology," in *Critique of the Political Economy of the Sign* [Saint Louis: Telos Press, 1981], 93).

6. In *The Philosophy of Money*, trans. Tom Bottomore and David Frisby (Boston: Routledge and Kegan Paul, 1978; originally published in German in 1907), 244, Georg Simmel describes the unique accessibility of money, its inability to harbor any secret or surprise:

We know more about money than about any other object because there is nothing to know about money and so it cannot hide anything from us. It is a thing absolutely lacking in qualities and therefore cannot, as can even the most pitiful object, conceal within itself any surprises or disappointments.

If money cannot conceal, according to Simmel, it cannot be concealed, according to *Dombey and Son*.

7. Michel Foucault, *The History of Sexuality Volume I: An Introduction*, trans. Robert Hurley (New York: Pantheon 1978), 32.

8. Edward Said, *Orientalism* (New York: Random House, 1979), 39. For an account of specifically literary constructions of the "third world" during the Victorian period, see Patrick Brantlinger, "Victorians and Africans: The Creation of the Dark Continent," *Critical Inquiry* (Autumn 1985), and *Rule of Darkness: British Literature and Imperialism 1830–1914* (Ithaca, N.Y.: Cornell University Press, 1988).

9. Charles Dickens, *Bleak House* (New York: Penguin Books, 1980), 85.

10. In addition to Said, for a discussion of the "orient" as spectacle for imperialist surveillance see, for example, Malek Alloula, *The Colonial Harem* (Minneapolis: University of Minnesota Press, 1986). See also Mark Seltzer's discussion of the construction of London's underground as exotic theater of supervision (*Henry James and the Art of Power* [Ithaca, N.Y.: Cornell University Press, 1984], 29–39).

11. Charles Dickens, *The Mystery of Edwin Drood* (Oxford: Oxford University Press, 1972), 1.

12. Dickens, "The Noble Savage," *Household Words* (June 11, 1853). All subsequent citations refer to this edition.

13. The embodiment of "oriental" exhibition that I am tracing in *Dombey and Son* is a common feature of Victorian fiction. In *Jane Eyre* Bertha Mason, the West Indian Creole, is cast as such an incarnation. The identification of physical "bulk" and "mask" as "oriental" exhibition appears again in *Villette*, when Brontë characterizes the painting of "Cleopatra" as utter carnality and contradistinguishes it from "Vashti," the emblem of disembodied theatrical energy. The embodiment of "oriental" exhibition appears in the sphere of the spectacle, as well as in the sphere of its spectator in *The Mystery of Edwin Drood* and Collins's *The Moonstone*. In Collins's novel the ingestion of opium produces the body of Franklin Blake as exhibit, and in

Drood this ingestion acts on the body of Jaspers to produce the spectacle that he sees. This is emphasized by Jaspers's "trembling frame," a phrase that conflates the body of the opium taker with the boundary of the spectacle. The spectacular "oriental" body may have been encouraged by what Christine Bolt calls the "hardening of race thinking" that takes place in the mid-Victorian period, the various ideological practices that surround the consolidation of the definition of "race" as a physical category. Bolt describes a crucial instance of this "hardening" in the activities of Dr James Hunt: "Rejecting the Enlightenment stress on the similarity of men's bodies, the new society's president, Dr James Hunt, and his followers endeavored . . . to prove the inferiority of blacks by means of craniology and comparative anatomy." ("Race and the Victorians," in *British Imperialism in the Nineteenth Century*, ed. C. C. Eldridge [New York: Macmillan, 1984], 129). Scientific programs of racial difference that developed in conjunction with evolutionary theory both relied upon, and helped reproduce the conception of the body as a sign, as itself a form of display. And, as Hunt's activities suggest, this conception concentrates on the "oriental" physique.

14. A provocative instance of the invocation of the "oriental" as a means of embodying sexuality appears in Jean Baudrillard's analysis of the erotic fetish object as the bodily site on which an abstract sexuality, "bound up in a general stereotype of *models of beauty* . . . the final disqualification of the body, its subjection to a discipline, the total circulation of signs" is reinscribed: "Tattoos, stretched lips, the bound feet of Chinese women, eyeshadow, rouge, hair removal, mascara, or bracelets, collars, objects, jewelry, accessories: anything will serve to rewrite the cultural order on the body; and it is this that takes on the effect of beauty." Baudrillard locates the erotic in the *embodiment* of the abstract, while Dickens, I am arguing, identifies the erotic as abstract, but in either case, whether it be Dickens's identification of the embodiment of sexuality, or Baudrillard's identification of the work of embodiment which is sexuality, the *"oriental"* body is constitutive. "Anything will serve to rewrite the cultural order on the body", but Baudrillard's own account begins with "Tattoos, stretched lips, the bound feet of Chinese women" ("Fetishism and Ideology", 94). A similarly ethnically ordered list appears a little later: "Levi-Strauss has already spoken of this erotic bodily attraction among the Caduveo and the Maori, of those bodies 'completely covered by arabesques of a perverse subtlety,' and of 'something deliciously provocative'" ("Fetishism", 95). My point, of course, is not that the order of Baudrillard's list accurately represents the actual history of the embodiment of sexuality, but rather that Baudrillard's own conception of this embodiment is founded on the "oriental" body.

15. Lane (London: Knight and Co., 1839–41).

16. "The Thousand and One Humbugs," *Household Words* (1855).

17. "The Thousand and One Humbugs." The significance for Dickens of the Arabian Nights as a form of exhibition is amplified by Deborah A. Thomas's report that Dickens was profoundly influenced by them as a model for story telling, seeking to emulate their form in his first fictional efforts. Deborah A. Thomas, *Dickens and the Short Story* (Philadelphia: University of Pennsylvania Press, 1982).

18. See the second entry for "awake" in *The Oxford English Dictionary*: "to rise from a state resembling sleep, such as death" (*The Compact Edition of The Oxford English Dictionary*, vol. I [Oxford: Oxford University Press, 1971], 590–91).

Susan Meyer

Colonialism and the Figurative Strategy of *Jane Eyre*

IN HER CHILDHOOD AND ADOLESCENCE in the late 1820s and 1830s, Charlotte Brontë wrote hundreds of pages of fiction set in an imaginary British colony in Africa. Her stories demonstrate some knowledge of African history and of the recent history of British colonialism in Africa: she makes reference to the Ashanti Wars of the 1820s, uses the names of some actual Ashanti leaders, and locates her colony near Fernando Po, which a writer for *Blackwood's Magazine* had been advocating as an apt spot for British colonization. Other aspects of Brontë's juvenile stories suggest her knowledge of events in the British West Indian colonies as well. Specific tortures used by West Indian planters on rebellious slaves appear in Brontë's early fiction, enacted on both black and white characters, and her most important black character, Quashia Quamina, who leads periodic revolutions against her white colonists, bears the surname of the slave who led the Demerara uprising of 1823 in British Guiana—as well as a first name derived from the racist epithet "Quashee."[1]

Colonialism is also present—and used figuratively—in each of Brontë's major novels. In both *Shirley* (1849) and *Villette* (1853), the men with whom the heroines are in love either leave or threaten to leave Europe for places of European colonization, and both men imagine their relationships with colonized people as standing in for their relationships with white women. In *Shirley*, Louis Moore proposes to go to North America and live with the Indians, and immediately suggests that he will take one of the "sordid savages," rather than Shirley, as his wife.[2] At the end of *Villette* M. Paul departs for the French West Indian colony of Guadeloupe, to look after an estate there, instead of marrying Lucy. Such an estate would indeed have needed supervision in the early 1850s, as the French slaves had just been emancipated in 1848. Brontë suggests the tumultuous state of the colony by the ending she gives the novel: M. Paul may be killed off by one of the tropical storms which Brontë, like writers as diverse as Monk Lewis and

Harriet Martineau, associates with the rage and the revenge of the black West Indians.³ If M. Paul is a white colonist, Lucy is like a native resisting control: Brontë has Lucy think of her own creative impulse as a storm god, "a dark Baal." On the level of these metaphors, the novel's potentially tragic ending becomes more ambiguous: it may not be entirely a tragedy if M. Paul *is* killed by a storm and does not return from dominating West Indian blacks to marry the Lucy he calls "sauvage."⁴

In *The Professor* (1846), white women's resistance to male domination is more overtly figured as "black." The novel begins as an unreceived letter, whose intended recipient has disappeared into "a government appointment in one of the colonies."⁵ William Crimsworth's own subsequent experiences among the young women of a Belgian *pensionnat* are represented as a parallel act of colonization. Crimsworth discreetly compares his Belgian-Catholic girl students to blacks whom he must forcibly keep under control. He likens one Caroline, for example, to a runaway West Indian slave when he describes her curling, "somewhat coarse hair," "rolling black eyes," and lips "as full as those of a hot-blooded Maroon" (86). Even the atypical half-Swiss, half-English Frances Henri whom Crimsworth marries shows a potential rebelliousness against male domination, and her rebelliousness is also figured as "black." Frances tells Crimsworth, with "a strange kind of spirit," that if her husband were a tyrant, marriage would be slavery, and that "[a]gainst slavery all right thinkers revolt" (255). This figure is even more explicit when Frances tells Hunsden, who is matching wits with her in an argument about Switzerland, that if he marries a Swiss wife and then maligns her native country, his wife will arise one night and smother him "even as your own Shakespeare's Othello smothered Desdemona" (242).

Even in the two existing chapters of Brontë's final and unfinished novel *Emma* (1853), race relations seem to be about to play an important figurative role: the heroine's suddenly apparent blackness suggests her social disenfranchisement due to her gender, age, and social class. The two chapters are set in a boarding school and focus on a little girl, known as Matilda Fitzgibbon, who appears at first to be an heiress, but whose father disappears after leaving her at the school and cannot be located to pay her fees at the end of the first term. Matilda is revealed, at the end of the second chapter, to be of a race, or at least a physical appearance, which renders her susceptible to the following insult:

> "[I]f we were only in the good old times," said Mr Ellin, "where we ought to be—you might just send Miss Matilda out to the Plantations in Virginia—sell her for what she's worth and pay yourself."⁶

This revelation has been prepared for by several previous passages. Matilda, the narrator has informed us, has a physical appearance which makes her inadequate as a wealthy "show-pupil," a physiognomy which repels the headmistress and causes her a "gradually increasing peculiarity of feeling" (312), and "such a face as fortunately had not its parallel on the premises" (313). Brontë has also given Matilda the name "Fitz / gibbon," a name which becomes a racist epithet when we realize that it arises out of the racist nineteenth-century scientific commonplace that blacks were low on the scale of being, closer to apes than to white Europeans: Matilda's patronymic brands her the illegitimate offspring of a monkey. Yet in a sense Matilda "becomes" of the race which suggests her liability to enslavement in Virginia only at the moment in the novel at which she loses her social standing: only then do any of those around her make any explicit references to her race or skin coloring, and only then does the reader become aware of what it is that is "repulsive" in her "physiognomy." When Matilda becomes isolated, orphaned, unrooted, and poor—and more vulnerable and sympathetic—she is transformed by the narrative into a black child. In *Emma*, Brontë may have been planning to write a novel which would make literal Jane Eyre's intuition that she is an outsider whom Mrs. Reed could not possibly like, that Mrs. Reed sees her as "an interloper, not of her race."[7]

Brontë uses references to colonized races in these novels to represent various social situations in British society: female subordination in sexual relationships, female insurrection and rage against male domination, and the oppressive class position of the female without family ties and a middle-class income. She does so with a mixture of both sympathy for the oppressed and a commonplace racism: Matilda's patronymic is a racial slur, yet the situation which provokes Mr. Ellin's harsh racism also evokes the reader's sympathy for Matilda. Lucy Snowe's strength of character is one of her most admirable traits—and yet to represent it Brontë invokes the Eurocentric idea of colonized savages. The figurative use of race relations in Brontë's fiction reveals a conflict between sympathy for the oppressed and racism, a conflict which becomes most apparent in *Jane Eyre* (1847).

*   *   *

The figurative use of race is so important to *Jane Eyre* that, much as it begins to be in *Emma*, the figure is enacted on the level of character. In representing an actual Jamaican black woman, Brontë finds herself confronting the non-figurative reality of British race relations. And Brontë's figurative use of blackness in part arises from the history of British colonialism: the function of racial "otherness" in the novel is to signify a generalized oppression. But Brontë makes class and gender oppression the overt significance of racial otherness, displacing the historical reasons why colonized races would suggest oppression, at some level of consciousness, to nineteenth-century British readers. What begins, then, as an implicit critique of British domination and an identification with the oppressed collapses into merely an appropriation of the metaphor of "slavery." But the novel's closure fails, in interesting ways, to screen out entirely the history of British colonial oppression.

This complex figurative use of race explains much of the difficulty of understanding the politics of *Jane Eyre*. In an important first reading of the significance of colonialism in this novel, Gayatri Chakravorty Spivak argues that "the unquestioned ideology of imperialist axiomatics" informs Brontë's novel and enables the individualistic social progress of the character Jane which has been celebrated by "U.S. mainstream feminists." Her reading describes Bertha as a "white Jamaican Creole" who can nonetheless be seen in the novel as a "native 'subject,' " indeterminately placed between human and animal and consequently excluded from the individualistic humanity which the novel's feminism claims for Jane.[8] While I agree with Spivak's broad critique of an individualistic strain of feminism, I find her reading problematic in its analysis of the workings of imperialist ideology and its relation to feminism, both in general and in *Jane Eyre*.

Spivak describes Bertha as at once a white woman and a colonized "native," that is, as what she terms, with little definition, a "native 'subject.' " She is thus able to describe Bertha as either native or white in order to criticize both Brontë's *Jane Eyre* and Jean Rhys's *Wide Sargasso Sea* as manifestations of exclusive feminist individualism. *Jane Eyre*, she argues, gives the white Jane individuality at the expense of the "native" Bertha; *Wide Sargasso Sea*, on the other hand, she contends, retells the story of *Jane Eyre* from Bertha's perspective and thus merely "rewrites a canonical English text within the European novelistic tradition in the interest of the white Creole rather than the native" (Spivak, 253). Bertha is either native or not native in the interests of Spivak's critique. Thus it is by sleight of hand that Spivak shows feminism to be inevitably complicitous with imperialism.

My own proposition is that the historical alliance between the ideology of male domination and the ideology of colonial domination which informs the metaphors of so many texts of the European colonial period in fact resulted in a very different relation between imperialism and the developing resistance of nineteenth-century British women to the gender hierarchy. *Jane Eyre* was written in response to the same ideological context which led Anthony Trollope, in his short story "Miss Sarah Jack of Spanish Town, Jamaica," to describe the fiancée of a post-emancipation West Indian planter with this resonant analogy: "Poor Maurice had often been nearly broken-hearted in his endeavours to manage his freed black labourers, but even that was easier than managing such as Marian Leslie."[9] In *Jane Eyre,* Brontë responds to the seemingly inevitable analogy in nineteenth-century British texts that compares white women with blacks in order, within the framework of a belief in racial hierarchy, to degrade both groups and assert the need for white male control. Brontë uses the analogy in *Jane Eyre* for her own purposes, to signify not shared inferiority but shared oppression. This figurative strategy induces some sympathy with blacks as those who are also oppressed, but does not preclude racism. Yet while for the most part the novel suppresses the damning British history of slavery and racist oppression, its ending betrays an anxiety that colonialism and oppression of other races is a "stain" upon English history and that the novel's own appropriation of the racial "other" for figurative ends bears a disturbing resemblance to that history. Thus while the perspective the novel finally takes toward imperialism is Eurocentric and conservative, I find in *Jane Eyre* not Spivak's "unquestioned ideology" of imperialism, but an ideology of imperialism which is questioned—and then reaffirmed—in interesting and illuminating ways.

An interpretation of the significance of the British empire in *Jane Eyre* must begin by making sense of Bertha Mason Rochester, the mad, drunken West Indian wife whom Rochester keeps locked up on the third floor of his ancestral mansion. Bertha functions in the novel as the central locus of Brontë's anxieties about oppression, anxieties that motivate the plot and drive it to its conclusion. The conclusion then settles these anxieties partly by eliminating the character who seems to embody them. Yet Bertha only comes into the novel after about a third of its action has taken place. As she emerges in the novel, anxieties which have been located elsewhere, notably in the character of Jane herself, become absorbed and centralized in the figure of Bertha, thus preparing the way for her final annihilation.

I read Bertha's odd ambiguity of race—an ambiguity which is marked within the text itself, rather than one which needs to be mapped onto it—as directly related to her function as a representative of dangers which threaten the world of the novel. She is the heiress to a West Indian fortune, the daughter of a father who is a West Indian planter and merchant, and the sister of the yellow-skinned yet socially white Mr. Mason. She is also a woman whom the younger son of an aristocratic British family would consider marrying, and so she is clearly imagined as white—or as passing as white—in the novel's retrospective narrative. And critics of the novel have consistently assumed that Bertha is a white woman, basing the assumption on this part of the narrative, although Bertha has often been described as a "swarthy" or "dark" white woman.[10] But when she actually emerges in the course of the action, the narrative associates her with blacks, particularly with the black Jamaican antislavery rebels, the Maroons. In the form in which she becomes visible in the novel, Bertha has *become* black as she is constructed by the narrative, much as Matilda Fitzgibbon becomes black in *Emma*.

Even in Rochester's telling of the time before their marriage when Bertha Mason was "a fine woman, in the style of Blanche Ingram: tall, dark, and majestic," there are hints, as there are in the early descriptions of Matilda Fitzgibbon, of the ambiguity of her race. Immediately after Rochester describes Bertha as "tall, dark, and majestic," he continues: "[h]er family wished to secure me because I was of a good race" (322). In the context of a colony where blacks outnumbered whites by twelve to one, where it was a routine and accepted practice for white planters to force female slaves to become their "concubines," and where whites on the island were consequently uneasily aware of the large population of mulattoes, Rochester's phrase accrues a significance beyond its immediate reference to his old family name. In this context the phrase suggests that Bertha herself may not be of as "good" a race as he.[11] Bertha is the daughter, as Richard Mason oddly and apparently unnecessarily declares in his official attestation to her marriage with Rochester, "of Jonas Mason, merchant, and of Antoinetta Mason, his wife, a Creole" (318).

The ambiguity of Bertha's race is marked by this designation of her mother as a "Creole." The word "creole" was used in the nineteenth century to refer to both blacks and whites born in the West Indies, a usage which caused some confusion: for instance, in its definition of the word the *OED* cites a nineteenth-century history of the United States in which the author writes: "There are creole whites, creole negroes, creole horses, &c.; and creole whites, are, of all persons, the most anxious to be deemed of pure white blood."[12] When Rochester exclaims of Bertha that "she came of a mad family; idiots and maniacs through three generations! Her mother, the Creole, was both a madwoman and a drunkard!" he locates both madness and drunkenness in his wife's maternal line, which is again emphatically and ambiguously labeled "Creole." By doing so, he associates that line with two of the most common stereotypes associated with blacks in the nineteenth century.[13]

As Bertha emerges as a character in the novel, her blackness is made more explicit, despite Rochester's wish to convince Jane, and perhaps temporarily himself, that "the swelled black face" and "exaggerated stature" of the woman she has seen are "figments of imagination, results of nightmare" (313). But when Jane describes to Rochester the face she has seen reflected in the mirror, the *topoi* of racial "otherness" are very evident: she tells Rochester that the face was

> 'Fearful and ghastly to me—oh sir, I never saw a face like it! It was a discoloured face—it was a savage face. I wish I could forget the roll of the red eyes and the fearful blackened inflation of the lineaments!'
> 'Ghosts are usually pale, Jane.'
> 'This, sir, was purple: the lips were swelled and dark; the brows furrowed: the black eyebrows widely raised over bloodshot eyes.' (311)

The emphasis on Bertha's coloring in this passage—she is emphatically not "pale" but "discoloured," "purple," "blackened"—the reference to rolling eyes and to "swelled," "dark" lips all insistently and stereotypically mark Bertha as non-white. Jane's use of the word "savage" underlines the implication of her description of Bertha's features, and the redness which she sees in Bertha's rolling eyes suggests the drunkenness which, following the common racist convention, Brontë has associated with blacks since her childhood. As Bertha's "lurid visage flame[s] over Jane" while she lies in bed, causing her to lose consciousness, the ambiguously dark blood Bertha has inherited from her maternal line becomes fully evident in a way that recalls a passage from Brontë's African juvenilia. In this passage in her *Roe Head Journal* the revolutionary black African leader Quashia has triumphed in an uprising against the white British colonists, and, having occupied the palace built by the colonists, revels drunkenly, in symbolic violation, on the "silken couch" of the white queen.[14] Like the rebellious Quashia, the Jamaican Bertha-become-black is the novel's incarnation of the desire for revenge on the part of the colonized races, and Brontë's fiction suggests that such a desire for revenge is not unwarranted. The association of Bertha with fire recalls Jane's earlier question to herself:

> What crime was this, that lived incarnate in this sequestered mansion, and could neither be expelled nor subdued by the owner?—what mystery, that broke out, now in fire and now in blood, at the deadest hours of the night? (239)

The language of this passage strongly evokes that used to describe slave uprisings in the British West Indies, where slaves used fires both to destroy property and to signal to each other that an uprising was taking place. White colonists of course responded to slave insurrections with great anxiety, like that expressed by one writer for *Blackwood's* in October 1823, in response to the news of the Demerara slave uprising:

> Give them [the abolitionists] an opportunity of making a few grand flowery speeches about liberty, and they will read, without one shudder, the narrative of a whole colony bathed in blood and fire, over their chocolate the next morning.[15]

Brontë finished writing *Jane Eyre* in 1846, eight years after the full emancipation of the British West Indian slaves in 1838. But the novel itself is definitely set before emancipation. Q. D. Leavis has shown that it may not be possible to pinpoint the closing moment of the novel further than within a range of twenty-seven years, between 1819 and 1846.[16] When Jane says, at the end of her autobiography, "I have now been married ten years," the date is at the latest 1846, the year in which Brontë finished writing the novel; thus Jane's marriage with Rochester takes place in 1836 at the latest. The year before their marriage, Rochester tells Jane that he has kept Bertha locked for ten years in his third-story room ("she has now for ten years made [it] a wild beast's den—a goblin's cell," as he puts it [336]). At the latest, then, Rochester first locked Bertha in that room in 1825, and since he lived with her before that for four years, again, at the latest, they would have been married in 1821. Brontë doubtless meant to leave the precise date of the novel ambiguous—she marks the year of Rochester and Bertha's wedding with a dash in Richard Mason's attestation to their marriage—but it is clear that even at the latest possible dates, events in the novel occur well before emancipation, which was declared in 1834 but only fulfilled in 1838. Brontë may have meant for the events of the novel to occur in the 1820s and 1830s, as I have suggested above, during the years in which, owing to the economic decline of the British sugar colonies in the West Indies, planters imposed increasing hardship on the slaves and increasingly feared their revolt. When Bertha escapes from her ten years' imprisonment to attempt periodically to stab and burn her oppressors, and as Rochester says, to hang her "black and scarlet visage over the nest of my dove" (337), she is symbolically enacting precisely the sort of revolt feared by the British colonists in Jamaica.

But why would Brontë write a novel suggesting the possibility of a slave uprising in 1846, after the emancipation of the British (though not the U.S.

or French) slaves had already taken place? Indeed, in 1846 it was evident that the British West Indian colonies were failing rapidly, and the focus of British colonial attention was shifting to India. While the novel's use of colonialism is most overtly figurative, nonetheless it in part does engage the issue of colonialism on a non-figurative level. The story of Bertha, however finally unsympathetic to her as a human being, nonetheless does indict British colonialism in the West Indies and the "stained" wealth that came from its oppressive rule. When Jane wonders "what crime . . . live[s] incarnate" in Rochester's luxurious mansion "which [can] neither be expelled nor subdued by the owner" (239), the novel suggests that the black-visaged Bertha, imprisoned out of sight in a luxurious British mansion, does indeed "incarnate" a historical crime. Rochester himself describes Thornfield as a "tent of Achan" (328), alluding to Joshua 7, in which Achan takes spoils wrongfully from another people and buries it under his tent, thus bringing down a curse upon all the children of Israel. The third floor of the mansion, where Bertha is imprisoned, Jane thinks, is "a shrine of memory" to which "furniture once appropriated to the lower apartments had from time to time been removed . . . as fashions changed" (137). The symbolically resonant language Brontë uses as Jane tours the house suggests that Thornfield, and particularly its third floor, incarnates the history of the English ruling class as represented by the Rochesters, whom Mrs. Fairfax, acting simultaneously as family historian and guide to the house—that is, guide to the "house" of Rochester in both senses—acknowledges to have been "rather a violent than a quiet race in their time." The atmosphere of the third floor of this "house" is heavy in the novel with the repressed history of crimes committed by a "violent race," crimes which have been removed from sight "as fashions changed." History keeps erupting into the language of this passage, as it does a few sentences later when Jane, climbing out onto the roof of the hall, finds herself on a level with the black rooks which live there, just above Bertha's head, and which are here referred to, with an eerie—and racist—resonance, as "the crow colony" (137). Jane's response to this place dense with history—she is intrigued but "by no means covet[s] a night's repose on one of those wide and heavy beds" (137)—suggests her awareness of the oppressive atmosphere of colonial history and her uneasiness lest she, by lying in the bed of the Rochesters, should get caught up in it.

*   *   *

Brontë's description of the room where Bertha has been locked up for ten years—without a window, with only one lamp hung from a symbolic chain—also reveals her awareness that the black-visaged Bertha, like

Quashia Quamina, has ample reason to be taking revenge on a "violent race." In these moments in *Jane Eyre* Brontë subtly suggests that the history locked up in the English "shrine of memory" is one of "crime incarnate" in Bertha. But the "slavery" which Bertha's coloring and imprisonment suggest has a more deliberate figurative function in the novel. The numerous parallels that Brontë draws between Bertha and other characters suggest that Bertha's most important narrative function is to "incarnate" these parallels, to give them a vivid and concrete form.

The "slave" uprisings that Bertha's nocturnal violence evokes also have a figurative significance. As in her juvenilia and, less prominently, in her other major novels, Brontë uses black slavery in *Jane Eyre* as a figure for economic oppression, a figure that the presence of Bertha illustrates and makes literal. Among those critics who have described issues of social class as central to the politics of *Jane Eyre*, Terry Eagleton finds the novel the most conservative. He sees in *Jane Eyre*, as in all Brontë's novels, a struggle between individualistic bourgeois values and conservative aristocratic values. Eagleton reads Brontë's novels as "myths" which work toward balancing these values, in part through conservative endings in which the protagonists "negotiate passionate self-fulfillment on terms which preserve the social and moral conventions intact" by taking positions within the social system that has oppressed them earlier in the novel.[17] Both Carol Ohmann and Igor Webb see a more radical thrust in *Jane Eyre*, in part because they both consider issues of gender to be as central to the novel as issues of class.[18] Ohmann argues that Brontë is concerned with gender and class "deprivation" in *Jane Eyre*, and that, caught between her conservatism and her radicalism, she offers a solution only on an individual level. But, Ohmann argues, "[i]n the very rendering of Jane Eyre's longing for fulfillment, Brontë conveys a moral imperative with broadly social implications," although the novel does not follow these out (762). Igor Webb sees Jane as the carrier of a "revolutionary individualism" through whom the novel struggles against inequality of gender and class. He too sees the novel as able to achieve revolutionary equality only on an individual level: "the full transformation of society seems daunting, and the novel retreats into its overgrown paradise. This paradise serves at once as a criticism of that other, public world and as an announcement of the deep dispiriting gulf between active self-fulfillment and social possibility" (86). With Ohmann and Webb, I find a more revolutionary impulse in *Jane Eyre* than does Eagleton, and I agree with their emphasis on the novel's dual struggle against class and gender inequality. Yet I find Brontë's struggle against inequality of class both more social and more limited than Ohmann and Webb do. *Jane Eyre* does suggest the need for a broader redistribution of wealth, but it also limits the recipients of this newly-equalized wealth to a specific group, the lower middle class. The novel's position on economic redistribution is worked out through the central figurative elements of racial "otherness," colonialism, and slavery.

As in her early African tales, Brontë uses slavery as an analogy not for the lot of the working class but for that of the lower middle class, for those who are forced into "governessing slavery" as Rochester puts it (298). Jane's governessing at Thornfield becomes like slavery to her only when Rochester arrives with his ruling class friends and she experiences the dehumanizing regard of her class superiors. Before this, those around Jane treat her as a social equal. Mrs. Fairfax helps Jane remove her bonnet and shawl when she first arrives, and Adèle is too young and also of too dubious an origin to treat her governess with superiority. Brontë specifically constructs the atmosphere among the three of them—though significantly *not* between the three of them and the servants—as a utopian retreat from a world where class hierarchy is constantly present. Mrs. Fairfax distinctly marks the exclusion of the working class from this classless utopia when she tells Jane, just after expressing her delight that Jane has come to be her "companion": "you know in winter times one feels dreary quite alone, in the best quarters. I say alone—Leah is a nice girl to be sure, and John and his wife are very decent people; but then you see they are only servants, and one can't converse with them on terms of equality; one must keep them at a due distance for fear of losing one's authority" (128). Some awareness of the costs even of having a class lower than one's own, a problem with which the novel is in general very little concerned, comes through in this passage.

For the most part, however, *Jane Eyre* pays scant attention to the working class. Instead it draws parallels between slavery and Jane's social position as one of the disempowered lower middle class. Both Jane and the narrator draw these analogies, not in response to the work Jane has to perform but in response to the humiliating attitudes of her class superiors. As a child when she first bursts out at John Reed, she cries: "You are like a murderer—you are like a slave-driver—you are like the Roman emperors!" and the adult Jane explains to the reader, "I had drawn parallels in silence, which I never thought thus to have declared aloud" (43). The adult Jane as narrator not only accepts the child's simile but makes it into a more emphatic metaphor when she continues, "I was conscious that a moment's mutiny had already rendered me liable to strange penalties, and, like any *other* rebel slave, I felt resolved, in my desperation, to go all lengths" (44, my emphasis). Later, when Jane has been placed by Brocklehurst on the stool, she thinks of herself as "a slave or victim." The novel itself draws a parallel between slavery and Jane's social position as a child through the character Bertha. Jane's sudden explosion of fury against her treatment at Gateshead occurs in her tenth year there: Mrs. Reed complains to the adult Jane, "to this day I find it impossible to understand: how for nine years you could be patient and quiescent under any treatment, and in the tenth break out all fire and violence" (267). Jane brings herself to "mutiny" and becomes a "rebel slave" in her tenth year, like Bertha who after ten years in her third-floor room "br[eaks] out, now in fire and now in blood."

The imagery of social class slavery recurs in Jane's adulthood in the context of her awareness of the economic inequality between her and Rochester. She comments after their engagement that receiving his valuable gifts makes her feel like a degraded slave, and when he boasts that he will cover her head with a priceless veil, she protests that if he does she will feel "like an ape in a harlequin's jacket" (288). Given the racist nineteenth-century association of blacks with apes, the apparition of Bertha's black face under the embroidered veil incarnates Jane's analogies.

This central passage, in which Jane glimpses Bertha's black face under the wedding veil, reflected in her own mirror, and then watches Bertha tear the veil in half, epitomizes the other form of slavery which Bertha both embodies for Jane and then enables her to avoid. Several feminist critics have commented on this passage, interpreting Bertha as either the surrogate or the double who expresses Jane's rage against the restraints of gender. Sandra Gilbert and Susan Gubar particularly elaborate on this pattern in the novel, describing Bertha as Jane's "dark double," the untamed, animal-like embodiment of Jane's flaming anger.[19] What I would add is an emphasis on the *darkness* of the double, on the way in which, by creating the "savage" Jamaican Bertha as Jane's "dark double," Brontë uses the emotional force of the idea of slavery and of explosive race relations following emancipation in the colonies to represent the tensions of the gender hierarchy in England.

The imagery of slavery is both pervasive in this context in the novel and closely tied to colonial actualities. When Rochester tells Jane, as he narrates the story of his life: "Hiring a mistress is the next worse thing to buying a slave: both are often by nature, and always by position, inferior: and to live familiarly with inferiors is degrading" (339), his words take on a startling resonance in the context of the story he has just told. Rochester acquired a

West Indian fortune by marrying a Jamaican wife and subsequently lived in Jamaica for four years. A wealthy white man living in Jamaica before emancipation would undoubtedly have had slaves to wait upon him, and his Jamaican fortune would have been the product of slave labor, so when Rochester discusses what it is like to buy and live with slaves he knows what he is talking about. When he compares his relationships with women to keeping slaves, then, the parallel is given a shocking vividness by his own history as a slave master. Rochester draws this parallel just after the reader, with Jane, has seen his wife's "black and scarlet" face emerging from her prison, an event that makes clear that it is not only Rochester's mistresses who are his "slaves." When Jane takes warning, then, from Rochester's analogy, Brontë suggests that Jane is learning more than that she would not be wise to become Rochester's lover without legal sanction.

*　　　*　　　*

Jane Eyre associates dark-skinned people with oppression by drawing parallels between the black slaves, in particular, and persons oppressed by the hierarchies of social class and gender in Britain. So far the narrative function of the dark-featured Bertha and of the novel's allusions to colonialism and slavery has a certain fidelity to history, although, as the association between blacks and apes reveals (to take only one example), these analogies are not free from racism. In addition, this use of the slave as a metaphor focuses attention not so much on the oppression of blacks as on the situation of oppressed whites in Britain. Nonetheless, the analogies at least implicitly acknowledge the oppressive situation of the non-white races subjected to the British empire. But oddly, the allusions to dark skin and to empire arise in precisely the opposite context in the novel as well, most strikingly in the descriptions of Blanche Ingram.

The haughty Blanche, with her "dark and imperious" eye (214), whose behavior makes Jane so painfully aware of her own social inferiority, is clearly connected with class oppression only in being of an oppressive class. Yet when Mrs. Fairfax describes Blanche to Jane, she emphasizes her darkness: "she was dressed in pure white," Mrs. Fairfax relates, she had an "olive complexion, dark and clear," "hair raven-black . . . and in front the longest, the glossiest curls I ever saw" (189). When Jane first sees Blanche, she too emphasizes her darkness—"Miss Ingram was dark as a Spaniard," Jane notes—adding that Blanche has the "low brow" which, like dark skin, was a mark of racial inferiority according to nineteenth-century race-science. Rochester directly associates Blanche with Africa: he might be speaking of

Bertha when he tells Jane, with unnecessary nastiness, that his apparent fiancée is "a real strapper . . . big, brown, and buxom; with hair just such as the ladies of Carthage must have had" (248).

These references to Blanche's darkness and to her other similarities to "inferior," dark races, make sense only in the context of the odd phrase "dark and imperious." The use of the word "imperious" to describe Blanche's ruling class sense of superiority evokes the contact between the British and their dark-skinned imperial subjects. In that contact, it was not the dark people who were "imperious," that is, in the position of haughty imperial power, but the British themselves. By associating the qualities of darkness and imperiousness in Blanche, Brontë suggests that imperialism brings out both these undesirable qualities in Europeans, that the British have been sullied, "darkened," and made "imperious" or oppressive by contact with the racial "other," and that such contact makes them arrogant oppressors both abroad, and, like Blanche, at home in England.[20] Blanche's white dresses, her mother's pet name for her ("my lily flower" [207]), and the meaning of her name all emphasize the ironic incongruity between what she tries to be and what she is: rather than embodying ideal white European femininity, this aristocratic Englishwoman is besmirched by the contagious darkness and oppressiveness of British colonialism.

The association of the class oppressor with "dark races" is hinted at in the descriptions of the Reeds as well as the Ingrams. John Reed reviles his mother for "her dark skin, similar to his own" (47), and John grows into a young man with "such thick lips" (122). Mrs. Reed's face in her last illness becomes, like Bertha's, "disfigured and discoloured" (270), while Lady Ingram, who derides governesses in front of Jane, and who within Jane's hearing pronounces that she sees in Jane's physiognomy "all the faults of her class" (206), has features, like Bertha's, "inflated and darkened"—with pride (201). Jane compares John to a Roman emperor; Lady Ingram has "Roman features," and is also associated with the British empire. She has, Jane says, "a shawl turban of some gold-wrought Indian fabric [which] invested her (I suppose she thought) with a truly imperial dignity" (201). The novel draws unflattering parallels between the British empire, evoked by Lady Ingram's Indian shawl, and the Roman empire, whose emperors, the young Jane has said, are murderers and slave drivers. The class oppressiveness of these wealthy Britons, and their dark features, arise, in the novel's symbolic framework, from their association with empire.

With this odd twist, racial "otherness" becomes also the signifier of the oppressor. By using dark-skinned peoples to signify not only the oppressed but also the oppressor, Brontë dramatically empties the signifier of dark skin in her novel of any of its meaning in historical reality and makes it merely expressive of "otherness." By assigning these two contradictory meanings to the signifier "non-white," the novel follows this logic: oppression in any of its manifestations is "other" to the English world of the novel, thus racial "otherness" signifies oppression. This is the most fundamentally dishonest move in the novel's figurative strategy, and the one that reveals the greatest indifference to the humanity of those subject to British colonialism. These passages that associate English oppressors with "dark races" are the most evasive about the reality of British participation in slavery and empire. The novel's anti-colonial politics, it becomes clear, are conservative. The opposition to colonialism arises not out of concern for the well-being of the "dark races" subject to British colonization—the African slaves in the West Indian colonies, the Indians whose economy was being destroyed under British rule—but primarily out of concern for the British who were, as the novel's figurative structure represents it, being contaminated by their contact with the intrinsic despotism and oppressiveness of dark-skinned people.

The novel also associates the gender oppressor with darkness, primarily through Rochester. Rochester's darkness, and the symbolic reason for it, emerge in the central charade passage. The first two scenes Rochester enacts are thinly disguised scenes from his own life. In the first, which enacts the word "bride," Rochester weds a tall, "strapping," dark woman. The second scene enacts the word "well" by representing the meeting of Eliezer with his intended bride, whom, as is the case with Rochester, Eliezer has been directed to wed by his father. The final scene, enacting the word "Bridewell," both suggests the imprisonment attendant upon making such a marriage and symbolizes the effects of Rochester's contact with dark-skinned people in search of fortune. In this scene Rochester is himself fettered like a slave and his face is "begrimed" by a darkness that has rubbed off onto him. That his contact with the colonies is the source of his situation is suggested both by the preceding scenes and by the description of his coat which looks "as if it had been almost torn from his back in a scuffle" (213), like the one he has with Bertha not long afterward.

Rochester's darkness is emphasized when his "begriming" past is alluded to and when he asserts the potentially oppressive power of his position in the gender hierarchy. During the period of Rochester's and Jane's betrothal, Brontë continues to use the imagery of slavery to represent Jane's lesser power in the relationship. But she veers away from making a direct parallel with the British enslavement of Africans by associating Rochester's dominating masculine power over Jane with that not of a British but of an Eastern slave master. This part of the novel is rich in images of Turkish and Persian despots, sultans who reward their favorite slaves with jewels, Indian wives forced to die in "suttee," and women enslaved in Eastern harems. The reality of British participation in slavery arises at one point in this part of the narrative—Rochester echoes the abolitionists' slogan when he tells Jane that she is too restrained with "a man and a brother"—but the novel persistently displaces the blame for slavery onto the "dark races" themselves, directly alluding to slavery only as a practice of dark-skinned people. At one point, for example, the novel uses strong and shocking imagery of slavery to describe the position of wives, but despite references to such aspects of British slavery as slave markets, fetters, and mutiny, the scenario invoked represents not British colonial domination but the despotic, oppressive customs of non-whites. Rochester has just compared himself to "the Grand Turk," declaring that he prefers his "one little English girl" to the Turk's "whole seraglio" (297), to which Jane responds with spirit:

'I'll not stand you an inch in the stead of a seraglio. . . . If you have a fancy for anything in that line, away with you, sir, to the bazaars of Stanboul, without delay, and lay out in extensive slave-purchases some of that spare cash you seem so at a loss to spend satisfactorily here.'

'And what will you do, Janet, while I am bargaining for so many tons of flesh and such an assortment of black eyes?'

'I'll be preparing myself to go out as a missionary to preach liberty to them that are enslaved—your harem inmates amongst the rest. . . . I'll stir up mutiny; and you, three-tailed bashaw as you are, sir, shall in a trice find yourself fettered amongst our hands: nor will I, for one, cut your bonds till you have signed a charter, the most liberal that despot ever yet conferred.' (297–98)

By associating Rochester's position at the top of the oppressive gender hierarchy, like Jane's position at the bottom, with dark-skinned peoples, the novel represses the history of British colonial oppression and, in particular, British enslavement of Africans, by marking all aspects of oppression "other"—non-British, non-white, the result of a besmirching contact with "dark races." Even when Rochester directly asserts his power over Jane, speaking of "attach[ing her] to a chain" (299), the novel compares him to a sultan, rather than to a white-skinned British slave master. All aspects of oppression, in this conservative twist in the novel's figurative strategy, become something the British are in danger of being sullied by, something foreign and "other" to them.

*   *   *

In opposition to this danger—the danger of becoming "begrimed" by the oppression which the novel associates with the dark-skinned—Brontë poses an alternative directly out of middle-class domestic ideology: keeping a clean house.[21] Clean and unclean, healthy and unhealthy environments form a central symbolic structure in the novel. In *Shirley,* Caroline's illness is anticipated by a passage about the arrival of "the yellow taint of pestilence, covering white Western isles with the poisoned exhalations of the East, dimming the lattices of English homes with the breath of Indian plague" (421). Similarly, in *Jane Eyre* Brontë consistently associates unhealthy, contagious environments with racial "otherness" and with oppression. When Rochester decides to leave Jamaica, where he has taken a wife as a "slave," participated in slavery, and become "blackened," the novel poses the opposition between oppressive Jamaica and pure England in terms of atmosphere. As Rochester recounts it:

> [I]t was a fiery West Indian night; one of the description that frequently precede the hurricanes of those climates. Being unable to sleep in bed, I got up and opened the window. The air was like sulphur streams—I could find no refreshment anywhere. Mosquitoes came buzzing in and hummed sullenly around the room . . . the moon was setting in the waves, broad and red, like a hot cannon-ball—she threw her last bloody glance over a world quivering with the ferment of tempest. I was physically influenced by the atmosphere. . . . I meant to shoot myself. . . .
>
> A wind fresh from Europe blew over the ocean and rushed through the open casement: the storm broke, streamed, thundered, blazed, and the air grew pure. I then framed and fixed a resolution. (335)

Under the influence of "[t]he sweet wind from Europe" Rochester resolves to return to England, to "be clean" in his own sight (334) by leaving this place of colonial oppression.

In a very similar passage Jane associates oppression and freedom with unhealthy and healthy environments. After she has fled Thornfield and settled at Morton, she reprimands herself for repining: "Whether it is better," Jane asks, "to be a slave in a fool's paradise at Marseilles—fevered with delusive bliss one hour—suffocated with the bitterest tears of remorse and shame the next—or to be a village schoolmistress, free and honest, in a breezy mountain nook in the healthy heart of England?" (386). Jane here imagines the gender and class slavery she would endure as Rochester's mistress as a feverish, suffocating, southern atmosphere.[22]

The damp pestilential fog of Lowood School is one of the novel's most drastically unhealthy environments; the atmosphere at this orphan institution where Jane thinks of herself as "a slave or victim" is the direct result of class oppression. After so many students die of the typhus fever fostered by the unhealthy environment, "several wealthy and benevolent individuals in the county" transform it into a less oppressive institution by the act of cleaning: a new building is erected in a healthier location, and "brackish fetid water" (115) is no longer used in preparation of the children's food.

Creating a clean, healthy, middle class environment stands as the novel's symbolic alternative to an involvement in oppression. As Rochester is engaging in his most manipulative attempt to assure himself of Jane's love, by bringing home an apparent rival, he also orders that his house be cleaned. A great fuss is made over cleaning the house that Jane had innocently thought to be already "beautifully clean and well arranged" (193). But what Rochester most needs to have "cleaned" out of his house as he is trying to obtain an Englishwoman's love is the dark-featured wife in his attic who represents his sullying colonial past, his "marriage" to the colonies. So despite all the cleaning—"such scrubbing," Jane says, "such brushing, such washing of paint and beating of carpets, such taking down and putting up of pictures, such polishing of mirrors and lustres, such lighting of fires in bedrooms, such airing of sheets and feather-beds on hearths, I never beheld, either before or since" (193)—the presence remains in Thornfield which makes Rochester call it "a great plague-house" (173). All that he can do with the "plague" in his house is to hire a woman to "clean" her away into a remote locked room. And as a reminder of this "plague," Grace Poole periodically emerges, amidst all the cleaning, from the third story—"damping" Jane's cheerfulness and causing her "dark" conjectures—in order, as both the most expert cleaner and the signifier of the great "stain" in the house, to give advice to the other servants: "just to say a word, perhaps . . . about the proper way to polish a grate, or clean a marble mantelpiece, or take stains from papered walls" (194).

The other great cleaning activity in the novel occurs as Jane decides to "clean down" Moor House (416), and it marks a more successful attempt at washing away oppression than the one at Thornfield. Jane cleans the house to celebrate the egalitarian distribution of her newly acquired legacy, which will enable her to live there happily with her new-found family. Brontë writes of Jane's "equal" division of her fortune using the rhetoric of a revolution against class oppression, although that division symbolically represents a redistribution of wealth in favor of only a limited group of people, the lower middle class. When St. John tells Jane that he, Diana, and Mary will be her brother and sisters without this sacrifice of her "just rights," she responds, in a tone of passionate conviction which Brontë obviously endorses:

> Brother? Yes; at the distance of a thousand leagues! Sisters? Yes; slaving amongst strangers! I wealthy—gorged with gold I never earned and do not merit! You, penniless! Famous equality and fraternization! Close union! Intimate attachment! (413)

This sort of redistribution of wealth, Brontë suggests, giving Jane the language of the French revolution—"Liberté! Egalité! Fraternité!"—will right the wrongs of the English lower middle class and clean from it the mark of blackness which represents oppression. Its women will no longer have to "slave" among strangers like blacks; its men will no longer have to venture into the distant, dangerous environment of the "dark races" in the colonies. With Jane, Brontë redefines the claims of "brotherhood," as her plot redistributes wealth: truly acknowledged "fraternity," the novel suggests, requires distributing wealth equally, not letting a brother or sister remain a penniless "slave."

But to only a limited group among those who might ask "Am I not a man and a brother?" does the novel answer "Yes." The plot of *Jane Eyre* works toward a redistribution of power and wealth, equalization, and an end to oppression just as Jane herself does, but its utopia remains partial; its "revolution" improves only the lot of the middle class, closing out both the working class and those from whom the figure of "slavery" has been appropriated in the first place. As Jane phrases her "revolution," it is one which specifically depends on erasing the mark of racial "otherness."

To signify her utopian end to economic injustice, Jane creates a clean, healthy environment, free of plague: her aim, she tells St. John, is "to *clean down* (do you comprehend the full force of the expression?) to *clean down* Moor House from chamber to cellar" (416). Jane works literally to "set her own house in order," creating a clean, healthy, egalitarian, middle-class, domestic environment as the alternative to oppression. This environment is not, however, to the taste of St. John, who wants to force Jane into an inegalitarian marriage and to take her to the unhealthy atmosphere of

British India (both of which she says would kill her) to help him preach to dark-skinned people his rather different values of hierarchy and domination. Jane recognizes this difference in mentality and their incompatibility when St. John does not appreciate her house-cleaning: "[t]his parlour is not his sphere," she realizes, "the Himalayan ridge, or Caffre bush, even the plague-cursed Guinea Coast swamp, would suit him better" (419).

Instead of deciding that it is her vocation to enter this new environment of plague, "dark races," and hierarchical oppression, Jane feels "called" to return to a house which, being larger and more stained by oppression, will be more difficult to "clean down"—Rochester's Thornfield. But of course when she gets there she finds that this "plague-house" has already been "*cleaned down.*" The plot of the novel participates in the same activity as Jane—cleaning, purifying, trying to create a world free of oppression. And Brontë's plot works precisely in the terms of the rhetoric of Jane's "revolution." It redistributes wealth and equalizes gender power, and it does so by cleaning away Bertha, the staining dark woman who has represented oppression.

In the ending of the novel, Brontë creates the world she can imagine free of the forms of oppression that the novel most passionately protests against: gender oppression and the economic oppression of the lower middle class. In the utopian ending of the novel lies much of the revolutionary energy which made its contemporary readers anxious: the novel enacts Brontë's conception of a gender and middle class revolution. The mutilation of Rochester (which interestingly has made critics of the novel far more uneasy than the killing of Bertha) together with the loss of his property in Thornfield redistributes power between him and the newly-propertied Jane. Jane tells her former "master" emphatically that she is now both independent and rich: "I am," she says, "my own mistress" (459). And in the last chapter Jane explicitly describes their marriage as egalitarian, unlike most: "I hold myself supremely blest beyond what language can express; because I am my husband's life as fully as he is mine" (475). The ending of the novel also severely punishes Rochester for his acquisition of colonial wealth. Fulfilling Rochester's own allusion to the accursed wealth wrongfully stolen by Achan, Brontë's ending enacts a purification like that of Achan who is "stoned with stones and burned with fire" (Joshua 7:25) for bringing the "accursed thing" into the camp of Israel. Unlike Achan, Rochester survives, but his "tent of Achan," his luxurious, oppressive "plague-house," is destroyed and his misbegotten wealth exorcised from the novel.

But this revolution against gender oppression and the economic oppression of the middle class, and even this purifying away of ill-gotten colonial wealth, is made possible by another sort of oppression and suppression. The revolution behind Jane's revolution is that of the black woman whom the novel has used to signify both the oppressed and the oppressor. Bertha institutes the great act of cleaning in the novel, which burns away Rochester's oppressive colonial wealth and diminishes the power of his gender, but then she herself is cleaned away by it, burned and purified from the novel. Brontë creates the racial "other" as the incarnate signifier of oppression, and then makes this sign, by the explosive instability of the situation it embodies, destroy itself.

Jane Eyre ends with a glimpse of the purified, more egalitarian world created by this figurative sacrifice of the racial "other," Brontë's complex working-out of culturally available metaphors. But the novel does not end as peacefully as we might expect after this holocaust of the sign of racial "otherness" and oppression. The ending betrays Brontë's uneasiness about her own figurative tactics, about the way in which her use of racial "otherness" as a signifier involves a brutal silencing, an erasing of the humanity of the actual people inside the bodies marked "other."

This uneasiness becomes evident in the way the spectre of the racial "other" remains to haunt the ending of the novel, although evaporated into the form of the "insalubrious" mist which hovers over Ferndean, where Jane and Rochester settle after the "cleaning down" of Thornfield (455). The dank and unhealthy atmosphere of Ferndean disrupts the utopian elements of the ending, indicating that the world of the novel is still not fully purified of oppression. And the oppression which that mist must signify now that it no longer refers to class or gender oppression, is that original oppression which on one level the novel has tried so hard to displace and repress: the oppression of dark-skinned people by the British.

The atmosphere of Ferndean recalls the fact that, even if Rochester's tainted colonial wealth has been burned away, the wealth Jane is able to bring him, enabling her to meet him on more equal terms—and the wealth she earlier distributes in such a scrupulously egalitarian and "revolutionary" spirit—has a colonial source. It comes from her uncle in Madeira, who is an agent for a Jamaican wine-manufacturer, Bertha's brother. And the location of Jane's uncle John in Madeira, off Morocco, on the West African coast, where Richard Mason stops on his way home from England, also evokes, through Mason's itinerary, the triangular route of the British slave traders, and suggests that John Eyre's wealth is implicated in the slave trade. The details of the scene in which Brontë has Jane acquire her fortune mark Jane's economic and literary complicity in colonialism as well. St. John announces Jane's accession to fortune by pulling the letter out of a "morocco pocket-book" (404), and he is able to identify Jane as the heiress because she has written her name, on a white sheet of paper, in "Indian ink" (407).

In this way the novel connects the act of writing with colonialism. Specifically writing "Jane Eyre," creating one's own triumphant identity as a woman no longer oppressed by class or gender—or writing *Jane Eyre,* the fiction of a redistribution of wealth and power between men and women—depends on a colonial "ink." Whether advertently or not, Brontë acknowledges that dependence in the conclusion of *Jane Eyre.* Like colonial exploitation itself, bringing home the spoils of other countries to become commodities such as Indian ink,[23] the use of the racial "other" as a metaphor for class and gender struggles in England commodifies colonial subjects as they exist in historical actuality and transforms them into East or West "Indian ink," ink with which to write a novel about ending oppression in England.

The eruption of the words "Indian ink" into the novel suggests, at some level, Brontë's uneasiness about the East Indian colonialism to which England was turning in 1848, as well as about the West Indian colonies which were by then clearly becoming unprofitable after the abolition of slavery. St. John, the East Indian missionary who is given the last words in the novel, writes them as he is dying—killed off by the "insalubrious" atmosphere of oppression in British India, as Rochester just misses dying when his West Indian plague-house collapses on him. Brontë's anxiety about British colonialism is everywhere apparent in the ending of *Jane Eyre.* The novel is finally unable to rest easily in its figurative strategy and its conservative anti-colonial politics: its opposition to a "contaminating" and self-destructive contact with the colonies, and its advocacy of a middle-class domesticity freed from some of the most blatant forms of gender and class oppression. *Jane Eyre* is thus a fascinating example of the associations—and dissociations—between a resistance to the ideology of male domination and a resistance to the ideology of colonial domination.

The critique of colonialism which the novel promises to make through its analogy between forms of oppression finally collapses into a mere uneasiness about the effects of empire on domestic social relations in England. That disquietude is the only remnant of Brontë's potentially radical revision of the analogy between white women and colonized races, and it is the only incomplete element in the ideological closure of the novel.

The insalubrious mist which suggests British colonial contact with the racial "other," diffused throughout the ending of the novel, betrays Brontë's lingering anxiety about British colonialism and about her own literary treatment of the racial "other," about the way in which, through oppressive figurative tactics, she has tried to make the world of her novel "clean."

Notes

1. See Christine Alexander, *The Early Writings of Charlotte Brontë* (Oxford: Basil Blackwell, 1983), 30. This work provides a detailed summary of the plots of Charlotte Brontë's juvenile writings as well as an analysis of Charlotte Brontë's development as a writer as manifested in this early fiction. Alexander is currently working on an authoritative edition of the Charlotte Brontë juvenilia, the first volume of which has now been published as *An Edition of the Early Writings of Charlotte Brontë: 1826–1832,* ed. Christine Alexander (New York: Basil Blackwell, 1987).

2. Charlotte Brontë, *Shirley* (1849; rpt. New York: Oxford University Press, 1981), 613.

3. In "The Isle of Devils," a thinly disguised verse-narrative about race relations in the British West Indies, Lewis creates a horrible monster, "black as the storm," who rapes a beautiful white virgin after her ship is wrecked near his island during a tempest. (Matthew Gregory Lewis, "The Isle of Devils" [1815], in his *Journal of a West India Proprietor* [London: John Murray, 1834], 261–87.) In Martineau's far more progressive and self-aware anti-slavery novel, *Demerara,* a West Indian hurricane enacts the rage the slaves themselves cannot: the slaves in her novel exult at the ravages the storm commits on their master's property, cry out with "horrid yells" as they watch their overseer drowning, and seem "like imps of the storm." (Harriet Martineau, *Demerara,* in *Illustrations of Political Economy* [London: Charles Fox, 1834], II: 109–12.) Brontë herself uses similar imagery in her juvenile *Roe Head Journal.*

4. Charlotte Brontë, *Villette* (1853; rpt. New York: Penguin Books, 1983), 404. For a discussion of the abolition of slavery in the French West Indian colonies, see F. R. Augier, S. C. Gordon, D. G. Hall, and M. Reckord, *The Making of the West Indies* (London: Longmans, 1960), 200–01 and J. H. Parry and P. M. Sherlock, *A Short History of the West Indies* (New York: Macmillan, 1957), 219. Parry and Sherlock note that "[t]he events of 1848–49, which marked the end of slavery, foreshadowed also the end of white political supremacy . . . in Martinique and Guadeloupe."

5. Charlotte Brontë, *The Professor,* ed. Margaret Smith and Herbert Rosengarten (1846; rpt. Oxford: Clarendon Press, 1987), 14.

6. Charlotte Brontë, *Emma,* appended to *The Professor,* ed. Smith and Rosengarten, pp. 322–23. Ellin's "joke" becomes even less amusing when we recall that Miss Wilcox would have been prevented from selling Matilda as a slave not because black slavery no longer existed in Virginia—slavery in the United States lasted through the end of the Civil War in 1865—but simply because England had abol-

ished the slave trade in 1808. For an account of the abolition and emancipation movements in England see Michael Craton, *Sinews of Empire: A Short History of British Slavery* (Garden City, New York: Anchor Books, 1974), 239–84.

7. Charlotte Brontë, *Jane Eyre* (1847; rpt. New York: Penguin Books, 1984), 48.

8. Gayatri Chakravorty Spivak, "Three Women's Texts and a Critique of Imperialism," *Critical Inquiry* 12 (Autumn 1985): 243–61. Two other critics have made brief allusions to the significance of race in *Jane Eyre*. In "Rochester as Slave: An Allusion in *Jane Eyre*," *Notes and Queries* 31 (March 1984) R. J. Dingley notes that Rochester uses the phrase "a man and a brother" in speaking to Jane (66). Dingley interprets the phrase as Rochester's impulsively premature declaration that the intensity of his passion makes him Jane's "slave." Patricia Beer frames the chapter on Charlotte Brontë in her *Reader, I Married Him: A Study of the Women Characters of Jane Austen, Charlotte Brontë, Elizabeth Gaskell and George Eliot* (New York: Barnes & Noble, 1974), 84–126, by suggesting that the novel draws an analogy between women and slaves and noting that Brontë, unlike Jane Austen, made "serious . . . comment" on this form of the "slave trade" (84), but she goes no further in exploring the analogy.

9. Anthony Trollope, "Miss Sarah Jack of Spanish Town, Jamaica," in his *Tourists and Colonials,* ed. Betty Jane Slemp Breyer (Fort Worth, Tex.: Texas Christian University Press, 1981), 8.

10. See, for example, Adrienne Rich's reference to Bertha's "dark sensual beauty," "Jane Eyre: The Temptations of a Motherless Woman," (1973) reprinted in her *On Lies, Secrets, and Silence: Selected Prose 1966–1978* (New York: Norton, 1979), 99, or Sandra Gilbert and Susan Gubar's description of Bertha as "a Creole—swarthy, 'livid,' etc. " (*The Madwoman in the Attic* [New Haven, Conn.: Yale University Press, 1979], 680 n).

11. For a discussion of the practices of and attitudes toward interracial sex and manumission in the English colonies, see Winthrop Jordan, *The White Man's Burden: Historical Origins of Racism in the United States* (New York: Oxford University Press, 1974), 70–73, and Craton, *Sinews of Empire*, 176, 181–86, 223–26.

12. J. M. Ludlow, *History of the United States* (1862), quoted in *The Compact Edition of the Oxford English Dictionary* (New York: Oxford University Press, 1981), I:601.

13. For the association of the racial "other" with madness, see Sander Gilman, *Difference and Pathology: Stereotypes of Sexuality, Race, and Madness* (Ithaca, N.Y.: Cornell University Press, 1985), esp. 131–49. A more lengthy discussion of the ambiguity of the word "Creole" appears in Christopher Miller, *Blank Darkness: Africanist Discourse in French* (Chicago: University of Chicago Press, 1985), 93–107.

14. Only excerpts from this journal entry, which begins "Well here I am at Roe Head," have been published. One excerpt appears in Alexander, *The Early Writings of Charlotte Brontë,* 148. A different, but partially overlapping, excerpt appears in Fannie Elizabeth Ratchford, *The Brontës' Web of Childhood* (1941; rpt. New York: Russell and Russell, 1964), 114.

15. "The West India Controversy," *Blackwood's Edinburgh Magazine* 14 (October 1823): 442.

16. Q. D. Leavis, "Notes," in *Jane Eyre,* 487–89.

17. Terry Eagleton, *Myths of Power: A Marxist Study of the Brontës* (New York: Barnes and Noble, 1975), 4, 16.

18. Carol Ohmann, "Historical Reality and 'Divine Appointment' in Charlotte Brontë's Fiction," *Signs* 2 (1977), 757–78 and Igor Webb, *From Custom to Capital: The English Novel and the Industrial Revolution* (Ithaca, N.Y.: Cornell University Press, 1981), esp. 70–86.

19. See Patricia Meyer Spacks, *The Female Imagination* (New York: Knopf, 1972), 64–65; Rich, 97–99; and Gilbert and Gubar, 336–71, especially 359–62.

20. For an excellent discussion of the European fear of "going native" in the colonies, which includes a discussion of Kurtz in Conrad's *Heart of Darkness,* see Patrick Brantlinger, "Victorians and Africans: The Genealogy of the Myth of the Dark Continent," *Critical Inquiry* 12 (Autumn 1985): 166–203, esp. 193–98. Brantlinger argues that "[t]he potential for being 'defiled'—for 'going native' or becoming 'tropenkollered'—led Europeans again and again to displace their own 'savage' impulses onto Africans" (196).

21. For two very interesting discussions of the Victorian bourgeoisie's equation of dirt and pollution with the "lower orders," see Leonore Davidoff's analysis of the relationship between the upper-middle-class A. J. Munby and his servant Hannah Cullwick in "Class and Gender in Victorian England," in *Sex and Class in Women's History,* ed. Judith L. Newton, Mary P. Ryan, and Judith R. Walkowitz (Boston: Routledge and Kegan Paul, 1983), 17–71, and Peter Stallybrass and Allon White, *The Politics and Poetics of Transgression* (Ithaca, N.Y.: Cornell University Press, 1986), 125–48..

22. Patricia Beer also notes that "the fresh air and the open countryside remain for [Jane] symbols of personal freedom and independence" which she opposes to the thought of suffocation as Rochester's "slave." Beer (see note 8, above), 126.

23. Ironically, the name "Indian ink" or "India ink" is a misnomer: the black pigment was actually made in China and Japan. The term entered the English language in the seventeenth century, according to the OED, when the word "India" was used more broadly for the region of southern Asia to the east of the Indus river, and the British were just beginning to engage in trade with the East.

Wai-chee Dimock

Ahab's Manifest Destiny

"IN MY PROUD, HUMBLE WAY—a shepherd-king,—I was lord of a little vale in the solitary Crimea; but you have now given me the crown of India."[1] With characteristic effusion Herman Melville writes to Nathaniel Hawthorne to thank him for his "joy-giving and exultation-breeding" letter about *Moby-Dick*. The effusion is characteristic, not only in sentiment but also in expression, because it is something of a habit for Melville to convey his authorial aspirations in the idiom of empire. Earlier, in *Mardi,* he has fancied himself a "monarch."[2] That fancy has apparently survived— *Redburn* and *White-Jacket* notwithstanding—and Melville now returns to it, to give it yet another airing. *Moby-Dick,* he says, is to be an "imperial folio," one designed to capture the "revolving panoramas of empire on earth."[3] The same conceit, and perhaps an attendant sense of kinship, seem also to have prompted his curious tribute to Nicholas the Czar, whose "ringed crown of geographical empire encircles an imperial brain" and in whose shadow "the plebeian herds crouch abased" (129).

Whatever hopes Melville might entertain about an "imperial brain," a "geographical empire" is clearly not his to have. Not an actual one, at any rate. Yet writing an "imperial folio" is in some ways almost as gratifying as ruling an empire, as his own experience in *Mardi* suggests. *Moby-Dick* will not, all the same, be as imperial or as free as *Mardi,* for unlike the sovereign author of the earlier book, Melville has no illusions now about his absolute dominion. The reception of *Mardi* and the writing of *Redburn* and *White-Jacket* have taught him at least a hostile regard for the reader. *Moby-Dick* is, in that sense, very much a sequel to its predecessors: it takes up old grudges, settles them, and compensates for them, but also derives from them a keener sense of the adversarial and, correspondingly, a subtler and more effective instrument of control. Where *Mardi* casually dismisses the reader as a docile specter, *Moby-Dick* is anything but casual. Having constituted his audience as a category of threat, the author must proceed to erect defenses.

The most powerful defense, for Melville, is the idea of an autonomous literary domain. If readers everywhere are tyrannous and despicable, if these "ocean barbarians" have taken over what he once claimed as his own, authorial freedom might be recovered only by positing a transcendent realm, at once independent of its environment and impervious to it. The spatial goal in *Moby-Dick* is therefore exactly the obverse of that in *Redburn* and *White-Jacket*. If Melville's project there is to designate a seat of malaise, his project in *Moby-Dick* is to locate an island of immunity. In either case, he is committed to an institution of the discrete, a faith in the self-contained and self-sufficient. This commitment accounts for the recurring images of charmed insularity in *Moby-Dick*. The ambergris is one such example: Melville marvels that the "incorruption of this most fragrant [substance] should be found in the heart of such decay" (343). No less marvelous, the doubloon, "nailed amidst all the rustiness of iron bolts and the verdigris of copper spikes, yet, untouchable and immaculate to any foulness, it still preserved its Quito glow" (359).

Untouchable and immaculate, eternally enclosed and eternally secure, ambergris and doubloon are emblems of the literary masterpiece Melville would like to produce. Like that masterpiece, they too are models of freedom: they are free from their environment, free from contagion and even from kinship. Such then is Melville's ideal image of the book, transposed, we might say, into material forms. Oddly, these material forms, transcendingly free as they are, nevertheless come equipped with an environment, understood to be corrupt and hostile, against which and in defiance of which they can measure their own freedom. For ambergris and doubloon happen to be surrounded by "decay" (343) and "foulness," "ruthless crew" and "ruthless hands" (359). To be the marvels that they are, they must be accompanied by something distinctly unmarvelous. The inviolate needs a corrupt world to prove its inviolability. Even in Melville's logic, freedom is always part of a complementary formation, set in a landscape of polarized attributes and discrete repositories. Freedom not only entails an obverse; it is itself constituted by that obverse.

The complementary logic here—the genesis of freedom alongside an obverse—is worth noting, for such a logic, I suggest, is ultimately not peculiar to doubloon and ambergris, and not peculiar to the literary text of which they are the material emblems. It is, more generally, the logic of the "imperial" self, and, even more generally, the logic of an "empire for liberty." In each case, freedom is only the positive pole within a double formation, a constitutive polarity of terms. Within this context, the emblematic polarity in *Moby-Dick*—the polarity between the incorruptible ambergris and the

surrounding corruption, between the untarnishable doubloon and its tar-
nished habitat—must appear as no more than a memorable variation on a
familiar theme. What animates this polarity, what gives it its characteristic
structure, is not merely a logic of the literary text, but equally a logic of the
self and, beyond the self, a logic of the nation: all three of them being double
formations, all three bodying forth, separately and together, a kindred logic
of freedom and dominion, sovereignty and subjection.

All of this would seem to align *Moby-Dick* directly with *Mardi,* a book
even more enamored of freedom, and even more haunted by freedom's
obverse. One important difference, however, sets the two books apart, and
makes them contrary testimonies in Melville's poetics. In *Mardi,* freedom is
primarily a sovereign right, something that the author claims for himself
and that enables him to write as he pleases. In *Moby-Dick,* however, freedom is primarily a disciplinary postulate, something that the author im-
putes to his characters and that enables him to judge them, as free agents,
responsible and punishable for their deeds. Freedom of this sort points to a
negative individualism: one that produces individuals as "subjects," figures
whose very freedom of action already constitutes the ground for discipline.

The self as "subject" is nothing new in Melville; in *Redburn* and *White-
Jacket* he has offered himself, the persecuted artist, as one such example. But
here, too, *Moby-Dick* seems to have departed from its predecessors and gone
beyond their purview, for if Melville has previously invoked the subjected
self as a token of the reader's dominion, he is now able to use the same
figure, paradoxically, as an instrument of his own sovereignty. The negative
individualism in *Moby-Dick,* then, is one that actually empowers its author,
allowing him to govern his characters, to dispense justice and assign destiny—and to do so by an internal mechanism, namely, by constituting his
characters as agents of that justice and that destiny. Under this new dispen-
sation, Melville's own exercise in freedom will entail a corresponding
attribution of freedom; his own authorial sovereignty will reside in the
creation of fictive characters as sovereign subjects.

Sovereign subjects abound in *Moby-Dick,* and not just human ones, but
specimens from the animal kingdom as well:

> It does seem to me, that herein we see the rare virtue of a strong individual
> vitality, and the rare virtue of thick walls, and the rare virtue of interior
> spaciousness. Oh, man! admire and model thyself after the whale! Do thou,
> too, remain warm among ice. Do thou, too, live in this world without being
> of it. Be cool at the equator; keep thy blood fluid at the Pole. (261)

If the whale had been human, it would have been applauded as a hero, a hero of Jacksonian individualism. Not being human, it is applauded in *Moby-Dick* as a heroic beast, a model of transcendent freedom, one that "live[s] in this world without being of it." But if the whale is free, its freedom is measured, nonetheless, not in and of itself, but over and against something else. Its "strong individual vitality" inheres, after all, in its ability to defy its environment, to stay cool at the equator and warm among ice. The whale is something of a defensive model, and from that standpoint its "thick walls" and "interior spaciousness" become vital assets.

Still, if this is a defensive model, the defense turns out to be not literal (since whales do get killed regularly in the course of the book), but literary. What the whale defies is the unworthy reader, the "timid untravelled man [who tries] to comprehend" it (378). To that reader, the whale "is an unwritten life" (118); it will always be "that one creature in the world which must remain unpainted to the last" (228). Even Ishmael, neither timid nor untraveled, finds himself utterly at a loss here: "If then, Sir William Jones, who read in thirty languages, could not read the simplest peasant's face . . . how may unlettered Ishmael hope to read the awful Chaldee of the Sperm Whale's brow?" (292–93). Melville has every reason, then, to call his book *Moby-Dick* (rather than *Ahab* or *Ishmael* or *The Fatal Voyage of the "Pequod"*), for as a literary model, especially a defensive one, the whale indeed has no match. It will always resist the reader, it will triumph over him, because its transcendent freedom is also a kind of transcendent illegibility: it cannot be read, because it refers to nothing other than itself. It luxuriates in what John Irwin calls "divine indeterminacy," a condition that prevails when the sign is simply its own representation.[4] The whale is doubly autonomous then, doubly self-contained, not only in its physical compass, but also in its circularity of reference.[5] Its "divine indeterminacy" reconstitutes the "imperial folio" as self-referential text.

Thus far, self-containment would seem nothing but a positive asset, something that protects both the whale and the book that is named after the whale from the unworthy and the sacrilegious. Yet, as we all know, protection is only half the story. For the whale also happens to be an engine of destruction. Only a few chapters earlier (chapter 76), its sublimely indeterminate head has appeared as a repository of "battering-ram power" (284), an "impregnable, uninjurable wall" capable of "inconsiderable braining feats" (285), the most spectacular of which is no doubt performed by Moby-Dick's "solid white buttress" (468). Self-containment, at least in the whale, is responsible for the "doom of boats, and ships, and men" (292). The "thick walls" that ensure freedom are also the "dead, blind wall" (284) that kills.

The strange conjunction here, between freedom as idealized privilege and freedom as destructive agency, should not surprise us, for it is just this conjunction, this yoking together of contrarieties, that commends the whale to Melville. In its alternate freedom and dominion, the whale is finally no more than an exceptionally enviable specimen in the gallery of double entities we have thus far examined. The achievement of *Moby-Dick* lies precisely in its ability to normalize this doubleness, by segregating it in such a way that the polarities seem to occupy two entirely different realms. Freedom, by this arrangement, becomes primarily a literary privilege: it belongs to the author, conferring on him a sovereignty he is understood to command absolutely. Dominion, on the other hand, becomes primarily a punitive consequence: it inflicts itself on the fictive individual, conferring on him a fate he is understood himself to have incurred.

In Ahab, we see both principles at work. The punitive logic dictates his end, of course, but the literary logic measures his offense. That offense is grave indeed—altogether unpardonable from a certain standpoint. Ahab is a monstrous reader, as a number of critics have suggested; his monomania threatens to reduce indeterminate text to determinate meaning.[6] His goal is to penetrate "that inscrutable thing" (144), the "impregnable, uninjurable wall" (285) that is both whale and text: "If man will strike, strike through the mask! How can the prisoner reach outside except by thrusting through the wall? To me, the white whale is that wall, shoved near to me" (144). If Ahab were to have his way, the category of the "inviolate" would exist no more, and neither doubloon, nor ambergris, nor even a literary text, could find refuge in it. That would be a blow indeed to Melville. For this, if for no other reason, Ahab is doomed never to have his way. *Moby-Dick*, in that respect, once again allegorizes the author's battle for sovereignty. It also allegorizes his revenge on the reader.

Ahab's sins, as a reader or otherwise, have been abundantly documented. My focus in this essay, however, will not be on those sins, but on the punitive logic his author administers. To dispatch Ahab, to disarm him, to make him die not only inevitably but also deservedly, Melville needs an executory instrument, a logic that explains and justifies the fate of this character. That logic is only too easy to come by, for it is already a provision in individualism. What we might expect to find in Ahab, then, is an individualism that afflicts its bearer, one that apprehends and incriminates, one that disciplines the self in its very freedom. And that, in fact, is what we do find.

Being a product of individualism, Ahab is by definition a free agent. But, since his individualism happens to be the negative variety, he is, also by definition, an overdetermined character. He is both doomed and free: free, that is, to choose his doom. This is a strange logic, to say the least, but within the terms of negative individualism, nothing is more reasonable, or more necessary, for such a logic—a logic that inscribes discipline in freedom—is just what makes the autonomous self governable as such. Embracing this logic, *Moby-Dick* will find itself in intimate communion with antebellum America, for both the text and the nation agree about what it means to be "doomed"—about the cause, character, and trajectory of that unfortunate condition.[7]

The narrative of doom in *Moby-Dick* comes into play even before Ahab appears. His ship is introduced with the accompanying information that "*Pequod*, you will no doubt remember, was the name of a celebrated tribe of Massachusetts Indians, now extinct as the ancient Medes" (67). The crucial words here are "now extinct"—and it is crucial, too, that the word should be "extinct," rather than "exterminated." "Extermination" betrays the work of an exterminator; "extinction," on the other hand, suggests a natural process, as if time alone were responsible for this fated course of events. Melville is not alone in favoring the word. Andrew Jackson, in his Second Annual Message (1830), had used the same word to defend his Indian policy. "To follow to the tomb the last of his race and to tread on the graves of extinct nations excite melancholy reflections," Jackson admitted, but quickly added that "true philanthropy reconciles the mind . . . to the extinction of one generation to make room for another."[8] The usefulness of the term becomes even clearer in the following observation by Benjamin Lincoln, the Revolutionary general from Massachusetts. Commenting on the imminent demise of the Indians, he predicted,

> [I]f the savages cannot be civilized and quit their present pursuits, they will, in consequence of their stubbornness, dwindle and moulder away, from causes perhaps imperceptible to us, until the whole race shall become extinct.[9]

Dying from "imperceptible" causes, Indians obligingly solved the problem for white settlers. "Extinction" is what happens in an autotelic universe: it naturalizes the category of the "doomed," not only by recuperating it as an evolutionary category but, most crucially, by locating the cause for extinction within the extinct organism itself.[10] If Indians die out it is their own fault. Their extinction is a function of their "stubbornness," their benighted refusal to quit their savage ways. This is the logic of blaming the victim; within the terms of our discussion, we might also call it the logic of negative individualism. The strategy here is to equate phenomenon with locus, to collapse cause and casualty into an identical unit, to make the Indian at once the scene and the agent of his own destruction. No less than the whale, the Indian too is a self-contained figure. He is both necessary and sufficient for his own condition: his impending doom refers to nothing other than his own savage self.

The Indian, as he is described by antebellum ethnographers and politicians, is therefore always the subject of a predestined narrative, in which he is responsible for, guilty of, and committed to a fated course of action, in which he appears not only as both victim and culprit, but also as a legible sign of his own inexorable end. Negative individualism could have found no better exponent. Ahab's kinship with the Indian is, under the circumstances, only to be expected. A single narrative works for both, for like the doomed savage, Ahab too is a product of negative individualism. He too is a victim of his own fault, and an instrument of his own fate. *Moby-Dick*, then, is not just a story of doom, but the story of a particular kind of doom, self-chosen and self-inflicted. As such, it has more than a little in common with another story of doom, Francis Parkman's *The Conspiracy of Pontiac*, a book also published in 1851, one written to record the "final doom" of those "destined to melt and vanish before the advancing waves of Anglo-American power."[11]

The *Pequod* is, for that reason, a "cannibal of a craft" (67), "apparelled like any barbaric Ethiopian emperor" (67), and manned by a "barbaric, heathenish, and motley" crew (109), repulsive in the "barbaric brilliancy of their teeth" (353) and their "uncivilized laughter" (353). Less civilized still are the five "tiger-yellow barbarians" (463) reserved for Ahab's whale-boat. Such barbaric trappings are obviously meant to suggest something about Ahab himself; in "The Try-Works" we are expressly told that "the rushing *Pequod*, freighted with savages, and laden with fire, and burning a corpse, and plunging into that blackness of darkness, seemed the material counterpart of her monomaniac commander's soul" (354). Ahab, indeed, is not without savage airs of his own. He walks on a "barbaric white leg" (110), for instance, and even though we do not ordinarily think of him as being animal-like, he has been shown on occasions to manifest a "sudden, passionate, corporal animosity" (160), and to emit a "terrific, loud, animal sob, like that of a heart-stricken moose" (143).

All the same, Ahab's barbarism has to do less with his "animosity" than with what Melville in *White-Jacket* has referred to as "barbarous feudal aristocracy," a condition associated with Czarist Russia, "immovable China," and to some extent England.[12] Ahab's "dictatorship" (129) is best understood in this context—in the equation between "barbarism" and "feudal aristocracy." Given such a definition, the repeated references to Ahab as "Khan of the plank" (114), "sultan" (130), and "Grand Turk" (130) are nothing if not ominous. More verdict than tribute, such allusions hardly describe Ahab: they merely brand him as a thing of the past. At once regal and barbaric, he takes his place among other candidates for extinction. "[S]ocial czarship" (131), "sultan's step" (130), and "Egyptian chest" (160) all conspire to make him a hopeless anomaly (and a sure casualty) in the age of the "Nantucket market" (143). Barbarians are doomed, in *Moby-Dick* as in antebellum America, because they have outlived their allotted time span, because their very nobility marks them as anachronistic. The Indian (John Quincy Adams called him the "lordly savage") perished not in spite of but because of his "stateliness," his "heroic virtues," his "fine figure, commanding voice, noble beauty."[13] Ahab perishes because he inhabits "the nameless regal overbearing dignity of some mighty woe" (111)—because, where feudalism equals barbarism, regality *is* woe.

The constellations of terms that seal Ahab's fate are therefore exactly those that sealed the fate of the Indians. Yet, seeing Ahab as an allegory of the Indian would be wrong, for the representational relation here is not so much one between the two as one encompassing both of them. Both are encompassed, that is, by a punitive representation of the self, what I have called negative individualism. Thus filiated in their genesis, Ahab and the Indians logically share a common end. We might speak of this punitive representation as broadly allegorical, for it operates through a set of signifying attributes, out of which it produces both "persons" and "destinies." Indeed, if we are right to detect in *Moby-Dick* a "hideous and intolerable allegory" (177) (whose existence Melville denies), that allegory works, I believe, primarily as an economy of ascription, as the production of narrative through the assignment of attributes. Ahab and the Indians are both bearers of attributes. They happen to inhabit two (apparently) disparate realms, one literary and the other social, but that fact finally matters less than the attributes they share. Those attributes make them analogous characters, produce them as analogous signs, and inflict on them analogous narratives—narratives of extinction.

Ahab's archaic speech (like the eloquence so often ascribed to Indians[14]) is therefore only another signifying attribute, another sign of his doom. At stake here is more than a question of language, for what the language embodies is actually an outmoded syntax of being. At its most memorable, this syntax takes the form of Ahab's famous resolve: to "dismember my dismemberer." This is the syntax of vengeance, we might say, and it makes Ahab the coeval of "sultans" and "Khans," for vengeance is the alleged code of the primitive. "[V]engeance, and fortitude . . . are duties which [Indians] consider as sacred," Jedidiah Morse reported in his much-reprinted article on "America" in the American edition (1790) of the *Encyclopaedia*. Francis Parkman agreed. "Revenge," he noted, was one of the "ruling passions" among Indians. It was this passion that he dwelled on, at the end of *The Conspiracy of Pontiac*, as he imagined the shade of Pontiac revisiting the scene of his murder and exulting in the "vengeance which overwhelmed the abettors of the crime," even as other tribes gathered to "revenge his fate."[15] In a somewhat different vein, René Girard also suggests that "primitive societies have only private vengeance."[16] It is this primitive obsession that sets Ahab apart and spells his doom. Captain Boomer of the *Samuel Enderby,* a man unburdened by such primitive obsession, appears, in this regard, not only as a contrast to Ahab, but also as a salient example of doom averted:

> "No, thank ye, Bunger," said the English Captain, "he's welcome to the arm he has, since I can't help it, and didn't know him then; but not to another one. No more White Whales for me; I've lowered for him once, and that has satisfied me. There would be great glory in killing him, I know that; and there is a shipload of precious sperms in him, but hark ye, he's best let alone; don't you think so, Captain?" (368)

Vengeance clearly means nothing to Captain Boomer. Indeed, if he were ever to hunt Moby-Dick again, it would not be for revenge, but for glory and profit—glory, in killing what no one has so far managed to kill, and profit, already beckoning in that "shipload of precious sperms." Both in what he values and in what he dismisses, Captain Boomer stands as a rebuke to Ahab. In that capacity he comically echoes Starbuck, for it is Starbuck, that eminently unprimitive character, who objects most strenuously to the idea of vengeance. What he says is this, "I came here to hunt whales, not my commander's vengeance. How many barrels will thy vengeance yield thee even if thou gettest it, Captain Ahab? it will not fetch thee much in our Nantucket market" (143).

Vengeance is wrong because it is unprofitable, Starbuck reasons. This is not simply crass materialism, either, for in spite of the talk about "barrels," about what vengeance will "yield" and "fetch," Starbuck is concerned with profit less as an end in itself than as a signifying economy, by which things can be calibrated, their meanings affixed and their values ascertained. Only such an economy will permit Starbuck to assess Ahab's vengeance and reject it for its deficient value. And only such an economy will permit violence to end. Starbuck's strategy, in other words, is always to resist vengeance-as-vengeance, always position it within a system of exchange. Vengeance can be validated, according to him, only if it can be substituted—only if it can be exchanged—for a different set of terms, like its value on the Nantucket market.

Ahab, of course, has no use for substitution and exchange.[17] His universe is one of mimetic repetition: in trying to dismember his dismemberer, he is trying to be like the whale, to do what the whale has done to him.[18] Vengeance affirms the primacy of temporal continuity, of mimesis in time. Starbuck, with no desire to imitate a "dumb brute," rejects not only mimesis but also the very idea of "continuity." Starbuck is an Emerson in the whaling business, we might say, and Emerson's defiant wish to be "an endless seeker with no Past at my back"[19] might have served equally well as his motto. Like Emerson, Starbuck cultivates the art of discontinuity, the art of discrete substitution.[20] Exchanging the whale (or vengeance on the whale) with what it will "fetch," he brings together two separate terms, the whale and its market value, and substitutes one for the other. There is no resemblance, of course, between the two terms, not even a logical connection, but that is precisely the point. Substitution, even as it exchanges one term for another, affirms the primacy of discontinuity.[21]

Discontinuity is also what Melville affirms as he proclaims himself "lord of [his] little vale." The freedom of the literary domain requires discontinuity, necessarily posits it, for the very possibility of freedom rests on the presumed ability of the literary artifact to set itself apart, to transcend mimesis, to rest within an impervious tissue of words. Melville and Starbuck would seem to be logical allies, at least on epistemological grounds. Starbuck, of course, is less worried about representation than about revenge: mimesis in time rather than mimesis in space is what he objects to. Unlike Melville, who values the discontinuous primarily as a spatial privilege—as the discrete separation of the literary object—Starbuck values the discontinuous primarily as a temporal privilege, as the privilege of not revenging, not repeating a prior event. Whether as spatial construct or as temporal postulate, however, discontinuity is, for both of them, the very condition of freedom: it liberates Starbuck from his antecedents, just as it liberates Melville from his surroundings. A common hope animates both, and if they were to win out, time and space in *Moby-Dick* would both observe the same law, the law of discontinuity.

Starbuck does not win out, although Melville does. Their differential fate points to a certain strain within *Moby-Dick,* to its contrary sense of possibilities and liabilities. And yet Starbuck need not have died. He (and indeed everybody else on the *Pequod*) could have survived without violating the logic of the plot. The fact that he does die, that his author deliberately makes it happen, suggests at once capitulation and control on Melville's part. For *Moby-Dick* manages, of course, to contain the terms of Starbuck's defeat within the terms of Melville's triumph—manages, that is to say, to contain its temporal disaster within a spatial order. Yet even that fact diminishes not at all the particular horror of Starbuck's defeat, a defeat his author scarcely "ha[s] the heart to write" (104). The "immaculate manliness we feel within ourselves" must "bleed[] with keenest anguish" at this tragic event, Melville says, for Starbuck's tragedy is the tragedy of American democracy itself:

> But this august dignity I treat of, is not the dignity of kings and robes, but . . . that democratic dignity which, on all hands, radiates without end from God Himself! The great God absolute! The centre and circumference of all democracy! His omnipresence, our divine equality!
> If, then, to meanest mariners, and renegades, and castaways, I shall hereafter ascribe high qualities, though dark; weave round them tragic graces . . . if I shall spread a rainbow over his disastrous set of sun; then against all mortal critics bear me out in it, thou just Spirit of Equality, which hast spread one royal mantle of humanity over all my kind! (104–05)

According to this passage, Starbuck's battle is the battle to enthrone democracy and to unseat the "dignity of kings and robes." It is a battle, we might infer, between the progressive and the primitive, between the "Spirit of Equality" and Ahab's barbaric "czarship." Given such an array of terms, there is no question what the outcome ought to be. Yet it is just this outcome that fails to materialize. In spite of its excited apostrophes, this celebrated passage on democracy actually predicts not victory but disaster. It is about the "dark" qualities, "tragic graces," and "disastrous set of sun" which await the democratic man.

Generalized as the defeat of American democracy, Starbuck's defeat is unbearable to contemplate because it represents a breakdown of what should take place, a reversal in the book's teleological opposition of terms. The tragedy here is the tragedy of failed succession, of deficient "valor" on the part of those slated for ascendancy, of "sultanism" stubbornly refusing to be deposed. It is the tragedy of the progressive failing to supplant the primitive. Instead of proceeding helpfully according to plan, time in *Moby-Dick* actually sides with Ahab's antiquated feudal barbarism. Even worse, that feudal barbarism seems quite capable of implicating the future in its wake. Time, it would seem, is resolutely, relentlessly continuous: there is no question here of substitution, no unexampled beginnings, no freedom even from vengeance. Starbuck's temporal economy—his dream of the discontinuous—fails abysmally.

Anxiety about the wayward workings of time is not peculiar to *Moby-Dick*. Antebellum expansionists expressed similar worries about the problem of succession, about the shape of America's future. If the Indian is allowed to be "lord paramount of that wide domain," Representative Strother speculated in an 1819 congressional debate on the Seminole War, "the progress of mankind is arrested and you condemn one of the most beautiful and fertile tracts of the earth to perpetual sterility as the hunting ground of a few savages."[22] This was a dismal prospect indeed, but not as dismal as what Representative Wilde of Georgia had in mind. If Indians were allowed to "perpetuate" themselves, he said, "a hundred or a thousand fold the number of white men would not be born" as a consequence.[23] Such dire events did not have to happen, of course, and the preventive measures seemed clear enough, at least in theory. In practice, however, the agency of time was problematic even to the most determined exponents of progress, as the following passage from *White-Jacket* demonstrates:

> The Past is dead, and has no resurrection; but the Future is endowed with such a life, that it lives to us even in anticipation. The Past is, in many things, the foe of mankind: the Future is, in all things, our friend. In the Past is no hope; the Future is both hope and fruition. The Past is the text-book of tyrants; the Future the Bible of the Free. Those who are solely governed by the Past stand like Lot's wife, crystallized in the act of looking backward, and forever incapable of looking before.[24]

The Past is demonstrably dead, Melville would like to suggest; and yet the demonstration, in its very obsessiveness, would seem to suggest the reverse. The passage offers neat serial categories ("the Past" and "the Future"), but the stubborn presence of what ought to be bygone jeopardizes the very notion of seriality. In its giddy dissonances, the passage anticipates the equally schizophrenic paean to democracy in *Moby-Dick*. The fear, in both cases, is that the Future might not become the future at all. Starbuck's defeat at the hands of barbaric "sultanism" gives that fear a palpable shape. Of course, by 1851 America's future was hardly likely to be threatened by Indians, but the anxiety in *Moby-Dick* remains real. Indeed, what the book articulates seems to be the inverse of what Representatives Strother and Wilde prophesied—not what savages might do to America's future, but what America's future might be like after savages have been done in.

Americans had always worried about the future of the American Empire. If that empire had so far been time's beneficiary, would it not (like other empires) ultimately also be time's casualty? Americans liked to think of their empire as unlike any other in history, unexampled both in character and duration. Its duration, as it turned out, had everything to do with its character, for in order to escape the proverbial fate of empires, America has to be imagined as a very special case indeed: not just any empire but an "empire for liberty," "an empire of reason," "an empire of virtue," "an empire of love."[25] By the same token, any territorial conquest by this "noble young empire" would have to be distinguished from other less laudable imperialist exploits. The text most often cited during the Congressional debates on Indian Removal in the 1820s and 1830s was Vattel's classic *Law of Nations,* in which the Swiss jurist had argued for the legality of the North American settlements:

> Thus, though the conquest of the civilized Empires of Peru and Mexico was a notorious usurpation, the establishment of many colonies on the continent of North America may, on their confining themselves within just bounds, be extremely lawful. The peoples of those vast countries of land rather overran them than inhabited them.[26]

Taking land away from the Indians constituted no territorial conquest, because Indian title "cannot be taken for a true and legal possession." For the same reason, Vattel added, "People have not, then, deviated from the views of nature, in confining the Indians within narrow limits."[27]

Those were reassuring words from an acknowledged authority. It was interesting, however, that those words had so often to be invoked and that expansionists felt so urgently called upon to defend themselves from the charge of aggression. The acquisition of Texas occasioned this editorial, for instance, from the *New York Morning News:*

> It is looked upon as aggression, and all the bad and odious features which
> the habits of thought Europeans associate with aggressive deeds, are at-
> tributed to it. . . . But what has Belgium, Silesia, Poland or Bengal in com-
> mon with Texas? . . . Rapacity and spoliation cannot be the features of this
> magnificent enterprise, not perhaps, because we are above and beyond the
> influence of such views, but because circumstances do not admit of their
> operation. We take from no man; the reverse rather—we give to man. This
> national policy, necessity or destiny, we know to be just and beneficent, and
> we can, therefore, afford to scorn the invective and imputations of rival
> nations.[28]

Such a frenzy of protest, of course, only affirmed what it denied. The
vehemence of the *New York Morning News* inversely registered the fear that
America had lost its character as an "empire of virtue" or an "empire of
love." This would bode ill indeed for its future, for its claim as the champion
of progress and the seat of permanence. What would be the fate of an
empire founded upon "aggression," "rapacity," and "spoliation"?

Emerson, seeker with no Past at his back, would have known how to
answer that question. The art of discontinuity, judiciously applied, clearly
has its political advantages. If time were no more than a series of discrete
units, if Past and Future were related only as disjunction, and if what ensues
had no reference to what preceded, one could indeed be absolved from
one's actions. Emerson and antebellum Americans wanted "the sense of an
ending," as Frank Kermode calls it, the condition in which "an act could be
without succession, without temporal consequence." But as Kermode also
says, "acts without 'success' are a property of the *aevum*. Nothing in time
can in that sense be *done,* freed of consequence or equivocal aspects."[29]
Antebellum Americans, defending themselves from charges of aggression,
rapacity, and spoliation, were especially haunted by the prospect of consequences, by the infinitude of action and reaction. Vengeance, mimetic
repetition in time, dramatized that infinitude as infinite retribution. America's very future was endangered by it. Even worse, the instrument of
vengeance was not to be the lordly savage (now happily on his way to
extinction), but his servile counterpart, one apparently meek and jolly, but
at heart as savage as the Indian himself.

"I tremble for my country," Jefferson wrote in 1782, "when I reflect that
God is just: that his justice cannot sleep for ever." He was speaking of
slavery. The slave uprisings in Santo Domingo some ten years later seemed
to confirm his fears. Jefferson foresaw "bloody scenes" for "our children
certainly, and possibly ourselves." Santo Domingo was only "the first

chapter," he thought, and thinking about other chapters to come, he predicted, "we shall be the murderers of our own children."[30] David Walker, author of *An Appeal to the Coloured Citizens of the World* (1829), made the same prediction from the other side. America's "victims of oppression," he said, were daily calling upon "the God of Justice, to be revenged":[31]

> I tell you Americans! that unless you speedily alter your course, you and your country are gone!!!!!! For God Almighty will tear up the very face of the earth. . . . I hope that the Americans may hear, but I am afraid that they have done us so much injury, and are so firm in the belief that our Creator made us to be an inheritance to them for ever, that their hearts will be hardened, so that their destruction may be sure.[32]

Walker's *Appeal* was nationally denounced as "one of the most wicked and inflammatory productions that ever issued from the press."[33] On June 28, 1830, he was found dead, apparently of poison, near the doorway of his shop. To the horrified nation, however, his hellish predictions seemed to have come true in August 1831, when Nat Turner led about seventy slaves on a rampage through Southampton County, Virginia, killing some sixty whites, more than half women and children.

Such bloody episodes of vengeance were kept very much alive in the public memory in the decades before the Civil War. Nat Turner was "a symbol of wild retribution," Thomas Wentworth Higginson reported. So potent was his threat, or the memory of his threat, that even "the remotest Southern States were found shuddering at nightly rumors of insurrection." Abolitionists, playing upon Southern fears, regularly made "vengeance" their theme—to such an extent that they even sometimes joked about it. An 1855 article ("About Niggers") in *Putnam's Monthly* argued, for instance, that the "terrible capacity for revenge" revealed in Santo Domingo proved that the "nigger" was "a man, not a baboon." Less playfully, black activist William Wells Brown invoked Nat Turner not only as the author of a "blood-thirsty and revengeful" insurrection but also as someone who "meditated upon the wrongs of his oppressed and injured people," and went on to issue this ominous warning: "Every iniquity that society allows to subsist for the benefit of the oppressor is a sword with which she herself arms the oppressed. Right is the most dangerous of weapons: woe to him who leaves it to his enemies."[34]

Vengeance as actual slave insurgence was horrible to contemplate. But increasingly, another kind of "vengeance" gained currency in the discourse about slavery. This vengeance also took the form of mimetic repetition, but in this case it came about, not in bloody revolt, not in the victim's imitation of his victimizer, but in familial reproduction, in the offspring's imitation of his parent. For Jefferson, the "unhappy influence" of slavery resided in just this sort of mimesis, one that turned the family itself into a vehicle of retribution:

> The whole commerce between master and slave is a perpetual exercise of the most boisterous passions, the most unremitting despotism on the one part, and degrading submissions on the other. Our children see this, and learn to imitate it; for man is an imitative animal. . . . The parent storms, the child looks on, catches the lineaments of wrath, puts on the same airs in the circle of smaller slaves, gives a loose to his worst of passions, and thus nursed, educated, and daily exercised in tyranny, cannot but be stamped by it with odious peculiarities.[35]

Slavery was its own retribution, then, as it enforced mimesis within the family, as it "stamped" the offspring, "an imitative animal," with the mark of the parent, in a kind of reproductive penalty. Jefferson was not the only one to think of "vengeance" in intrafamilial terms. Harriet Beecher Stowe had much the same idea in *Uncle Tom's Cabin* (1852). "It is perfectly outrageous,—it is horrid, Augustine! It will certainly bring down vengeance upon you," Miss Ophelia assures her slave-owning cousin.[36] And "vengeance," in Stowe as in Jefferson, works from within the family and inflicts its punishment reflexively on the slave owner himself. This is no doubt why we find, in *Uncle Tom's Cabin,* a character like Henrique, little Eva's ungentle cousin. Henrique, aged twelve, is already in the habit of striking his slave boy Dodo "across the face with his riding-whip" and speaking to him in the following tones: "There, you impudent dog! Now will you learn not to answer back when I speak to you? . . . I'll teach you your place!"[37] Henrique exemplifies precisely what Jefferson fears. An "imitative animal," he is already a juvenile copy of the brutal master, will grow up to be an adult copy, and will in turn produce more copies of his own. Slavery, ensconced within the family, reproduces itself with a vengeance.

By locating mimesis within the family, by imagining the slave owner as someone who punishes himself in the mere act of reproduction, Jefferson and Stowe come up with another model of "vengeance," a circular model, one in which the master enslaves himself and genealogy is its own retribution. This prospect is by no means pleasing, but there is something reassuringly tautological about it all the same. For if genealogy is already its own retribution, and the master already his own slave, any further act of vengeance would seem unnecessary. Slave rebellion is not so much wrong as gratuitous here, because the master, especially such a one as Augustine St. Clare, has assuredly been punished enough. And because that self-punishing master is eternally reproduced through the family, slave rebellion is eternally unnecessary. For Stowe especially, retribution runs its course within the compass of a single individual, the master himself; any repetition in time would simply reenact that spatial figure. As a self-contained unit, a model of discrete closure—at once agent and victim of his own fate—the self-punishing master is not unlike the self-victimizing Indian. Both are products of Jacksonian individualism, the ultimate institution of the discrete. But whereas the self-victimizing Indian is erased from history, the self-punishing master eternally remains. Vengeance as tautology, as the circular agency within a single person, displaces vengeance as reciprocity, as the action and reaction between persons, and preserves the master who so conveniently punishes himself. Stowe offers no bloody scenes of vengeance, only Uncle Tom.

Published just a year before *Uncle Tom's Cabin, Moby-Dick,* too, is a meditation on vengeance: on the deflection of it and the deterrence of it. Melville is fascinated, however, by the savage energy of the undeflected and the undeterred. And so he ends up parting company with Stowe after all. *Moby-Dick* will have no Uncle Tom, only Captain Ahab. Ahab believes in vengeance. He refuses to locate it, moreover, in a circuit of identity, in the reflexive self-punishment of the victimizer. For him, the dismembered and the dismemberer are mutually engendering but by no means identical. His "vengeance" is a question of relation, not to oneself but to someone else; it is also a question of action, inflicted on another and perhaps returned in kind by that other.[38] Such a model entails not the spatial containment of victim in victimizer, but the temporal reversal of positions between the two. In short, Ahab's syntax of vengeance invokes the agency of time not only to preserve both victim and victimizer but, more crucially, to constitute one as the potential of the other. The two will trade places in time. Change is possible, indeed logical, as far as Ahab is concerned. It will not be absolute change, of course—his world will always have two positions, victims and victimizers—but one can at least move from one position to the other. Against Stowe's closed circuit, Ahab offers instead a temporal sequence, a sequence of reversals operating in time and through time. What he says to the "clear spirit of clear fire" might have been said to Stowe as well: "There is some unsuffusing thing beyond thee . . . to whom all thy eternity is but time" (417). Claiming time as his medium and ally, he can invoke another temporal phenomenon, what he calls the "genealogies of these high mortal miseries" (386), to champion his cause:

> Nor, at the time, had it failed to enter his monomaniac mind, that all the anguish of that then present suffering was but the direct issue of a former woe; and he too plainly seemed to see, that as the most poisonous reptile of the marsh perpetuates his kind as inevitably as the sweetest songster of the grove; so, equally with every felicity, all miserable events do naturally beget their like, . . . Mortal miseries shall still fertilely beget to themselves an eternally progressive progeny of griefs beyond the grave. (385)

It is altogether fitting that these thoughts should come from Ahab—and Melville is careful to attribute them to his "monomaniac mind"—for such a "genealogy," cheerless as it might seem, actually turns out to be the best hope for a doomed man. Not only does it affirm Ahab's sense of injury (his action is the "direct issue of a former woe" rather than the crazy dilatations of a monomaniac), it also offers him vicarious life beyond his own preordained death. Ahab might be killed off, but his wrong will never die out, since it will "beget" an "eternally progressive progeny of griefs beyond the grave." Individuals perish, their positions remain: Ahab dies only to give birth to a thousand other Ahabs. The model here is not the primacy of the self but the primacy of relation; not the discrete spatiality of Jacksonian individualism, but an interweaving sequel that "naturally beget[s] their like."

Ahab's "genealogy" represents an apparent tautology that refuses to be one. His syntax of vengeance—"to dismember my dismemberer"—turns out to be anything but circular. It activates, on the contrary, a temporal process, a process of reversals at once inevitable and interminable. Against and around this temporal menace, Melville would have to erect other spatial forms of defense. The most effective form, he discovers, turns out once again to be the form of the tautology, for nothing works better as a vehicle of containment, and nothing keeps Ahab's vengeance under tighter control. And tautologies are easy enough to come by. All Melville needs is five short words: "Ahab is for ever Ahab" (459). Those are Ahab's own words, defiantly spoken; ironically they are also the words that condemn him. From our standpoint, these words must stand as the very epigraph of negative individualism, the punitive logic centered on the autonomous self. That punitive logic, we can now see, is tautological almost by necessity: it begins and ends with the self, a self constituted here not only as the seat of agency but also as the circuit of discipline. The version Melville comes up with—"Ahab is for ever Ahab"—therefore operates as two related tautologies, both of which begin and end with Ahab, and condemn him in just that circularity. Both are vehicles of containment, mobilized to contain Ahab's syntax of vengeance, and we might speak of them, accordingly, as the syntax of fate and the syntax of self.

Fate begins, in Ahab's case, with the name itself. Such a name is clearly "not without meaning," as Melville might say, and it is just this meaning that dooms its unlucky bearer. Ishmael and Peleg allude to that meaning even before Ahab appears. In response to Peleg's remark that "Ahab of old, thou knowest, was a crowned king!" Ishmael replies, "And a very vile one. When that wicked king was slain, the dogs, did they not lick his blood?" (77). No nineteenth-century reader would have missed the meaning of such a name, and few of them would have been surprised by what happens to Ahab at the end. Ahab can only mean what his name says he means: he is characterized by that name, summarized by it, and doomed by it. As a bearer of meaning, at once unmistakable and immutable, Ahab is less a living thing, perhaps, than a legible sign. He is a personified name, a human receptacle invested with a signifying function. That signifying function is quite literally his fate: he lives in it and dies in it, since his whole life is really nothing more than a recapitulation of what his name has made abundantly clear at the outset. To be called Ahab is to inhabit a narrative tautology, in which the ending is already immanent in the beginning, and in which all temporal development merely reenacts what is in place from the very first.

Ahab, of course, has hoped for change. He has hoped that time will help him. He should have known better, for his own name ought to have taught him the futility of his hope. Personifying that name, Ahab can have only one narrative, not a narrative of vengeance, but a narrative of doom.[39] His story is therefore (as Elijah says) "all fixed and arranged a'ready" (87), already inscribed in the fate of his Biblical namesake. Ahab is right, then, to say, "This whole act's immutably decreed. 'Twas rehearsed by thee and me a billion years before this ocean rolled" (459). The passage of time ("a billion years") brings no change, no prospect of vengeance, for time turns out to be completely unavailing here. Its status is summed up in the five words, "Ahab is for ever Ahab," a tautology that, quite literally, puts time in its place, in the spatial confines of the personified name. Ahab's story can only be a story of fate, because personification is, in effect, a vehicle of predestination. Under its dictates, time counts only as duration, not as potentiality. The circuit of identity between "Ahab" and "Ahab" marks the circuit from immanence to permanence, and affirms a timeless design, the design of "for ever."

Earlier, we spoke of personification as a procedure that spatializes time. In Ahab we see that procedure at work. Through him we also see, perhaps more clearly than anywhere else, the context as well as the function of such spatializations. For it is just this procedure that authorizes the category of "fate" in *Moby-Dick:* authorizes it, in a temporal landscape in which the future appears, already inscribed, composed, demarcated, almost as a fact of geography. This is what Melville in *White-Jacket* has called "the wilderness of untried things,"[40] a wilderness that materializes, apparently, when time is converted into space. Signs and omens hail from this region; prophets make their way into it, like so many venturous prospectors, mapping its terrain, claiming it as virtual property. Prophecy in *Moby-Dick* is a territorial enterprise. To be a prophet one must survey the future, with an eye to ownership. And it is in the jealous tones of a proprietor that Elijah accosts Ishmael: "Didn't ye hear a word about them matters and something more, eh? No, I don't think ye did; how could ye? Who knows it? Not all Nantucket, I guess" (87).

What is odd is that Elijah's field of knowledge actually lies not in the future but in the past: he pities Ishmael for having heard "nothing about that thing that happened to [Ahab] off Cape Horn, long ago, when he lay like dead for three days and nights; nothing about that deadly skrimmage with the Spaniard afore the altar in Santa?—heard nothing about that, eh? Nothing about the silver calabash he spat into?" (87). Prophecy in *Moby-Dick* enlarges upon the past. But that, too, is what one should expect from a spatial ordering of time. Indeed, the future is knowable to the prophets only because it has been converted into a spatial category, part of a known design. Prophets are prospectors and colonizers because they are emissaries of the known, because their mission is to expand and assimilate, to annex the "wilderness of untried things" into the domain of the existing. They can function as prophets only by reducing the potentiality of sequence to the legibility of design, only by reading time as space.

In that regard Melville's prophets are perhaps less prophets of the future than spokesmen for their own age, for spatialized time was the very condition for Manifest Destiny. What Albert Weinberg calls America's "geographical determinism" operated by equating geography with destiny, an equation that, in conflating time and space—in harnessing time to space— at once recomposed time and incorporated it as a vehicle for spatial aggrandizement. The familiar strategy for antebellum expansionists was to invoke some version of "Providence," whose plans for the future happened to coincide exactly with America's territorial ambitions. American expansion in space and providential design in time turned out to be one and the same. In the famous words of John L. O'Sullivan, it was America's "manifest destiny to overspread the continent allotted by Providence for the free development of our yearly multiplying millions."[41] This manifest destiny had no spatial limits, for as another expansionist enthusiastically put it, America was bounded "on the west by the Day of Judgment."[42] For this hopeful soul, and for many others, spatialized time legitimized and empowered. Yet the same mechanism could just as easily victimize and destroy. For Indians, too, happened to be subjects of spatialized time. As much as America, they were "destined"—destined, that is, "to melt and vanish." Representative Wilde of Georgia found that destiny only too manifest: "Jacob will forever obtain the inheritance of Esau. We cannot alter the laws of Providence, as we read them in the experiences of the ages."[43] Within the spatialized time of providential design, the fate of the doomed savage became legible as a text.

Spatialized time is also what *Moby-Dick* invokes to make Ahab's fate legible. Reading that fate, Melville's prophets turn Ahab, too, into a doomed figure, spatializing his temporal endeavor into a timeless script. Melville's "imperial folio," then, logically shares the same temporal economy with its imperial environment, for a structure of dominion is inseparable from a structure of time, as J. G. A. Pocock has reminded us.[44] Fate in *Moby-Dick* and Manifest Destiny in antebellum America are kindred constructs. Ahab and America, bearers both of a timeless destiny, mirror each other in familial likeness.

Of course, the relation here cannot be anything other than *mirroring*, for if Ahab and America are in one sense kindred, kindred in their timelessness, in another sense they are also diametrically opposed. The destiny that afflicts Ahab is, after all, nothing like the destiny that awaits America. It resembles rather the fate of those whose "doom" America dictates. But even here, America's destiny and Ahab's are not so much opposed as complementary. One exists as the companion to the other, the necessary condition for the other's possibility. Putting this another way, we might say that America and Ahab represent the two poles in a single narrative, the narrative of spatialized time, a narrative that (not surprisingly) also has two contrary provisions: for sovereignty as well as for subjection, the doom of the one being no more than a measure of the other's fated ascendancy.

In this regard Ahab, too, might be said to have a Manifest Destiny of his own. Because this was the nineteenth century, however, Manifest Destiny could also appear in guises other than the providential. The fixed disposition of the natural—the "identity" of a person, or a race—could serve equally well as a sign of doom. The naturalized category was more effective, in fact, as we will discover both in antebellum America and in *Moby-Dick*. In both cases, the narrative of fate is supplemented by a narrative of self, a naturalized vehicle that produces much the same outcome as its providential counterpart, for it, too, is a vehicle of predestination. It, too, dictates doom, as we can see all too clearly in the genesis of the Indian "character" and the narrative it underwrites. Whether described positively as showing "bravery and fortitude," "commanding energy and force of mind," "firmness, courage, and decision of character," or negatively as "intractable," "fixed and rigid,"[45] the Indian was represented as a creature stuck with such a timeless identity that his very immutability spelled his doom. Francis Parkman put this most dramatically:

> The Indian is hewn out of a rock. You can rarely change the form without destruction of the substance. Races of inferior energy have possessed a power of expansion and assimilation to which he is a stranger; and it is this fixed and rigid quality which has proved his ruin. He will not learn the arts of civilization, and he and his forest must perish together. The stern, unchanging features of his mind excite our admiration from their very immutability; and we look with deep interest on the fate of this irreclaimable son of the wilderness.[46]

For Parkman the naturalist, "immutability" of identity was a sounder and much more useful argument than the "immutable decree[s]" of fate. Naturalized and internalized, fate now operated within the self as a sort of internal mechanism of doom. Of course, for that doom to come about, Indians would need to be immutable—they would have to be posited as such even if they appeared otherwise—as the "mutable" Cherokees found out when they tried to use their "civilized" way of life as an argument against dispossession.[47] What seems clear, from the example of the Indians, is the extent to which "identity" might be a product of attribution. What seems also clear is the extent to which that process is itself "interest[ed]" in every sense of the word. Identity, for that reason, would seem never to be merely neutral or objective. Harnessed always to meanings and trajectories, its attribution might turn out to be just as fatal as denomination. To be called "immutable" is as good as to be named "Ahab."

Ahab, as it turns out, is not only named Ahab but also called "immutable." Indeed, in an uncanny parallel, he seems to have been fashioned out of just those attributes that antebellum Americans bestowed on the Indian. In Ahab, Melville tells us, "There was an infinity of firmest fortitude, a determinate, unsurrenderable wilfulness, in the fixed and fearless, forward dedication of that glance" (111). "The path to my fixed purpose is laid with iron rails," Ahab himself says at one point (147). Elsewhere he is said to be "made of solid bronze, and shaped in an unalterable mould" (110). He commands an "iron soul" (438) and an "iron voice" (439); his face is "set like a flint" (369). To Parkman, the Indian seemed "hewn out of a rock"; to Melville, Ahab's very coat appears "stone carved" (438).

The startling correspondence here suggests, once again, not thematic correspondence—not a deliberate decision on Melville's part to make Ahab an allegory of the Indian—but rather the cultural genesis of Ahab and Indians as analogous "characters."[48] Both are generated by a common representational form of the self, one that produces not only literary meanings but also social meanings, and not only fictive casualties but also casualties of flesh and blood. I have referred to that representational form as personification: in a different register, we might also call it negative individualism. In the "persons" of Ahab and the Indians, we see what such a form can do, and why it might be useful. Personification, then, would seem to operate in a much broader domain than we ordinarily think. It is as much a social phenomenon as a literary one. It comes into play both in the "dooming" of Ahab and in the "dooming" of the Indians. It assigns analogous destinies to analogous selves.[49]

The tautology "Ahab is for ever Ahab" functions here, not as the syntax of fate, then, but as something altogether analogous to it, what we might call the syntax of self. At once subject and predicate, instrument and embodiment of his own misfortune, Ahab stands convicted the moment he is ascribed with a self, the moment he is bound, himself to himself, by "is for ever." The verb here can only be "is," only the present tense, for the syntax of self, like the syntax of fate, invokes a timeless regime, a circuit of identity. Following Lacan, we might say that such an identity is itself the mark of alienation, that it "symbolizes the mental permanence of the I, at the same time as it prefigures its alienating destination."[50] That unhappy fate is what afflicts Ahab, and what afflicted the Indians. "Identity," in both cases, would thus seem to be as much a sociopolitical category as a psychoanalytic one. Certainly it has its sociopolitical uses. Negative individualism, the punitive logic based on the autonomous self, cannot operate outside its province.

For the punitive logic must reside in the very identity of selfhood. As a self-contained unit, the self is the seat of agency, we have said, but, as we can also see, such a unit is no less the seat of penalty. Within its circuit of identity, as Ahab and the Indians embody it, the self encapsulates both cause and consequence, both injury and blame. Even as it generates a circuit of closure, the attribution of identity would seem also to generate, in the same process, a circuit of discipline, one that regiments the self, fashions it into the seat of "self-government." This it accomplishes not just by enclosure but equally by exclusion: by marking the self's boundary against a companion domain, that of the "extraneous," posited as outside the self. As we shall see, it is in tandem with this companion category, paradoxically, that the self bodies forth its most powerful punitive logic.

Starbuck gives voice to that logic when he advises Ahab, "let Ahab beware of Ahab; beware of thyself, old man" (394). In a sense, this is merely another way of saying what Ahab has already said about himself—"Ahab is for ever Ahab"—for Starbuck's injunction, too, centers on "Ahab," the all-encompassing, all-responsible individual self. What is striking about Starbuck's formulation, however, is what it manages to exclude, and, in the process of exclusion, where it manages to locate blame. According to Starbuck, Ahab must beware of himself, presumably because he is his own worst enemy. There is no mention here of Moby-Dick, no mention of what has been done to Ahab, no mention, in short, of either adversary or antecedent. Relation and temporality alike are excluded in Starbuck's formula for selfhood. Portrayed as such, Ahab indeed has no one to fear but himself, and no one to blame but himself. His fate is a "consequence of [his] stubbornness," his refusal to "quit [his] present pursuits." If this sounds familiar, that is because we have heard it before, in Benjamin Lincoln's indictment of the Indians. Starbuck's indictment of Ahab follows the same logic. The instrument of indictment, in both cases, is the very figure of selfhood, a figure that both encloses and excludes: a tautology, finally, within whose confines one always is what one is.[51] Denied either potentiality in time or relation in space, denied any hope of change or any notion of injustice, the self must bear the full burden of its own condition. It must undertake to doom itself.

What we are witnessing is that most pervasive and persistent of phenomena: the phenomenon of blaming the victim. Starbuck dramatizes the connection between that phenomenon and the institution of "selfhood." It is no accident that the spokesman for "Nantucket market" should be a champion of the autonomous self, no accident that such a self should be exhorted as the seat of agency, and no accident, either, that the same self should be invoked as the grounds for damnation. Starbuck only advises Ahab, "beware of thyself," but he might also have said, "help thyself." The two mottoes go hand in hand. If the latter ushers in the self-reliant entrepreneur, the former dispatches the self-victimizing savage. There is no contradiction here: for self-reliance and self-victimization, too, are kindred, the freedom of the one making up the fate of the other, the penalty for one being the other's reward. To make the self the seat of agency is to invoke the agency of both.

Even in *Moby-Dick,* we see not just the spectacle of self-victimization but also the spectacle of self-reliance. We see it, quite graphically, in the whale, the proud owner of "thick walls" and "interior spaciousness," who lives "in the world without being of it" (261). We see it, less graphically, in the book named after the whale—or rather, we see it in Melville's image of the book. The image remains ideal, however, for Melville, his dream of freedom notwithstanding, is haunted always by its obverse. Ahab's death is, for that reason, not quite the last word in *Moby-Dick,* and certainly not the last word as Melville goes on to reconsider it in *Pierre.* In that book the doomed savage returns, in logic if not in person, but vengeful as ever. What triumphs in *Pierre* is what is defeated in *Moby-Dick:* genealogy as Ahab imagines it, genealogy as a sequel of reciprocal relations, as the reversal of positions and even the circulation of attributes. For Melville, that is utter nightmare. Something of that horror is already suggested in *Moby-Dick,* in the image of Tashtego, "the submerged savage," extending a "red arm and hammer" in his "death-grasp" to bring down a sky-hawk with "his imperial beak thrust upwards" (469). That image of reciprocity is negated, of course, by the final image of Ishmael, "orphan[ed]" by the catastrophe but surviving all the same as an autonomous self.[52] *Pierre,* whose protagonist is likewise "orphan-like"—indeed, an "infant Ishmael"—will come to very different conclusions.

Notes

Portions of this chapter appeared in Wai-chee Dimock, *Empire for Liberty: Melville and the Politics of Individualism* (Princeton, N.J.: Princeton University Press, 1989). Copyright © 1989 by Princeton University Press. Reprinted by permission.

1. Melville to Nathaniel Hawthorne, November 17, 1851. *Letters,* 141.

2. *Mardi, and a Voyage Thither* (1849; rpt. Evanston and Chicago: Northwestern University and the Newberry Library, 1970), 368.

3. The citations are from *Moby-Dick,* ed. Harrison Hayford and Hershel Parker (1851; rpt. New York: Norton, 1967), 378–79. All further references to this edition appear in the text.

4. John Irwin, *American Hieroglyphics: The Symbol of the Egyptian Hieroglyphics in the American Renaissance* (Baltimore: Johns Hopkins University Press, 1980), 305. Without disagreeing with Irwin's point that the whale embodies indeterminacy, I would like to suggest that the very notion of "indeterminacy"—especially Melville's articulation of it—should itself be contextualized and historicized. The book-whale analogy is by no means a new argument, of course. See, for example, Edgar A. Dryden, *Melville's Thematics of Form: The Great Art of Telling the Truth* (Baltimore: Johns Hopkins University Press, 1968), 83–113; and David Hirsch, *Reality and Idea in the Early American Novel* (The Hague: Mouton, 1971), esp. 199–219. For a reading of the whale as text even more determinedly deconstructive than Irwin's, see Rodolphe Gasché, "The Scene of Writing: A Deferred Outset," in *Glyph* 1 (Baltimore: Johns Hopkins University Press, 1977), 150–71. Charles Feidelson's *Symbolism and American Literature* (Chicago: University of Chicago Press, 1953) remains the best discussion of American "symbolism" as textual self-reference.

5. For an interesting account of Derridean deconstruction as a "metaphysics of the discrete"—as, indeed, "an extension of Locke's doctrine of contiguity and the associationism that ensued"—see Charles Levin, "La Greffe du Zèle: Derrida and the Cupidity of the Text," in *The Structural Allegory: Reconstructive Encounters with the New French Thought* (Minneapolis: University of Minnesota Press, 1984), 201–27.

6. See, for example, James Guetti, *The Limits of Metaphor: A Study of Melville, Conrad, and Faulkner* (Ithaca, N.Y.: Cornell University Press, 1967), 34–41; and Richard Brodhead, *Hawthorne, Melville, and the Novel* (Chicago: University of Chicago Press, 1976), 137–38.

7. Virtually all "political" readings of *Moby-Dick* have chosen to see Ahab as villain. See, for instance, C. L. R. James, *Mariners, Renegades, and Castaways: The Story of Herman Melville and the World We Live in* (London: Allison & Busby, 1953); Alan Heimert, "*Moby-Dick* and Political Symbolism," *American Literature* 15 (Winter 1963): 498–534; and, more recently, Carolyn L. Karcher, *Shadow Over the Promised Land: Slavery, Race, and Violence in Melville's America* (Baton Rouge: Louisiana State University Press, 1980); Joyce Sparer Adler, *War in Melville's Imagination* (New York: New York University Press, 1981); Michael Paul Rogin, *Subversive Genealogy: The Politics and Art of Herman Melville* (Berkeley: University of California Press, 1983); James Duban, *Melville's Major Fiction: Politics, Theology, and Imagination* (Dekalb: Northern Illinois University Press, 1983). My deepest disagreement with these critics has to do with my sense of Ahab not as villain but as victim. A new and important reading of *Moby-Dick* from this perspective is Donald Pease, "*Moby-Dick* and the Cold War," in *The American Renaissance Reconsidered: Selected Papers from the English Institute, 1982–83,* ed. Walter Benn Michaels and Donald E. Pease (Baltimore: Johns Hopkins University Press, 1985), 113–55. Pease, however, sees Ahab only as Ishmael's victim. I see Melville himself as being implicated in the process of victimization.

8. Andrew Jackson, Second Annual Message, December 6, 1830, in *The State of*

the Union Messages of the Presidents, 1790–1966, 3 vols. (New York: Chelsea House, 1967), 1: 335.

9. *Massachusetts Historical Society Collections,* ser. 3, 5 (1836): 138–39. Quoted in Roy Harvey Pearce, *The Savages of America: A Study of the Indian and the Idea of Civilization* (Baltimore: Johns Hopkins University Press, 1965), 69.

10. Gillian Beer discusses the importance of the idea of "extinction" to the nineteenth-century novel in her fascinating *Darwin's Plots: Evolutionary Narrative in Darwin, George Eliot and Nineteenth-Century Fiction* (London: ARK Paperbacks, 1985), 123–48. The American context, however, makes "extinction" not so much a danger to be averted (Beer's emphasis) as a desired, perhaps even eagerly awaited, end—at least for certain groups of people.

11. Francis Parkman, *The Conspiracy of Pontiac,* 2 vols. (1851; rpt. Boston: Little Brown, 1909), 1: x, xi.

12. *White-Jacket, or, The World in a Man-of-War* (1850; rpt. Evanston and Chicago: Northwestern University Press and the Newberry Library, 1970), 146, 144, 150.

13. Adams's phrase is from his much cited *Oration Delivered at Plymouth* (Plymouth, Mass.: J. Avery, 1820), 17. The other three phrases are from Parkman, *Conspiracy,* 1: 234, 48, and Henry Rowe Schoolcraft, *The American Indians: Their History, Condition, and Prospects* (Rochester, N.Y.: Wanzer, Foot and Co., 1851), 150.

14. See, for instance, Parkman, *Conspiracy,* 1: 191; 2: 329; Schoolcraft, *The American Indians,* 15.

15. The Indians' "ruling passions," according to Parkman, are "Ambition, revenge, envy, jealousy." See *Conspiracy,* 1: 45. Pontiac's vengeful shade is described in *Conspiracy,* 2: 329.

16. René Girard, *Violence and the Sacred,* trans. Patrick Gregory (Baltimore: Johns Hopkins University Press, 1977), 15.

17. I differ here from Michael Gilmore, who sees Ahab as being implicated in exchange. See *American Romanticism and the Marketplace* (Chicago: University of Chicago Press, 1985), 117.

18. René Girard also relates vengeance to mimesis; see "From Mimetic Desire to Monstrous Double," in *Violence and the Sacred,* 143–68.

19. The quotation is, most appropriately, from "Circles," an essay that in many ways theorizes about what Melville is practicing in *Moby-Dick.* See *Selections from Ralph Waldo Emerson,* ed. Stephen E. Whicher (Boston: Houghton Mifflin, 1960), 176.

20. For an account of Emerson's art of discontinuity, see James Cox, "Ralph Waldo Emerson: The Circles of the Eye," in *Emerson: Prophecy, Metamorphosis, and Influence,* ed. David Levin (New York: Columbia University Press, 1975), 57–81; and, more recently, Julie Ellison, *Emerson's Romantic Style* (Princeton, N.J.: Princeton University Press, 1984), 160–74. Harold Bloom stresses the importance of discontinuity to poetic freedom in *The Anxiety of Influence* (New York: Oxford University Press, 1973), 39–40. I depart from these critics in emphasizing the social function of discontinuity.

21. David Simpson also sees *Moby-Dick* as "a book about substitution on the grandest scale." See *Fetishism and Imagination: Dickens, Melville, Conrad* (Baltimore: Johns Hopkins University Press, 1982), esp. 81–82. Ramon Saldivar gives a useful

(though somewhat predictable) account of Ishmael's commitment to metaphoric substitution in *Figural Language in the Novel: The Flowers of Speech from Cervantes to Joyce* (Princeton, N.J.: Princeton University Press, 1984), 141–51. My own sense is that Starbuck, Ishmael, and Melville are all practitioners in metaphoric substitution, while Ahab is not.

22. *Annals of Congress*, 15th Congress, 2nd session (1818–19): 838.

23. *Register of Debates in Congress*, 21st Congress, 1st session (1829–30): 1103.

24. *White-Jacket*, 150.

25. These astonishing phrases are collected by Sacvan Bercovitch in *The American Jeremiad* (Madison: University of Wisconsin Press, 1978), 114.

26. Emmerich de Vattel, *The Law of Nations* (New York: Samuel Campbell, 1796), 1: 94.

27. Ibid., 161.

28. *New York Morning News*, October 13, 1845. Quoted in Frederick Merk, *Manifest Destiny and Mission in American History* (New York: Knopf, 1963), 25.

29. Frank Kermode, *The Sense of an Ending: Studies in the Theory of Fiction* (New York: Oxford University Press, 1966), 86.

30. Winthrop D. Jordan, *White Over Black: American Attitudes Toward the Negro, 1550–1812* (Baltimore: Penguin Books, 1969), 433–34.

31. David Walker, *Appeal, to the Coloured Citizens of the World* (1829; rpt. New York: Hill and Wang, 1965), 49.

32. Ibid., 39–40.

33. This comment came, significantly enough, from the *Columbian Sentinel* of Boston. See Charles M. Wiltse's "Introduction" to Walker's *Appeal*, x.

34. Thomas Wentworth Higginson, "Nat Turner's Insurrection," in *Black Rebellion: A Selection from "Travellers and Outlaws"* (1889; rpt. New York: Arno, 1969), 276; "About Niggers," *Putnam's* 6 (December 1855): 608–12; William Wells Brown, *The Negro in the American Rebellion* (1867; rpt. New York: Kraus Reprint, 1969), 24, 36.

35. Jefferson, *Notes on the State of Virginia* (1787; rpt. New York: Norton, 1972), 162.

36. Stowe, *Uncle Tom's Cabin* (1852; rpt. New York: Bantam, 1981), 218.

37. Ibid., 264.

38. I am here concurring with Ramon Saldivar's observation about Ahab's "reliance on action." See *Figural Language*, 124–41. This "reliance on action," I further suggest, has a historical context, for instance, that of slave rebellion.

39. It is no accident, surely, that—even though he is really a victim—Ahab is nevertheless given the name of a biblical aggressor doomed by his deeds of aggression.

40. *White-Jacket*, 151.

41. The statement here, marking the first time the phrase "manifest destiny" was used, appeared in the July 1845 issue of the *United States Magazine and Democratic Review*. The anonymous article was attributed to John L. O'Sullivan. See Weinberg, *Manifest Destiny*, 111–12.

42. *A Treasury of American Folklore*, ed. B. A. Botkin (New York: Crown Publishers, 1944), 276.

43. *Register of Debates in Congress*, 21st Congress, 1st session (1829–30): 1103.

44. J. G. A. Pocock's idea about time as a political category is developed in *Politics, Language, and Time* (New York: Atheneum, 1971), and, more crucially, in *The Machiavellian Moment: Florentine Political Thought and the Atlantic Republican Tradition* (Princeton, N.J.: Princeton University Press, 1975).

45. Samuel Stanhope Smith, "Of the Natural Bravery and Fortitude of the American Indian," Appendix to *An Essay on the Causes of the Variety of Complexion and Figure in the Human Species* (1787; rpt. Cambridge: Harvard University Press, 1965), 213; Parkman, *Conspiracy,* 1: 191; Schoolcraft, *The American Indians,* 150; Parkman, *Conspiracy,* 1: 160, 48.

46. Parkman, *Conspiracy,* 1: 48.

47. The Cherokees, who had not only farms but printing presses, schools, and churches, were censured for having become *too* civilized, and were accordingly dispossessed. For an account of the dumbfounding logic presented to justify their dispossession, see Weinberg, *Manifest Destiny,* 85–89.

48. Jonathan Arac discusses an analogous process in Hawthorne's use of "character." See "The Politics of *The Scarlet Letter,*" in *Ideology and Classic American Literature,* ed. Sacvan Bercovitch and Myra Jehlen (Cambridge: Cambridge University Press, 1986), esp. 255–59.

49. My sense of personification as a vehicle of control and even a vehicle of subjection differs from Bainard Cowan's view of allegory as "a cultural activity that arises at moments of crisis in the history of a literate people," an activity that permits that culture to "recogniz[e] its necessary discontinuity with received tradition." See his *Exiled Waters: Moby-Dick and the Crisis of Allegory* (Baton Rouge: Louisiana State University Press, 1982). In focusing on personification as a vehicle of dominion, I am in some sense addressing the underside of the phenomenon Cowan discusses, not the project of redemption at the moment of crisis, but the project of control.

50. Jacques Lacan, "The Mirror Stage," in *Ecrits,* trans. Alan Sheridan (New York: Norton, 1977), 2.

51. My discussion of the self here uses many of the terms Sharon Cameron discusses in *The Corporeal Self: Allegories of the Body in Melville and Hawthorne* (Baltimore: Johns Hopkins University Press, 1981). My somewhat different conclusions come from my different sense of the self's status and function.

52. In virtually ignoring Ishmael, I am departing from a tradition in Melville criticism that has focused on Ishmael not only as the center of *Moby-Dick* but, in one way or another, as its figure of redemption. Important works along this line include Walter Bezanson, "*Moby-Dick:* Work of Art," in "*Moby-Dick*": *Centennial Essays,* ed. Tyrus Hillway and Luther S. Mansfield (Dallas, Tex.: Southern Methodist University Press, 1953), 30–58; Paul Brodtkorb, *Ishmael's White World* (New Haven, Conn.: Yale University Press, 1976); Edgar Dryden, *Melville's Thematics of Form* (Baltimore: Johns Hopkins University Press, 1968); Warwick Wadlington, "Godly Gamesomeness: Selftaste in *Moby-Dick,*" in *The Confidence Game in American Literature* (Princeton, N.J.: Princeton University Press, 1975). One important exception to this tradition is the already cited essay by Donald Pease, "*Moby-Dick* and the Cold War," whose skeptical view of Ishmael I share.

Lisa Lowe

Nationalism and Exoticism: Nineteenth-Century Others in Flaubert's *Salammbô* and *L'Education sentimentale*

Orientalist Text as Cultural Artifact

THE NECESSARILY DIVERSE WAYS in which we construct and approximate the "macropolitical" field in nineteenth-century studies vary not only according to the national culture through which one approaches the field, but certainly also according to the nature of the materials through which one reads, reconstitutes, and perhaps, invents the "macropolitical"—whether they be historical, literary, or para-literary materials. The "macropolitical" can be extrapolated then as a heterogeneous composite of the diversity of "micropolitical" descriptions; we arrive at one sense of "macropolitics" through a variety of analyses of specific textual moments in the nineteenth century. In my study, I consider the means and strategies through which different types of otherness—national, cultural, historical, and sexual—are rhetorically postulated and parodied in the texts of Flaubert. Flaubert's texts are cultural artifacts that dramatize some of the dynamics peculiar to the nineteenth-century culture by which they are produced, and which they, in turn, produce; the urgent concerns with a national identity distinguishable from culturally, economically, and sexually different Others, emerges at this moment from French involvements in North Africa and the rivalries between France and other continental nations, as well as from the conflicts between classes and ideologies within the unstable French state itself. Figurations of the oriental, the woman, and the barbarian masses, as Others of a national bourgeois identity, textualize the desires of French national identification in an age of instability, as much as this textualizing contributes to, and further determines, the convention of establishing a national identity in the projection of different Others. The orientalism in Flaubert's texts does not merely indicate how an Orient is constructed as an Other of the Occident as a means of establishing a coherent European national identity; it also provides some illustrative statements about the kinds of macropolitical circumstances which generate the narratives of Occident and Orient, male and female, and bourgeois and worker, in nineteenth-century France.

The importance of the Orient as a *topos* in Flaubert's work has been noted in a number of recent studies both of Flaubert and of orientalism.[1] Particularly the *Voyage en Orient* (1849–52), an account of Flaubert's travels through Egypt and the Middle East, and *Salammbô* (1862), his novel set in Carthage after the First Punic War, occupy influential positions in the French tradition of orientalism. It is a tradition that includes literatures as different as eighteenth-century travel fictions by Montesquieu or Voltaire, nineteenth-century narratives of pilgrimages to the Orient by Volney or Chateaubriand, the diversely orientalist twentieth-century novels of Pierre Loti, André Malraux, or Marguerite Duras, and the more theoretically self-conscious representations of Japan and China by Roland Barthes or Julia Kristeva. The Orient evoked in the last three centuries of French literature is alternately figured as a powerfully consuming unknown, a forbidden erotic figure, a grotesquely uncivilized world of violence, and a site of incomprehensible difference. In all senses, the place of the Orient is a richly literary space, where French culture inscribes its various myths and preoccupations by invoking an imaginary and culturally different Other.

The diversity of narratives about the Orient reflects different states of urgency in the history of French nationalism; the importance of defining a fixed and prominent identity among other western European nations changes in different ages, and the French representations of the Orient vary as territories, boundaries, and empires change. In eighteenth-century travel literature, for example, the Orient is often figured as a metaphorical reflection of a notion of occidental Self, geographically displaced onto a fictional land; the colonial concern with land and empire is expressed in this geographical trope. In contrast, during the nineteenth-century, the Orient is frequently represented as a female figure, and the narrative of Occident and Orient is figured in the rhetorical framework of the romantic quest; the female Orient is a metonymical reduction of what is different from and desired by the masculine European subject. For example, in *Salammbô,* the occidental regard for a constructed oriental opposite is not only eroticized, but figured as the quest for the forbidden female priestess Salammbô; the spatial logic of eighteenth-century travel literature—which asserts the geographical centrality of Europe and distances non-European Others—becomes, in the nineteenth century, a hetero-erotic and gendered relationship. Orientalist techniques of figuration resonate and collude with the nineteenth-century literature which constitutes women as romantic and sexual objects. The projection of Others as not simply culturally but sexually different constitutes a figuration of social and political crises in a rhetorical register of sexuality: for example, the instability of the regimes oscillating between revolution and reaction after 1789, the crisis of class definition in a bourgeois age, the changes in family, gender, and social structure in a time of rapid industrialization, urbanization, and emigration—these may all be figured in the concerns with the centrality and coherence of masculine individuality over and against a powerfully different feminine Other. The problematic tensions within the French identity are rhetorically condensed into the *topoi* and rhetorics of cultural difference between France and other nations, and the sexual difference between male and female.

In 1853, Flaubert wrote to Louise Colet of the Egyptian courtesan, Kuchuk-Hânem, one of the subjects of the *Voyage en Orient*. His description of "la femme orientale" is paradigmatic of the vivid intersection and collusion of the discourses of orientalism and colonial domination, and that of romantic desire and the sexual domination of women: "La femme orientale est une machine, et rien de plus; elle ne fait aucune différence entre un homme et un autre homme. . . . C'est nous qui pensons à elle, mais elle ne pense guère à nous. Nous faisons de l'esthétique sur son compte."[2] In Flaubert's letter, "la femme orientale" is invented as an exaggerated sensuality and sexuality against which "civilized man" may be distinguished, but in this invention, she only generates sexuality, she is unable to comprehend its pleasures. There is no correspondence between "la femme orientale" and women of North Africa and Asia; rather, the representation "la femme orientale" is a metonymy of an invented opposite to an imagined European masculinity, an otherness whose referent is not femininity but rather the construction of masculinity based upon the notion of masculine desire. Further, the equation of the oriental woman and the highly prized object of the industrialized nineteenth century, the machine, reduces and dehumanizes Kuchuk-Hânem, and renders her the technology, and sexual pleasure the surplus value, for which the "femme/machine" is exploited. But the portrait of the Egyptian woman is a representation of a European masculine desire to master, and in the unsuccessful mastery of "her"—"she" does not recognize Flaubert, he does not succeed in inscribing himself on the oriental world, it overwhelms him, is complete without him—it is an equal and concomitant statement about the Frenchman's anxiety about a failure of this desire, against which the desire to master is articulated.

The last decade of criticism on orientalism,[3] particularly since Edward Said's influential study (*Orientalism*, 1979), suggests that these literary Orients are invented, and that "the cultures and nations whose location is in the East" are dominated by means of these fictions, or constructed misrepresentations. Orientalism is a discourse, Said argues, which is, on the one hand, homogenizing—the Orient is leveled into one indistinguishable entity; and is, on the other hand, anatomizing and enumerative—the Orient is an encyclopedia of details, divided and particularized into manageable parts; the discourse manages and produces information about an invented Other, which locates and justifies the power of the knowledgeable European Self. My essay, following Said's notion of orientalist discourse, considers a moment of the French orientalist tradition to describe how texts, as cultural artifacts, construct cultural narratives about the relationship between Occident and Orient. However, I depart from Said's critique in several respects. First, European productions and managements of difference are not limited to inscriptions of cultural difference, but take the forms of ascriptions of gender, class, caste, race, and nation, as well. For example, in different texts by Flaubert, the oriental figures enunciate the structuring themes of quite different discourses: the representation of Kuchuk-Hânem in the *Voyage en Orient* (1850) and *Correspondance* (1853) figures her oriental otherness in both racial and sexual terms; whereas in *Salammbô* (1862) the drama of the barbarian oriental tribes builds upon a concurrent discourse about the French working class revolts of 1848; and in *L'Education sentimentale* (1869), the oriental motif is invoked as a figure of sentimental and romantic desire, offering a literary critique of this *topos*. In this sense, I would like to foreground gender and class as two equally important valences of difference within nineteenth-century French orientalism, to propose that the constructions of "woman" as the Other of man, and the barbarian mass as the Other of the bourgeois commercial class, are ideological tropes as powerful as the orientalist constructions, and to suggest that, in this regard, marxist and feminist theories provide crucial methods of deconstructive reading.[4]

Secondly, if we understand from this observation of the importance of class and gender that inscription and domination are not uniform, but multivalent, operating through a plurality of discourses at different moments, this heterogeneity contradicts the notion of orientalist discourse as discrete, monolithic, and mastering. The cultural text of Flaubert's orientalism exemplifies that any "discourse of orientalism" is bound up with, indeed reanimates some of the structuring themes of, other discourses that emerge in the nineteenth century: e.g., the colonial and scientific discourses concerning "race," the medical discourses about "sexuality," the commercial discourses of industry and class. Further, discourses are not univocal, they include not only dominant formations, but challenges to those dominant formations. The orientalizing formations articulated in Flaubert's *Salammbô* and *Voyage* are reiterated and parodied at another moment in the corpus, in *L'Education sentimentale*. Flaubert's divided corpus exemplifies one instance of the greater discursive field that is heterogeneous, dynamic, and dialectical. The notion of orientalist discourse as mastering generates readings that render orientalist texts unequivocally appropriative or dominant with regard to the one cultural Other treated by the texts; whereas a consideration of orientalist discourse as a heterogeneous, rather than homogeneous, series of rhetorics, tropes, and literary traditions through which the management and production of many Others take place, permit us readings in which we trace not only the desires for mastery, but the critiques of these desires as well. In other words, the critique of orientalism is not simply a late twentieth-century post-colonial critical position retrospectively applied to a tradition: the societies and historical moments which produced these texts are already divided and already self-critical, and the tensions between the desires of orientalism and the failures of these desires are already thematized within the texts of these societies. In this sense, my readings of Flaubert's corpus do not consider it as a unified, purely "colonizing" corpus which exemplifies a misrepresentation and appropriation of women, non-Europeans, and the working class; rather, my reading concentrates on the ways in which the various texts reflect different states of conflict in the history of French nationalism. While the *Voyage, Correspondance,* and *Salammbô* exemplify nineteenth-century orientalisms which figure the Orient as female or barbarian Others, the later work, *L'Education sentimentale,* thematizes and critically observes orientalism; the narrative of *L'Education* thematizes Frédéric's use of the oriental motif, and calls attention to it as an emblem of Frédéric's sentimentalism. As my reading of the novel's final reminiscence of the bordello of "La Turque" suggests, orientalism is ultimately targeted in *L'Education* as a regressive *topos* of sentimentality, a posture of subjective and cultural instability in the figuration of an Other. Flaubert's corpus, considered as a series of orientalist moments, reflects the divided and conflicted nature of nineteenth-century French culture itself; the orientalism of the various texts is multivalent and heterogeneous, expressing a plurality of ideologies. The texts of orientalism themselves contain critiques of orientalist logics and rhetorics.

Thirdly, it seems necessary to revise and render more complex the thesis that an ontology of Occident and Orient appears in a consistent manner throughout all cultural and historical moments,[5] because the operation which grants this kind of uniform coherence and closure to any discourse risks misrepresenting the far more heterogeneous conditions and operations of discourses. When Michel Foucault posits the concept of "discursive formations"—the regularities in groups of statements, institutions, operations, and practices—he is careful to distinguish it as an *irregular* series of regularities which produce objects of knowledge. In other words, a phenomenon, such as the notion of the Orient, is said to be constituted by a "regularity"—the conjunction of statements and institutions (maps, literary narratives, treatises, missionary reports, diplomatic politics, etc.) pertaining to the Orient; however, the manner in which these materials conjoin to produce the category "Orient" is unequal to the conjunction constituting it at another historical moment, or in another national culture.[6] In a like manner, I would argue against the "historical desire" to view the occidental conception of the oriental Other as an unchanging *topos*, the origin of which is European man's curiosity about the non-European world. The misapprehension of an identical construction of an object through time does not adequately appreciate that the process through which an object of difference—the Orient—is constituted, is enabled precisely by the non-identity through time of such notions, Occident and Orient. That is, the identification of a static dualism of identity and difference as the means through which a discourse expresses domination and subordination, upholds the logic of the dualism and fails to account for the "differences" (internal discontinuities, heterogeneity) inherent in each term. In the case of orientalism, the misunderstanding of uniformity prohibits a consideration of the plural and inconstant referents of both terms—Occident and Orient; the binary opposition of Occident and Orient is a misleading perception which serves to suppress the specific heterogeneities, inconstancies, and slippages of each individual notion.[7]

In addition, the assumption of a unifying principle—even one that we must assume to be partly true, that the representation of the Orient expresses the colonial relationships between Europe and the non-European world—leaves uninvestigated the necessary possibility that social events and circumstances other than the relationships between Europe and the non-European world are represented in the literature about the Orient, and that the relative importances of these other conditions differ over time and by culture. Allegorizing the meaning of the representation of the Orient as if it were exclusively and always an expression of European colonialism analyzes the relationship between text and context in terms of a homology, an overdetermining of meaning such that every signified must have one signifier, and every narrative one interpretation. Such a totalizing logic represses the heterologic possibilities that texts are not simple reproductions of context—indeed that "context" is plural, unfixed, unrepresentable—and that orientalism may well be an apparatus through which a variety of concerns with differences are figured. I consider the "Orient as Other" as a literary trope that may register a variety of national crises—at one time, the race for colonies; at others, class conflicts and workers' revolts, or changes in the sexual roles in a time of rapid urbanization and industrialization. Orientalism facilitates the inscription of many different kinds of differences as oriental otherness, and the use of oriental figures at one moment may be distinct from their use in another historical period, in another set of texts, or even at another moment in the same corpus.

A very important and necessary political statement is contained in the thesis that orientalism is an expression of European imperialism. Yet, when we polemically propose that the discourse of orientalism is both discrete and monolithic, this falsely isolates the discourse and ignores the condition that discourses are never singular; discourses operate in conflict, they overlap and collude, they do not produce fixed or unified objects. For this reason, my essay treats orientalism as one discourse in a complex intersection. My reading of the heterogeneity of orientalism, based on this nineteenth-century moment represented by the corpus of Flaubert, does not dispute the orientalist criticism that argues that there is a discernible history of European representation and appropriation of the Orient; I do, however, problematize the assumption that orientalism *monolithically* constructs the Orient as Other of the Occident. The purpose of making this distinction is to challenge the critical perception of a single univocal discourse that dominates and controls forms of cultural difference. My essay ultimately rejects the totalizing paradigm that grants such authority to a managing discourse, because this kind of paradigm tends to understand all forms of resistance to be contained within the discourse.

The Orient as Woman: Salammbô and Kuchuk-Hânem

The novel *Salammbô* concerns the Carthaginian priestess Salammbô and Mâtho, the leader of the mercenary army who falls in love with her. Salammbô is the daughter of the Carthaginian ruler Hamilcar and is betrothed by her father to a rival leader. In the story of Mâtho's impossible desire for Salammbô, the oriental woman is exoticized as distant, forbidden, and inaccessible, and is objectified as the prize or bounty of Mâtho's war against Carthage. The Barbarians' efforts, under Mâtho's leadership, to penetrate barricaded Carthage, to puncture the city's aqueduct, and to steal the sacred veil of Tanit are contemporary with Mâtho's growing desire for the virgin priestess Salammbô; the simultaneity of the two conquest themes contributes to the figuration of the oriental city of Carthage as the woman, Salammbô. The cultural and historical alterity of Carthage as the Orient, are figured in the sexual alterity of Salammbô, as woman. Salammbô is, as woman, a complicated representation of multivalent and intersecting inscriptions: she is a forbidden object of desire as well as a material object of exchange, the barricaded city and the virgin priestess, the infinite beauty of "la nature" and the sacred, violent, oriental world. She is a fiction of European man's Other, represented as the seducer and recipient of Mâtho's desire, as the prey and object of men's social exchange in war, and as a metonym of the wealthy city of Carthage who starves its mercenary children.

Two separate descriptions of Salammbô's entrances emblematize her different functions in the novel as eroticized woman and as object of exchange in war. The first occurs when she enters the courtyard where the mercenary soldiers are feasting at her father's house in his absence. During the feast, the soldiers have proclaimed the injustice of the Carthaginian republic in having neglected to pay them for their labor during the war with Rome. They curse Hamilcar's wealth and power; they kill the sacred fish of the Barca family.

> Enfin elle descendit l'escalier des galères. Les prêtres la suivirent. Elle avança dans l'avenue des cyprès, et elle marchait lentement entre les tables des capitaines, qui se reculaient un peu en la regardant passer.
>
> Sa chevelure, poudrée d'un sable violet et réunie en forme de tour selon la mode des vierges chananéenes, la faisait paraître plus grande. Des tresses de perles attachées à ses tempes descendaient jusqu'au coins de sa bouche, rose comme un grenade entr'ouverte. Il y avait sur sa poitrine un assemblage de pierres lumineuses, imitant par leur bigarrure les écailles d'une murène. Ses

bras, garnis de diamants, sortaient nus de sa tunique sans manches, étoilée de fleurs rouges sur un fond tout noir. (12)

In this passage, Salammbô is described in a vertical descension, from her hair, to her mouth, her breasts, her arms, and finally her ankles. The descriptive gaze of the narrator anatomizes, particularizes, and sequesters isolated parts of Salammbô. The gems of her "costume" are an ironically conspicuous display of her market value as an object, her significance as Hamilcar's daughter. The attention to the "perles," "pierres lumineuses," and "diamants" of Salammbô's dress marks her as the embodiment of Hamilcar's hoarded wealth, the "war-chest" desired by the mercenary soldiers as she enters the scene. And yet the narration remains at a distance from her; the gaze does not penetrate into the interior of Salammbô, but remains fastened upon the jewels, textures, and fabrics of her dress. Salammbô, although described in particulars, is not a character in the immediate world of the novel as others might be, but rather a represented figure which calls attention to itself as representation, unknowable, eccentric, and extravagant to the narrator and the mercenary soldiers. Salammbô is compared to "un tour," "une grenade," and "une murène"; while the metaphors attempt to capture Salammbô, she is nonetheless rendered quite strange by these comparisons. The metaphor of the tower evokes height, but at the same time, the comparison renders the woman excessively tall and unfamiliar, almost dwarfing the men below. Salammbô is paradoxically distanced and isolated, objectified and desired by the narrative description. "Salammbô" is a figure for contradiction; she is concrete and worldly, like her gems, but she has a remote unworldly aspect which resists possession and referentiality.

The *topos* of the descending oriental woman, both eroticized and materially objectified, appears also in the *Voyage en Orient* in Flaubert's first encounter with the Egyptian courtesan, Kuchuk-Hânem.[8]

> Sur l'escalier, en face de nous, la lumière l'entourant et se détachant sur le fond bleu du ciel, une femme debout en pantalons roses, n'ayant autour du torse qu'une gaze d'un violet foncé.
> Elle venait de sortir du bain, sa gorge dure sentait frais, quelque chose comme une odeur de térébenthine sucrée. . . .
> Ruchiouk-Hânem est une grande et splendide créature, plus blanche qu'une Arabe, elle est de Damas; sa peau, surtout du corps, est un peu cafetée. Quand elle s'asseoit de côté, elle a des bourrelets de bronze sur ses flancs. Ses yeux noirs et démesurés, ses sourcils noirs, ses narines fendues, larges épaules solides, seins abondants, pomme. (487–88)

Between 1849 and 1851, Flaubert traveled in Egypt and the Middle East. Among his most notable portraits is the one of Kuchuk-Hânem, who appears in both the letters from Egypt and the *Voyage en Orient*. Kuchuk-Hânem is said to be the model for Salammbô, and Flaubert wrote *Salammbô* upon his return from his travels. And yet the Orient that Flaubert writes about in his travels and articulates in the letters about Kuchuk-Hânem is an Orient received from cultural myths and a literary tradition. As with the descent of Salammbô, the Egyptian woman enters the narrative gaze from an elevated position on the staircase. There is an allusion to her height, as well, in "[elle] est une grande et splendide créature." However, it is not simply in her height that she is rendered strange. She is called a "créature," as if she is a different species, not human, animal. Further, her eyes are "noirs et démesurés," and their scale and color seem to make them icons of her difference. The perspective from which the Egyptian woman is regarded is a disturbingly immediate one, and the writer of the *Voyage* emphasizes her otherness not through the use of distancing metaphors (as in the passage introducing Salammbô) but through the intimacy of the bodily and sensual detail in the descriptions of her race and her sex. In "Quand elle s'asseoit de côté, elle a des bourrelets de bronze sur ses flancs," the narrator constitutes not only her otherness as an Egyptian in the attention to the color of her skin "un peu cafetée," but her otherness as a woman, as an erotic object scrutinized very near, as well. A perspective of close proximity is utilized to aestheticize her image, to reduce her as object; the very details—"n'ayant autour du torse qu'une gaze d'un violet foncé," "seins abondants, pomme"—establish and privilege the artist's eye and constitute Kuchuk-Hânem as object. It is upon the objectivity of Kuchuk-Hânem that the subjectivity, the "métier" and identity of Flaubert, is established.

In the passage describing Salammbô's second descent, she greets her father Hamilcar when he returns to Carthage after the First Punic War.

> Salammbô descendait alors l'escalier des galères. Toutes ses femmes venaient derrière elle; et, à chacun de ses pas, elles descendaient aussi.
> Hamilcar s'arrêta, en apercevant Salammbô. Elle lui était survenue après la mort de plusieurs enfants mâles. D'ailleurs, la naissance des filles passait pour une calamité dans les religions du Soleil. (139–40)

The two descents—the one before the mercenary soldiers, Mâtho, and Narr'Havras, the other before Hamilcar—indicate two dimensions of Salammbô's objectification as woman. In the first passage, she is a remote, inaccessible sexual object; in the second, as she greets her father, she is a material object of exchange, useful only to Hamilcar as wealth to barter. In the first, the woman is beloved, sought, and desired; in the second, she is daughter, disdained and exchanged for a better price. The objectification of the woman as material possession is particularly evident in Hamilcar's attitude toward Salammbô when he receives the rumor that his daughter may have lost her virginity to the leader of the Barbarian tribes. Hamilcar's rage at imagining his daughter's violation mixes with his anger about the theft of the sacred veil, as well as his indignation that his properties and riches have been mismanaged in his absence: "malgré ses efforts pour les bannir de sa pensée, il retrouvait continuellement les Barbares. Leurs débordements se confondaient avec la honte de sa fille" (153). For Hamilcar, hearing of his daughter's alleged rape is equal to his discovery that property from his home has been stolen. It is the combined effect of acknowledging all of his losses—his material loss of property, as well as the loss of ownership of Salammbô, which the hypothetical loss of her virginity represents to him—which moves Hamilcar to accept the command of the Carthaginian armies against the Barbarian tribes. When Hamilcar enlists the aid of the Numidian tribes, he offers his daughter as bride to Narr'Havras, the Numidian king, saying "En recompense des services que tu m'as rendus, Narr'Havras, je te donne ma fille." Narr'Havras' gratitude is described: "[Il] eut un grand geste de surprise, puis se jeta sur ses mains qu'il couvrit de baisers." (235) Salammbô is the prize, the bounty, exchanged between men at war. The economy of war between men is based upon the woman as territory which is bartered and exchanged. The man is granted the possession of the woman when he kills for another man. Although "ses mains" is somewhat ambiguous in its reference, it is presumably Hamilcar's hands which Narr'Havras kisses; through the exchange of Salammbô, the two men are erotically united.[9] Salammbô is described as being "calme comme une statue, semblait ne pas comprendre" (235)—she is the token whose receipt seals the contract that the Numidians will kill for the Carthaginians.

French Barbarians in *Salammbô*

Salammbô takes place in 240 BC, after Carthage loses to Rome in the First Punic War, when the various North African tribes who had been employed as mercenaries by Carthage revolt against the Carthaginian Republic. The novel describes the wars between Carthage and these Barbarian tribes. At the time of the First Punic War, Rome and Carthage are competitors for trade in the western Mediterranean. Although a world which is historically and geographically other to nineteenth-century France is evoked, it is not difficult to recognize in *Salammbô* echoes of themes from Flaubert's France. Just as Carthage is a commercial republic competing with Rome for markets and empire, so too is early nineteenth-century France an emerging commercial force, threatening and being threatened by Great Britain. Napoleon's defeats by the British are echoed in Carthage's repeated defeats, under Hamilcar, and then his son Hannibal, in the First (264 BC), Second (218–201 BC) and Third (149–146 BC) Punic Wars. The decline of Carthage is due as much to its losses to Rome as to the revolt of the Barbarian tribes of North Africa, just as the instability of France after its international losses in the periods of bourgeois revolt (1830) was shaken further by the workers' revolts during the Revolutions of 1848. Yet while the Roman Republic is a forceful determinant in the war between Rome and Carthage and its mercenaries, Rome is conspicuously absent from the novel, which focuses strictly on the war between Carthage and the Barbarians.[10] Rather than figuring France's Roman Other, the Barbarian tribes in *Salammbô* may be understood as a simultaneous figuration of the two "internal" and "external" Others constituted as threats by French bourgeois society in the mid-nineteenth-century: on the one hand, the volatile and emergent French working class whose concerns erupt in 1848, and on the other hand, the North African colonies violently occupied by French armies in the 1830s and 1840s. The extreme brutality of the battle scenes in *Salammbô* alienates the slaughter of rioting masses in 1848 onto a very distant historical setting, at the same time that the location of the violence in North Africa curiously "confesses" the equally violent French activities in North Africa and Egypt during the first half of the nineteenth century. The French occupation and military subjugation of Algeria in the 1830s and 1840s, which included systematic massacres of the native populations, is de-familiarized in the portrait of Carthage's commercial and military exploitation of the nomad peoples outside the walls of the city. Internal class violence and external nationalistic violence are thematized in the novel, but the responsibility for those violences is quite apart from France when it is detoured into the oriental world of Carthage and the surrounding Barbarian tribes. A world of war—determined by commercial greed and the desire for empire, and founded upon the subjugation of other lands and other peoples—is removed by the exotic context of *Salammbô*.

The fascination with the themes of war in the novel—the subjugation of many races of people by the Carthaginian Republic, the penetration of the walled-in city, war as the alliances and enmities among men, the status of women as the bounty of the war between men—reveals a particular displacement of both French fascination with, and denial of its own nineteenth-century war efforts, in North America, Africa, and continental Europe, as well as in France itself. Because the historically distant Orient is not contemporary with modern Europe, the slaughter of the warring factions can be distanced and aestheticized. In the novel's juxtaposition of two powerful populations, Carthage and the Barbarians, the structure of the novel portrays each as equal to the other: each is involved in a frenzy of violence, each disapproves of the other's violence, and does not recognize that the other community's barbarism is thoroughly present within their own group. In the wars between Carthage and the Barbarians, the novel itself thematizes the process by which one group's violence is expelled in the image of the threatening and different Other.

The dynamic by which one group is constituted as "outside" or Other to the hegemonic culture is represented by the description of the nomad peoples who live just outside of Carthage. These nomads are described as Mâtho and the Barbarians approach the walls of the city.[11]

> Il y avait en dehors des fortifications des gens d'une autre race et d'une origine inconnue,—tous chasseurs de porc-épic, mangeurs de mollusques et de serpents. Ils allaient dans les cavernes prendre des hyènes vivantes, qu'ils s'amusaient à faire courir le soir sur les sables de Mégara, entres les stèles des tombeaux. Leur cabanes, de fange et de varech, s'accrochait contre la falaise comme des nids d'hirondelles. Ils vivaient là, sans gouvernement et sans dieux, pêle-mêle, complètement nus, à la fois débiles et farouches, et depuis des siècles exécrés par le peuple, à cause de leurs nourritures immondes. (*Salammbô*, 60–61)

This passage contains an inventory of the means by which a group of nomads who live outside the walls of the city are classified and constituted as Other—as barbarian—by the Barbarians themselves, who are approaching the fortifications. They are described as "d'une autre race," a difference and exteriority marked by their position outside the walls of the city of Carthage, and "d'une origine inconnue," beyond Mâtho's people's territory of information and experience. They are outside of history, and eccentric to culture and civilization. They retreat into caves to hunt "leurs nourritures immondes"; they eat prohibited, unclean, wild foods, like porcupines, shellfish, and snakes. Their dwellings, "de fange et de varech," are made of materials which are coded as primitive and natural. Hayden White discusses the cultural function of the Other as "savage" as a "technique of ostensive self-definition by negation. . . . If we do not know what we think 'civilization' *is*, we can always find an example of what it is not."[12] In a complementary observation, Mary Louise Pratt notes that there are very particular ethnographic "tropes"—literary figures or commonplaces—which characterize the reports of European anthropologists encountering native, "primitive" cultures.[13] This description of the nomads as "sans gouvernement et sans dieux . . . complètement nus" exemplifies a number of tropes, used throughout the eighteenth and nineteenth centuries, for constituting cultural and historical otherness as a chaotic "nature," before language, society, and law. The notion of the "primitive" which evolves throughout European philosophical, political, and literary discourses (like the notions of the "oriental") comprises a genealogy of myths, a series of signifiers, which refer to the desire of European culture to define itself through negation, in terms of what it fears it is, and desires not to be. Rousseau's descriptions of primitive man in the state of nature in the second *Discourse,* or Montesquieu's Troglodytes in the *Lettres persanes,* express less about the origins of western civilization than they do about the dilemma of national self-representation and French cultural desires during the Enlightenment. To the extent that these tropes are recognizable as established rhetorics for constituting difference, *Salammbô* thematizes its own orientalism and the displacement of French barbarism—against both North African and working class Others—into a novel about oriental violence. That the novel levels the two sides of the conflict between Carthage and the Barbarians, revealing each to be equally barbaric, suggests that nationalism and war depend upon the representation of one's own barbarism in the Other. The "othering" of the nomads by the Barbarians is repeated in the attitudes of Carthage and the Barbarians towards one another: the disdain for the Other, the inability to recognize the Other's crimes as one's own.

Carthage's violence towards the Barbarians is described in sensualized, particularized detail, as are the Barbarian tortures of Carthaginians. Descriptions of the brutality waged by one group against the other are also present in the accounts of the slaughter of soldiers and workers during the June battles of 1848 in *L'Education sentimentale,* and suggest that the battle scenes in *Salammbô* are curious statements about the failures and loss of human life in 1848, as well as symptoms of the preoccupation with and unsuccessful denial of the French massacres in North Africa. But of interest is the remarkable rhetorical equality of Carthaginian and Barbarian tortures of their foes. Both sides are grotesque and barbaric, and neither more so than the other. The equality of the two warring groups suggests a reflection of the one group's sadism in the brutality of the Other. Carthage's torture of the Barbarians is described:

> Les deux milles Barbares furent attachés dans les Mappales, contre les stèles des tombeaux; et des marchands, des goujats de cuisine, des brodeurs et même des femmes, les veuves des morts avec leurs enfants, tous ceux qui voulaient, vinrent les tuer à coups de flèche. On les visait lentement, pour mieux prolonger leur supplice: on baissait son arme, puis on la relevait tour à tour; et la multitude se poussait en hurlant. . . .
> Puis on laissa debout tous ces cadavres crucifiés, qui semblaient sur les tombeaux autant de statues rouges. (184)

The sadism of the Barbarian troops is likewise described in painful detail:

> Les hommes y vinrent ensuite, et ils les suppliciaent depuis les pieds, qu'ils coupaient aux chevilles, jusqu'au front, dont ils levaient des couronnes de peau pour se mettre sur la tête. . . . Il envenimaient les blessures en y versant de la poussière, du vinaigre, des éclats de poterie: d'autres attendaient derrière eux; le sang coulait et ils réjouissaient comme font les vendangeurs autour des cuves fumantes. (241)

In both passages, one community of soldiers perceives the other community, and there is a condemnation of the lack of conscience, of the extent to which the torturers are unmoved by their own violence and the suffering of the Other. In the first passage, describing the Carthaginian tortures, the prisoners are a spectacle for the by-standers to enjoy, and several merchants make profits by selling to the crowds the arrows with which they will render the "cadavres crucifiés." In the second, describing the Barbarians putting vinegar and irritants in the soldiers' wounds, the torturers are described as being as joyful as winemakers. Neither faction is privileged in the representation of the fascination with the other's violence, and in this sense, in Flaubert's text *Salammbô* the workers' revolts are as cynically condemned as they are in *L'Education sentimentale*. The mutual fascination and equality of violence represent a description of the means by which Others are regarded and objectified in the constitution of the national class and cultural identity. The manner in which Carthage constitutes the Barbarians as sacrilegious and sexually violent, and the Barbarians consider Carthage to be cruel and hoarding, are themselves emblems of the process by which the oriental world of *Salammbô* is produced, and enjoyed as a spectacle of displaced violence, by the novel.

The Oriental Motif as Sentimentalism: *L'Education sentimentale*

Flaubert's texts reflect the divided and conflicted nature of the nineteenth-century culture in which they are produced and which they, in turn, produce. As cultural products, a variety of ideologies coexist within Flaubert's texts just as a multiplicity of positions compete within the culture; in this sense, the orientalism in Flaubert's texts is multivalent and heterogeneous, expressing a plurality of often contradictory concerns. For example, Flaubert may have traveled to and written about the Orient as an attempt to escape from bourgeois society and to find a position from which to criticize French society; in this sense, the appearance of the Orient in his work is one representation of cultural self-criticism, of an anti-bourgeois position.[14] But the figuration of the oriental as Other in Flaubert's texts equally textualizes the cultural preoccupation with defining a coherent national identity—and bourgeois identity—at a moment when its stability is challenged by external rivalries with other nations, and internal upheaval and social dislocations during and following the revolutions of 1848. As I suggest earlier, the construction of the Orient as "les Barbares" in *Salammbô* is, on a cultural level, a bourgeois projection of the internal threat in 1848 by workers and revolutionaries (and continuing beyond 1848 to the Paris Commune), as much as the figuration of the Orient as an exteriority may equally register French anxiety about the wars between the French and other nations. In addition to the plurality of ideological positions represented, the narrative styles of the texts are themselves complexly ironic and divided. In *L'Education sentimentale* (1869), for example, the "style indirect libre"[15] for which Flaubert is so famous, merges narratorial and subjective modes to achieve the greatest elimination of distance between narrator and character. The result is a subtly ironic narrative that in one description preserves the subjective perspective of Frédéric's thoughts as it simultaneously represents a narratorial commentary and critique of that perspective, through mimicry of Frédéric's idiom and through the ironic juxtaposition of different contexts in which these idioms occur. Thus, while Frédéric has a penchant for oriental symbols, and orientalism is present in *L'Education* as an aspect of Frédéric's world, at the same time, I suggest that the orientalist posture which associates the Orient with eroticism is established in the narrative as Frédéric's posture; and as a mark of Frédéric's sentimentalism, the use of the oriental motif is mocked, parodied, and ultimately criticized.

Oriental motifs—a painting of a Turkish odalisque by Ingres, a Chinese parasol, an Egyptian tarbouche—occur in the novels as fragments of an exotic world elsewhere, signifiers of "l'au-delà," references to oriental contexts eccentric to the scenes in which they are invoked. These motifs accompany and come to characterize the young man's erotic interest: Léon imagining he finds in Emma's shoulders "la couleur ambrée de l'*Odalisque au bain*"; the harpist playing "une romance orientale, où il était question de poignards, de fleurs et d'étoiles" during Frédéric's first sight of Madame Arnoux; or the "chaînette d'or" between the ankles of Salammbô seen by Mâtho when she first enters the group of soldiers. As fragments, they quote from the detailed iconographies of other orientalist texts which associate certain motifs with the Orient: nude slaves, daggers, gold ankle chains. They are incomplete, partial quotations, and their fragmentary natures underscore their standing as marks of incompletion, and hence, as marks of desire. For example, in *Madame Bovary* (1856), Léon's imagination of Emma's shoulders as those of the Turkish odalisque in Ingres's painting does not refer to a woman in a Turkish harem. In imagining Emma as Ingres's subject, Léon expresses his desire by invoking an already established association of the oriental and the erotic; the erotic relationship of present lover and absent beloved, and eroticism as the transgression of prohibition and taboo, are expressed in an oriental motif. The association of orientalism and this particular type of eroticism is not coincidental, for the two situations of desire—the occidental fascination with the Orient, and the young adulterer's passion for Emma Bovary—are structurally similar. Both paradigms depend upon a binary structure which locates the Other— as woman, as oriental scene—as inaccessible, different, beyond. In addition, Léon's desire for Emma reveals desire as fundamentally a matter of cultural quotation, or the repetition of cultural signs; the metaphor of Emma's shoulders as those in Ingres's painting is twice-distanced: itself a quotation of an orientalist painting, it signifies orientalism in order to signify erotic desire. Just as Emma learns her desiring posture from popular novels,[16] Léon casts this moment of his desire in an orientalist and equally literary mode. Ironically enough, Ingres never traveled to North Africa or the Near East, but derived the colors and textures for his bathers, odalisques, and Islamic interiors "from the eighteenth-century illustrations and the descriptions found in the letters of Lady Mary Wortley Montagu and in

Montesquieu's *Lettres persanes* (1721)."[17] In the sense that Ingres received his Orient from literary sources, it is a "literary" Orient that he painted, and Léon's notion of desire is as "literary" as that of Emma. The oriental motif is the distinguishing mark of sentimentalism in Flaubert—a sentimentalism which longs for a memory of earlier innocence, an impossible union, a lost wholeness in which European culture is faithfully reflected in its oriental Other. This paradigm of sentimentalism, represented by the oriental motif, is exemplified, critically observed, and ultimately mocked by the occurrences of the motifs in *L'Education sentimentale*.

The oriental motif, though perhaps not central to *L'Education*, emerges nonetheless as the mark which characteristically expresses and initiates Frédéric's erotic desire. The first time Frédéric meets Madame Arnoux aboard the steamboat, a harpist plays an oriental ballad. The narration of this scene begins, "Il la supposait d'origine andalouse, créole peut-être," which establishes the figuration of Madame Arnoux as exotically Other as Frédéric's perceptive mode, and this passage describing the oriental melody, though undesignated by a pronoun as belonging to Frédéric, continues his romantic idiom and postures. The throbbing of the boat's engine makes loud and uneven noises so that the harpist must play louder to compensate:

> les battements de la machine coupaient la mélodie à fausse mesure; il pinçait plus fort: les cordes vibraient, et leur sons métalliques semblaient exhaler des sanglots et comme la plainte d'un amour orgueilleux et vaincu. (41)

Frédéric's adulterous desire for Madame Arnoux is signified, as is Léon's in *Bovary,* by the quotation of fragments from orientalism; not only is the ballad a fragment, an emblem of incompletion and desire, but in this image, the Orient of its origin is also associated with a lost, threatened past. Frédéric's impossible passion for Madame Arnoux is personified in the sobbing sounds of the plucked notes as the musician attempts to be heard over the engine noises. In this image, the narrative observes Frédéric's conflation of several kinds of censorship and prohibition: the noises from the engine impinge upon the delicate sounds of the ballad, as the bourgeois Arnoux obstructs Frédéric's passion for Arnoux's wife, and even more grandly, as western industrial society supersedes an earlier oriental age of plenitude and sensuality. Frédéric's plight is dramatized as the plight of a lost, earlier oriental civilization. Desire is figured in a romantic opposition: an earlier temporality is juxtaposed with a corrupted present, an unknown plenitude opposed to a known world. The oriental ballad is always already tortured and sad; from the first moment, Frédéric's desire for Madame Arnoux is already characterized as loss and impossibility. Frédéric's idealization of Madame Arnoux is continually characterized by an exaggerated drama about loss, and is underscored by the hyperbolic language used to express his infatuation: "Plus il la contemplait, plus il sentait entre elle et lui se creuser des abîmes. Il songeait qu'il faudrait la quitter tout à l'heure, irrévocablement, sans avoir arraché une parole, sans lui laisser même un souvenir!" (43) The intensity of Frédéric's desire is represented by the growing enormity of the abysses he imagines opening between them; the moment of contact with her is overdetermined by the inevitable subsequent separation. The narrative critically observes Frédéric creating his sublime sentiment for Madame Arnoux by dramatizing her inaccessibility in the inversion of two moments—the future in which Madame Arnoux is gone is substituted for the present moment of contact. She is constituted as already lost, the moment of contact thoroughly desired because it is irrevocably past. The oriental motif is the mark under which Frédéric's sentimentalizing posture takes place.

The oriental motif occurs at other moments in the novel, as well. Frédéric's passion for Madame Arnoux is continually associated with travel to distant oriental lands: he imagines that he and Madame Arnoux will travel to "des pays lointains . . . au dos des dromadaires, sous le tendelet des éléphants" (101), and he dreams of her "en pantalon de soie jaune, sur les coussins d'un harem" (102). Later, a bawdy party attended by Frédéric and his young friends takes place in "moresque" rooms, under "une toiture chinoise" where Hussonet speaks the now typical conflation of the erotic and the oriental by suggesting "un raout oriental" (105). When he is not able to attend Madame Arnoux's birthday, Frédéric selects for her "une ombrelle . . . en soie gorge-pigeon, à petit manche d'ivoire ciselé, et qui arrivait de Chine." (112) The motifs are completely heterogeneous fragments—camels and elephants, bits of Moorish interiors, a Chinese silk parasol with carved handle—they are incomplete quotations of disparate orientalisms, and their fragmentary qualities as *motifs* call attention to their importance as signifiers and as marks of desire. Further, the orientalist texts themselves, to which these motifs refer, also represent postures of incompletion, ultimately sentimental paradigms which constitute the invented Orient as a sublime ideal, a lost otherness, a time and space removed from the occidental world. The oriental motif calls attention to itself as a signifier which does not correspond or refer to "cultures and nations whose location is in the East,"[18] and, in effect, does not signify except to signify orientalism (a larger tradition of postures of incompletion). It is an emblem of the desire to signify desire, as if the structure and character of desire is—as Lacan suggests[19]—a perpetual series of linguistic and social postures of incompletion, which does not find its completion in objects but renews itself in the signification of other desiring postures. That the novel represents desire as inhering in the metonymic substitution of one signifying posture for another is echoed in Frédéric's voyage from one love interest to another: from the infatuation with Madame Arnoux, to the desire for Rosanette, to the interest in Madame Dambreuse. Frédéric's love-choices parallel his efforts to rise into the society of the "haute bourgeoisie"; he wishes to signify himself and his social standing by the possession of women from particular classes (or women possessed by other men of particular classes); his efforts are unsuccessful, and the progress of his desire is the repeated substitution of one woman for another, or one signifying posture for another. Indeed, in a single day, he visits all three women, going from one residence to the next (IIc:ii), and on the day of the fateful rendez-vous with Madame Arnoux on la rue Tronchet, Frédéric makes love with Rosanette "dans le logement préparé pour l'autre" (307).

After Frédéric has deserted Rosanette, spurned Madame Dambreuse, and refused finally to consummate his love with a much older Madame Arnoux, the novel ends with Frédéric's "atrophie sentimentale" (394). The Revolutions of 1848 have given way to the installation of Louis Napoléon in 1851. It is not only the young men in the novel who do not achieve their ambitions, but their society does not achieve the ideals of equality and liberty—lost first in 1789 and now again in 1848. Frédéric's disillusionment in love corresponds to the political disillusionment after the virtual restoration of the old structures of wealth and privilege during the Second Empire. The failure of the revolutions and the betrayal of revolutionary ideals by the bourgeoisie is most poignantly figured when Frédéric witnesses the death of his working-class friend Dussardier at the hands of Sénécal, a former revolutionary turned "agent de police." Frédéric's long desire for and pursuit of Madame Arnoux is one model of sentimental idealism observed throughout the novel, but the novel also draws an analogy between Frédéric's education in love and the political education of the French society which has suffered two thwarted efforts at revolutionary social change. Frédéric's love quest, a process of desire already marked by the loss of the object, is compared to the story of the failure of the revolutions of 1848 to achieve the egalitarian society already desired and lost in 1789.[20] In this metaphor of the young man's sentimentalism and his society's aspirations, the revolution and its political idealism are judged severely.

The oriental motif which marks Frédéric's and Deslauriers' reminiscence of the bordello at the end of the novel, provides the final commentary on the oriental figuration of erotic desire. The two friends' remembrance of their first visit to a house of prostitution in 1837 is introduced by an explanation of how the woman who ran the house had come to be called "la Turque": many people believed her to be a Muslim from Turkey, and as this "ajoutait à la poesie de son établissement" (444), she was from that point known as "la Turque." Hearsay embellished the house with an exotic flair, endowing it with an intriguing erotic quality.

> Ce lieu de perdition projetait dans tout l'arrondissement un éclat fantastique. On le désignait par des périphrases: «L'endroit que vous savez,—une certaine rue,—au bas des Ponts.» (445)

Frédéric and Deslauriers recall that the townspeople would use euphemisms when speaking of the house of prostitution. Ambiguous, non-referential phrases like "l'endroit que vous savez" were used to signify the prohibited site of sexuality. "La Turque" also serves the purpose of a periphrasis, a turning or deferring of meaning, used to signify the unknown sexuality within the house of prostitution. The oriental motif of "la Turque" does not refer to the woman who manages the house (indeed, she does not appear in their reminiscence), nor does it refer to Turkey; "la Turque" is the periphrasis used by the young boys to signify the plenitude of unknown women and sexual practices. It is also the *motif* under which Frédéric and Deslauriers reconstitute the adolescent position of curiosity, still uninterrupted by failure and disillusionment. The remembered scene has value as a reconstructed moment of pure idealism and innocence: Frédéric presents a bouquet "comme un amoureux à sa fiancée" (445), and, flustered by the presence of so many women, he ultimately flees.[21] Frédéric leaves the establishment of "la Turque" a virgin, still inexperienced, with all desire and all disappointment ahead of him. The irony of this final scene in which Frédéric and Deslauriers invoke a lost moment of plenitude, is punctuated by their final declarations: "C'est là ce que nous avons eu de meilleur!" In a characteristically romantic strategy, the two friends perform a dialectic of presence and absence, rhetorically substituting a constructed past—"c'est là"—for their fallen, corrupted present states. The invocation of the house of "la Turque" as the place where they had their happiest times replaces their condition of loss with a reconstituted plenitude of adolescent virginity. The novel portrays Frédéric in an endless repetition of these desiring postures, marked by the oriental motif, as an unsignifying signifier of incompleteness. This final use of the motif suggests Frédéric's ultimate lack of change; though older, more weary—having lived under Louis Philippe, through the revolutions, and now under Napoléon III—Frédéric invokes once more the adolescent oriental motif to recall an earlier state of desire.

Flaubert's texts—especially the representations of the Egyptian courtesan in the *Voyage en Orient* (1850) and *Correspondance* (1853), and *Salammbô* (1862)—exemplify a nineteenth-century orientalism which figures the Orient as an erotic female Other. The later work, *L'Education* (1869), departs from this orientalism, thematizing rather than strictly exemplifying the orientalist posture; the narrative observes Frédéric's use of the oriental motif, and calls attention to it as an emblem of Frédéric's sentimentalism. The scene in which Frédéric remembers "la Turque" is entirely in contrast to Flaubert's description of the courtesan Kuchuk-Hânem in the *Voyage* and the *Correspondance*. The scene from *L'Education* exposes Frédéric's invention of oriental exoticism as sentimentality. In a sense, it offers us a retrospective critique of orientalism within the Flaubertian corpus itself, while the earlier description of "la femme orientale" in the *Correspondance* most vividly exemplifies the orientalizing posture which both desires and debases its culturally and sexually different object. To the degree that orientalism and sentimentalism are equated in *L'Education,* the narrative criticizes the ultimate delusion and regression of the orientalist posture. It is as if the various texts in the "oeuvre" of the author Flaubert were themselves different orientalist moments on a continuum in which, to greater and greater degrees, the narrative calls attention to orientalism as a posture, and ironically contextualizes that posture. With *L'Education,* the orientalist imagery is no longer performed by the narrative, but is instead mocked as a function of the protagonist. The final reminiscence of a reconstituted ideal moment under the signifier of "la Turque" (the name itself is a received hearsay, a periphrastic reference to another orientalist text), illustrates the utility of the oriental motif as sentimentalism, as much as the reminiscence emphasizes how the oriental motif indeed fails to signify throughout the novel. The narrative's use of the oriental motif to signify Frédéric's sentimentalism is appropriate, because the individual paradigm of sentimentalism is structurally similar to the cultural paradigm of orientalism: each substitutes an invented otherness for a present condition of failed self-possession or unstable cultural identity.

Orientalist Criticism

It is not sufficient to merely characterize the shapes, rhetorics, and postures of French orientalism, however, for, in a sense, these criticisms may contribute further to a static notion of the "discourse of orientalism." I would prefer instead to apply my readings of Flaubert—as plural, conflicted multivalent texts in which representations of class, culture, and gender overlap and intersect in a variety of ways—towards the project of challenging the very idea of a "discourse of orientalism."

At particular moments in critical theory in the United States, the notion of "the Other" has been powerful, illuminating, transformative. For example, in feminist debates, these moments are marked by the publication of works such as Juliet Mitchell's *Psychoanalysis and Feminism* (1974), or Nancy Chodorow's *Reproduction of Mothering* (1978), or Gayatri Chakravorty Spivak's important introduction to her translation of Jacques Derrida's *Of Grammatology* (1976). Similarly, Edward Said's *Orientalism* (1979) and his analysis of the construction of "the Orient as Other" initiated a questioning of scholarly assumptions in several academic disciplines—in modern and classical literary studies, in history—not the least of which is a serious ongoing interrogation of ethnographic practices within the field of anthropology.[22] Analyses of how races, cultures, economic groups, or sexualities are marked and figured as "other," or as the subordinated counterpart of dominant privileged categories, are absolutely essential to our current project of cultural criticism. Yet I believe we risk certain dangers in continuing to use monolithic notions of both "discourse" and "the Other": on the one hand, the production of more of this kind of theory may enunciate and be deeply implicated in the powerful hegemonies it seeks to criticize; and, on the other hand, these theories may greatly underestimate other points and positions of struggle and resistance operating in the discourse at all moments. The view that a dominant discourse produces and manages the Other, univocally appropriating and containing all dissenting positions within it, underestimates the tensions and contradictions within a discourse, the continual play of resistance, dissent, and accommodation by different positions. This type of dominant discourse theory minimizes the importance of minority group counter-representations and counterideology, and continues to subsume the minority to the majority. The idea that a dominant discourse monochromatically misrepresents and produces a minority ties us too strictly to the very literal notion that cultural politics and ideological changes are always a matter of numbers (a greater number has a greater voice), and perpetuates the over-determined mythology that minority interests are always represented by the majority. This cannot be the case if we recognize that local regions of economic, sexual, and racial minorities are continually resisting and contesting particular uses of the classification of "otherness" and thematizing the very misuse of the classification as a powerful means of altering its function. To begin to account for this resistance while continuing to recognize the functioning category of the "Other" in discourse, I believe we must consider instead the heterogeneity of acts of representation. On the one hand, marks of difference and otherness are multivalent; the mark of difference which is at one time a mode of exclusion may at another historical moment or in another set of social relations be an enabling mark of inclusion.[23] On the other hand, discourses are what I would call "heterotopical"; discourses are heterogeneously and irregularly composed of statements and restatements, contestations and accommodation, generated by a plurality of writing positions at any given moment. The theoretical problem facing us in cultural criticism is not how to fit anomalous positions into a fixed dualistic conception of dominant ideology and counter-ideology, or discourse and counter-discourse. Rather, it is the other way around; heterogeneities and pluralities are givens in culture. These non-equivalences and non-correspondences are not the objects to be explained; they must constitute the beginning premise of any analysis.

It is my contention that the accepted usage of the idea of a closed discourse which manages and produces a single object has left the dynamics of dissent, intervention, resistance, and change inadequately theorized. In other words, the use of the notion of a dominant discourse is incomplete if not accompanied by a critique which explains why some positions are easily co-opted and integrated into apparently-dominant discourses, and why others are less likely to be appropriated. I believe that the critical work identifying a "discourse of otherness" should include a discussion of reification and hegemony, as well as an analysis of how the reification of categories such as "otherness" and "difference" incorporates within them the very logics of domination and subordination, hegemony and counter-hegemony. The premise that representations of difference and otherness are multivalent—that they can be at one time marks of exclusion, at other times used in arguments for enfranchisement, and still at others appropriated again as different means of exclusion—has direct ramifications for how we, in literary and cultural criticism, construct our future arguments. For when the *topos* of "the Orient as Other" is used as a mode of argument to analyze the power of orientalism, this mode of argument itself may contribute to the very logic it seeks to criticize. In this sense, the ultimate aim of my essay is to challenge and resist the "logic of otherness" and to historicize the critical strategy of identifying the representations of otherness as a discursive mode of production itself. For if we understand the "logic of otherness" as an apparatus in which is inscribed a logic of domination and subordination, then we must also question the continuing efficacy of using this logic as a critical method. By interrogating the utility and responsibility of the concept of "the discourse of the Other," we can begin to rethink the notion of discourse and work toward the theorizing of change and resistance within discourse.

Notes

1. Jean Bruneau, Le "Conte oriental" de Gustave Flaubert (1973); Edward Said, Orientalism (1979); Richard Terdiman, Discourse/Counter-Discourse (1985); Naomi Schor, Breaking the Chain: Women, Realism and the French Novel (1985).

2. Flaubert, Correspondance in Oeuvres complètes de Gustave Flaubert, 313–14.

3. The 1984 Essex conference on the Sociology of Literature, entitled "Europe and Its Others" and focused on representations of colonial and imperial power, is a fine example of the aftermath of orientalist criticism and the attention given to Said's work. Topics covered in the published volume of papers include orientalist painting, Flaubert in Egypt, Islam and the idea of Europe, the Chinese and Japanese in the USA, aspects of India under the British, and multiculturalism in Australia. Said, also, presents a reconsideration of Orientalism in the light of its reception. (Colchester: University of Essex, 1985.)

The Group for the Study of Colonialist Discourse, out of the University of California, Santa Cruz and Berkeley, is a network responsible for concentrating and generating some recent anti-colonialist criticism and other responses to orientalism.

"Race," Writing and Difference, ed. Henry Louis Gates, Jr. (1986) constitutes another forum responding to the implications and consequences of Said's theory of otherness.

The debates in anthropology and cultural criticism represented in two collections of essays, Writing Culture: The Poetics and Politics of Ethnography, ed. James Clifford and George Marcus (1986), and Anthropology as Cultural Critique: An Experimental Moment in the Human Sciences, ed. George Marcus and Michael M. J. Fischer (1986), are also clearly marked by Said's work. Indeed, of all the modern disciplines, perhaps it is the anthropological project of one culture authoritatively rendering another culture, which has been most shaken by Said's notion of orientalist discourse.

4. Notable and important work that explores this nexus of colonialist discourse with discourses about class and gender includes Malek Alloula, The Colonial Harem (1986); Gayatri Chakravorty Spivak, In Other Worlds (1988); Lata Mani's work on the discourse on "sati" in nineteenth-century Bengal; Trinh T. Minh-ha, Woman,

Native, Other: Writing Postcoloniality and Feminism (1989). See also *Inscriptions* Nos. 3/4 (1988) entitled "Feminism and the Critique of Colonial Discourse."

5. This is one implication of Said's *Orientalism*, in which he writes: "Orientalism is a style of thought based upon an ontological and epistemological distinction made between 'the Orient' and (most of the time) 'the Occident.' . . . in short, Orientalism as a Western style for dominating, restructuring, and having authority over the Orient." (2–3) The inference that Orientalism is a constant and monolithic discourse is illustrated by others' interpretations of Said: e.g., James Clifford, 1988; B. J. Moore-Gilbert, 1986. Moore-Gilbert, for example, argues for the need to reappraise Said's presentation of orientalism as monolithic by calling attention to the incongruity between the West's relationship to Arabs and Islam and Britain's relationship to India.

However, in the work subsequent to *Orientalism*, Said has turned his attention to situations of post-colonial emergence, making it clear that he is not a proponent of the kind of monolithic rendering that does not account for resistance. See "Identity, Negation and Violence," *New Left Review* (December, 1988); and the forthcoming *Culture and Imperialism*. At the same time, Said's work does continue to stress the homogeneity and dominance of an imperialism of a single character, and to de-emphasize what I would consider equally important, the heterogeneity of different imperialisms and specific resistances.

6. With the idea of an "irregular series," Foucault emphasizes that both the conditions of discursive formation and the objects of knowledge are neither identical, static, nor continuous over time. In this way, Foucault devises a project that avoids some of the primary idealities of traditional historical study—the desire for origins, unified developments, or causes and effects. Conceiving of history as an irregular series of discursive formations is an alternative method that takes into account non-linear events, discontinuity, breaks, and the transformations of both the apparatuses for producing knowledge and what is conceived of as "knowledge" itself. After having rejected four hypotheses concerning the unifying principles of a discursive formation—reference to the same object, a common style in the production of statements, constancy of concepts, and reference to a common theme—Foucault characterizes the active principle of discourse as "dispersion."

> Whenever one can describe, between a number of statements, such a system of dispersion, whenever, between objects, types of statement, concepts, or thematic choices, one can define a regularity (an order, correlations, positions and functionings, transformations), we will say, for the sake of convenience, that we are dealing with a *discursive formation*. . . . The conditions to which the elements of this division (objects, mode of statements, concepts, thematic choices) are subjected we shall call the *rules of formation*. The rules of formation are conditions of existence (but also of coexistence, maintenance, modification, and disappearance) in a given discursive division. (*Archaeology of Knowledge* 38)

7. This is borne out most simply in the different meanings of the "Orient" over time: in many eighteenth-century texts, the Orient signifies Turkey, the Levant, and

the Arabian peninsula occupied by the Ottoman Empire, now known as the Middle East; in the nineteenth-century literature, the notion of the Orient additionally refers to North Africa; and in the twentieth century, more often to Central and Southeast Asia. Notions such as "French culture," "the British Empire," or "European nations," are replete with ambiguity, conflicts, and non-equivalences, as well. And we will see that the nineteenth-century British literature about India is marked by an entirely different set of conventions, narratives, figures, and genres, from the French literature about Egypt and North Africa of the same period. For the British and French cultural contexts for producing such literatures at that particular moment are distinct: not only are there many non-correspondences between the individual national cultures and literatures, but in the nineteenth century, Britain's century-old colonial involvement in Indian culture, economy, and administration, and France's more recent occupation of North Africa, exemplify non-equivalent degrees of rule and relationship.

8. Flaubert, *Voyage en Orient* in *Oeuvres complètes de Gustave Flaubert*, 487–88. The name of "Kuchuk-Hânem" appears variously and inconsistently in the *Voyage* and the *Correspondance*.

9. In a most interesting manner, in *La femme dans les romans de Flaubert: mythes et idéologie* (1983), Lucette Czyba associates the reduction of Salammbô as an object of exchange with the homoeroticism of war. She argues that "La femme est la proie, la victime désignée dans l'univers de violence masculine et sadique qui caractérise la guerre et qui mêle indissolublement la volupté à la mort." (130) Czyba suggests that the sadism of war in *Salammbô*, may be the obverse aspect of erotic bonding between men. Both male "eros" and "thanatos" have the common characteristic of excluding women from a closed society of men; the two parts of the war economy are compatible and mutually productive.

10. In *Improvisation sur Flaubert* (1984), 117, Michel Butor suggests that Carthage is "la face cachée de la Rome antique," at once denied and suppressed by Rome, the precursor of France, and yet signifying Rome, and by implication, France. One may think of Carthage as the oriental Other of Rome, the Other of Christianity and classical antiquity. The absenting of Rome decenters Rome as the western origin, and presents the French tale in the oriental disguise of Carthage.

11. All quotations from *Salammbô, Madame Bovary,* and *L'Education sentimentale* are from editions of Garnier-Flammarion, Paris.

12. Hayden White, "The Forms of Wildness: Archaeology of an Idea," and "The Noble Savage Theme as Fetish," in *Tropics of Discourse* (1978), 150–96.

13. Mary Louise Pratt, "Fieldwork in Common Places," in *Writing Culture,* ed. Clifford and Marcus (1986), 27–50.

14. This interpretation of Flaubert's orientalism is offered by Richard Terdiman in *Discourse/Counter-Discourse,* Part II, Chapter 5.

15. The discussions of Flaubert's style are many. For particularly lucid explications, see: Roy Pascal, *The Dual Voice: Free Indirect Speech and Its Functioning in the Nineteenth-Century European Novel* (1977); Dominick LaCapra, *"Madame Bovary" on Trial* (1982).

16. That Emma takes her particular notion of romantic desire from the clichés of

popular novels, and from the songs she sang in the convent as an adolescent, has been noted by many critics, including: Victor Brombert, *Flaubert* (1971); Jonathan Culler, *Flaubert: The Uses of Uncertainty* (1974); Tony Tanner, *Adultery in the Novel* (1979).

17. From *The Orientalists: Delacroix to Matisse*, ed. MaryAnne Stevens (1984), 17, catalogue to the exhibit of nineteenth-century orientalist paintings at the National Gallery in Washington, D.C. in 1984. The exhibit included in its collection several paintings of odalisques by Jean-Auguste-Dominique Ingres even though he, like many orientalist painters, "never travelled to North Africa or to the Near East."

18. Said, *Orientalism* (1979).

19. The notion of the "signifying chain" is clearly articulated in "Agency of the Letter in the Unconscious or Reason Since Freud," *Ecrits* (1977), 146–78.

Lacan's subject is situated in and by language, language being the most determining structure in the Symbolic, or social realm. Lacan discusses signification in the Symbolic as a process in which every signifier corresponds not to a signified, but to another signifier: "no signification can be sustained other than by reference to another signification." (150) Desire inheres in the chain of signifiers, and more particularly in the incommensurability of word and thing, the failure of metaphoric similitude and the determined succession of metonymic associations. "It is in the word-to-word connexion that metonymy is based." (156) The metonymic structure, or the connection between signifier and signifier "permits the elision in which the signifier installs the lack-of-being in the object relation, using the value of 'reference back' possessed by signification in order to invest it with the desire aimed at the very lack it supports." (164)

20. For a discussion of historical representation in Flaubert's novel and Marx's *Eighteenth Brumaire of Louis Bonaparte*, see Hayden White, "The Problem of Style in Realistic Representation: Marx and Flaubert," in *The Concept of Style* (1979), 213–22.

21. Faced with so many women available to him, the young Frédéric is speechless, and when the women laugh, he flees thinking they are mocking him: "d'un seul coup d'oeil, tant de femme à sa disposition, l'émurent tellement, qu'il devint très pâle et restait sans avancer . . . il s'enfuit." (445) Victor Brombert, *Flaubert* (1971), 98–100, has noted that the final reminiscence of the bordello is "un résumé en miniature" of many of the previous themes in the novel: Frédéric's flight when confronted with choices is a tendency echoed throughout the novel, in his repeated inability to choose a woman to whom he can be committed or a vocation to which he can be tied, in his fear of humiliation and his obsession with reputation.

22. The significant debates in anthropology are represented in two volumes: Clifford and Marcus (1986); Marcus and Fischer (1986). For Said's response to these debates, see "Representing the Colonized: Anthropology and its Interlocutors."

23. By "multivalent," I mean that marks denoting social class, race, culture, or gender differences acquire distinct significances in different contexts; these marks may in one period or culture be used to exclude and marginalize a social group, while in another they may be appropriated as marks of privilege or empowerment. I discuss the problem of multivalence with regard to the position of Asian Americans in the university, in "Differences: Theory and the University."

Stuart Hall has remarked that the names "black" and "coloured" signify quite differently in the distinct contexts of England and the Caribbean. He observes that in the English system, organized around a binary dichotomy which reflected the colonizing order of "white/not-white," the terms "black" and "coloured" are more or less synonymous, while in the Caribbean system, where race is organized in an ascending spectrum of classifications, "black" and "coloured" denote different points on the scale rising towards the ultimate "white" term. See "Signification, Representation, Ideology: Althusser and the Post-Structuralist Debates," *Critical Studies in Mass Communication* (June, 1985).

Another example is the construction of "race" in contemporary U.S. society, which has changed since the 1950s, as the result of many factors, including the civil rights movements of the 1950s and 1960s. In *Racial Formation in the United States: From the 1960's to the 1980's* (1986), Michael Omi and Howard Winant argue persuasively that previous paradigms for analyzing racial formation—an ethnicity-based theory, a class-based theory, and a nation-based theory—are not sufficient. Omi and Winant theorize a process of "racial formation," in which social, economic, and political forces determine the content and importance of racial categories and racial meanings, through the examination of the different meanings of race from the 1950s to the 1980s.

There is also multivalence and non-correspondence in the signification of gender. For example, in middle-class literary discourse in early eighteenth-century England, the classification of female connoted domesticity, sexual fidelity, passive virtue. By the early nineteenth century, when female authority had asserted itself in the domestic sphere, in courtship, in family relations, marks of femininity had different meanings and different categories of female identity emerged. For study of the role of gender in culture and its relation to political change in eighteenth- and nineteenth-century England, see Nancy Armstrong, *Desire and Domestic Fiction* (1987).

Works Cited

Alloula, Malek. *The Colonial Harem*. Trans. Myrna Godzich and Wlad Godzich. Minneapolis: University of Minnesota Press, 1986.

Armstrong, Nancy. *Desire and Domestic Fiction*. New York and Oxford: Oxford University Press, 1987.

Brombert, Victor. *Flaubert*. Paris: Seuil, 1971.

Bruneau, Jean. *Le "Conte oriental" de Gustave Flaubert*. Paris: Denoël, 1973.

Butor, Michel. *Improvisation sur Flaubert*. Paris: Editions de la Différence, 1984.

Clifford, James. *The Predicament of Culture: Twentieth-Century Ethnography, Literature, and Art*. Cambridge, Mass.: Harvard University Press, 1988.

Clifford, James and George Marcus, eds. *Writing Culture: The Poetics and Politics of Ethnography*. Berkeley: University of California Press, 1986.

Culler, Jonathan. *Flaubert: The Uses of Uncertainty*. Ithaca, N.Y.: Cornell University Press, 1974.

Czyba, Lucette. *La Femme dans les romans de Flaubert: mythes et idéologie*. Lyon: Presses Universitaires de Lyon, 1983.

Flaubert, Gustave. *Oeuvres complètes de Gustave Flaubert*. Volumes 10 and 13. Paris: Club de l'Honnête homme, 1973.

———. *Madame Bovary*. Paris: Garnier Flammarion, 1979 (1856).

———. *L'Education sentimentale*. Paris: Garnier Flammarion, 1969 (1869).

———. *Salammbô*. Paris: Garnier Flammarion, 1961 (1862).

Foucault, Michel. *The Archaeology of Knowledge*. Trans. A. M. Sheridan Smith. New York: Pantheon, 1972.

Gates, Henry Louis, Jr., ed. *"Race," Writing and Difference*. Chicago: University of Chicago Press, 1986.

Hall, Stuart. "Signification, Representation, Ideology: Althusser and the Post-Structuralist Debates." *Critical Studies in Mass Communication* (June, 1985).

Lacan, Jacques. *Ecrits*. Trans. Alan Sheridan. New York: Norton, 1977.

LaCapra, Dominick. *"Madame Bovary" on Trial*. Ithaca, N.Y.: Cornell University Press, 1982.

Mani, Lata. "The Construction of Women as Tradition in Early Nineteenth-Century Bengal." In *Minority Discourse*. Ed. Abdul Jan Mohamed and David Lloyd. Oxford: Oxford University Press, 1990.

Marcus, George and Michael M. J. Fischer, eds. *Anthropology as Cultural Critique: An Experimental Moment in the Human Sciences*. Chicago: University of Chicago Press, 1986.

Minh-ha, Trinh T. *Woman, Native, Other: Writing Postcoloniality and Feminism*. Bloomington: Indiana University Press, 1989.

Moore-Gilbert, B. J. *Kipling and "Orientalism."* London: Croom Helm, 1986.

Omi, Michael and Howard Winant. *Racial Formation in the United States*. London: Routledge, 1986.

Pascal, Roy. *The Dual Voice: Free Indirect Speech and Its Functioning in the Nineteenth-Century European Novel*. Manchester: Manchester University Press, 1977.

Said, Edward. *Orientalism*. New York: Random House, 1979.

———. "Identity, Negation and Violence." *New Left Review* (December, 1988).

———. "Representing the Colonized: Anthropology and its Interlocutors." *Critical Inquiry* (Winter, 1989).

Schor, Naomi, *Breaking the Chain: Women, Realism and the French Novel*. New York: Columbia University Press, 1985.

Spivak, Gayatri Chakravorty. *In Other Worlds*. London: Routledge, 1988.

Stevens, MaryAnne, ed. *The Orientalists: Delacroix to Matisse*. London: Weidenfeld and Nicolson, 1984.

Tanner, Tony. *Adultery In the Novel*. Baltimore: Johns Hopkins University Press, 1979.

Terdiman, Richard. *Discourse/Counter-Discourse: The Theory and Practice of Symbolic Resistance in Nineteenth-Century France*. Ithaca, N.Y.: Cornell University Press, 1985.

White, Hayden. *Tropics of Discourse*. Baltimore: Johns Hopkins University Press, 1978.

———. "The Problem of Style in Realistic Representation: Marx and Flaubert." In *The Concept of Style*. Ed. Berel Lang. Philadelphia: University of Pennsylvania Press, 1979.

Loren Kruger

Attending (to) the National Spectacle: Instituting National (Popular) Theater in England and France

> une seule condition est nécessaire pour le théâtre nouveau, c'est que la scène, comme la salle, puisse s'ouvrir à des foules, contenir un peuple et les actions d'un peuple. [The new theater should fulfil only one condition: stage and auditorium should alike be open to the masses, contain a people and the actions of a people.]
>
> Romain Rolland

THE IDEA OF REPRESENTING THE NATION in the theater in the double sense of summoning a representative audience which will in turn recognize itself as nation on stage offers a compelling if ambiguous image of national unity, less as an indisputable historical fact, than as an object of speculation. The notion that a stage picture might constitute as well as reflect the nation, might represent (stand in for) the evident lack of national unity, persists throughout the nineteenth century from Schiller and Coleridge on, but becomes increasingly prominent in discussion during the last quarter of the century, in the wake of militant and organized challenges to national unity. Although these debates may not arise in *direct* or *immediate* response to the growth of mass parties antagonistic to the status quo, they nonetheless articulate attempts to address the crisis in the legitimacy of ruling class hegemony provoked by mass mobilization, by asserting the popular validity of national unity in the theater.

Clearly the key term in this schema is the role of the popular audience. The debates revolve around two key issues whose relationship seems at once natural and hotly in dispute: is the audience spectator or participant? incoherent crowd or mature nation? and conversely, does "mature nationhood" call for participation or simply assent? What, in other words, is the force of the people as *agent* of national representation? Populist discourse owes its power (and its ambiguity), as Ernesto Laclau has shown, to its *potential* transformation into an antagonistic class agency of political as well as cultural change, a potential that may nonetheless be absorbed as the neutral acknowledgment of mere diversity within the unified nation.[1]

These questions traverse the discourse of theatrical nationhood in Western Europe but receive particular attention in the France of the Third Republic. The discourse of popular sovereignty is the foundation of the republican tradition; indeed this is the discursive formation that legitimates the Republic *as* tradition, as what Foucault has called the "background of permanence" against which emergent practices can be identified and articulated within the discursive formation,[2] in this case, of a *Republican* populism. The force of this formation as tradition is such that appeals to national identity tend to at least *traverse* if not unconditionally endorse the notion of popular support.

Even if it does not ensure participatory democracy on a national scale, the traditional invocation of the First Republic opens up a public space in which the popular voice and, in particular, popular *dissent* can be rendered politically and culturally *legitimate* in the Third Republic. As Eric Hobsbawm has argued, the advent of mass party politics in the last quarter of the nineteenth century demanded strategies of mass mobilization, from state initiatives such as primary education and public displays of patriotism such as Bastille Day to oppositional intervention such as the May Day parade and the strike.[3] At the same time, however, it is clear that this notion of "the people" is no stable ground on which to erect the nation or the nation's theater, but rather the field of contention for legitimate representation. These public ceremonies have the ambiguous status of what Hobsbawm calls "invented traditions": they may be "mass-produced" to generate public consent to the state and social relations that effectively exclude mass representation, or they may be "mass-produc*ing*," a lightning rod for mass opposition to the state.

The rhetorical force of political appeals to popular representation informs the appeals of popular theater's advocates: theater groups performing for the working-class register their claim to legitimately represent hitherto unrepresented citizens by asserting their popularity. Representatives of the established theater and advocates of a centralized national theater counter by asserting that a theater is truly of the people only when it ceases to be specifically popular (democratic and, in particular, proletarian) in its appeal. Neither assertion, however, can be simply reduced to a particular class position; both claim to address and *therefore* to represent the people as such. On the other hand, the notion of popular theater is not a mere ideological cipher pressed into the service of any and every political appeal; rather it articulates a larger social dispute over the legitimate role of the people. In fact, we can measure the power of this "people" in the extent to which it exceeds the status of an *object* of dispute and emerges instead as the *subject* uniquely capable of articulating national unity.

In order fully to appreciate the significance of this dispute in France and its implications for a macropolitics of popular theater on a national scale, we might begin by looking briefly at the rather different shape that the national theater debate takes on in England. Here, the issue of national (and international) representation in the theater resonates with the full consciousness of Empire. The National Theatre was understood by Parliamentary representatives and National Theatre advocates alike to be the appropriate place and occasion for national contemplation, as legitimate a House as Parliament itself. Yet, as I have shown elsewhere,[4] attempts to summon the "general populace" to join the engineers of Empire as one Nation in the theater were compromised from the start by the populace's resistance. The desire to "invite the masses into history" was haunted by the nagging doubt that the masses would respond to the summons only under duress, a doubt borne out by the coercive undertow in the appeals by such exemplary figures as Matthew Arnold and Harley Granville-Barker, who identified themselves as the "imaginative few" best able to call for national reconciliation in the theater.

Faced with the divided nation that does not recognize itself as exemplary audience of the National drama, Arnold turns to France and its theatrical ambassador, the Comédie française, hoping that this *inter*national exemplum will elevate the British stage and recapture the middle class public that had abandoned the theater earlier in the century:[5]

> This great class . . . is now awakening to the sure truth that the human spirit . . . has a vital need [not only] for religion, . . . but also for expansion, for intellect and knowledge, for beauty. . . . The revelation of these needs brings the middle class into the theatre.
>
> The revelation was indispensable, the needs are real and the theatre is the mightiest means of satisfying them, and the theatre, therefore, is irresistible.[6]

Arnold does not simply acknowledge the fact of the divided nation; he endorses the division by deliberately replacing the actual "riff-raff" currently still attending the theaters with the ideal attendance of the middle class, even as he asserts that the need for beauty is a general truth.

After this explicit and apparently exclusive focus on the middle class as appropriate public for the national theater, the return to the "people" comes as a surprising *après coup:*

> When the institution in the West of London becomes a success, then plant another of its kind in the East. The people *will* have a theatre, then make it a good one.[7]

Arnold's belated inclusion of the working class in the national audience has the effect of neutralizing its opposition. By legitimating as exemplary fine art the kind of theater represented by the Comédie française and dismissing alternatives as "mere entertainment," "amateurism," or simple vulgarity, he appears to want to coerce an indifferent majority into accepting a particular canon as representative of a universal heritage, thus dissolving the dissident cultural (and political) identity of this majority.

If we follow Arnold's example and turn to contemporary developments in France, we encounter a dominant tradition that represents the broad masses, not as "riff-raff" disrupting the spectacle, but as the point of reference for the nation as a whole. Instead of the Comédie whose historical association with a national audience falls far short of Arnold's expectations, a rather different image emerges: the tradition of collective participation in national celebration, perceived and instituted as France's revolutionary republican inheritance. We can see this tradition articulated in reflections from Michelet's retrospective celebration of the people's participation in and even inauguration of the Revolutionary *fêtes* on the eve of the Second Republic (1846–48), to the debates during the Third Republic about the character and needs of national popular audiences and the attempts to address them—in the experiments of Maurice Pottécher (1892), Louis Lumet (1898), and the projects suggested by Eugène Morel (1900) and Romain Rolland (1903), for a popular theater on a national scale—to the foundation of the Théâtre National Populaire begun by Ferdinand Gémier (1921) and consolidated by Jean Vilar (1951). This republican tradition of national festival claims to speak more forcefully to the broad masses and, in so doing, explicitly mobilizes the discourse of "le peuple souverain," displacing the metropolitan elite as subject and object of national theatrical representation.

✳   ✳   ✳

We can sense the weight of this popular rhetoric in Revolutionary legislation promoting and regulating *fêtes publiques* in which the goal of public edification is to be achieved, not by the contemplation of an exemplary dramatic text (on the Enlightenment model of Mercier's "tableau moral" of a "beau moment dans la vie humaine")[8] but rather in the *occasion* of summoning the people to a festival deemed appropriate to the commemoration of significant moments of the Revolution. While the National Convention and the Comité de Salut Publique endorsed exemplary "tragédies républicaines" such as Schiller's *Wilhelm Tell* or Voltaire's *Brutus,* for their appropriate *subject matter,* they went beyond the representation of republican themes, to assert that, in order to command the assent of the people, in other words, "éveiller dans l'âme des citoyens toutes les sensations libérales, toutes les passions généreuses et républicaines,"[9] the Republic should demand active civic participation in ceremonial re-presentations of the Revolution. To this end, the Convention appropriated and orchestrated popular celebrations of the Revolution to produce commemorative pageants, following the precedent set by the Fête de la Fédération on the first anniversary of the Fall of the Bastille and culminating in the Fête de l'Unité orchestrated by David at the beginning of Year II of the Republic (August 10, 1792).[10]

Although Revolutionary theatrical policy never uniformly endorsed pageants to the exclusion of dramatic representation, and indeed returned, in the wake of the Terror, to a traditional emphasis on the canon of classical tragedy, purified of the contemporary republican trappings during the heady days of *sans-culotte* power,[11] this legislation confirms the already evident disruption of the theatrical order of the *ancien régime.* This order was essentially defined by a clear distinction between the legitimate *théâtres,* in particular the Théâtre français, which held an initially absolute monopoly on the performance of dramatic literary works (or *poésie dramatique*) and the small houses on the Boulevard du Temple, where only melodrama (including "comédies larmoyantes," tear-jerkers with appropriate musical interludes) and "spectacles" (from pantomime to variety) were permitted. By 1780, however, the granting of theater licenses to selected boulevard houses had already blurred the line between the "legitimate theater" and its other. Thus, the National Assembly's abolition, in 1789, of the official theaters' monopoly control over the representation of canonical dramatic works helped accelerate the change already underway, by encouraging the boulevard theaters to produce the classics (rather than importing "spectacle" into the Français).[12]

While Revolutionary legislation thus confirmed rather than initiated changes in the repertoire, its most radical consequence reflected in microcosm the macropolitical disruption of the social and political order: the levelling of the theater audience. Whereas, during the *ancien régime,* freedom of access functioned in one direction only, in that the aristocracy frequented the Boulevard as well as the Français and the Opéra, whereas the people attended the small houses only, during the Revolution, the sans-culottes not only *attended* the Français, but endorsed and encouraged the producers to tailor the classical texts to republican taste, most explicitly by choosing appropriate subjects such as Voltaire's *Brutus* and substituting "citoyen" for any form of address deemed unsuitably aristocratic.

Whereas comparable developments in England unleashed a torrent of laments about the decline of the drama,[13] effectively foreclosing any legitimate discussion of the specificity of popular needs and tastes, the Revolutionary designation of the people as nation in France provided a crucial foundation for subsequent reflection on the issue. The key debates that dominate nineteenth (and to a certain extent, twentieth) century discussion—about repertoire (the appropriate balance of classical "universal" drama and the contemporary local appeal of melodrama and vaudeville), location (the claims of the working-class *quartiers* against the metropolitan center of Paris) and appropriate response (edification or diversion) were all interpretations of this original conception of the people. The image of the "peuple souverain" participating in and even writing the national drama, which informs every project for popular theater in France from the nineteenth century to the present, has its most explicit formulation in retrospective accounts of the civic festivals of the Revolution, in which the people ideally present themselves to themselves as nation without the need of symbolic mediation or staging.

*   *   *

Michelet in particular, whose reflections on popular representation, in *Le Peuple* as well as in *The History of the French Revolution,* had an exemplary influence on later theory and practice, returns again and again to the original miracle of popular revolutionary action.

> Nothing is more grand than to see this people advancing towards the light, without any law, but hand in hand. They advance, but do not act; . . . The mere sight of their immense movement causes everything to recoil before them; every obstacle vanishes, and all opposition is removed. Who would think of standing up against this pacific and formidable apparition of a great nation in arms?[14]

What first appears in this account is Michelet's identification with the spontaneous immediacy in the Revolutionary advance. As the account progresses, however, this spontaneous uprising of the people as Revolutionary subject becomes the object of the historian's gaze: it is finally not the action of the crowd, but rather the way it comes into view that interests this historian, who alone can name this spectacle as the "apparition of a great nation in arms."

This illumination of immediate and spontaneous revolution is further refracted by Michelet's concession to the people's apparent need for exemplary leadership and *edification,* in spite or perhaps because of their spontaneous response to nationhood, as his appeal on behalf of a popular theater suggests:

> Tout ensemble, mettez-vous à marcher *devant* le peuple. Donnez-lui l'enseignement souverain qui fut toute l'éducation des glorieuses cités antiques: un théâtre vraiment du peuple . . . le théâtre est le plus puissant moyen de l'éducation, du rapprochement des hommes; c'est le meilleur espoir de la rénovation nationale. (emphasis added)

> All together, take up position in the vanguard of the people. Give them the sovereign instruction that constituted the education of the glorious city-states of antiquity: a theater that was truly of the people . . . the theater is the most powerful means of instruction, for bringing men together; it is [our] best hope for national renewal.[15]

While this exhortation echoes the emphasis, in *Le Peuple,* on the natural wisdom of the people, which needs only to be educed, rather than inculcated by enlightened leaders, the reference to "ancient city states" is significantly ambiguous. While Michelet no doubt intends to invoke the familiar example of classical Greek theater as a representation of organic nationhood, his description conjures up instead the image of the triumphal procession, which corresponds less to a spontaneous celebration than to an orchestrated festival. This gesture repeats rather than resolves this tension between the spontaneous uprising of popular subjects and the orchestration of passive participants, a tension which he inherits from the Revolution,[16] leaving us with a sense of the incommensurability of popular education and spontaneous uprising in Michelet's terms.

Michelet's defense of the spontaneous patriotism of the people and his call for general popular education through the theater are alike grounded in the ambiguous if compelling assumption of the essential unity of the people. This assumption provides the premise for his *History;* it also underlies the argument in *Le Peuple* that, despite *apparently* opposed interests, the various social groups in France (Michelet would not call them *classes*), ideally come together in loyalty to a nation in common. Michelet defends the *natural* character of popular patriotism by insisting not only on this essential unity, but also on its basis in the unmediated simplicity of the rural peasant as exemplary patriot, who escapes the corruption of materialism, which taints the industrial worker and capitalist boss alike.[17] Threatened by the industrial social and productive relations that Michelet identifies as *English,* the peasant turned factory worker runs the risk not only of physical weakness, but also of moral degeneration, which Michelet attributes to the combined effect of broken family ties and the temptations of urban entertainment.

Michelet nonetheless reluctantly concedes that the peasant must first be displaced if he is to gain the solidarity of his peers as worker.[18] His acknowledgment of a new (and troubling) industrial proletarian presence already suggests the split that the Revolution of 1848 and the advent of the Second Empire would reveal between bourgeois liberals and what came to identify itself as the working class.[19] At the same time his nostalgic link between the conditions of rural labor and moral robustness prefigures a recurring if contradictory image of the target audience in the people's theater projects. Acknowledging the ambiguous cast of Michelet's celebration of the people as both natural and historical entity and the ideological problematic of a political position that also claims to be a kind of "second nature,"[20] we should nonetheless note that this appeal for popular unity continues in the course of the nineteenth century to be invoked even by representatives of a militant working class, in the socialist party and in the various *théâtres du peuple.* Michelet's exemplary citizen, the physically and morally robust peasant, undergoes a metamorphosis in these invocations: the object of their attention, the urban worker, ideally retains the robustness inherited from family life in the countryside, while gaining strength, specifically *virility,* from the solidarity offered by mass movements.

*   *   *

Taking its cue from political representation, by way of universal (i.e., male) suffrage (in France from 1875), which radically changed the social and political space of the masses and led directly to the founding of the Socialist Party a year later,[21] a sort of mass performance emerges in the spectacular representation of class identity, not so much in "lower class" dramatic protagonists, but in the growing popularity of workers' festivals culminating in the state institution of May Day parades in 1890. Public ceremonies such as May Day parades organized by socialist groups in France (from 1878; officially sponsored from 1890) or Bastille Day celebrations organized by the state of the Third Republic (from 1880) have the ambiguous status of "invented traditions." They may be mass-produced to generate mass patriotic consent to social relations that continue to exclude effective mass representation (in this scenario, the right to strike is translated into and contained within the May Day parade) or they may be the authentic expression of mass movements, providing a focal point for mass action (in which case, every May Day parade carries the threat—or the promise—of the original strike).[22]

This sense of the power of the "proletariat organisé" exemplified in the May Day parade's representation of a *potential* general strike clearly motivates explicitly socialist reflections on a hypothetical popular socialist theater. Unlike the advocates for the English National Theatre, who generally see the National Theatre as a repository of the dramatic heritage represented by Shakespeare and thus as an exemplary, selective, and ultimately exclusive enterprise, and who tend to see the working class as an obstacle to this enterprise or at best the object of coercion,[23] Jean Jaurès, leader of the French Socialist Party, conceives of the antagonism between bourgeoisie and proletariat as the necessary condition for the exemplary status of the proletariat. In a speech on "Le Théâtre social" published in *Revue d'art dramatique* in 1900, he characterizes the separation of bourgeois and proletarian interests in 1848 as the first step toward the proletariat's assumption of its world-historical role, not merely as a "personnage avec sa figure distincte" but rather as the "classe portant en soi l'espoir de l'humanité de demain . . . , le grand ressort du progrès."[24] In other words, the proletariat is set to succeed the bourgeoisie as *the* appropriate representative of humanity as a whole.

Despite this claim for universality, Jaurès's image of this vanguard and its appropriate theatrical representation has a distinctly masculine cast. He criticizes the current dramatic vanguard (especially Ibsen and Zola) not simply because their characters and milieu are generally bourgeois (this would not be quite true in Zola's case), but because the thematic and dramaturgical form of the plays unquestionably reproduces bourgeois drama's focus on the individual and the domestic sphere. Against this sphere, Jaurès claims that the demonstration or the meeting, the domain of fraternal collectivity, is the proper setting for social(ist) drama. He argues that contemporary drama's task is not to portray individual workers at home, but rather as members of a class on the move. Michelet had found the origin of Revolution in the "domestic hearths of the people" and thus placed women, however ambiguously, in the "van of our Revolution";[25] Jaurès, on the other hand, locates the Revolutionary crucible on the (homo)social terrain of the enfranchised masses. The defining metaphor for social relations is no longer family feeling, but the collective test of manhood in the class struggle.[26]

Jaurès's argument keeps a certain skeptical distance from contemporary experiments in popular theater, which multiplied in the last decade of the nineteenth century. While he concentrates on the theatrical representation of the working class as an appropriate supplement of its representation by the Party, the theater practitioners debating the issue focus their attention on the more specifically theatrical coordinates of the representation. While all agree that making the theater accessible to the broad masses would be a desirable asset of a democratic republic, and while many explicitly endorse the Socialist Party,[27] their disagreements as to the precise character and needs of a democratic theater remain significant. In a series of articles in the influential *Revue d'art dramatique,* culminating in 1900 with Eugène Morel's exhaustive blueprint, "Projet pour un théâtre populaire," and Romain Rolland's historical analysis "Le théâtre du peuple et le drame du peuple," we can chart the persistence of this idea as well as its salient contradictions in debates about the location and repertoire as well as appropriate audience response for a national popular theater.

These contradictions surface most immediately in the question of the theater's location. In order to grasp the dimensions of the problem, we need to recall that Baron Haussmann's urban developments beginning in 1862 had all but destroyed the old working class *quartiers* of St. Antoine and Temple, displacing their inhabitants to the peripheral neighborhoods of Clichy and Belleville as well as to the suburbs of St. Denis and Asnières.[28] Instead of the little theaters of the Boulevard du Temple that had served the motley and as yet undifferentiated popular audience during the first half of the century, the new theatrical landscape was divided among the official theaters in the center, the bourgeois theaters on the new boulevards, and, towards the end of the century, the small experimental theaters in Montmartre and Montparnasse (in particular, Antoine's Théâtre libre—1887—and Lugné-Poë's Théâtre de l'oeuvre—1893). The working class periphery made do with melodrama theaters and music halls, such as the Ambigu, the Bataclan, the Moulin de la Galette and the Elysée Montmartre (rather than the progressively more expensive Folies-Bergères) as well as a growing number of "cafés-concerts" and, by 1900, cinemas as well.[29]

In the last decade of the century, however, new "théâtres du peuple" emerged, claiming to represent the needs of the masses only recently granted legitimate entry into French political life. These theaters were set up in existing, often non-theatrical buildings in working-class areas to meet local rather than metropolitan needs and operated without government subsidy, although with informal connections to the socialist movement. As Jaurès's speech makes clear, the socialists aimed first of all to use any means to mobilize working men as *citizens,* voters, and demonstrators in the public sphere. Less immediately obvious, but no less significant, was their endeavor to penetrate beneath the *public occasion* of mass mobilization to its motivation in the workers' everyday life and leisure. In this context, a socialist theater (defined interchangeably as "théâtre social" and "théâtre socialiste" to stress the general social import of socialist aspirations) would not simply propagate socialist ideas, but also engage the working class's attention by representing their experience on stage,[30] and by staging this representation within the context of working-class work and leisure. According to Louis Lumet, director of the Théâtre civique and editor of *L'Enclos,* a socialist magazine:

> Avec les sports et le parliamentarisme, le théâtre est une des plus importantes manifestations de la vie sociale contemporaine; il participe à l'existence *journalière* comme les courses . . . et les débats des Chambres. (emphasis added)

> Together with sports and parliamentarism, theater is one of the most important aspects of contemporary social life; it participates in *daily* life like [horse] races . . . and the debates in the Houses.[31]

Gaining the allegiance of working men requires something more than strictly political appeals. To be popular, a socialist theater would have to make contact with what Bourdieu has called the *habitus* of this group (the general disposition of habits and attitudes that constitute the class [and gender] character of cultural practice)[32]: in this case, finding a way to fit theater into daily work and leisure, without abandoning the special potential of theater to *edify* the worker and make of him an enlightened spectator.

This construction of workers as active recipients of culture is, however, accompanied by the intellectuals' suspicion of workers' actual leisure activities, in particular their frequentation of "cafés-concerts," where entertainment, usually singing, could be had for the price of a beer (c. 50 centîmes). Despite their explicitly expressed faith in the working class as the vanguard of humanity generally, their suspicions about working men bring the socialist intellectuals somewhat closer to popular theater advocates who follow Michelet in their concern for the moral lassitude of the urban populace. They share a nagging concern that the sexualized spectacle and alcohol consumption characterizing café-concert and especially music hall fare (with the almost obligatory "chachut" or "cancan") will undermine the workers' wholesome virility and thus their capacity for daily work as well as occasional political mobilization.[33] Although this anxiety rarely figures as more than an elliptical aside to the loftier claims for a popular theater, it returns to haunt the invocations of the unifying force of such a theater or of its potential for social(ist) mobilization, despite the fact that *employed* workers tended to limit their consumption.[34]

Whatever this anxiety, the stress on *local place* is crucial. The Théâtre civique's project attempts to refashion the Revolutionary tradition of *fêtes publiques* to include indoor performances in the local *quartiers.* By proposing performances in a variety of sites, including well-known places of entertainment, rather than one fixed theater, Lumet defends the principle of engaging the popular majority on its own territory: the urban hall rather than the village green invoked by Rousseau and rural popular theater practitioners such as Maurice Pottécher (see below). To emphasize this point, Lumet staged the first performance of the Théâtre civique (July 1897)—a mixed program including traditional songs, music by Haendel and Delibes, and *La Révolte,* a one-act play by bohemian Villiers de l'Isle Adam—in the Maison du peuple, a meeting hall in Montmartre.[35]

In addition to highlighting the importance of *place* in the determination of a popular theater, Lumet's practice and critical reflections seek to redefine the *occasion* of theater-going for an audience that is no longer an incoherent crowd, but rather *citizens* who desire a national theater.[36] Lumet goes on to argue that by themselves, neither plays on working class themes, nor the mere location of their performance necessarily makes the occasion of theater popular. Instead, the Théâtre civique not only offered a variety program that juxtaposed material familiar to working class readers, especially plays by Hugo and Dumas, with new material with popular aspirations, in particular Rolland's *Danton;* Lumet also organized this material around topical issues or events in the democratic or specifically proletarian calendar, in the tradition of the May Day parade: in 1899, at the height of the Dreyfus debate, he offered a program centered on "Justice" and in 1900, his production of Rolland's *Danton* was attended by an enthusiastic audience in support of striking textile workers in the North.[37]

The Théâtre civique experiment and the debates in the *Revue d'art dramatique* set the terms for subsequent projects in Paris.[38] Despite continued debate on the nature of a popular repertoire—ranging from the classical tradition (especially Molière) to an invented tradition of national epic (such as Rolland's projected *Théâtre de la Révolution*) as against the representation of everyday life in "drames sociaux" or melodrama (in the work of Brieux or Dumas)—the popular theater practitioners and their advocates agree on the fundamental importance of low seat prices and location in the *quartiers* as a necessary condition that later theaters with national popular aspirations cannot ignore. Subsequent calls for cheap seats invoke the goal of democratic access to the theater as a "maison du peuple," while opposition to price reduction—especially prevalent in England—tends to be defended as the necessary means of maintaining "standards."

*   *   *

This relocation of popular theater within what we might call proletarian time and space, effected less by the choice of texts than by the geographical *place* of the theater and the theatrical *occasion*'s acknowledgment of an alternative history, clearly has the potential to alter the theatrical landscape of Paris and perhaps the macropolitical terrain as well. The centrifugal pull towards local representation for working class audiences in their own space is diverted somewhat, however, by a persistent drift towards centralization, both in the geographical location and in the choice of repertoire. Regretting petit-bourgeois resistance to theaters frequented by working class audiences in Clichy, Rolland suggests that a more "popular," that is, more general, audience might be better reached by large central theaters on the model of the Berlin *Volksbühne* which, while supported in part by Socialist Party member subscriptions, also accommodated the professional and industrial bourgeoisie in the stalls and performed national classics ostensibly for the edification of all.[39]

This conflation of popular and general continues to challenge the association of popular and working-class in the "théâtre populaire" projects. Maurice Pottécher, for example, whose account of popular theater in Paris reveals a persistent bias against the diverting spectacles entertaining the urban populace, wishes to relegate such entertainment to the periphery of the city. He insists that, by virtue of its location in the capital (the nation's representative city), a theater for the people can be truly national only when it is exemplary, that is, when it treats general subjects accessible not only to citizens of France but to those of the world. Pottécher thus casts doubt on the legitimacy of popular venues and demands by dismissing them as local and *therefore* divisive: "le théâtre populaire s'adresse plus spécialement aux éléments populaires de la nation, la classe la moins cultivée" whose "préférences, préjugés *tyranniques*"[40] (emphasis added) threaten to displace general interests. Instead of the alleged tyranny of these "special interests" represented by a "théâtre *populaire*," Pottécher proposes a "théâtre *du peuple*":

> qui entend mêler des classes et, loin d'exclure l'élite, il la croit indispensable à assurer aux spectacles un caractère artistique élevé. . . . Tandis que la foule . . . apporte sa fraîcheur d'impressions et sa faculté d'enthousiasme, . . . l'élite intelligente et instruite corrige le goût de la foule.

> a theater of the people that entails mixing classes. Far from excluding the elite, this theater believes it to be indispensable in lending to the performances an elevated artistic character. . . . While the masses bring their freshness of response and their capacity for enthusiasm, the intelligent and educated elite corrects the taste of the masses.

By stripping the larger part of the population of the legitimating name "le peuple" and dismissing it as a crowd with special, antagonistic interests, by shifting the responsibility for popular edification to an agency outside the people, and, finally, by blaming the masses rather than the elite for exercising a tyranny of taste, Pottécher *disenfranchises* the masses. His argument threatens to cancel the challenge exerted by a "théâtre populaire" to the canonical sites as well as the forms of theatrical hegemony. This threat continues to surface even in those texts explicitly endorsing popular claims.

Despite the challenge to the traditional place and occasion of theater, then, the picture within the frame—the dramatic dimension of the theatrical representation—remains remarkably tied to the canon. In particular, while Rolland and his contemporaries continually invoke the people as arbiters as well as spectators of the national spectacle, they tend to skirt the issue of popular taste in the construction of the *tradition* of exemplary texts. In dismissing classical tragedy, Racine in particular, as the residue of the culture of the court during the ancien régime,[41] they recapitulate the familiar Enlightenment strategy, pursued in particular by Diderot and Mercier, of challenging the class (court) bias of the classical tradition that ridicules the middle class and rejects all but the nobility as worthy subjects for drama.

In its stead, Rolland, Pottécher, Lumet, and Morel do not so much endorse Mercier and Diderot's proposals—the serious dramatic representation ("tableaux moraux") of ordinary citizens ("citoyens moyens")—as hesitate between two apparently incompatible projects. On the one hand, they negotiate, in varying degrees (but in all cases to a far greater extent than anything in England), the question of popular taste. All programs for popular theaters in this period express the need to confront if not wholly to endorse the claims of melodrama and music hall (variety, vaudeville) as a legitimate popular form of theater,[42] popular, not in the sense of a (rural) folk tradition "arising from the people" as Michelet might have it, but in so far as it is clearly conceived for and identified by popular urban audiences in terms, however mediated by the market, of a (largely urban) entertainment in the vernacular. On the other hand, they follow Michelet's reading of the Revolutionary inheritance, calling for a repertoire that reflects the historical significance of the French people, in the form of "épopées nationales" (Michelet) or "tragédies républicaines" (Robespierre) on the model of *Wilhelm Tell*[43] and Rolland's own *Danton*. This second project—of edification—to revive the Revolutionary tradition of celebratory national festival tends in practice to succeed rather in terms of the first: as an entertaining (and incidentally enlightening) "spectacle" rather than as an occasion for the people's participation in national representation.

In his discussion of the appropriate response to a theater of the people, Rolland returns to this tension between enlightenment and diversion or, in its late nineteenth-century version, between "théâtre populaire" and "théâtre du peuple." While he does not resolve the problem, and while the title of his book suggests his allegiance to a "théâtre du peuple" (an edifying theater *for* rather than *of* the people), he nonetheless opens up this rather rigid opposition by granting the claims of and for diversion far greater weight than one might expect from his Enlightenment inheritance. Where Mercier (and his Revolutionary inheritors, among them David and Robespierre) marks moral edification, as distinct from the rhetorical diversion of the court theater, as the touchstone of the appropriate response,[44] and where Pottécher finally endorses the full legitimacy (effective universality) of elite cultural norms as against the mass debasement of the popular,[45] Rolland hesitates to follow their example. Instead he acknowledges that diversion may well be an appropriate, if not completely desirable response to entertainment produced as a diversion from the monotony of industrial labor, and he therefore grants the legitimacy of working class taste for the emotional release of empathy and tears and for entertaining spectacle rather than enlightening "tableaux moraux":

> La première condition d'un théâtre populaire est d'être un délassement. . . .
> Que d'abord il fasse du bien, qu'il sois un repos physique et moral pour le
> travailleur fatigué de sa journée.
>
> The primary obligation of a popular theater is to be diverting. Above all, it
> should please (its audience), should provide physical and moral rest for the
> worker tired by a day's labor.[46]

At the same time, however, he reiterates the Enlightenment axiom that "le
théâtre doit être une lumière pour l'intelligence" stimulating the workers'
minds even while their bodies are resting from the day's labor.

Ideally, edification and diversion are to meet in a third term: the *energy* of
the event. Rolland glosses "energy" as the engine generating the collective
experience of the performance as well as the evidence for that experience.
Yet the relationship between this desirable energy and the evident exhaus-
tion of the working audience remains obscure. Rolland is clearly reluctant
to jeopardize his cherished picture of the hard-working but enthusiastic
laborer by capitulating to the conventional wisdom (which even Michelet
endorses), which blames the worker for moral lassitude allegedly brought
on by his exhausting and confusing working conditions. To be sure, Rolland attempts to interpret strenuous work as the necessary and even sufficient condition for a "vrai et viril idéalisme" that might trounce what he
sees as the decadence of fin-de-siècle life and art,[47] but this interpretation is
undone by his acknowledgment that the conditions of capitalist production
and the emergent culture industry do not allow the worker the leisure for
this "enlightened virility."

Instead of a *class* fortified with a critical knowledge of its own condition
as well as its strength in numbers, Rolland can see only a crowd, whose
inner workings he cannot penetrate. His identification of the members of
the Socialist Party Congress (1900) as the "éternel peuple de Shakespeare,
brouillard, irréflechi, sans aucune suite des idées"[48] suggests an uneasy
awareness that his ideal audience may be beyond his grasp. Significantly
Rolland's final praise at this meeting goes not to Jaurès (whom he otherwise
supports), but to the Guèsdiste opposition, whom he characterizes as
"moins intelligents, moins sympathiques" but *"moralement supérieurs"*;
their intransigence *"les défendait contre les compromis de la politique.* [defends
them from political compromises]"[49] (emphasis added). Rolland attributes
the moral superiority of popular virtue not to the people's legitimate
struggle for social and theatrical representation, but to a brutish rather than
enlightened virility. Far from *"fusing* eighteenth century rationalism and
fin-de-siècle vitalism" in the image of *popular sovereignty,* this notion of the

audience as crowd conjures up stubborn, incoherent muscle power; instead of representing the people as a social whole, to which he ought to commit himself, Rolland's image of the "océan populaire" simultaneously evokes a fear of the people as an overwhelming natural force, and a desire to reduce popular energy to proportions that enable him to incorporate and neutralize if not annihilate the force of this ocean.[50]

This characterization of the energy of the people not only defines their virility at the expense of legitimate defence of their sovereignty; emphasizing virile *rather than* rational political subjectivity short-circuits the claim that theater might indeed incite the people to act:

> Qu'en délassant le peuple, le théâtre le rende plus propre à agir le lendemain. Des êtres simples et sains n'ont d'ailleurs pas la joie complète sans l'action.
>
> In relaxing the people, may the theater render them more capable of activity on the following day. Simple and healthy creatures do not experience happiness without activity.[51]

This appears at first glance to be a call to arms, arousing the people to action that will change the status quo. When we recall, however, that the first action (the theater's) is subjunctive: "Qu[e] . . . le théâtre le *rende* plus propre à agir" and that the subject of the desired second action is defined as a simple creature capable only of impulsive behavior, we can no longer see the verb "agir" sustaining the meaning "to act" in the sense of "to change what is." It takes on instead the sense of the circumscribed activity of daily labor (*travail*). In this context, Rolland's wishful exhortation takes on a curiously utilitarian cast; instead of rousing the people to act and take control of the productive and social relations that bind them, the theater may well serve best to prepare them to return to their labor, within existing relations of production.

Within this controlling frame, the popular audience's response can only be passive; its role is defined by its oft mentioned naivete and fresh response to education, rather than by any critical intervention: "l'éducation exige la *répétition*. Pour agir éfficacement sur le public, il faut l'avoir constamment en main [To act effectively on the audience, one must take them continually in hand]."[52] This suggestion of restraint and control carries over to the apparently generous invitation to the masses:

> En somme, une seule condition est nécessaire, à mon sens, pour le théâtre nouveau, c'est que la scène, comme la salle, puisse s'ouvrir à des foules, *contenir* un peuple et les actions d'un peuple. De cette condition, tout le reste

découle. Il faut évidemment que les pièces représentées devant plusieurs milliers de spectateurs soient adaptées à l'optique et l'acoustique de ces vastes étendues. (emphasis added)

In my opinion, the new theater should fulfil one condition: the stage and auditorium should alike be open to the masses, should contain a people and the action of a people. Everything will follow from this condition. Obviously, plays performed for several thousand spectators should be adapted to the aural and visual dimensions of these vast spaces.[53]

Thus, even in his generosity, Rolland's pronouncements on popular repertoire and audience for his new theater in fact depend on the audience's passive enclosure face to face with the spectacle on a vast, ideally national scale, not on their own participation in its making. The subscription system would appear to support the precepts of participation, not only by encouraging the workers' education through repeated exposure, but by regularly responding to subscribers' criticism of performance and suggestions for the repertoire, but the effect of these outreach endeavors in Paris (and even more so in Berlin) was to build a body of enlightened "consumers" of edifying spectacles.

Lest there be any doubt, Rolland makes it clear that direct participation, far from complementing a national theater, would entail its disruption:

Je ne veux pas dire que le peuple doive nécessairement prendre part à l'action. . . . Ceci est une question très complexe, où interviennent des considérations non seulement esthétiques, mais morales. S'il s'agit de grandes fêtes nationales ou populaires, rien de plus naturel que la participation directe du peuple à ces spectacles . . . sans distinction de classe. Mais dès qu'il est question d'un théâtre régulier, cette participation du peuple a beaucoup plus d'inconvénient que d'avantage.

I don't mean that the people should necessarily take part in the action. That is a very complex question, involving not only aesthetic, but also moral considerations. In the case of national or popular festivals on a grand scale, nothing is more natural than the direct participation of the people in these shows . . . without any class distinctions. As soon as we are in the realm of the legitimate theater, this popular participation would be more disruptive than useful.[54]

Rolland's concession to metropolitan standards of professional excellence is also a concession to the exclusive high culture that such notions tend to support: this is clear in a revealing distinction between "théâtre régulier" (legitimate theater) on the one hand, and his unexpected conflation of "fêtes nationales" and "spectacle" on the other (alike in their appeal to popular tastes rather than to the needs of the people as a whole nation). This move threatens to undermine his earlier assertion—that the growing visibility of the masses in the theater heralds social as well as theatrical progress by "opening the doors to the crowd [*la foule*] on and off stage" and so consolidating the sovereignty of the people—bringing him surprisingly close to a conservative position (such as that dominant in England) that sees the popular audience as a potential force for disruption.

This contradiction at the heart of "popular theater" continues to manifest itself into the twentieth century. Although Gémier's intentions in founding the Théâtre National Populaire were explicitly to provide the suburbs and provinces with theater of both a classical and popular cast by means of a touring "théâtre ambulant,"[55] he remains devoted to his spectacles on a grand (national?) scale such as *Oedipe* at the Cirque d'Hiver (1919; modelled on Reinhardt's production at the Circus Schumann in Berlin, 1910).[56] Despite his willingness to accommodate popular entertainment in the national repertoire, his chief concern is still the ideal reunification of the nation through edifying spectacle:

> l'art dramatique doit s'adresser à tout le peuple . . . j'y entend pas seulement la classe ouvrière mais toutes les catégories sociales à la fois. . . . je crois que la plus haute mission du théâtre est de réunir tous les auditeurs dans les mêmes idées et les mêmes sentiments.

> The dramatic arts should address the people as a whole . . . by that I mean not only the working class, but all social classes at once . . . I believe that theater's highest mission is to reunite all the members of the audience in the same ideas and feelings.[57]

The means of this reunification are not simply ideal, however; Gémier, like Rolland, finds the material correlative of the idea in the practice of orchestrating masses on stage, which is intended to represent (stand in for) a "grande synthèse sociale."

This reconciliatory moment in Gémier's reflections appears to differ from the English appeals to a "general need" for a National Theatre in two important respects. First, the acknowledgment of the legitimacy of a specific working class culture (even if that specificity is ultimately to be transcended) and, second, the claim that national reconciliation through theater has to *ground* itself in a faith in the "sensibilité et l'intelligence de la classe prolétaire."[58] In the English case, the "general need" is framed by the exclusive pretensions of the "imaginative few" for whom the "Theatre in the East [End]" (to use Arnold's words) is essentially a supplemental afterthought to the exemplary and exclusive "theatre in the West [End]."[59] The French case differs from the English not only in the ideal acknowledgment of the proletarian class as the legitimate heirs of the Revolutionary "peuple" and hence the legitimate representatives of the French nation, but also, beyond the rhetorical appeals to the people in general, concretely in the proposals for workers' subscription and performances in the *quartiers* of the working class and hence in the attempt to democratize actual audience formation from Eugène Morel's 1900 proposal to the practice of Gémier and Jean Vilar.[60]

The question remains, however, whether one can *simply* reconcile the claims of the national popular theater to represent the gathering of the sovereign working class while edifying its members with the very classical tradition that the Enlightenment had rejected as classist. Although the tradition of popular sovereignty does indeed play a more significant role in the various incarnations of the Théâtre (National) Populaire than in anything we might want to identify as its English counterpart, not simply because of its ideological power as the legitimate echo of Revolutionary republicanism, but also in so far as this tradition is concretely if imperfectly realized in attempts to democratize the theater institution, the discourse of the popular theater seems finally unable to escape the persistently patronizing rhetoric of general edification. Whatever their evident commitment to *reaching* new audiences, Michelet, Rolland, and their contemporaries, as well as their successors in the twentieth century, all tend to formulate this democratization in terms that approach its opposite. Their emphasis on containing and constraining as well as educing the audience's response for its own good corresponds, despite their liberating claims, to the ruling desire, formulated, for example, by Turguet, Minister of the Beaux Arts in the 1880s, to (in)form the populace as nation, only recently literate and enfranchised, but nonetheless loyal to the central power of the Third Republic, and thus to contain and defuse the antagonistic moment embodied in the popular assembly outside the confines of the theater.

While I would hesitate to follow Hobsbawm's example completely in ascribing to the French state the deliberate manipulation of the Revolutionary tradition[61] (in the theater or elsewhere) to keep the populace in line, I would nonetheless suggest that these appeals to the "sovereign people" in the theater do indeed constitute an "invented tradition." The repeated inscription of the "sovereign people" as *audience* rather than active participants in the National spectacle in the theatrical and social space, as well as thematized in exemplary dramatic texts, effectively rearticulates— even in an explicitly socialist discursive context—the ideological gap between people and national protagonist. Present already in Enlightenment and Revolutionary reflections on theater, in the late nineteenth century this theater nostalgically represents the irredeemable loss of a unified public sphere in the simulacrum of the captive spectator, attending but still not attending to the National spectacle.

Notes

Unless otherwise stated, all translations are mine.

1. Ernesto Laclau, *Politics and Ideology in Marxist Theory* (London: Verso, 1979), Ch. 4, esp. 161, 173—75. Despite its generality, Laclau's argument has the theoretical advantage over recent accounts of the ideological articulation of the national popular such as Tom Nairn's *The Break-Up of Britain* (London: Verso, 1981) and Benedict Anderson's *Imagined Communities* (London: Verso, 1983), in that he refuses to reduce the "popular" to a free floating signifier that can be filled with any content to achieve political ends; rather, he insists that the discourse of populism is grounded in the contradiction between different class claims to transcend class. Populist ideology cannot be reduced to a particular "class expression," but neither can it transcend class conflict (175).

2. Michel Foucault, *The Archeology of Knowledge*, trans. A. Sheridan Smith (London: Tavistock, 1971), 21, 27.

3. Eric Hobsbawm, "Mass-Producing Traditions: Europe 1870–1914," in *The Invention of Tradition,* ed. Eric Hobsbawm and Terence Ranger (Cambridge: Cambridge University Press, 1983), 283ff.

4. Loren Kruger, *"Our National House*: The Ideology of the National Theatre of Great Britain," *Theatre Journal* 39:1 (1987).

5. Matthew Arnold, "The French Play in London," *The Nineteenth Century* 30 (August 1878): 238–43. There are two distinct and significant moments in the subtext and context for Arnold's reflections: first, the increasingly rowdy character of the audience following (not necessarily a consequence of) the enlargement of the Covent Garden, Drury Lane and new theaters and their concentration on spectacle, in the first half of the nineteenth century; second, the gentrification of theaters and audiences in the latter half of the century, as the music hall siphoned off the industrial working-class audience and as the newer, more intimate theaters substituted stalls and circle for the pit and gallery to attract and accommodate a more affluent and respectable audience. See George Rowell, *The Victorian Theatre, 1792–1914* (Cambridge: Cambridge University Press, 1978) and Michael Booth, *Prefaces to Nineteenth Century Theatre* (Manchester: Manchester University Press, 1980).

6. Arnold, "The French Play," 240.

7. Arnold, "The French Play," 243.

8. Louis-Sébastien Mercier, *Du théâtre: ou nouvel essai sur l'art dramatique* (Amsterdam: van Harreveld, 1773), 105–16.

9. Sessions of the National Convention on August 2, 1793 and November 5, 1793, *Archives parlementaires de 1787–1860*, ed. M. J. Madeval (Paris: 1862–1919), série 1, vol. 22.

10. For an indication of the debate on this event, see Frederick Brown, *Theater and Revolution* (Princeton, N.J.: Princeton University Press, 1982), 77–79, and Mona Ozouf, *La Fête révolutionnaire* (Paris: Gallimard, 1983). The exact charge of this appropriation is difficult to determine. While Ozouf's critical archaeology of the Fête de l'Unité as an instance of the National Assembly's attempt to enforce national unity in the face of the Terror is doubtless a more accurate assessment than Brown's uncritical enthusiasm for the theatricality of the event, the crucial point— for an investigation of later theater projects with national ambitions—is the persistent power of this image, to which all subsequent endeavors pay homage, of the people summoned in celebration of their collective identity as nation, despite the actual historical precarity of that identity.

11. See Michèle Root-Bernstein, *Boulevard Theatre and Revolution in Eighteenth Century France* (Ann Arbor: UMI Research Press, 1984), 232ff.

12. Root-Bernstein, *Boulevard Theatre and Revolution,* 190ff.

13. Rowell, *The Victorian Theatre,* 12ff, 38ff.

14. Jules Michelet, *History of the French Revolution,* trans. Charles Cocks, ed. Gordon Wright (Chicago: University of Chicago Press, 1967), 441.

15. "Le Théâtre et le peuple," *L'Etudiant* (1847–48); quoted by Romain Rolland in *Le Théâtre du peuple* (Paris: Fayard, 1903), 85–86.

16. For a rigorous discussion of the ideological implication of the triumphal procession as Revolutionary exemplum, see Ozouf, *La Fête révolutionnaire,* 98ff.

17. Jules Michelet, *Le Peuple* (Paris: Hachette, 1846), 107–11.

18. Michelet, *Le Peuple,* 112–13.

19. Marx's account in *The Eighteenth Brumaire of Louis Napoleon* (Moscow: Progress Publishers, 1935) demonstrates how the apparently impossible seizure of power by Louis Napoleon was facilitated precisely by the liberals' ultimate refusal to maintain the alliance with the workers (especially in Paris) that had made the Revolution of 1848 possible.

20. For an analysis of this problematic, see Patricia McCallum, "Michelet's Narrative Practice: Naturality, Popular and Intellectual," *Cultural Critique* 1 (1984): 147ff.

21. George Rudé, *The Crowd in History: 1730–1848* (London: Lawrence and Wishart, 1981), 6–7, notes that the industrial proletariat differs from the pre-industrial crowd, precisely in that the former identifies itself and is in turn identified as a class (represented by general manhood suffrage and the growth of socialist parties in Western Europe), whereas the latter still appears too heterogenous and without general allegiances.

22. Hobsbawm, "Mass-Producing Traditions." As Hobsbawm's remarks imply, this scenario reinforcing the political signficance of the May Day parade is characteristic of those Western European nations that can boast (or lament) an organized

and militant working class, in particular, France and Germany. Although Hobsbawm does not then account for the absence of the official May Day in England, the implications of this apparent anomaly for the present argument are considerable.

23. This exclusivity and corresponding resistance to popular tastes as "simple vulgarity" is clear in reflections on English theater during the nineteenth century from Coleridge to Granville Barker and continues to color twentieth-century debate, as the Parliamentary Debates on the National Theatre and the administrative policies of the National Theatre demonstrate; see "Our National House."

24. Jean Jaurès, "Le Théâtre social," *Revue d'art dramatique* (December 1900): 1073–75.

25. Michelet, *History,* 163, 288.

26. Jaurès, "Le Théâtre social," 1065, 1072–74.

27. See Maurice Pottécher, "Théâtre populaire à Paris," *Revue d'art dramatique* (September 1899); Romain Rolland, "Théâtre du peuple et drame du peuple" and Eugène Morel, "Projet pour un théâtre populaire," *Revue d'art dramatique* (December 1900); Louis Lumet, *Le Théâtre civique* (Paris: Ollendorf, 1903).

28. For a thought-provoking account of the effects of this displacement on the urban space and its inhabitants' changed perceptions, see Marshall Berman, *All That is Solid Melts into Air* (New York: Simon and Schuster, 1982).

29. For a description of available performance entertainment in this period, see Eugen Weber, *France: Fin de Siècle* (Cambridge, Mass.: Harvard University Press, 1986), 159–77. For a detailed account of the repertoire, location, price structure, and audience of live popular entertainment and the increasingly powerful influence of cinema, see Charles Rearick, *Pleasures of the Belle Epoque: Entertainment and Festivity in Turn of the Century France* (New Haven and London: Yale University Press, 1985).

30. See Jaurès, "Théâtre social," 1065.

31. Louis Lumet, in *La Plume* (November 1897), excerpted by the author in *Théâtre civique,* 36. Note that while workers were certainly betting on horses by 1900 (Rearick, *Pleasures,* 90–91), their participation in government was largely limited to voting.

32. For a definition of "habitus," see Pierre Bourdieu, *La Distinction* (Paris: Minuit, 1979); trans R. Nice (London: Routledge and Kegan Paul, 1982); for his analysis of the relationships among *habitus,* lifestyle, and the cultural hegemony of the taste for "literature" and "art," see especially 9–105.

33. See Lumet, *Théâtre civique,* 6; Pottécher, "Théâtres populaires à Paris," 402; and Rolland, *Théâtre du peuple,* 114.

34. Rearick, *Pleasures* (97), notes that patrons (women and sometimes children as well as working men) in establishments in the proletarian neighborhoods (as distinct from the big music halls where workers might spend a holiday) tended to drink little and leave early.

35. See Lumet, *Théâtre civique,* 17ff.

36. Lumet, *Théâtre civique,* 10.

37. Rolland, *Théâtre du peuple,* 90–100. Rolland responded somewhat ambivalently to this socialist appropriation of his play, which was performed, as he put it,

"au profit de je ne sais plus quels ouvriers grévistes " (*Mémoires* [Paris: Albin Michel, 1966], 313).

38. The two most significant subsequent developments were Emile Berny's "théâtre du peuple" in the working class neighborhood of Belleville and Henri Beaulieu's theater of the same name in the mixed class area of the Batignolles, both founded in 1903, the year Rolland published *Le Théâtre du peuple*. The success of both was short-lived due to lack of subscribers; nonetheless, the *location* of Berny's theater encouraged working class attendance, even though he explicitly eschewed Beaulieu's socialism. See Berny, "Théâtre populaire: Belleville," *Revue* (June 1903): 200–203, Rolland, *Théâtre du peuple*, 99–107, and Fisher, "Origins," 474–76.

39. Rolland, *Théâtre du peuple*, 106.

40. Maurice Pottécher, *Théâtre du Peuple à Bussang* (Paris: Stock, 1913), 10–11.

41. Rolland, *Théâtre du peuple*, 9ff.

42. This confrontation typically takes the form of an uneasy recognition of the popularity of vernacular forms, coupled with a desire to secure their legitimacy (i.e. potential for "general appeal") by "elevating them" out of too close a contact with the perceived vulgarity of working class preferences. See Pottécher, "Théâtre populaire à Paris," 402, Rolland, *Théâtre du peuple*, 114ff.

43. Michelet, "Le Théâtre et le peuple."

44. Mercier, *Du théâtre*, 105, 117

45. Pottécher, *Théâtre du Peuple à Bussang*, 10–11

46. Rolland, *Théâtre du peuple*, 113–14.

47. Rolland, "La Poison idéaliste," "Introduction à une lettre de Tolstoy," *Compagnons de route* (Paris: Sablier, 1936), 21, 191–97.

48. Rolland, *Mémoires* (Paris: Albin Michel, 1956), 300. He goes on to compare the workers to the crowd in David's *Horatians*, emphasizing, on the one hand, their submission to orchestration from above and, on the other, their appearance to a spectator. This contradictory image fundamentally marks Rolland's dramatic as well as critical representation of the people, as his *Danton* reveals (see below).

49. Rolland, *Mémoires*, 301.

50. In his recent biography, *Romain Rolland and the Politics of Engagement* (Berkeley and London: University of California Press, 1988), David Fisher claims that Rolland was possessed of a sort of "oceanic feeling" that expresses his "deepest longing for union" with the Revolutionary crowd and thus "made him a Socialist" (12, 22), while at the same time asserting that this "oceanic feeling was essential for maintaining . . . individual independence." Fisher's identification with Rolland as an intellectual at once *engagé* and olympian apparently blinds him to the anxiety that saturates Rolland's reaction to the crowd and to the incommensurability of his image of the people as "océan populaire" with any notion of the people as rational political subjects "seizing hold of their own destiny" (23).

51. *Théâtre du peuple*, 115.

52. *Théâtre du peuple*, 109.

53. *Théâtre du peuple*, 119–20.

54. *Théâtre du peuple*, 127n. Even Maurice Pottécher, creator and orchestrator of rural festivals for and by the people, stressed that amateur performance would not

do for the nationally representative theaters of the metropolis. See Pottécher, "Le Théâtre du peuple," *Revue d'art dramatique* (January–March 1899): 415.

55. Ferdinand Gémier, "Lettre à propos d'un théâtre populaire," *Le Théâtre populaire* 2 (1953): 24–26.

56. Ferdinand Gémier, *Le Théâtre* (entretiens réunis par Paul Grell) (Paris: Grasset, 1925), 65, 117. Also Michael Hays, *The Public and Performance: Theatre and Society 1871–1914* (Ann Arbor: UMI Research Press, 1982), 114–15.

57. Gémier, *Le Théâtre*, 65.

58. "Lettre . . . ," 26.

59. Kruger, "Our National House," 23; see also Granville-Barker's and Shaw's comments, quoted on p. 24 and p. 25 of the article.

60. Eugène Morel, "Projet d'un théâtre populaire: exposé sommaire," *Revue d'art dramatique* (December 1900): 1116–20; Jean Vilar, *Le Théâtre: service public* (Paris: Gallimard, 1975). As Vilar's reflections on his experience suggest and as the comments of Roger Planchon, his successor at the TNP, confirm, the problematic and potentially patronizing character of this "democrat*ization*" in the face of local demands for cultural democracy persists all the same, but is a topic more suited to discussion of theater in the twentieth century.

61. "Mass-Producing Traditions," 269.

Chris Bongie

Exotic Nostalgia: Conrad and the
New Imperialism

> Do you see him? Do you see the story? Do you see anything? It
> seems to me I am trying to tell you a dream . . .
>
> *Heart of Darkness*

NEAR THE END OF HIS LIFE, Joseph Conrad wrote a brief preface for a book
of travels by his friend Richard Curle.[1] In his reading of *Into the East* (1922),
Conrad sketches out a deeply pessimistic and overtly nostalgic analysis of
the "spirit of modern travel" that he feels the book embodies. Nowadays, he
notes, "many people encompass the globe"; they go rushing through the
world with blank notebooks and even blanker minds. And this should
hardly come as a surprise for, after all, what remains to be done in the way
of traveling "on this earth girt about with cables, with an atmosphere made
restless by the waves of ether, lighted by that sun of the twentieth century
under which there is nothing new left now, and but very little of what may
still be called obscure" (88)?

Certainly nothing as grand or noble as what such "infinitely curious and
profoundly inspired men" as Barth, Denham, Clapperton, and Mungo Park
accomplished in their journeys through "darkest Africa." The days of "heroic travel" are gone, Conrad assures us, and the exotic settings that these
explorers once envisioned have long since been despoiled of "their old black
soul of mystery"; soon they will be "bristling with police posts, colleges,
tramway poles." Curle would seem to be perfectly suited to the task of
chronicling this "marvellously piebald" world:

> He is very modern, for he is fashioned by the conditions of an explored earth
> in which the latitudes and longitudes having been recorded once for all have
> become things of no importance, in the sense that they can no longer appeal
> to the spirit of adventure, inflame no imagination, lead no one up to the very
> gates of mortal danger. (90)

Appealing to the "spirit of adventure," inflaming the imagination, leading one's reader up to "the very gates of mortal danger": such are the possibilities that remain open to those writers who were not yet fashioned by "the conditions of an explored earth."

But where, we might ask, does Conrad himself stand in relation to this ongoing process of decline? The rather condescending tone he adopts toward the younger Curle would certainly lead us to believe that Conrad considers himself to be something rather less than "very modern." I would like to suggest, however, that this preface gains its full resonance only if we consider the possibility that Conrad's portrait of Curle is first and foremost a piece of displaced autobiography. Shunted off onto the generation of writers that has followed in his tracks is a problem that, from the beginning, "fashions" his own work as a writer: namely, the problem of a truly *global* modernity. Everywhere and in everything, this modernity necessarily cancels out whatever might once have differed from it. As David Simpson has argued, convincingly to my mind, Conrad writes from *within* an undifferentiated world:

> Conrad has reduced all the potentially dialectical elements in the antithesis of primitive and civilized societies, whereby each might function as an image of what the other is not, to a state of monotonous, undifferentiated oneness. . . . The fetishized world of the colonial nations has imposed itself upon the far-flung corners of the earth, creating a commerce in the images of its own alienation.[2]

Within the (global) space of this "monotonous, undifferentiated oneness" goods take the form of commodities, mechanically reproducible; value is present only as that which has already been lost; and we ourselves seem no more than the interchangeable parts of a mass society whose fate is inseparable from the impersonalized machinations of the bureaucratic State.

The "truth-value" of Conrad's analysis of modernity is not of immediate concern here. What needs to be emphasized, rather, is the reduction, or the erasure, of the possibility of a dialectical encounter between the "primitive" and "civilized" (and I will henceforth spare the reader the quotation marks that ought to be placed around these and other such loaded words) that any such global analysis necessarily involves. Such an encounter was, as I have argued elsewhere and in some detail, the dream of *exoticism*.[3] Very briefly, we can define exoticism as a nineteenth-century literary and cultural practice that posits another space (the space of the Other) outside the boundaries of a society that to some observers, in the aftermath of the political and technological revolutions at the end of the eighteenth century, seemed inalterably modern and deeply alienating. The project of exoticism is to salvage values and a way of life that had vanished, without hope of restoration, from post-Revolutionary society (the realm of the Same) but that might, beyond the confines of modernity, still be figured as really possible.

The initial optimism of the exoticist project, however, gives way in the later part of the century to a massive pessimism, as colonial power—and with it, all the consumeristic, technological trappings of modernity—spread to the four corners of the earth. The acute phase of territorial expansion referred to as the "New Imperialism," and most commonly associated with the scramble for Africa, marks the definitive crisis-point of exoticism: how can one hope to step outside of a process that has become global, and apparently irreversible? This New Imperialist crisis is Conrad's point of departure as a writer, and for this reason, as Simpson goes on to say, he "does not tend to show us the genesis of this process of [colonial] exportation; to do so would be to introduce the energetic antithesis of innocence and corruption which he clearly means to avoid." To write from within an undifferentiated world means foregoing the sort of energetic ideological oppositions that were at the base of the exoticist project. The difference between innocence and corruption, or between civilization and savagery, is from this perspective no difference at all; it is something *unreal*.

But I would argue that Simpson's claim needs to be nuanced in at least two ways. First, there are indeed many signs of such "energetic antitheses" in Conrad's very first novels (*Almayer's Folly* [1895], *An Outcast of the Islands* [1896]), although they are constantly, as it were, self-deconstructing.[4] Conrad's early inability to write an heroic, exotic, or "romantic" novel is a consequence of the undifferentiated perspective that is already his, from the time he first takes pen to paper, but that he will only come to grips with in *Heart of Darkness* (1899) and *Lord Jim* (1900). In these later works, the matter of guilt and innocence is no longer at issue; it can never again be an issue for one who takes a world-wide modernity as his starting point. But—and here is the second (and all-important) nuance that must be attached to Simpson's claim—the passage from exotic difference to colonial indifferentiation is nonetheless not forgotten in these more properly Conradian works. The "energetic antitheses" of exoticism continue to haunt the world of Conrad's novels, in spite of his by now complete awareness of their unreality. Conrad "de-energizes" these oppositions, hollowing them out, and thereby conserving them in the only possible way—a way that leads through the impossible. They inhabit the text as absence, as what has been canceled out of an indifferent world girt round by wires and enlightened by the sun of modernity. In this essay, I will attempt to show, to begin to show, this conservative strategy at work in *Heart of Darkness,* without making a case for its potentially ethical significance (although I believe such a case can, and must, be made). In order to reach *Heart of Darkness,* however, we must first take a rather large detour through the despotic imaginary of Victorian politics.

*   *   *

A major dispute in eighteenth-century political theory revolved around the applicability of the word "despotism" to the governance of European nations. The founder of the Physiocrats, François Quesnay, when meditating on the best method of government, spoke approvingly of a "despotisme légal." Rousseau's response to Quesnay was immediate and virulent: the first term, he affirmed, killed the second; they were "deux mots contradictoires qui, réunis, ne signifient rien."[5] Here we have a stark opposition between two Enlightenment ideologies: one tending toward despotism, the other toward liberalism. The fundamental intervention of the French Revolution in many ways tipped the scale for Rousseau's exorcism of the despotic from the realm of legality. The modern European State would be founded upon liberal principles; liberalism and despotism were no longer engaged in a dialogic struggle for mastery (as with Rousseau and Quesnay) but definitively opposed to each other as legality to illegality. Enlightenment was henceforth to be judged only according to the standards of democracy; despotism, as a positive political alternative, was banished from much of the continent. However, although the liberal position achieved dominance within Europe, the idea of a "legal" or "enlightened" despotism maintained a certain validity in the realm of "unenlightenment," that is to say, abroad. During the first half of the nineteenth century, the legal despotism favored by Quesnay still seemed, to most politicians, an appropriate way for metropolitan Europe to administer its peripheral territories.

In a parliamentary speech of July 10, 1833, the future Lord Macaulay, then-Secretary of the East India Company's Board of Control, gave a succinct formulation of the difference between British rule at home and abroad when he affirmed that India was governed as an "enlightened and paternal despotism."[6] From the standpoint of a Rousseau, Macaulay's simultaneous appeal to both enlightenment and despotism could only appear as politically regressive; and yet, as long as enough spatial distance obtained between center and periphery, it was a regression that might easily be tolerated. Early- and mid-nineteenth-century colonialism—or what we can conveniently, if somewhat misleadingly, refer to as the "Old Imperialism"—incorporates the possibility of a despotic as opposed to liberal authority in its formal or informal dealings with peripheral societies. As John Stuart Mill put it later on in the century, in an article entitled "A Few Words on Non-Intervention" (1859):

> The sacred duties which civilized nations owe to the independence and nationality of each other are not binding towards those to whom nationality and independence are a certain evil, or, at best, a questionable good.[7]

For Mill, an imperial system remained the most suitable means of governing those peoples who had not yet learned to represent themselves abstractly as members of a democratic State. At some point, however, as Macaulay himself made clear, native peoples would indeed arrive at this point: he goes on to affirm, in the name of an eventually self-governing India, that "we are free, we are civilised, to little purpose, if we grudge to any portion of the human race an equal measure of freedom and civilisation."

At the time of Macaulay's speech, a year after the first Reform Bill, liberal democracy in England was still in its initial phases: even on the domestic front, constitutionalism was as yet conceivable, as it were, only in the form of an "enlightened paternalism." In Macaulay's call for an "enlightened and paternal despotism" the word "paternal" mediates between the modernity of enlightenment and the antiquatedness of despotism, enforcing a familial image that both softens the imperial connotations of despotism and guards against a too liberal enlightenment—a mediatory role it continued to fill in a country where the third term of Macaulay's formula, despotism, had dropped out of sight. But as the century drew on, and as the process of enfranchisement and of democratization unfolded, paternalism itself came to seem an unsatisfactory way of describing how a truly modern State functioned. Suggesting as it does an imbalance of power in what should— one man, one vote—be a situation of equality, paternalistic authority itself falls victim to the increasingly democratic imperatives of twentieth-century Europe (resurfacing, to be sure, as part of political salvage projects like fascism). The modern State must be represented as neither despotic nor paternal, but merely enlightened. What effect, we might ask, would this shift have on a turn-of-the-century Macaulay's portrayal of colonial rule?

Following through on our logical progression—that is to say, on the logic of progress—we can imagine this hypothetical turn-of-the-century politician speaking, from the standpoint of a new unqualified enlightenment, about an India well on the path to democracy: an India ruled according to the dictates of an enlightened paternalism from which the archaic figure of the despot has definitively disappeared. By this logic, the founding contradiction of the Old Imperialism—the twofold postulate of democracy at home and despotism abroad—had to give way, or at the very least be *represented* as giving way, to a more "civilized" relationship between metropolitan and peripheral territories. This change in the ground rules for portraying European power did not, of course, necessarily correspond to a real democratization of colonial rule—in fact, the opposite is most often the case: as Philip Darby has pointed out, for instance, "increasingly, towards the end of the nineteenth century, there was a tendency for British rule in India to become more authoritarian," not less.[8] The idea of self-government, which Macaulay held out to Indians (despite, or precisely because of, his despotic perspective), slips, as Darby puts it, "into the distant, unforeseeable future" (43). Regardless of this real backsliding, though, the despotic sobriquet itself could no longer adequately fill the representational needs of a political power committed to figuring itself as benignly paternalistic in its treatment of "the nations to whom nationality and independence are a certain evil, or, at best, a questionable good."

In 1876, at the mid-point of a transitional decade in which "the inner-directed era of European nation building gave way to the outer-directed age of global conflict,"[9] the opposition between new and old ways of figuring imperialism surfaced very emphatically in the parliamentary debates leading to the proclamation of the Royal Titles Act. If Victoria's controversial adoption of the title "Empress of India" symbolically confirmed the tendency of mid–nineteenth-century imperialism (enlightenment at home, despotism abroad), the intense opposition that many parliamentarians mounted against the passage of this Act was a signal that the old-style imperialism favored by Disraeli was proving less and less palatable to "enlightened" minds. Throughout the course of these debates, the battle-line is strongly drawn between a *despotic* and a *liberal* interpretation of the imperial idea, and out of the extensive amount of material generated therein we can cite a typical instance of each position.[10]

First the despotic interpretation:

We stand in the relation of the paramount Power towards them [the Indian principalities] as what may be called, roughly, feudatory and subordinate States and . . . we occupy towards them that position which is most accurately described—of all the titles that I am aware of—by that of Emperor. (Sir S. H. Northcote, Chancellor of the Exchequer, 228: 91)

In its most extreme version the position was ably summarized by Sir George Campbell, who asserted that it was time for Victoria to assume in name as in effect "the position hitherto occupied by the Great Mogul in India"—albeit not as absolute Sovereign but as Representative of the British Nation. Those who supported the new title inevitably stressed that it was not meant to signify an individual, but only to mark the fact of having an empire; but if this were truly the case, those taking up the liberal position countered, then what need was there of such a factious term? As Robert Lowe, one of the few MPs who thought it conceivable that Britain might some day lose India, pointed out:

> The Emperors of Hindostan were Mahomedan conquerors. Would it be wise or prudent in us to confound in name our wise and beneficent government with that of the Rulers who preceded us? (227: 414)

Here Lowe is appealing to standards of wisdom and beneficence compatible with, if in some ways different from, the enlightened values that were (ostensibly) at work in the governance of most European nations. The battleground, then, is clearly marked out: Percy Wyndham asserts without qualms that "the Government of India is essentially a despotic Government as administered by us, although it includes more than one individual" (227: 1736); Gladstone replies that this is indeed the case, but goes on to lament it as "our weakness and our calamity."

Victoria would have her way; the word "Empress" entered Britain's political vocabulary, and to "the substance of ancient greatness" was added "the glitter of modern names," as one parliamentary commentator derisively put it (228: 106). But, ironically, even as it achieved this nominal confirmation, the Old Imperialism of a Disraeli was on the point of giving way to its New Imperialist successor. Lord Rosebery's gradual conversion to the cause of Empire is a key gauge of the change in official colonial policy that marked the last decades of the nineteenth century:

> In Disraeli's time Rosebery had been opposed to the way the Government then used the word Empire, a word about which he felt 'a gloomy foreboding.' It then lacked liberty and smacked of oriental despotism. It was too closely associated with India.[11]

By 1895, however, he had established himself as one of the leading voices of a "Liberal Imperialism" in which the despotic idea, if not the imperial name, was to be excised from the story of territorial acquisition and rule.

Ridding the Empire of its imperial vestiges is the paradoxical imperative of the New Imperialism, as it engages in and is engaged by a process of rationalization that must (in theory, to be sure) lead to the transformation of an enlightened despotism into an even more luminous paternalism, one more suited to the global pretensions of colonial power in the age of the New Imperialism. And it is here, on the point of this transformation, that we can begin to tell Conrad's story; but before doing so, we must take one last brief look back at the fundamental turning between the eighteenth and nineteenth centuries that was our point of departure in this section.

What is *modern* about the enlightened State is that the locus of power has shifted from the despotic body of a sovereign figure to an abstract entity representing the people. Roberta Maccagnani has pointed this out in an excellent discussion of the Marquis de Sade's relation to the exoticist project:

> The sort of sovereignty of the subject laid claim to by Sade is that of the ancient despot, the absolute monarch of the *Anciens Régimes,* who based his power on his dominion over bodies and his capacity for their total subjection. With the fall of these regimes and the advent of modern egalitarian democracies, the subject loses the idea of sovereignty since it has been completely absorbed in the body of the State, which posits itself as the only, and abstract, holder of all the forms of power.[12]

With the coming of modern egalitarian democracies the sovereignty of the *ancien régime* subject (figured most dramatically by the absolute monarch) disappears from the immediate political horizon. Sade's post-Revolutionary protagonists at once model themselves after this archaic subject and yet find themselves at an insuperable distance from their model. Figures of and in crisis, they are the embodiment of an entirely new sort of subject: namely, the modern *individual.*

Paolo Valesio has argued persuasively that individualism "was (re)born as a revolt against the mass rebellion that erupted into history as the French Revolution"[13]; modernity presides over the individual's birth, but for that very reason the revolt of the individual is an impossible one, from the beginning conditioned by the definitive loss of that state of affairs under which his sovereignty might be (re)realized. The individual can never be what he models himself after. Aware that he is alienated from the conditions of his own authenticity, the individual—at least in his first, heroic phase—nonetheless blinds himself to the necessity of this crisis. Disregarding the constitutive nature of his "untimeliness," he goes off in search of a remedy for what is irremediable, attempting to recuperate a wholeness from which he has, as it were, been separated at birth. Exoticism is one such nineteenth-century attempt at "curing" the individual: where better to escape the ills of mass society than in those "unenlightened" locales in which, as we have just seen, the archaic model of subjectivity still persisted as a political system? But the individual is always-already incurable: his dream of passing over the boundaries of modernity is never more than that, never more (or less) than an impossible dream. And yet, it is perhaps a dream worth telling, and telling over again, even in the clear light of a New Imperialist day when its unreality has become apparent to one and all.

∗   ∗   ∗

The imperial system that we have discussed in the previous section acted as a buffer between the two very distinct realms of civilization and savagery; situated between the two, it served to differentiate the one from the Other and thereby confirmed the real existence of both. By the turn of the century, though, liberal democracy could no longer have recourse to this mediatory system; confronting the contradiction of equal rights at home and inequality abroad became imperative. Those who had formerly been subject to the rule of an "enlightened and paternal despotism" had now to be represented anew, according to the discursive criteria of what I termed "enlightened paternalism": savagery, and its difference, was to be brought into line with the now global pretensions of European democracy. This discursive position was adopted by at least one of the participants in the Royal Titles debate who asserted that

> there were many educated Natives who recognized and appreciated our institutions, and was this title of Empress to be sent to them as a message of peace and goodwill? Was the house to stamp that despotic title upon them in perpetuity . . . ? (Mr. Anderson, 228: 140)

The liberal directives underlying this parliamentarian's speech are at work in much of the literature that would be written about the colonies during the age of the New Imperialism. For the most part, turn-of-the-century colonial literature can be read as an attempt to come to terms with the challenge of speaking paternalistically rather than despotically about the subjects of imperial rule: as Martin Steins has remarked, it sets out to make this familial image "prevail over the resentments and phobias that public opinion had inherited from the nineteenth century."[14]

In contrast to this assimilating and "enlightened" approach a work like Conrad's *Heart of Darkness* continues to put into play apparently phobic representations of natives as "savages." As I will argue, Conrad's decision to portray natives in this way is a corollary of his Romantic belief in the individual's sovereignty—a belief that was ever more at odds with the New Imperialist world in which he found himself writing. From this disjunction between personal ideology and historical reality arises the basic ambiguity of Conrad's position when it comes to the matter of European expansion, which Terry Eagleton has summed up quite nicely: "Conrad neither believes in the cultural superiority of the colonialist nations, nor rejects imperialism outright."[15] We must now consider a little more closely the reasons behind this ambiguous attitude.

Following Avrom Fleishman's classic interpretation, we can say that Conradian ideology is traceable back to the "organicist doctrine of self-realization through identification with the community."[16] Organicism affirms the unity of the individual and his society, positing at the head of this community a charismatic figure who embodies the positive qualities of all its members. In Conrad, the exemplary instance of this social relationship is the hierarchy established between a ship's captain and his crew. Marlow's description in *Chance* is typical and illuminating: the captain is "a remote, inaccessible creature, something like a prince of a fairy-tale, alone of his kind, depending on nobody, not to be called to account except by powers practically invisible and so distant, that they might well be looked upon as supernatural for all that the rest of the crew knows of them, as a rule."[17]

But, we must ask ourselves, has this unity of the individual and his community ever been a present possibility; have the conditions for its realization not always-already come and gone? Is it not the nostalgic construction par excellence? The organicist doctrine is, and cannot help being, a belated ideology. The individualistic project of "self-realization," of being rescued from the ills of an atomized society, could itself never have arisen until *after* the dissolution of that traditional community in which the "untimely" individual places his empty hope. For all its desirability, the authentic community envisioned by Romantic organicism is no more accessible to modernity than is the archaic subject upon whom the post-Revolutionary individual has modelled himself.

Returning to Eagleton's remark, then, we can say that for Conrad the "colonialist nation" could never be a manifestation of cultural superiority because it was so obviously the antithesis of a genuine community; it was a modern State, founded upon abstract principles and "material interests."

However, imperialism, at least a certain imperialism, held out a slim hope for Conrad's organicist imagination: where an (enlightened) despotism held sway, modernity might yet be averted. But if the project of (re)instituting a community, and thereby (re)creating the conditions for the individual's "self-realization," was still conceivable in the world of the Old Imperialism—the world of Conrad's youth (and of his ideology)—the unrealizable nature of this project had become all too clear by the end of the century. Conrad the writer thus finds himself torn between the appeal of an imperial system that offered the individual a chance (but, as I argued earlier, the individual has no *real* chance) and the necessity of registering its, for him, repelling successor.

We can bring out the complexity of Conrad's position by referring to a double-barreled distinction made early on in *Heart* between, on the one hand, "efficiency" and "inefficiency," and, on the other, "conquerors" and "colonists." Marlow makes these distinctions in the course of his evocation of the Romans' encounter with the "utter savagery" of darkest Britain: they would have felt, he asserts, the "fascination of the abomination."[18] This "fascination" is clearly the same as the "horror" that Kurtz, in his sovereign solitude, has been able to sense and express, and that Marlow, enfolded within the colonialist enterprise, has lost all direct contact with (though he will be able to record its traces in the language and the gestures of Kurtz). Marlow admits as much: none of "us," he assures his listeners aboard the *Nellie,* would have felt this fascination, saved as we are by our *efficiency,* "the devotion to efficiency." Now, Conrad, in a letter of December 31, 1898, to his publisher Blackwood, had charged those tackling "the civilizing work in Africa" with "the criminality of inefficiency"[19]; but a careful reading should lead us to see that, in the sense defined by the text itself, both Marlow *and* the Company are "efficient." Both, that is, are blind to the horror that Kurtz and the Romans feel—blind to "savagery" as a force that must be reckoned with. Kurtz's ability to feel the horror, then, is a sign of his "inefficiency" within the economy of late-nineteenth-century colonialism.

The word "efficiency" obviously has a positive valence for Marlow: it was, as Ian Watt has pointed out, the watchword of the Liberal Imperialists[20]; it was also the motivating force behind Benjamin Kidd's immensely popular *Social Evolution* (1894). Efficiency justifies the British effort. But at the same time, as their shared blindness to the horror shows, it is impossible to make a distinction on the basis of mere efficiency between the "real work" being done in British colonies and the reprehensible work of the Company; efficiency is a necessary but not sufficient condition for licit territorial expansion. Hence, Marlow hastens to add another distinction that would draw a definitive line between the two: the opposition between efficiency and inefficiency is supplemented by one between conquerors and colonists.

Not only were the Romans inefficient, they were conquerors to boot; their administration was little more than a "squeeze." They were not, Marlow sums up, "colonists." Conquest is not just the affair of the Romans, however, but a present concern—even if, as in the case of the Company, it has become what we might call an "efficient conquest":

> The conquest of the earth, which mostly means the taking it away from those who have a different complexion or slightly flatter noses than ourselves, is not a pretty thing when you look into it too much. What redeems it is the idea only. An idea at the back of it; not a sentimental pretence but an idea and an unselfish belief in the idea—something you can set up, and bow down before, and offer a sacrifice to . . . (31–32)

The colonist, as opposed to the conqueror, is redeemed by the "idea"; it forms the necessary complement of "efficiency." Again, idealism was a common battlecry of the day, as we can see from the following passage in John Seeley's *Expansion of England* (a famous series of lectures originally given in the early 1880s):

> The material basis of a Greater Britain might indeed be laid, that is, vast territories might be occupied, and rival nations expelled from them. In this material sense Greater Britain was created in the seventeenth and eighteenth centuries. But the idea that could shape the material mass was still wanting.[21]

However, everything depends on who or what would embody this idea. For Seeley, here showing himself in total accord with the spirit of his age, "individuals are important in history in proportion, not to their intrinsic merit, but to their relation to the State"; Conrad's position is, at heart, a very different one.

Once we begin to think Marlow's two sets of opposing terms together, though, the unviability of this position becomes apparent. Combining these terms, we come up with four logical possibilities, two of which are patently unsatisfactory: the inefficient and efficient conquests undertaken by the Romans and the Company, respectively.[22] What possibilities remain? The ideal resolution, clearly, would be an "efficient colonization"; the novelty of Conrad's approach, however, lies in at once affirming the necessity of this efficient colonization and showing it to be the one thing missing from the text and, by extension, from political life. And here is where our discussion of Conrad's ideological starting point—namely, a Romantic valorization of the individual's place in society—becomes especially relevant. For Conrad, the individual and not the State must be the repository of "ideas": hence, the absolute necessity of finding (or inventing) a figure like Kurtz—an individual who is possessed of "ideas" and who exists at a more or less complete distance from the efficient world of New Imperialist conquest that, at least in the first half of *Heart*, occupies the entire horizon of Marlow's experience. But, writing as he was from within an undifferentiated world, Conrad was unable to fully credit the demands of his own ideology; under these circumstances, Kurtz's sovereign difference, his capacity for operating outside the (global) boundaries of civilization, can in the final analysis be no more than a "hollow," "deficient" fiction.

Conrad turns Kurtz into the very embodiment of an *inefficient colonist* (the fourth term of our *combinatoire*), one who still feels the horror of "utter savagery" and indeed has himself reverted to it. But despite his inefficiency, Kurtz provides a disconcerting counter-balance to the efficient yet reprehensible conquest of the Company in all its technocratic anonymity; he conjures up—if only for an instant, an instant that has always-already passed away—the figure of that efficient colonist who is necessarily missing from the text. The slot of the efficient colonist proves an empty one. Any attempt to think this "imperialist" future can only lead back to the past—to a time, that is, when one could still believe in what has become unbelievable: namely, the sovereign individual and the possibility of an Other way of life. Unable to follow the lead of much turn-of-the-century literature about the colonies, which subscribes to the assimilatory language of paternalism and subordinates the authority of the individual to that of the State, Conrad is forced, through the chiasmus of efficient conquerors and an inefficient colonist, to represent the incompatibility of efficiency and the saving idea. The efficient colonist can only be figured through his disfigurement—a rendering hollow of the heroic individual who should, ideally, be the vehicle of a redeemed imperialism.

Intimately connected to the individual's hollow presence in *Heart* is the portrayal of natives as "savages." I have said that with the shift to a paternalistic way of speaking about colonized peoples a word like "savage" ceased to fill the same political and representational needs that it did earlier on in the century; once the colonial nations have apportioned the entirety of the earth's suface, savagery is necessarily *ex*-cluded from the world as a real alternative and *in*-cluded, under another name, as a (lesser) part of a newly global civilization. Inadequate to the discursive needs of the New Imperialism, savagery nonetheless remained a central trope in turn-of-the-century popular culture. Indeed, a jingoistic insistence on savagery and the civilizing mission becomes, if anything, aggravated outside governmental circles; as David Daniell notes, "late in the century, a change quite clearly comes over the popular literature of all kinds: it becomes aggressively, and defensively, imperialist."[23] Conrad's conservation of savagery, a natural corollary of his attachment to the exoticist project, thus leads to a curious overlap between his own writing and the pulp literature of his day in which, among other things, the figure of the *hero* retained a positive consistency that "serious" writers had long since put into question: the hero of adventure stories and romances unproblematically communicates with alternative worlds of fantasy and savagery, a mediating role that Kurtz himself plays. But with the latter—and here is the critical difference—the "energetic antithesis" of savage and civilized worlds no longer holds true: it can be no less hollow than the individual who at once keeps these worlds apart and joins them together.

The great distance between these two worlds is dramatized in *Heart* by two very different ways of occupying territory, of "filling the earth." On the one hand, we have the abstract method of territorialization practiced by the State. Marlow points out near the beginning of the novella that the "many blank spaces on the *earth* had got *filled* since my boyhood with rivers and lakes and names" (33, italics mine). The blank spaces of mystery that the heroic individual could conceive, as it were, of coloring in on his own have been covered over by an abstract informational network that controls and orders the entire globe. The earth has been partitioned into various national domains, marked in Britain's case by "a vast amount of red." This graphic moment is in direct contrast to a later incident which occurs when Kurtz is being dragged away from the Inner Station. A "savage" spectacle breaks out; the natives, Marlow asserts, "*filled* the clearing, covered the slope with a mass of naked, breathing, quivering, bronze bodies." They are led by three men "plastered with bright *red earth* from head to foot" (108, italics mine). The opposition between an immanent earth and the earth as a graphic abstraction given a transcendent unity by the colonialist nations could not be more striking. Marlow, as an envoy of civilization, already a part of the colonial machine, is at a complete remove from this savagery: it has, in fact, *ceased to exist for him*. The natives, he says, are absolutely incomprehensible, shouting out "strings of amazing words that resembled no sounds of human language."

With the coming of the New Imperialism, "savagery" drops out of sight, recedes into the inhuman. Or, rather, as the "savages" disappear back in time and beyond the pale of humanity, they are recoded within a new discourse, as objects of a benign paternalism (or, alternatively, as exploited members of a capitalist work force). The reality of the "savage" can only be grasped through the despotic mediation of a Kurtz: Marlow, appalled by the deep murmurs of "that wild mob," and hearing the shouts of the helmeted woman, must have recourse to the "atrocious phantom" of the sovereign subject if he is to make any sense of this archaic experience. " 'Do you understand this?' . . . 'Do I not?' " Kurtz replies, "gasping, as if the words had been torn out of him by a supernatural power." Kurtz alone is able to come between Marlow and this primitive world; he demarcates a (textual) space in which they can still be thought together. Two worlds meet in this one figure to whom the native chiefs offer up "unspeakable rites" and the civilized, efficient Marlow comes to attach himself with almost filial piety.[24]

Kurtz maintains the lines of contact with a world that no longer has a place in our own; this contact with what has come before us, of course, is no more real than Kurtz himself, no more real than this individual who has been canceled out of the Company's New Imperialist world and for this reason can be conceived of only in terms of "hollowness" and "deficiency." Marlow, in turn, mediates between "us" and this "atrocious phantom," making us see (and think) the ghost of what would otherwise be forever relegated to the darkness of the past: a sovereign individual who has gone beyond the (uncrossable) boundary of a modern world, a world without difference. Marlow thus participates in two stories: he shuttles back and forth between a non-heroic New Imperialist narrative in which the range of his actions is contingent upon the orders handed down to him by the Company, and another, eroticized tale of fascination for a hero of sorts. He is at once successor to the Dane Fresleven in a story of efficient conquest, and witness to Kurtz's archaic, inefficient colonization—doubly incriminated by the value-less contract he has signed with an impersonal overseer, and the damning allegiance that he feels toward a disgraced and (reversing the biological norm) illegitimate father. In his duplicity, Marlow is, ultimately, a figure of the author himself: Conrad, who finds himself uneasily situated between what he can no longer believe in and what defies belief, between (as he would put it near the end of his life) "the single-minded explorers of the nineteenth century, the late fathers of militant geography whose only object was the search for truth" and "the vilest scramble for loot that ever disfigured the history of human conscience and geographical exploration."[25]

That these "late fathers" were only engaged in the "search for truth" is, of course, the sort of overtly nostalgic assertion that a work like *Heart of Darkness* in no way bears out. The banal conservatism of Conrad's old age stems from the fact that he has forgotten his own modernity: as I suggested in my discussion of his preface to Curle's book, he shunts the problem of modernity off onto the younger generation. What is absent from the later work is a sense of the writer's own duplicity, an awareness of his simultaneous allegiance to what is impossible and complicity in what is all-too-possible; the ambiguous and unreal space that we have seen him opening up in *Heart of Darkness,* a space situated *between* his exotic beliefs and the modernity that has always-already displaced them, gives way in late Conrad to an unproblematical affirmation of the past. He completely sides with the world the way he says it once was (no more simplistic a move, I might add, than throwing one's ideological lot in with the world the way it supposedly will be). This sterile nostalgia of his last years is a far cry from the troubled and troubling memories that haunt the colonial present in *Heart of Darkness* or *Lord Jim.* What is at stake in these properly Conradian narratives is the double work of memory, which at once de-energizes every belief and every idea of difference and yet at the same time inalterably disturbs the colonial present; we are thus led up to the very gates of mortal danger, which are the gates of change, in what is for Conrad the only possible way—a way that must lead through the impossible.

Does this fin-de-siècle politics of the impossible have any relevance for us today? My own answer to this question should by now be obvious. As Fredric Jameson remarked in *The Political Unconscious,* "the peculiar heterogeneity of the moment of Conrad" consists in its being a point of transition from subjective to collective values (280); Conrad registers this shift, and yet is unwilling either to place his trust in the colonial nation-states or utopically to project himself beyond his historical moment in a vision of some more "genuine" collective. He chooses, rather, to follow up on the traces of a past that is at once unreal and yet necessary in its difference from the present. To argue for the continued relevance of Conrad's work in our own age of multinational capitalism is to suggest that the problem of a global modernity has not become any less inexorable, or any less pressing, than when it first emerged in the days of the New Imperialism. It is to suggest that the moment of our own neo-colonial present is itself still "peculiarly heterogeneous," still situated, tragically, between an obsolete subjectivity and collective values that consistently fail to materialize in a world where "there is nothing new left now, and but very little of what may still be called obscure."

Notes

1. "Travel," *Last Essays* (London: Dent, 1955), 84–92.

2. *Fetishism and Imagination: Dickens, Melville, Conrad* (Baltimore: Johns Hopkins University Press, 1982), 119.

3. In my book, *Exotic Memories: Literature, Colonialism, and the Fin de siècle* (Stanford, Calif.: Stanford University Press, forthcoming); for a good account of the dialectical foundations of the exoticist project, see also Gianpiero de Vero, "Esotismo e dialettica," in *Esotismo e crisi della civiltà*, ed. Berta Cappelli and Enzo Cocco (Naples: Tempi moderni, 1979), 205–31.

4. On this point, see the relevant chapters in Benita Parry's *Conrad and Imperialism: Ideological Boundaries and Visionary Frontiers* (London: Macmillan, 1983), a book which, despite its rather strident tone, contains far and away the best critical discussion of colonialism in Conrad's work.

5. Quoted in François Bluche, *Le Despotisme éclairé* (Paris: Fayard, 1968), 338.

6. *The Works of Lord Macaulay*, ed. Lady Trevelyan (London, 1879) 8: 139 and, for the following quotation, 141.

7. *Dissertations and Discussions: Political, Philosophical, and Historical* (New York, 1874) 3: 252.

8. *Three Faces of Imperialism: British and American Approaches to Asia and Africa, 1870–1970* (New Haven, Conn.: Yale University Press, 1987), 39.

9. Raymond F. Betts, *The False Dawn: European Imperialism in the Nineteenth Century* (Minneapolis: University of Minnesota Press, 1975), 72.

10. The various debates from February through May 1876 are recorded in *Hansard's Parliamentary Debates (Third Series)*, vols. 227–229 (London, 1876). References will be given in the text according to volume and page number.

11. Richard Koebner and H. D. Schmidt, *Imperialism: The Story and Significance of a Political Word* (Cambridge: Cambridge University Press, 1964), 194.

12. "Esotismo-Erotismo—Pierre Loti: dalla maschera esotica alla sovranità coloniale," in Anita Licari, Roberta Maccagnani, and Lina Zecchi, *Letteratura Esotismo Colonialismo* (Bologna: Cappelli, 1978), 68. Translation mine.

13. "The Beautiful Lie: Heroic Individuality and Fascism," in *Reconstructing Individualism: Autonomy, Individuality, and the Self in Western Thought*, ed. Thomas C. Heller, Morton Sosna, and David E. Wellbery (Stanford, Calif.: Stanford University Press, 1986), 175.

14. "Entre l'exotisme et la négritude: la littérature coloniale," *L'Afrique littéraire* 58 (1981): 75. Translation mine.

15. *Criticism and Ideology* (London: Verso, 1978), 135.

16. *Conrad's Politics: Community and Anarchy in the Fiction of Joseph Conrad* (Baltimore: Johns Hopkins University Press, 1967), 68.

17. *Chance* (Harmondsworth: Penguin Books, 1974), 241–42.

18. *Heart of Darkness* (Harmondsworth: Penguin Books, 1983), 31.

19. *Collected Letters of Joseph Conrad*, ed. Frederick R. Karl and Laurence Davies (Cambridge: Cambridge University Press, 1983–), 2:139–40.

20. *Conrad in the Nineteenth Century* (Berkeley: University of California Press, 1979), 216.

21. *The Expansion of England: Two Courses of Lectures* (London, 1884), 72 and, for the following quotation, 7.

22. The theoretical justification for this combination of terms (or *combinatoire*) derives, of course, from the semiotics of A. -J. Greimas, although I do not wish to insist upon his structuralist procedure here; for a technical application of this aspect of Greimas's work to literature in general and Conrad in particular, see Fredric Jameson, *The Political Unconscious: Narrative as a Socially Symbolic Act* (Ithaca, N.Y.: Cornell University Press, 1981), especially 46–49, 166–68 and 253–57.

23. "Buchan and 'The Black General,'" in *The Black Presence in English Literature*, ed. David Dabydeen (Manchester: Manchester University Press, 1985), 141.

24. As one example of a similar mediation at work in contemporary theory, I refer the reader to Deleuze and Guattari's portrait of the Barbarian Despotic Machine, "the common horizon for what comes before and what comes after it": namely, savagery and civilization. In their study "Savages, Barbarians, Civilized Men" (see *Capitalisme et schizophrénie: L'Anti-Oedipe* [Paris: Minuit, 1972], 163–324), Deleuze and Guattari distinguish between capitalist and primitive representation. The former involves such things as the universal circulation of abstract signs (most prominently, money) and the unlimited transmission of information via non-immanent media. The latter, in direct contrast to capitalist representation, is marked by a limited exchange of material goods (barter) and the inscription of bodies in a theater of cruelty as a means of conveying information (e.g., tattooing). The emergence of the despot from primitive society marks the foundation of the State but also anticipates a new, capitalist State from which he will be excluded. Primitive society is subsumed by capitalism, and ceases to exist in itself. Any return to this pre-capitalist world, any re-presentation of it, is necessarily polemical, and unreal; it is one such unlikely return that Conrad effects in *Heart of Darkness*.

25. "Geography and Some Explorers" (1924), *Last Essays* 10, 17.

James F. Knapp

Irish Primitivism and Imperial Discourse: Lady Gregory's Peasantry

IN 1916, as the first World War engaged the principal European powers in increasingly bloody stalemate, James Connolly, the Irish labor leader, wrote an article in which he defined Ireland's place at that moment of history: "We shall continue, in season and out of season, to teach that the 'far-flung battle line' of England is weakest at the point nearest its heart, that Ireland is in that position of tactical advantage, that a defeat of England in India, Egypt, the Balkans or Flanders would not be so dangerous to the British Empire as any conflict of armed forces in Ireland, that the time for Ireland's Battle is NOW, the place for Ireland's Battle is HERE."[1] Within a few months he and others would make good on that promise of armed insurrection. But rather than following the men and women of Easter week into the twentieth century, I would like to turn back to the last decades of the nineteenth, and to examine some of the ways in which the Irish situation did force to awareness—close to home—issues of empire and of resistance to empire which had been safely distanced by what we might call an ideology of the exotic, that powerful discourse of Otherness which has been most fully described by Edward Said.

When the Irish Literary Revival began to gather toward the end of the 1880s, it announced a movement which would eventually act as a kind of bridge between nineteenth-century Romanticism and the various Modernisms of the twentieth century. One prominent thread in all these movements was a fascination with the primitive. By the nineteenth century, earlier notions of the Noble Savage had been elaborated by extensive colonial experience of exotic parts, and by the emergence of disciplines (philology, comparative religion, anthropology, for example) which took as their task the production of "knowledge" about primitive life and thought. By the time Sir James Frazer began to write *The Golden Bough*, the proper matter for such study was understood to include the folk culture of the European peasantry as well as the customs of the so-called "savage tribes."

Wordsworth's peasant could be juxtaposed quite appropriately with Polynesian myth and African rite. If the Irish were less advanced in scholarly terms than the great continental folklorists, they nevertheless constructed out of archaic myth and contemporary folk materials a body of texts which was unparalleled elsewhere for its artistic fruitfulness or its usefulness to nationalist ideology.

In the many attempts to understand the significance of the Irish Revival's use of "primitive" materials, however, one issue has emerged as crucially important. Perhaps the simplest way to define it would be to question the basic premise underlying the construction of a study such as *The Golden Bough*. By juxtaposing countless examples drawn from vastly different times and places, Frazer would seem to be assuming a human essence which in some senses, at least, transcends history. His narrative of evolutionary progress may then be seen to be articulated against a norm of human identity which "we" (that is, the male European intellectual) still share with all other men and women, no matter how remote from us in time or space. It is precisely this sense, that to turn to the "primitive" is to turn away from historical difference and toward a realm of timeless essence, that underwrites the dominant critical understanding of the Irish Revival's particular version of primitivism, from the folk collections of Lady Gregory, to the peasant drama of John Synge, to the poetic mythology of W. B. Yeats. No one has put it more clearly than Conor Cruise O'Brien: "The revivalists sought in Ireland the kind of dignity and the kind of health that the industrialized world, the modern world, had lost; the Ireland they loved had an enormous West Coast and no North-east corner. They belonged with variations of emphasis to the Ascendancy and their thought for good and ill was in the perspective of the Ascendancy, the rural-to-universal perspective."[2]

The notion that there is an inevitable logic transforming rural into universal is a common one, as the work of numerous critics could demonstrate. For example, an influential early critic of Synge's writing asserts that "literary cosmopolitanism enabled Synge to express Irish life so completely that his peasant characters are lifted from the narrow boundaries of their petty Robinson-Crusoe-island provinciality into a kind of universal and dateless dreamworld which makes them representative of human nature everywhere."[3] The comparison of Ireland to Crusoe's distant micro-colony is apt, insofar as the encounter with the primitive functions in each case to obscure historical struggle and change by privileging the idea of transcendent human essence. While this reading of artistic primitivism as essentially an escape from history is a powerful one, it does not ultimately do justice to the complexity with which writers at that time deployed the primitivist discourse which had begun to assume new cultural prestige.

Lady Gregory is a particularly important figure for understanding the way in which broad new developments in the production of art and knowledge contributed to the emerging nationalist resistance to empire at the end of the nineteenth century. Like Yeats and Synge, Lady Gregory seemed to occupy an anomalous position, as a member of the Protestant Ascendancy—that class which had ruled Ireland throughout the nineteenth century—and at the same time as a supporter of the Irish struggle for independence. Her position was richly precedented, of course, in a long tradition of Irish Protestant leadership of the agitation and rebellion against English rule. Moreover, she represented a kind of social formation which has complicated the process of de-colonization as it has appeared in such widely different shapes as those of the creole elites of Latin America, the whites of Rhodesia, or the French planters of New Caledonia. Like all these others who found themselves in opposition to as well as alliance with both colonizer and colonized, Lady Gregory offers an exemplary instance of why "nationalism" cannot be understood as a trans-historical concept independent of the specific social and cultural interests in which, at any given moment of history, it is deployed.

The initial question raised by the work of Lady Gregory and that of the other members of the Irish Literary Renaissance, is whether or not theirs was a "genuine" nationalism of the people, that is, a movement emerging out of the experience of subject classes and serving the aspirations of those classes for liberation from colonial domination. The alternative is what Benedict Anderson calls "official nationalism—an anticipatory strategy adopted by dominant groups who are threatened with marginalization or exclusion from an emerging nationally-imagined community."[4] The nationalism of the Literary Revival has certainly been characterized in this second sense by critics who have regarded it as perpetuating the traditional English domination of the Catholic majority. The journalistic agitation at the time of the riots surrounding Synge's *Playboy of the Western World* might serve as one example of this view, as would Daniel Corkery's 1931 book on Synge's writings. By the end of the nineteenth century, however, the Protestant Ascendancy was not in fact a ruling class any longer, but rather a community doubly threatened: by the rising Catholic nationalism of Ireland on the one hand, and, on the other, by the destabilizing advance of English capitalism into new forms of world-wide dependency which left little place, even in agriculture, for the archaic economy of great-house and tenant. Rather than serving as the voice of either British imperial power (as the nationalist press tended to assert), or native Irish nationalism (as their own simplistic justifications occasionally tried to have it), the leaders of the Literary Revival thus faced the challenge of appropriating the discourse of nationalism in such a way as to control its potential *both* for social liberation and for social containment. Only such a complex and apparently paradoxical deployment of nationalist discourse could serve their historical interests.

Lady Gregory's writing offers a particularly good opportunity to observe the way in which the contending interests of a time of great historical change may be inscribed in literary texts. Her efforts in support of the Irish language, and her extensive work of gathering and translating ancient Celtic tales and peasant lore alike, distinguish her as one of those early modernist explorers of what I might call the "exotic familiar"—that cultural world of folktale and peasant lore which had been virtually invisible to "civilized" eyes until it suddenly began to be seen in the reflected light of nineteenth-century Europe's fascination with the more distant exoticism of its world-wide imperial realms. And yet, unlike any of her fellow explorers of bog and cottage, she had also been close to the very center of British imperial power. As the wife of a former Royal Governor of Ceylon, she had known the Empire and its highest administrators firsthand, though her relation to such power was sometimes an uneasy one. In Egypt, during the early 1880s, she had supported the nationalism of Colonel Arabi, until the British finally ended his threat by occupying the country in 1882. Of that time, she later wrote:

> This was the end of my essay in politics, for though Ireland is always with me, and I feared and then became reconciled to, and now hope to see even a greater independence than Home Rule, my saying has been long, "I am not fighting for it, but preparing for it." And that has been my purpose in my work for establishing a National Theatre, and for the revival of the language, and in making better known the heroic tales of Ireland. For whatever political inclination or energy was born with me may have run its course in that Egyptian year and worn itself out; or it may be that I saw too much of the inside, the tangled threads of diplomacy, the driving forces behind politicians. But I am glad to have been in that fight for freedom, and glad my husband took freedom's side, it was of a piece with his nature.[5]

In ostensibly renouncing politics, Lady Gregory employed a transformation which was highly ambiguous: "fighting for" becomes "preparing for." If this was in some sense an attempt to shift the arena of struggle from politics to culture (as opposed to adopting a merely passive attitude of waiting), then the question it poses for her writing is whether there can be such a thing as the textual resistance to imperial power. Certainly, there are many examples in her autobiographical writings suggesting that she understood, and sought to deconstruct, the rhetoric of empire. She might deflate the high style of official speech, or, by referring to upper class table-talk as "folklore," she might subtly undermine the crucial hierarchy dividing ruling class and common folk. Or again, writing to Wilfred Blunt in 1886, she might speak about the Indians as "gentle people 'made to be ruled,'" her own quotation marks around "made to be ruled" pointing to the political nature of this arbitrarily imposed human difference, an insight which the discourse of empire must necessarily efface.

In 1903 she published *Poets and Dreamers,* a volume which is in many ways typical of the late nineteenth-century efforts to recover materials perceived as exotic to mainstream European culture—whether through their distance in time, as with archaic myth and legend, or through their existence in oral traditions normally invisible to ruling class culture. In one of his reviews, Yeats praised the book as "one which will always be a part of our canon,"[6] but he appropriated it for the aestheticism which so characterized his own writing around the turn of the century: "And because one is not always a citizen there are moods in which one cannot read modern poetry at all; it is so full of eccentric and temporal things, so gnarled and twisted by the presence of a complicated life, so burdened by that painful riddle of the world, which never seems inexplicable till men gather in crowds to talk it out." He goes on to suggest that sometimes "one is convinced that all good poems are fruit of the Tree of Life, and all bad ones apples of the Tree of Knowledge. I find in this book many fruits of the Tree of Life, and am content that they offer me no consolation but their beauty" (301). In fact, *Poets and Dreamers* turns to the rural and the archaic without finally surrendering to "the universal" as a way of escaping those troubling questions of imperial power and nationalist resistance. In spite of the power of Yeats's rhetoric, which has exerted such influence over subsequent views of the Irish Revival, Lady Gregory's book by no means leaves "the presence of a complicated life" out of account in order to pursue some elusive vision of Fairyland.

Poets and Dreamers is a collection which ranges from translations of the wandering Gaelic poet Raftery, to traditional ballads, to Lady Gregory's interviews with residents of the local workhouses, to the lore of "herb-healing." But we might begin with a section to which the *Spectator* objected in its review as being too politically controversial. Entitled "Boer Ballads in Ireland," the chapter prints a number of popular ballads associated with the war which had concluded only the previous year, along with a commentary consisting mostly of an account of the common people's attitudes toward the war and toward these songs. While far from Ireland, and only very imperfectly understood (Lady Gregory quotes an Irish woman who insists that the Boers must be Catholic, or the English would not be their enemies), the Boer War was perceived to be a colonial conflict onto which the Irish opposition to British imperialism might easily be displaced. Hostility toward England is generalized in these ballads to include all the subject peoples of the British Empire:

For the people of India
(Pitiful is their case);
For the people of Africa
She has put to death.

For the people of Ireland,
Nailed to the cross;
Wage for each people
Her hand has destroyed.   (78)

Some of the ballads celebrate the Irish Brigade, which, under the leadership of John MacBride, actually fought on the Boer side: "And Erin watches from afar, with joy and hope and pride, / Her sons who strike for liberty, led by John MacBride."

In addition to such overt political content, however, there is a more subtle critique of the cultural imperialism which modern tourism can represent:

Oh! Paddy dear, and did ye hear
The news that's going round?
No cheers for brave Paul Kruger
Must be heard on Irish ground.

No more the English tourist at
Killarney will be seen,
Unless you join the pirate's cause,
And chaunt "God save the Queen."   (72–73)

Douglas Hyde's speech on "The Necessity for De-Anglicising Ireland" is only the most famous version of many contemporary attempts to describe the phenomenon of cultural imperialism. Even George Moore, who had always been more interested in Parisian aestheticism than in Irish politics, could join in this critique, writing that "The commercial platitude which has risen up in England, which is extending over the whole world, is horrible to contemplate. Its flag, which Mr. Rhodes has declared to be 'the most valuable commercial asset in the world,' is everywhere. England has imposed her ideas upon all nations, and to girdle the world with Brixton seems to be her ultimate destiny."[7] As Tom Nairn has argued in his book on resurgent nationalism within the United Kingdom, Irish nationalism has seemed increasingly typical of anti-imperialist struggle in the twentieth century, the economic relations between the two nations being particularly important: "Although unusually close geographically to the metropolitan center, Southern Ireland had in fact been separated from it by a great socio-political gulf, by that great divide which was to dominate so much of the epoch: the 'development gap.'"[8] Throughout the nineteenth century, Ireland had been subjected to an increasing flow of English goods, becoming, as F. S. L. Lyons puts it, "an integral, if backward, part of the United Kingdom economy."[9] It could be argued, however, that "backward" is not so much a qualification of Ireland's integral status within the United Kingdom economy, but rather a description of precisely how Ireland did function as integral to that larger economy.

In one sphere at least, it was precisely Ireland's economic backwardness which allowed it to fill a rather advanced role. Pointing out the fact that while heavy industry (the usual symbol of the industrial revolution in Britain) was not present in southern Ireland, modern structures of communication, advertising, and mass consumption were very advanced indeed, W. J. McCormack has recently emphasized "the extent to which the metropolitan colony within the United Kingdom of Great Britain and Ireland was devoted to the manufacture of ideology."[10] The growth of literacy and of the distribution of such media as newspapers, periodicals, and mail-order catalogues was considerable in Ireland during the nineteenth century[11] and in fact drew considerable fire from social critics at the time. For example, in the same volume of essays edited by Lady Gregory in which George Moore had denounced the spread of English materialism, D. P. Moran attacked the rise of the popular English periodicals which had increasingly begun to flood the Irish market, and, in his view, to shape the Irish imagination.

It was during this period of accelerating modernization that tourism also arose, and the Boer ballad's warning of the withdrawal of English tourism as punishment for Irish support of the Boers reveals a new kind of economic dependency. But tourism is more than an economic exchange which subordinates seller to buyer. Like the new mass media which Moran attacks, it functions to undermine local cultural traditions, while at the same time appropriating, and in a sense rewriting, those traditions. A similar process had already taken place in France, for example, as the urban bourgeoisie constituted Celtic Brittany as a place of archaic remainders, a "primitive" object for their aesthetic contemplation—regardless of the fact that the province had experienced half a century of substantial economic growth and modernization. Tourism may thus be seen as part of the larger discourse of imperialism, which depends on a delineation of difference between high civilization and a more "primitive" society composed of men and women who are "known" only through civilization's gaze.

In this sense, the overt, but quite limited, political content of a book like *Poets and Dreamers* is in some ways less important than its attempt to authorize the language of men and women who (according to the logic of empire) should be merely seen—picturesquely—rather than heard. One of the notions through which Lady Gregory links her selections concerns the Anglo-Irish blindness to the people and their language: "'Eyes have we, but we see not; ears have we, but we do not understand.' It does not comfort me to think how many besides myself, having spent a lifetime in Ireland, must make this confession" (43). In order to understand the extent to which Lady Gregory is attempting to initiate an oppositional discourse, we might consider her comment in introducing a poem concerning a man about to be executed: "I do not know who the following poem was written about, or if it is about anyone in particular; but one line of it puts into words the emotion of many an Irish 'felon.' 'It is with the people I was; it is not with the law I was.' For the Irish crime, treason-felony, is only looked on as a crime in the eyes of the law, not in the eyes of the people" (69). The dichotomy which Lady Gregory defines here between the law and the people is congruent with an oppositional rhetoric which accepts the Empire's appropriation of Reason, Law, and Enlightenment to itself, but which then counters those notions with an idealized version of peasant purity and solidarity.

The image of a primitive essence of "the People" is defined most clearly by the book's first chapter, which concerns the life of the blind poet Raftery, who had died sixty years earlier. His value is specifically understood to consist in his difference from the traditional canons of civilized art and learning:

> I hear the people say now and then: "If he had had education, he would have been the greatest poet in the world." I cannot but be sorry that his education went so far as it did, for "he used to carry a book about with him—a Pantheon—about the heathen gods and goddesses; and whoever he'd get that was able to read, he'd get him to read it to him, and then he'd keep them in his mind, and use them as he wanted them." If he had been born a few decades later, he would have been caught, like other poets of the time, in the formulas of English verse. As it was, both his love poems and his religious poems were caught in the formulas imported from Greece and from Rome; and any formula must make a veil between the prophet who has been on the mountain top, and the people who are waiting at its foot for his message. The dreams of beauty that formed themselves in the mind of the blind poet become flat and vapid when he embodies them in the well-worn names of Helen and Venus. (26–27)

In this rather familiar formulation, the domination of English culture is set over against the possibility of recovering a continuing, but suppressed, native tradition. Exalting a "Natural," unlearned tradition as the logical contrary to a culture which has successfully identified its own interests with enlightened reason and education, this counter-tradition constitutes itself as a Romantic primitivism which has displayed its effectiveness over the course of the past hundred years.

The political implications of this kind of rhetorical gesture which attempts to recover a suppressed cultural continuity are highly problematic, however. For example, this is how one recent critic regards the Revival's romantic peasantry:

> But our present dilapidated situation has borne in upon us more fiercely than ever the fact that discontinuity, the discontinuity which is ineluctably an inheritance of a colonial history, is more truly the signal feature of our condition. One could, finally, add to this the remark that the dream of an evolutionary continuity in a civilization which fetches its origins from some misty past is also a characteristic of the conservative politics which the main line of European Romanticism has always held in considerable affection.[12]

By creating "the People" and the blind, untutored poet as trans-historical subjects, Lady Gregory and others attempted to invent a rhetoric capable of opposing the Instrumental Reason of imperialism. This is an instance of what Tom Nairn has characterized as the tendency of nationalists to seek to advance by going backward, so to speak, to indulge in an archaic and myth-making populism as an effective way of rallying mass support for their struggle.[13] Such a tactic may be necessitated by the fact that few resources other than ethnic difference, language, traditional folklore, and so on are available to them. The danger, as Seamus Deane points out, is that such a validation of essence and continuity simply inscribes a mythic closure which obscures the actual contentions of history which lead to domination and subjection.

The manner in which such mythic closure is accomplished, however, may reveal a great deal about the historically specific nature of the political intervention which is in fact taking place. For example, in her commentary on a selection of "West Irish Ballads," Lady Gregory suggests that "the very *naïveté,* the simplicity of these ballads, made one feel that the peasants who make and sing them may be trembling on the edge of a great discovery; and that some day—perhaps very soon—one born among them will put their half-articulate, eternal sorrows and laments and yearnings into words that will be their expression for ever" (53–54). She goes on to equate that imagined achievement with the language of the Bible. Insofar as the folk approach the condition of naivete and simplicity (the familiar romantic equation of the primitive with the childhood of the race), their utterance may become as timeless as the "thirty-seventh Psalm," or the "Song of Solomon." But however close they may be to that originary state, they are represented as not yet having attained it, as perhaps never attaining it. In the meantime, they must remain only "half-articulate," and therefore ultimately dependent upon the mediation of a figure such as Lady Gregory herself, who offers not only translations of the Irish texts, but interpretive and evaluative commentary as well. While the peasants are thus accorded a status which is mythic, but only potential, Lady Gregory attains a cultural authority which is quite real and present. This authority is a form of what David Cairns and Shaun Richards have recently termed the "positional superiority" which the discourse of Celticism made possible for the Anglo-Irish as well as the English.[14]

The complexity of Lady Gregory's discourse regarding "the People" may be seen most clearly in a chapter entitled "The Wandering Tribe," which concerns the Irish tinkers. The question of where the reader is positioned is crucial here, particularly in light of the typical nationalist effort to bring about an emotional and unquestioning identification with the figure of the traditional peasantry. The chapter begins with Lady Gregory's initial perception of the tinkers as distinctly other than the world of British modernity, which (as I noted earlier) is typically figured by "newspapers" and "law and order": "When poor Paul Rutledge made his great effort to escape from the doorsteps of law and order—from the world, the flesh, and the newspaper—and fell among tinkers, I looked with more interest than before at the little camps that one sees every now and then by the roadside for a few days or weeks" (94). In their traditional lives outside the realm of law and the newspaper, the tinkers would seem to be an archetypal figure for the People. Offering a series of quotations from her peasant neighbors, Lady Gregory does indeed portray the tinkers as living close to some sort of natural origin, as possessing a kind of uncivilized vitality ("they are as hardy as goats or as Connemara sheep").

However, her interest in these people immediately becomes problematic, as she acknowledges that the Irish country folk are, in general, hostile to the tinkers: "And I wondered why our country people—who are so kind to one another, and to tramps and beggars, that they seem to live by the rule of an old woman in a Galway sweet-shop: 'Refuse not any, for one may be the Christ'—speak of a visit of the tinkers as of frost in spring or blight in harvest." In juxtaposing the traditional country folk with a still more "primitive" people—the tinkers—a margin is defined which has the effect of seriously undermining unitary notions of "the People," and making it very difficult to subsume the Irish peasantry into the timeless continuity of myth. To view the tinkers as these men and women do is in fact to replicate, in some sense, the traditional position of the colonizer with regard to the colonized subject. The tinkers become the exotic Other, hated and feared, and yet in many ways the objects of desire as well as of loathing. Their existence beyond the constraints of civilized law is recounted in a way which seems to combine denunciation with envy: "They have no marriage at all; but their women might be ten times better than the rural women for all that, and true to their men." Their men, however, are said to "sell their wives to one another; I've seen that myself."

If in one sense *Poets and Dreamers* shapes an image of the People as oppositional to domination by British imperialism, it would seem that the same image, when problematized as an opposition such as that between the tinkers and the country folk, may allow a reinscription of the ideology of empire. In their primeval condition ("They are a class of themselves," says another man, "and they have been there ever since the world began"), the tinkers define a supposed original state of child-like, amoral desiring and acquisitiveness which it is precisely the task of civilization to limit and control. Lady Gregory's book thus seems to construct a mythic image of the People as a nationalist weapon, and yet at the same time to call upon certain underlying assumptions of imperialism to set a limit to those nationalist aspirations for liberation.

The section of *Poets and Dreamers* which presents the most extensive collection of traditional tales is entitled "Workhouse Dreams," and this very title would seem to express the ambiguity of nationalist efforts to resist imperial power by recuperating ancient native traditions. In framing the folktales which she had collected in her visits to the local workhouse, Lady Gregory begins with a familiar evocation of the superior imaginative powers of the People: "Last June I had a few free days, and I chose to spend them among the imaginative class, the holders of the traditions of Ireland, country people in thatched houses, workers in fields and bogs" (98). "Class" is the pivotal word in this statement, as an aristocratic lady able to choose how to spend her free days situates herself in relation to informants who are described as "workers in fields and bogs." By designating the workers as an "imaginative" class, however, Lady Gregory once again invokes the peasantry as a primary source of cultural value, while at the same time making clear that they are in some way disabled or constrained. Though she speaks of "country people in thatched houses," in fact, all the stories come from the inmates of a workhouse, and before she begins to retell the tales, she leaves no doubt about the economic condition of her informants: "But as I listened, I was moved by the strange contrast between the poverty of the tellers and the splendours of the tales." And, strictly speaking, it was not even a question of the poverty of life on the Irish land: a "workhouse" was not a place where the world's work was done at all. On the contrary, it was a last refuge for those who had no place in the economy of their society, for those beyond the margins of productive labor.

Still, if W. J. McCormack is correct in the assertion which I discussed earlier—that the metropolitan colony of Ireland was engaged in the manufacture of ideology—then perhaps another kind of work was indeed taking place, not in the workhouse itself, but in discourse such as that of Lady Gregory. The old men who tell the tales are said to receive a special, visionary gift: "I think it has always been to such poor people, with little of wealth or comfort to keep their thoughts bound to the things about them, that dreams and visions have been given. It is from a deep narrow well the stars can be seen at noonday; it was one left on a bare rocky island who saw the pearl gates and the golden streets that lead to the Tree of Life" (99). The rhetorical potentialities of such a formulation are ambiguous. On the one hand, such a vision is certainly congruent with the nationalist attempts to rally support behind an image of noble peasantry, cruelly oppressed, but possessed of a spiritual superiority which places it on the side of the angels. Padraic Pearse, for example, in his essay "The Coming Revolution," asserted that "peoples are divine and are the only things that can properly be spoken of under figures drawn from the divine epos," and he traced the origins of his movement to the spiritual insights available to an oppressed people: "we had first to learn to know Ireland, to read the lineaments of her face, to understand the accents of her voice; to re-possess ourselves, disinherited as we were, of her spirit and mind, re-enter into our mystical birthright." The essay concludes with an exhortation to armed rebellion, and to the enthusiastic embrace of bloodshed.[15]

On the other hand, of course, the image of destitute but visionary peasants had long been used by another kind of nationalism which focused only on the effects of capitalist modernization, divorcing that process from the imperialism which was its context, and thus effectively accepting British domination by leaving the realm of politics altogether. This is the poet AE, writing on "Nationality and Imperialism":

> The shout of the cockney tourist sounds in the cyclopean crypts and mounds once sanctified by druid mysteries, and divine visitations, and passings from the mortal to immortal. Ireland Limited is being run by English syndicates. It is the descent of a nation into hell, not nobly, not as a sacrifice made for a great end, but ignobly and without hope of resurrection. If we who watch protest bitterly at the racial degradation—for we have none of us attained all the moral perfections—we are assured that we are departing from the law of love. We can have such a noble destiny if we only accept it. When we have lost everything we hoped for, lost our souls even, we can proceed to spiritualise the English, and improve the moral tone of the empire.[16]

To see the stars from the bottom of a deep well of oppression may be to discover the divinity of the people, and so begin to move toward armed insurrection, or it may be to discover that the divinity of the people constitutes a spiritual superiority which relegates the merely political arrangements of empire to secondary status. Both possibilities are mythic insofar as their discursive strategies subordinate the materiality of history to ideal categories which are trans-historical and absolute. Pearse's famous statement that "we may make mistakes in the beginning and shoot the wrong people; but bloodshed is a cleansing and a sanctifying thing,"[17] is only the most striking instance of this kind of myth-making.

The effect of "Workhouse Dreams," however, is finally quite different. In its narrative techniques, the chapter evades mythic closure by locating its peasant storytellers firmly within the realm of historical contingency. Through intrusive devices such as summarizing segments which she acknowledges to be dull, or allowing us to see the sometimes derisive audience reaction to the tales, Lady Gregory retains her own position of authority, superior to both the tellers and the tales. Most important in assuring this position is the inscription of social hierarchy which I noted above:

> And then the old man, whose brother has fought for the king, and hasn't sent him anything, said: "Peace is made. That's my story. Will you give me tobacco for that?"

> But this being the last day, they all had tobacco—story-tellers and all. (132)

In refusing to tell a story, but requesting tobacco anyway, the old man resists the social situation in which he finds himself. His resistance is contained, however, by the rhetorical tradition of the amusing peasant anecdote which certainly governs this reported exchange. The peasant is a charming rascal, but a rascal nonetheless, and so necessarily requires the kind of animal-trainer system of rewards and deprivations which Lady Gregory has employed. Her act of generosity in giving all the men tobacco as a parting gesture simply reinscribes a relationship of domination and dependence. If stories which only "the People" can provide are essential to the emerging cultural nationalism which Lady Gregory would deploy against the British Empire, it remains equally essential that social relations of domination within Ireland should not be subjected to similar attack.

The questions posed by this book should not be of concern only to a small group of Anglo-Irish specialists. *Poets and Dreamers* was part of a larger rewriting of Romantic primitivism which would soon become an important constituent of the Modernist movement. But Lady Gregory's text was also involved in the complex discourse of nationalist resistance to European imperialism. That discourse countered the authority of imperial civilization with notions of the archaic wholeness and solidarity of the People. And yet that populist rhetoric was in many ways the inversion of a premise equally useful to the apologists of empire: that subject peoples were essentially Other, persisting in a "primitive" or child-like state outside of history—and the Irish were no less subject to the paradigm than were the Egyptians or the Indians (whose kinship with the ancient Celts, it might be added, had recently been established by "Orientalist" scholars). As a member of the Protestant Ascendancy, Lady Gregory was in some sense both colonizer and colonized, and in her own attempts to explore the exotic familiar, she displays the fact that none of these rhetorical counters—not the People, not the simple tales of country folk, not the archaic originality of myth—is possessed of the kind of essential meaning which Imperial Governor and nationalist rebel alike assumed. If her work demonstrates some of the ways in which a colonizing discourse may itself be colonized and subverted, it also teaches us that the struggle for liberation is not everywhere and always the same. Historically specific, often contradictory, it is, in this case too, many things at once. The attempt of an amateur folklorist to place the nineteenth-century tradition of romantic—and revolutionary—primitivism at the service of Irish nationalism is a central part of it. But so too is the struggle by a member of a threatened class to contain that revolutionary change which she feared as well as urged. And finally, it is the struggle of a writer just beginning to find ways to inscribe within her texts that corrosive skepticism about all the myths of social power which would so characterize the decades to come.

Notes

1. James Connolly, "What Is Our Programme?" in *1000 Years of Irish Prose,* ed. Vivian Mercier and David H. Greene (New York: Devin-Adair, 1952), 242–43.

2. Conor Cruise O'Brien, ed., *The Shaping of Modern Ireland* (1960; rpt. New York: Barnes and Noble, 1970), 21.

3. Maurice Bourgeois, *John Millington Synge and the Irish Theatre* (London: Constable and Co., 1913), 63.

4. *Imagined Communities: Reflections on the Origin and Spread of Nationalism* (London: Verso, 1983), 95.

5. *Seventy Years: 1852–1922: Being the Autobiography of Lady Gregory,* ed. Colin Smythe (New York: Oxford University Press, 1974), 54.

6. W. B. Yeats, *Uncollected Prose,* vol. 2 (New York: Columbia University Press, 1976), 300; Lady Gregory, *Poets and Dreamers* (New York: Oxford University Press, 1974).

7. "Literature and the Irish Language," in *Ideals in Ireland,* ed. Lady Gregory (New York: AMS Press, 1978), 50–51.

8. *The Break-Up of Britain: Crisis and Neo-Nationalism* (London: New Left Books, 1977), 11–12.

9. "Yeats and Victorian Ireland," in *Yeats, Sligo and Ireland,* ed. Norman Jeffares (Totowa, N.J.: Barnes and Noble, 1980), 117.

10. *Ascendancy and Tradition in Anglo-Irish Literary History From 1789 to 1939* (Oxford: Clarendon Press, 1985), 299.

11. Joseph Lee, *The Modernisation of Irish Society 1848–1914* (Dublin: Gill and Macmillan, 1973), 13.

12. Seamus Deane, "The Literary Myths of the Revival: A Case for Their Abandonment," in *Myth and Reality in Irish Literature,* ed. Joseph Ronsley (Waterloo, Ontario: Wilfred Laurier University Press, 1977), 325–26.

13. *The Break-Up of Britain,* 348.

14. David Cairns and Shaun Richards, *Writing Ireland: Colonialism, Nationalism and Culture* (Manchester: Manchester University Press, 1988), 50.

15. In *1000 Years of Irish Prose,* 234–35.

16. AE [George Russell], "Nationality and Imperialism," in *Ideals in Ireland,* 20.

17. *1000 Years of Irish Prose,* 237.

Contributors

JONATHAN ARAC is Professor of English at the University of Pittsburgh and a member of the *boundary 2* editorial collective. Editor of *Postmodernism and Politics* (1986) and *After Foucault* (1988), he is the author of *Critical Genealogies* (1987). His study of "Prose Narratives, 1820–1870" appears in volume 2 of the new *Cambridge History of American Literature*, and he is completing a book on "*Huckleberry Finn* and the Functions of Criticism."

CHRIS BONGIE is Assistant Professor of Comparative Literature and English at the College of William and Mary. He is the author of *Exotic Memories: Literature, Colonialism, and the Fin de siècle* (1991). He is working on a study entitled "Islands and Exiles: The Creole Identities of Post/colonial Literature."

WAI-CHEE DIMOCK is the author of *Empire for Liberty: Melville and the Poetics of Individualism* (1989) and *Cognition and Justice: American Literature, Law, Political Philosophy* (1995). She teaches at Brandeis University.

BRUCE GREENFIELD is Associate Professor of English at Dalhousie University. He is the author of *Narrating Discovery: The Romantic Explorer in American Literature, 1790–1845* (1992) and is continuing work on eighteenth- and nineteenth-century travel writing.

MARK KIPPERMAN is Associate Professor of English at Northern Illinois University. He is the author of *Beyond Enchantment: German Idealism and English Romantic Poetry* (1987) and is currently working on Byron, Shelley, and the utopian strain in romantic political thought.

JAMES F. KNAPP, Professor of English at the University of Pittsburgh, is the author of *Erza Pound* (1979) and *Literary Modernism and the Transformation of Work: Innovation in the Age of Scientific Management* (1988). His articles have appeared in such periodicals as *Modern Language Quarterly, Sewanee Review, Twentieth Century Literature, College English, Comparative Literature*, and *boundary 2*.

LOREN KRUGER teaches drama and critical theory at the University of

Chicago. She is the author of *The National Stage: Theatre and Cultural Legitimation in England, France, and America* (1992) and the translator of *The Institutions of Art* by Peter and Christa Berger (1992). She is currently working on a book provisionally entitled "Drama and Modernity in South Africa."

LISA LOWE is Associate Professor of Comparative Literature at the University of California, San Diego. She is the author of *Critical Terrains: French and British Orientalisms* (1991). Her essays on postcolonial and U.S. minority literatures have appeared in *Diaspora* and *Yale French Studies*.

SUSAN MEYER is Assistant Professor of English at Wellesley College. Her book *Imperialism at Home: Race as a Metaphor in the Fiction of Charlotte Brontë, Emily Brontë, and George Eliot* is forthcoming from Cornell University Press.

JEFF NUNOKAWA is Associate Professor of English at Princeton University. He is the author of *The Afterlife of Property: Domestic Security and the Victorian Novel* (1994).

HARRIET RITVO is Professor of History at the Massachusetts Institute of Technology and author of *The Animal Estate: The English and Other Creatures in the Victorian Age* (1987). Her essays have appeared in such journals as *Victorian Studies, Representations, BioScience, Comparative Studies in Society and History,* and *History of the Human Sciences*.

MARLON B. ROSS, Associate Professor of English at the University of Michigan at Ann Arbor, is the author of *The Contours of Masculine Desire: Romanticism and the Rise of Women's Poetry* (1989). He is currently working on a book about reading habits in the eighteenth and nineteenth centuries.

NANCY VOGELEY, Professor of Spanish at the University of San Francisco, has published articles on Mexican literature and culture of the early nineteenth century in *Bulletin of Hispanic Studies, Hispania, Ideologies and Literature,* and *PMLA*.

SUE ZEMKA is Assistant Professor of English at the University of Colorado at Boulder. Her book *Victorian Testaments: The Bible in Early Nineteenth-Century British Culture* is forthcoming from Stanford University Press.

Index

Library of Congress Cataloging-in-Publication Data
Macropolitics of nineteenth-century literature:
nationalism, exoticism, imperialism / edited
by Jonathan Arac and Harriet Ritvo.
p. cm. — (New Americanists)
Includes index.
ISBN 0-8223-1612-9 (pbk. : alk. paper)
1. Literature, Modern—19th century—History and
criticism. 2. Politics and literature. 3. Nationalism in
literature. 4. Exoticism in literature. 5. Imperialism
in literature. I. Arac, Jonathan, 1945– . II. Ritvo,
Harriet, 1946– . III. Series
PN761.M23 1995
809'.93358—dc20   94-41318   CIP